Cambridge Studies in Social and Emotional Development

General Editor: Martin L. Hoffman

Advisory Board: Nicholas Blurton Jones, Robert N. Emde, Willard W. Hartup, Robert A. Hinde, Lois W. Hoffman, Carroll E. Izard, Jerome Kagan, Franz J. Mönks, Paul Mussen, Ross D. Parke, and Michael Rutter

Children's understanding of emotion

Children's understanding of emotion

Edited by

CAROLYN SAARNI
Sonoma State University

PAUL L. HARRIS
University of Oxford

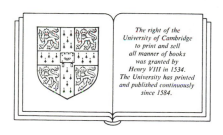

The right of the
University of Cambridge
to print and sell
all manner of books
was granted by
Henry VIII in 1534.
The University has printed
and published continuously
since 1584.

CAMBRIDGE UNIVERSITY PRESS
Cambridge
New York   Port Chester   Melbourne   Sydney

Published by the Press Syndicate of the University of Cambridge
The Pitt Building, Trumpington Street, Cambridge CB2 1RP
40 West 20th Street, New York, NY 10011, USA
10 Stamford Road, Oakleigh, Melbourne 3166, Australia

First published 1989
First paperback edition 1991

Printed in the United States of America

Library of Congress Cataloging-in-Publication Data

Children's understanding of emotion / edited by Carolyn Saarni, Paul
L. Harris.
p.   cm. – (Cambridge studies in social and emotional
development)
1. Emotions in children.   2. Emotions.   3. Child psychology.
I. Saarni, Carolyn.   II. Harris, Paul L.   III. Series.
BF723.E6C48   1989   88–7887
154.4′12 – dc19   CIP

British Library Cataloguing in Publication Data

Children's understanding of emotion.—
(Cambridge studies in social and emotional
development)
1. Children. Emotions. Development.
I. Saarni, Carolyn
II. Harris, Paul L.
155.4′12

ISBN 0-521-33394-6 hardback
ISBN 0-521-40777-X paperback

Contents

Part IV The control of emotion

Part V Emotion, empathy, and experience

Part VI The role of culture and socialization practices

Contributors

Jackie Gnepp
Department of Psychology
Northern Illinois University

Steven L. Gordon
Department of Sociology
California State University
at Los Angeles

Paul L. Harris
Department of Experimental
Psychology
Oxford University

Susan Harter
Department of Psychology
University of Denver

Janellen Huttenlocher
Department of Education
University of Chicago

Michael Lewis
Institute for the Study of
Child Development
Department of Pediatrics
University of Medicine and Dentistry
of New Jersey

Mark S. Lipian
Department of Psychiatry
University of California
Los Angeles

Mark Meerum Terwogt
Developmental Psychology
Free University
The Netherlands

Tjeert Olthof
Department of Social Sciences
State University of Utrecht
The Netherlands

James A. Russell
Department of Psychology
University of British Columbia

Carolyn Saarni
Department of Counseling
Sonoma State University
California

Patricia Smiley
Department of Education
University of Chicago

Nancy L. Stein
Department of Behavioral Sciences
University of Chicago

Janet Strayer
Department of Psychology
Simon Fraser University
British Columbia

Tom Trabasso
Department of Behavioral Sciences
University of Chicago

Ross A. Thompson
Department of Psychology
University of Nebraska

Nancy Rumbaugh Whitesell
Department of Psychology
University of Denver

Preface

The theme of this book is one which had been relatively neglected in developmental psychology until this last decade, but since the late 1970s research on the topic of children's understanding of emotion has been considerable. Surprisingly, there has been no single volume pulling together the threads (much less weaving a tapestry) of how children come to comprehend emotional experience across childhood, starting with infancy and extending into early adolescence. The present volume seeks to remedy this omission and, with that purpose in mind, we have gathered together individuals whose work has influenced how problems in children's understanding of emotion have been conceptualized.

These individuals have also participated with us in symposia at meetings of the Society for Research in Child Development and in assorted panels and discussion groups of the International Society for Research on Emotions. There are a number of other influential contributors to the field of children's understanding of emotion, and we regret not being able to include them here in a truly comprehensive volume.

We look forward to the continuing expansion of research methods and theoretical accounts offered for how and why children understand emotional experience as they do. As a result of this burgeoning research in children's understanding of emotion, we also anticipate more refined clinical applications for remedying deficits in emotion understanding and educational curricula that facilitate children's insight and responsiveness to those in need. We think this volume will promote more incisive and sophisticated models of emotional development and stimulate still greater interest in the field of emotional development as a whole. We trust the reader will share our enthusiasm and excitement in reading this book.

Carolyn Saarni
Paul L. Harris

Part I

Introduction

1 Children's understanding of emotion: an introduction

Paul L. Harris and Carolyn Saarni

Research on the child's understanding of emotion has steadily increased in the last decade to the point where it seems appropriate to draw some of the main contributors together. Our goal is to provide, within a single volume, a fairly comprehensive review of recent research and the theoretical assumptions that have guided it. In doing so, we seek to underline not only the considerable consensus that has emerged but also important areas of disagreement that only future research will resolve. In this introductory chapter, we sketch the historical background to contemporary research. We also indicate, where appropriate, the ways in which contributors have questioned some of the restrictive assumptions that were prevalent in that earlier research. Following our review of the historical background, we attempt to identify the key issues raised in each of the succeeding parts of the volume.

Historical background

Sympathy and empathy

Contemporary work on the child's understanding of emotion stems, in part, from a long-standing research tradition concerned with children's sympathetic and empathic responses. Since the 1930s, we have known from the classic observations of Lois Murphy (1937) that young preschool children are sympathetic to peers who are in distress. Murphy also observed that children vary markedly in the frequency with which they display sympathy. Since that time, there has been a continuing investigation of two fundamental questions raised by Murphy's observational work: Are there stable individual differences in sympathetic responsiveness to another person's emotional state? And, by what mechanism does the young child come to feel the same emotion as another person (i.e., respond empathically) or feel and act in an appropriate fashion when someone is

We thank the contributors who helped us in the preparation of this chapter by commenting on earlier drafts.

distressed (i.e., respond sympathetically)? Current research on these two issues has been recently reviewed by Eisenberg (1986); Eisenberg and Strayer (1987), and Radke-Yarrow, Zahn-Waxler, and Chapman (1983). Research on children's understanding of emotion has relied on this body of work, but it has increasingly begun to ask a prior question. Although it is important to identify when and how the child is moved by another person's distress, such empathic understanding is only one part of a much more wide-ranging understanding of emotion that children begin to show in the early years. The understanding of another person's emotion may sometimes result in the empathic arousal of a similar emotion or in the offer of sympathy or comfort, but it may also lead to nicely calculated strategies for teasing, hurting, and upsetting another person (Dunn, 1988). It is also important to stress that young children often exhibit an obvious interest in the emotions of another person that does not necessarily lead them to engage in either pro- or antisocial behavior. They frequently turn to watch when they see an emotionally charged exchange (Dunn, 1988; Zahn-Waxler & Radke Yarrow, 1982). Indeed, their interest may assume a wary, frozen intensity (Cummings, 1987; Cummings, Iannotti, & Zahn-Waxler, 1985) but they do not necessarily do anything. Their interest in emotion is also apparent in the comments and questions that they produce about the emotional states of other people (Bretherton, Fritz, Zahn-Waxler, & Ridgeway, 1986). Viewed in this light, the child's understanding of emotion becomes an object of study in its own right, rather than an intervening variable that might explain pro- or antisocial behavior. Most of the contributors to parts II and III of this volume adopt this essentially cognitive perspective.

Expression and recognition of emotion

A second important tradition acknowledged by several contributors is research on the expression and recognition of emotion. In the early 1970s, evidence was gathered supporting the hypothesis that there is a set of discrete emotional expressions that are universally recognized as conveying particular emotional states (Ekman, 1973; Izard, 1971). On the assumption that this expressive repertoire is part of a species-specific native endowment, more recent research has examined the infant's capacity to both produce (Campos, Barrett, Lamb, Goldsmith, & Stenberg, 1983; Izard & Malatesta, 1987) and recognize these emotional expressions (Nelson, 1987).

The availability of such a biologically grounded signaling system suggests that children's early concepts of emotion might be anchored to facial expressions. According to this line of thinking, children will, irrespective of culture, focus on the same set of emotions: those core emotions such as happiness, sadness, and anger that can be conveyed easily by means of facial expressions. Indeed, a considerable body of research has been directed at finding out just how rapidly and accurately children can identify such facial expressions.

Research that narrowly focuses on the recognition of facial expression – or on the recognition of any supposedly universal expressive cues such as tone of voice or body posture – suffers, however, from two hidden assumptions. First, the capacity to distinguish among different expressions of emotion is not tantamount to the possession of a concept of any of the discriminated emotions. Admittedly, it is possible – certainly Darwin argued as much – that infants have an innate capacity not simply to recognize particular facial expressions of emotion but also to identify the emotional state that they convey. There is little contemporary evidence, however, to back up the claim (Nelson, 1987). It seems safer to view the infant as being well tuned to the discrimination of emotional expressions but requiring considerable instruction in their *significance*. In keeping with that distinction, several contributors (e.g., Smiley & Huttenlocher, Stein & Trabasso, Russell) focus not on the child's capacity to identify facial expressions per se but on the child's capacity to recognize such expressions as a reflection of a person's internal states. More generally, facial expressions are seen as only one component of a repertoire of expressive behaviors, and such behaviors are, in turn, recognized as being part of a temporally organized script that can include an appropriate cause, a subjective emotional state, and ensuing behavior.

The second weakness of research that focuses on the recognition of facial expression is that it gives us a restricted view of the conceptual task facing the child, and possibly a restricted view of what the child actually understands. For example, in English, we make a conceptual distinction between the emotions of *pride* and *relief*. There is no compelling evidence showing that we distinguish these emotions in terms of the facial, postural, or vocal cues that are associated with them. Admittedly, both emotions might often be accompanied by a happy facial expression or other signs of positive affect, but there is not evidence to show that the two emotions are accompanied by distinctive as well as similar modes of expression. On the other hand, it is quite easy to think of situations that would provoke one emotion but not the other. Recent evidence shows that young children can also perform this task: They can cite situations that would lead to *pride* but are not obviously associated with *relief* and vice versa (Harris, Olthof, Meerum Terwogt, & Hardman, 1987). The implication is that the emotional repertoire the child understands rapidly moves beyond those emotions that are linked to a distinctive facial expression. In acknowledgment of this extended repertoire, several contributors (e.g., Harter & Whitesell, Thompson, Russell, Gordon) consider emotions outside of the basic set emphasized by psychologists who study the facial expression of emotion.

Metacognition and the child's theory of mind

A third influential line of investigation has its home, properly speaking, in the study of cognitive development. During the 1970s, it became clear that the large differences that could be observed between younger and older children in memory performance often had little to do with the basic mnemonic mechanisms available to the child at different ages, but were instead attributable to differences in the way particular age groups deployed those mechanisms. Older children were more planful and far-sighted in their efforts to remember or retrieve information, particularly information that lacked an easily assimilable and meaningful structure. Flavell (1971) claimed that such differences in strategy were, at least in part, due to differences in metamemory: knowledge about the variables that affect the course of remembering. Older children were more sensitive to their mnemonic limitations and more knowledgeable about ways to circumvent those limitations. More generally, it seemed likely that older children would have a deeper and broader knowledge of all sorts of cognitive processes. Hence, the study of metacognition was born.

How is work on metacognition pertinent to the child's understanding of emotion? We can think of the child as a spectator of another person's emotion, a spectator who may or may not discern the person's facial expression and its significance, a spectator who may or may not empathize with the person's emotion and intervene. However, as soon as we acknowledge that the young child is a highly emotional participant and not simply a spectator, the work on metacognition has an immediate relevance. Given that the older child is likely to have a wider knowledge of the causes and the time-course of emotion, does that knowledge enter into the capacity for emotional self-control, which even casual observation suggests is much more extensive in the older child as compared with the preschooler? Several contributors (e.g., Saarni, Meerum Terwogt & Olthof, Harris & Lipian) consider this question.

While investigators have been engaged in applying the conceptual tools of work on metacognition to the study of emotion, the study of metacognition has itself undergone an important revolution. As we have mentioned, an early theme in the study of metamemory was the notion that older children are more knowledgeable about what to do when the more or less automatic processes of memory were inadequate for the task at hand, be it one of encoding or recall. Thus, the older child's psychological knowledge was regarded as strategic in content and application. More recently, it has become clear that there is much to gain if we relax the tight conceptual link between metacognition and strategic self-control. Psychological knowledge can serve other purposes. Thinking once more of the child as a participant in social life, seeking to understand the mental lives of caretakers and companions, the child must develop what has come to be known as a "theory of mind" (Premack & Woodruff, 1978) – a theory about the psychological processes that underlie everyday social activities.

Recent research has shown that an understanding of two of the key components of that theory – beliefs and desires – is in place at the end of the preschool period (Astington, Harris, & Olson, 1988). Those components not only help the child to predict another person's actions, but also to make sense of another person's emotions and emotional displays (Harris, 1987; Harris & Gross, 1988). Several contributors (e.g., Smiley & Huttenlocher, Stein & Trabasso, Gnepp) place their research in that wider context by asking how the child's understanding of emotion borrows from and contributes to the child's general theory of mind. In particular, they claim that basic emotions such as happiness, sadness, or fear imply a specific relationship between desire and reality, and that such relationships are understood early in the preschool years. For example, sadness usually involves the loss of an object that the person wanted to keep or a failure to attain that desired object. By attending to the relationship between desire and reality, young children can grasp that all sorts of different situations can elicit sadness so long as they all lead to the loss of a desired object. Conversely, the same situation may elicit sadness depending on whether it does or does not match a person's desires.

The social context

A final influence derives from the study of emotion within its social context. Many psychologists have been inclined to search for invariant, biologically grounded aspects of emotion, particularly through the study of facial expression or through supposedly universal aspects of our emotional experience, such as loss or frustration. Nevertheless, colleagues in social psychology (Schachter & Singer, 1962), sociology (Hochschild, 1983), and anthropology (Rosaldo, 1980; Lutz, 1987) have emphasized the plasticity of our emotional experience and the interpersonal frame of reference within which that experience develops. Such a frame of reference may include the cultural or personal schemata that are employed in appraising a situation, the norms and values of one's culture regarding particular emotions and their expression, and one's own interpersonal history and self-evaluation. There are both "radical" and "moderate" interpretations of the impact of this frame of reference upon what one feels and whether one expresses what one feels. Radicals argue that emotions and expressive behavior can only be constituted within a frame of reference that is socially defined, whereas moderates claim that the social context has an organizing or moderating influence on universal predispositions.

Our view of the task facing the child in understanding emotion will depend quite critically on our conception of the nature of the social context. One might argue that the social context, even if it exerts an influence, can only do so within certain limits. Irrespective of the culture that they grow up in, all children will appraise reality in terms of its coincidence with their goals. As a result, all children will experience the anger that arises when another person deliberately blocks their goal; they will inevitably experience the sadness that occurs at the loss of a desired object or a temporary separation from an attachment figure; and they will all experience the joy of obtaining a desired object and being able to keep it for a certain length of time. Because all children will appraise reality in terms of its match with their desires, and because they will necessarily experience these various relationships between desire and outcome, it is reasonable to insist that there is a set of focal or basic emotional experiences, just as the conjunction of our perceptual apparatus and the color spectrum gives rise to a set of focal or basic colors. Starting from such a universal base, we may assume, as do Stein and Trabasso, that certain key features of emotional understanding will be present from an early age. Alternatively, like Harter and Whitesell, we may adopt a quasi-Piagetian position, and assume that the child will proceed through various stages in the development of a theory that reflects that universal base with increasing adequacy. From either of these perspectives, social experience is likely to be, at most, a general facilitator or inhibitor of cognitive development, rather than a major determinant in its own right.

"Moderate" social constructivists, by contrast, insist that development may be much more culturally variable even though they too allow that the child may start from a pancultural base. For example, Russell claims that irrespective of their culture children are universally constrained to interpret emotional episodes in terms of two dimensions: pleasure–displeasure, and arousal–sleepiness. However, he also goes on to argue that depending on their culture children may take divergent paths during development. In particular, depending on the emotional scripts they learn within their culture, they will develop emotion categories at quite different loci within the universal two-dimensional grid. Thus, Russell makes no claim to the effect that certain focal scripts will be universally found and similarly located in conceptual space.

Contributors of a more "radical" persuasion (e.g., Saarni, Gordon) claim that the child can have little understanding of emotion that is not socially transmitted. First, the emotional experiences that a child has will be generated within a social context. Second, communities are likely to elaborate indigenous cultural beliefs and practices about the causes and effects of emotions. Such indigenous psychologies (Heelas & Lock, 1981) or "emotional cultures" (Gordon, this volume) will be conveyed to the developing child through a host of social prescriptions and explanations. Thus, both the content and the interpretation of emotional experience will vary from culture to culture, leaving little scope for a pancultural base.

To sum up this review of historical influences, the study of children's understanding of emotion has built upon at least four areas of research. In doing so, it has increasingly adopted a set of assumptions and questions that are distinct. We – and most of the contributors to this volume – subscribe to the following basic assumptions. Young children exhibit an interest in and an understanding of the emotional reactions of other people that extends beyond whatever capacity for empathy or sympathy they might display. Their understanding also amounts to much more than an ability to discriminate among facial expressions; it involves a grasp of the causal links that bind particular situations, subjective emotional states, and expressive signals into coherent emotional experiences. Their understanding appears to have at least two important functions. It can gradually help efforts at strategic self-control, whether aimed at the outer expression or the inner experience of emotion. Second, it is an important component in the child's theory of mind, which is a vital acquisition if the child is to participate fully in social life. Finally, there is little consensus on the nature of the domain that the child seeks to understand. Some see it as invariant in important ways across cultures, whereas others insist that emotion can only arise within a social context, and, because those contexts can vary dramatically from culture to culture, the nature of what is to be understood about emotional experience in oneself and others must vary across cultures.

We now turn to a discussion of the particular themes that are taken up in each part of the volume.

Part II: Early understanding of emotion

In the past 10–15 years, enormous progress has been made in our understanding of concept acquisition. To summarize that achievement briefly, it now seems clear that in a variety of domains adults form concepts that are organized around a prototype that need not correspond to a specific instance but synthesizes the average or most frequently occurring features of a set of instances (Smith & Medin, 1981). The capacity for forming such prototypes appears to be available early in infancy, at least when the infant is presented with a variety of instances of a particular category of physical object (Harris, 1983a; Younger & Cohen, 1985).

The prototype approach does not depend on the availability of any essential features, but it does presuppose the existence of frequently recurring features. Smiley and Huttenlocher (chapter 2) emphasize that the child who is acquiring emotion categories faces a difficult task in identifying helpful recurrent features across the various instances of emotion that he or she encounters. Emotion categories, and indeed other categories relating to persons, involve two distinct types of instance. On the one hand, there are instances involving the self, which we shall call first-person instances, that consist centrally in a set of internal states in reaction to particular events. By contrast, instances involving other people (third-person instances) consist of the external expressive behaviors of those people and the circumstances that surround them; the internal states of other people cannot be experienced directly by an observer. Thus, there is a clear asymmetry in the features that are present in first- and third-person instances.

Second, even if we confine our attention to third-person instances, considerable heterogeneity will still be encountered. The expressive behavior, particularly the facial expression that accompanies particular emotional states, may be stable across different instances of a given emotion, but the circumstances in which that emotion occurs can be quite diverse. Consider, for example, the range of situations in which a child might observe a sibling feeling sad or upset: not getting a particular food, breaking a toy, seeing a parent leave. It is difficult to identify any perceptual features that recur across these various situations, and yet the preschooler must somehow come to appreciate that each is a likely elicitor of sadness.

On the basis of existing evidence, Smiley and Huttenlocher tentatively propose a developmental sequence for the acquisition of emotion concepts. At first, the child uses words like *sad, mad,* and so forth in relation to current internal states of the self. Next, the child notices the invariant external cues to other people's emotional experiences, including facial and bodily expressive behaviors. Thus, the child begins to describe people who look or act in a distressed or angry fashion as *sad* or *mad.* Finally, instead of categorizing only the overt behaviors that other people express, the child begins to appreciate that other people can feel a given emotion in a variety of circumstances. Thus, even watching an unfamiliar person in a novel situation, the child can figure out whether they are *mad,* as opposed to *scared* or *sad.*

How does the child come to detect similarities across first- and third-person instances? Smiley and Huttenlocher make two tentative suggestions. The first is that the linking of first- and third-person instances can be made by analogy, and the second is that the child may notice that other people exhibit the same sorts of expressive behaviors (e.g., crying or laughter) as the self. Similarities in the observable, expressive aspects of first- and third-person instances might be used to infer, by analogy with the self, that other people have internal experiences when they display emotion. The ability to identify recurrent features across diverse situational elicitors of emotion requires a different mechanism. The child may need to appreciate that other people have goals and desires that can be advanced or thwarted by external circumstances. Sadness typically involves the loss of an object that one desires to have or keep; what remains constant across the various situations that elicit sadness is not the particular object or event involved, but a particular relationship between desire and outcome.

In their chapter, which is concerned with somewhat older children, Stein and Trabasso (chapter 3) also assume that children infer a person's emotional state by reference to the goals and desires of that person. They make explicit contact with recent work on the child's theory of mind by arguing that preschool children and certainly 6-year-olds do not focus exclusively on the external outcome or situation. Rather, their results suggest that children appreciate that as external outcomes change, so the relationship between goals and outcomes changes, and as a result the emotion experienced by the protagonist also changes. Thus, 6-year-olds appreciate that someone may shift from intense happiness to intense sadness (or the reverse) in the course of an episode, given that a goal is initially satisfied but then blocked. They can also infer some of the likely mental sequelae of such emotional states: They appreciate that particular emotions lead to a particular pattern of wishing and planning. In sum, 6-year-olds are sensitive to the mental antecedents and to the mental consequences of emotion. Their concept of emotion extends forward and backward in time. In that respect, their conceptualization of emotion is similar to that of a script. It involves knowledge of a temporally and causally organized sequence of events. We return to the construct of emotion scripts in part VI.

Pulling together the two contributions to part II, an important common theme can be identified. The child's concept of a particular emotion, even during the preschool years, cannot rely on particular perceptual features, such as a given facial expression, to unite the various instances of that emotion. To successfully identify the various instances of an emotion such as happiness or sadness, the child must attend to the goals and intentions whose satisfaction or frustration leads to the experience of emotion. Briefly stated, children cannot understand the most basic emotional states unless they penetrate beyond the expression of those states.

Part III: Developmental changes in understanding emotion

Part II shows that the preschool child has a good understanding of the causes and consequences of basic emotions such as happiness, sadness, fear, and anger. During the school years, this basic knowledge is elaborated in three important ways. First, the child begins to appreciate that such basic emotions are not mutually exclusive. More than one emotion can be experienced at the same time in response to a given person or episode. Second, the child starts to engage in a fuller examination of the events that have led up to a particular emotionally charged outcome, so that a finer diagnosis of the emotion becomes possible. Third, the child becomes increasingly sensitive to the personal history that will modulate any given individual's emotional reaction to a situation. Each of these developments requires that the child engage in a more exhaustive analysis of the events that cause emotion. The child must achieve greater "causal depth" (R. M. Gordon, 1987).

In chapter 4, Harter and Whitsell present an updated account of their findings concerning the first development: children's understanding of mixed feelings. They find that between the ages of 5 and 12 years, children move through a five-step sequence. At first, children claim that two feelings cannot occur at all, or can only occur one after the other. At the end of the sequence, at about 11 years, they acknowledge that a single situation can elicit positive and negative feelings concurrently, or, if not, in rapid alternation. Harter and Whitesell explain this development in terms of two factors: changes in the way the child represents the links between situations and emotions, and the child's increasing capacity for simultaneously keeping in mind two such mental links.

Although Harter and Whitesell emphasize that the cognitive limitations of the 6-year-old prevent any genuine admission of simultaneous mixed feelings, Stein and Trabasso argue that approximately half of their 6-year-old subjects did make such an admission. How can we explain this discrepancy? One possibility is that the stories involving successive changes in the emotional state of the protagonist served as a prime for Stein and Trabasso's subjects. A more likely explanation, however, is that Harter and Whitesell used a more stringent criterion for the understanding of ambivalence; they required subjects to provide an example where the eliciting components took place concurrently and where the emotions would be concurrent or at least experienced in an oscillating fashion over a given span of time.

Despite this apparent discrepancy between the two chapters, there is one area of substantial agreement: An understanding of successive feelings toward a given target precedes and probably sets the stage for an understanding of simultaneous or mixed feelings toward that target. What might serve as a developmental bridge between the understanding of simultaneous and successive feelings? Stein and Trabasso create story episodes where the later emotion (e.g., happiness at having what one wanted) effectively deletes and replaces an earlier emotion (e.g., sadness at not having it). Yet such total replacement is not always likely. Consider, for example, the episodes devised by Donaldson and Westerman (1986) and Harris (1983b; Experiment 2). In these episodes, an earlier negative emotion was likely to persist so as to be felt concurrent with a later-aroused positive emotion. For example, in one of the stories devised by Donaldson and Westerman (1986), the protagonist loses his or her kitten and is then given another kitten to replace the first. In this story, the sadness aroused by the initial loss will probably persist so that it will be felt alongside the positive feelings aroused by the new kitten. Such hybrid episodes where the eliciting situations are successive but the feelings end up being concurrent may be an important stepping-stone toward an understanding of feelings that are both elicited and also experienced simultaneously.

In a later section of their chapter, Harter and Whitesell consider how the child's understanding moves beyond the basic emotions of happiness, sadness, anger, and fear. Specifically, they provide an intriguing account of the emergence of the child's understanding of pride and shame. At around 6–7 years, children show some understanding of the two emotions but judge that they will only arise when the protagonist commits an act (be it shameful or pride-worthy) in the presence of a disapproving or approving person such as a parent. Later, this external audience is augmented by an internalized or imagined audience, so that children appreciate that pride and shame can be experienced even when the protagonist is alone. Two points are especially noteworthy about these findings. First, they offer an important glimpse of the likely impact of key socializing agents such as parents (we will consider their role in more detail when we introduce the final part of the book). Second, although Harter and Whitesell do not interpret their findings in this way, it seems likely that there is some connection between the child's understanding of mixed emotions and the child's understanding of pride and shame. Specifically, pride involves an acknowledgment of two successive, causally linked emotions: the approval or happiness expressed by another person (whether present or imagined) and the resultant happiness felt by the self. Similarly, shame also implies two emotions: the disapproval or anger expressed by another person (present or imagined), and the resultant sadness or fear experienced by the self. Here we also find the implicit notion of a script, albeit a script that has two players: protagonist and audience. Harter and Whitesell's results suggest that when this script has been well-rehearsed one of the players may be dispensed with, because the child can mentally assume that part as well as his or her own.

Thompson (chapter 4) also examines how children acquire a more differentiated understanding of emotions. From the standpoint of attributional theory, he asks whether there is an age-dependent shift from a narrow focus on outcomes – which would only permit the correct attribution of outcome-dependent emotions, such as happiness and sadness – to a more comprehensive analysis of the causes of those outcomes – which would permit the correct attribution of emotions such as pride and guilt. Contrary to the expectations of attribution theory (cf. Graham & Weiner, 1986), his findings show that such a broad shift does not occur. There are circumstances when even young children aged 6–8 years are quite sensitive to the cause of an outcome and not just to the outcome itself. For example, when they attribute gratitude or anger to someone, they appreciate that these emotions often depend not just upon the presence of a given outcome but also upon how the outcome was brought about, particularly if it was due to an intervention by another person.

However, young children are likely to attribute pride and guilt on the basis of outcomes associated with success and failure, ignoring the question of who or what caused the outcome. They think that a person will feel pride or guilt in relation to purely adventitious outcomes. Older children acknowledge that pride and guilt depend upon personal responsibility for success or failure.

Overall, Thompson's chapter shows that young children do not entirely ignore the question of causation; for certain emotions they can execute the relevant analysis but for other emotions, which turn on an appreciation of personal responsibility, their analysis may be too crude to make appropriate attributions. Accordingly, although there is no developmental watershed marking the point when causes are taken into account, there is a lot to be gained by asking just what causal sequences young children do and do not understand, because the appropriate attribution of certain emotions depends critically on the analysis of causal sequences.

The results described by Harter and Whitesell and by Thompson show that self-directed affects – pride, shame, guilt – may be especially interesting candidates for developmental and social analysis. First, each chapter shows that the acquisition of a full understanding of these emotions is quite protracted. In addition, Harter and Whitesell emphasize that there are marked individual differences in the rate of progress. It seems quite likely that parents play an important role in offering children feedback for successes or failures and, as we have seen, children gradually internalize that role. What is unclear is how parents might foster a mature understanding. On first reflection, it seems likely that absent or neglectful parents will not help development because they are not available to serve as an external audience, and will therefore delay the process of internalization. However, it is also possible for parents to slow development by overly generous feedback. If they praise their child's success irrespective of the effort or ability that was needed for success, the child may fail to link pride with personal responsibility. Equally, if they express anger or criticism toward the child when he or she fails, irrespective of whether the failure was avoidable, the child may be slow to develop a more selective, responsibility oriented, concept of guilt or shame. We believe that future research will be especially revealing if it seeks to combine an analysis of the cognitive prerequisites for understanding particular affects with an analysis of the socialization practices that would foster or suppress a grasp of those prerequisites.

In chapter 6, Gnepp examines a further set of developmental changes in the child's understanding of the link between situation and emotion. Harter, Whitesell, and Thompson ask children to predict a *typical* response by an unspecified other person to a given situation. Thus, they ask children to examine the situation facing the protagonist without reference to the preferences, the personality, or the history of the protagonist. Gnepp points out, however, that the emotional reaction of a given individual to a particular situation can be moderated by all these factors. She asks whether children take these factors into account in making their predictions. In a comprehensive review, she finds that children do increasingly take such information into account. What is particularly interesting is that young children appear to take certain types of personal information into account much more easily than others. Thus, preschoolers often ignore personal information altogether, with one important exception: They do appear to take into account the preferences – the likes, the dislikes, and the desires – of an individual. In the early school years, children begin to lay the foundations for a more extensive use of personal information: they realize that different people respond differently to certain, equivocal situations, and they also recognize that a person's past behavior and past experience offer clues to their appraisal of a current situation. Yet, despite the availability of this background knowledge, young children often ignore it in predicting emotion. Finally, older children – from 8 to 12 years – put this background knowledge to use more actively. They acknowledge that someone might feel more than one way about a situation and that his or her reaction will be based on appraisals born of past encounters.

Part IV: The control of emotion

In chapters 7 and 8, Meerum Terwogt, Olthof, and Saarni ask what children understand about the strategic control of emotion. Despite their focus on a common problem, the starting point for each chapter is somewhat different. Meerum Terwogt and Olthof adopt the working hypothesis that the link between situation and emotional behavior is normally quite smooth and automatic. They point to the existence of well organized emotion "programs" in the young infant. Given such preexisting programs, the child's task is to break into and redirect a program that is already in operation. As a result, these authors view the process of self-regulation as a self-reflexive process. The child must – to use Bartlett's memorable phrase – turn around on his or her own schemata. Viewed in this light, the process of self-regulation will depend upon the child's introspective abilities. To be sure, the social community will also alert the child to possible strategies for self-regulation and to the consequences of failing to apply them, yet for Meerum Terwogt and Olthof, such knowledge, like a good deal of so-called education, may often lead to a sterile and fragmentary understanding, as compared with the more dynamic and functional knowledge that comes from self-reflection. Finally, in line with the notion that self-regulation requires a reflection upon preexisting processes, Meerum Terwogt and Olthof acknowledge explicitly that in the absence of such self-reflection there may often be a developmental lag between the expression or experience of emotion and knowledge about emotion.

Saarni starts her chapter by immediately placing the child in a social context. That social context influences the child in various ways. It provides feedback about what type of emotional expression is desirable but, even more importantly, it provides the child with information about what to feel in response to otherwise ambiguous or neutral situations. Such information can be provided verbally or can be communicated nonverbally to infants via their capacity for social referencing. Thus, contrary to Meerum Terwogt and Olthof, Saarni does not make the assumption that there is a very tight or automatic relationship between situation and emotion. Instead, she assumes that the child's parents or the surrounding culture will often provide a gloss on a particular situation, and that gloss will effectively teach the child what to feel. Such socially mediated learning may be especially important for the acquisition of emotion blends and for complex emotions such as pride and guilt. In the absence of any automatic emotion program, the developmental issue is not how the child breaks into an otherwise operational program in order to redirect it. Rather, the issues are: By what mechanism(s) does the surrounding community convey to the child information about what emotion it is appropriate to feel, and how does the child become attuned to the different expectations and constraints that operate in particular interpersonal settings?

Having sketched this contrast in working hypotheses, we must also underline certain ways in which the two chapters are complementary to one another. Saarni presents her work as an extension and elaboration of some of her earlier findings on display rules. The control of the external expression of emotion is, in certain respects, sharply different from the control or redirection of the underlying affect itself. At the risk of simplification, we can say that subjective experience will often reflect the operation of the automatic emotion program especially when basic emotions are involved, whereas the outward expression of emotion will be more subject to the social influences that Saarni underlines. The very existence of a discrepancy between overt display and experience strongly suggests that, social pressure notwithstanding, there are certain parts to the emotion program that do run untrammeled by the prescriptions of parents and peers. In short, the child's emotions enjoy or suffer a life of their own, albeit a life that is often hidden from view. This discrepancy between overt expression and actual feelings is sufficiently potent that 6-year-olds are quite articulate about it: They realize that the two need not coincide and that appearances may therefore mislead others about their true feelings (Harris & Gross, 1988). Thus, the control of emotion may operate at two levels. On the one hand, the process of introspective self-reflection that Meerum Terwogt and Olthof see as critical to self-regulation may be especially important for interrupting the automatic link between situation and subjective experience; on the other hand, the socially mediated learning stressed by Saarni may be especially important for the control of overt affective displays.

Part V: Emotion, empathy, and experience

In several chapters of the volume, children's understanding of emotion is approached in terms of the accurate diagnosis of another person's emotional state. The question of what emotion the perceiver experiences before, during, or after such a diagnosis is not considered. In the two chapters that comprise Part V, Harris and Lipian (chapter 9) and Strayer (chapter 10) tackle this issue head-on. Harris and Lipian ask whether a child who is currently facing an emotionally charged experience will be thereby hindered or helped in understanding his or her own emotions or those of other people. Thus, Harris and Lipian treat the presence of an emotionally charged situation and, by implication, the current experience of emotion, as an independent variable that could have an impact on the child's understanding of emotion.

Harris and Lipian questioned children in two emotionally charged settings: in a hospital and in a boarding school. They note that despite important similarities between these two settings – insofar as they each confront the child with a strange environment that he or she must in large measure negotiate without the support of parents and friends – there are also important differences. Children entering a hospital typically do so unexpectedly, perceive few positive aspects to the experience, and anticipate leaving the hospital as soon as they have recovered. By contrast, children entering a boarding school usually know well ahead of entry that their life will change; they see distinct advantages to the new environment, and they see it as a permanent change.

Marked differences in the understanding of emotion were associated with the two different environments. In particular, children in the hospital exhibited a slippage or regression in their understanding of emotion, whereas no such phenomenon was found in the boarding school. Harris and Lipian tentatively attribute the slippage effect to the feelings of distress experienced and reported by children in the hospital. They suggest that such feelings are the source of a pervasive cognitive bias that leads the child to be pessimistic about the likelihood of experiencing or displaying positive feelings.

Strayer raises a different issue about the role of current emotion. She points out that there has been a lengthy tradition of research looking at the degree to which children respond empathically to the emotional state or, more generally, to the plight or circumstances of another person. Much of this research has focused on the extent to which the observer responds to another person's situation by feeling either the same emotion (perhaps with a different intensity) or an emotion of the same valence. Strayer makes the important point that although such affective matching has been seen as a critical element of empathy, measures that focus exclusively on the presence or absence of matching may miss important developmental differences in the way such matching is achieved. In short, Strayer's chapter can be read as an essay on the question of whether and to what extent the experience of emotion – and more specifically matching emotion – is sufficient to define empathy.

Strayer presented 5-, 8-, and 13-year-olds with six films depicting people describing or encountering various emotionally charged experiences. The children described the emotions of the protagonist in each film and said how they themselves felt and why they felt as they did. Thus, it was possible to measure affective matching with the protagonist in the traditional fashion, but it was also possible to assess how the child had arrived at his or her emotional reaction to each film. Affective matching was quite frequent at all ages, although its prevalence varied to some extent depending on the age of the child and on the particular emotion attributed to the protagonist. More striking was the fact that the apparent route by which children achieved that match varied quite markedly with age. The majority of 5-year-olds either failed to explain their supposedly empathic feeling, offered irrelevant reasons, or focused on the outward events depicted in the film rather than on the situation as perceived by the main character. By contrast, the majority of children in the two older groups were much more likely to take the perspective of the main character into account: They mentioned the particular situation facing that character or the particular feelings of that character.

Part VI: The role of culture and socialization practices

In different ways, Russell (chapter 11), Gordon (chapter 12), and Lewis (chapter 13) consider the impact of culture and socialization practices. Gordon and Lewis return to a dilemma that we also identified in part IV. What is the nature of the domain that the child is trying to understand? Does it consist of a universal set of biologically given discrete emotion programs, with each program specifying a tight link between a particular situation and a particular emotion? Alternatively, does it consist of a set of loosely arranged scripts whose organization is chiefly specified by the culture? If the first description is correct, we might describe the child as accurately or inaccurately recognizing a set of schemata that are biologically grounded and effectively culture-free. If, however, the second description is more appropriate, we might speak in terms of the child's gradual construction of a conceptual scheme that is culture-specific. As Russell (chapter 11) points out, however, an accurate characterization of the domain of emotion (even if we could achieve it) cannot automatically tell us exactly how the child will set about understanding that domain; for example, the child might try to impose discrete categories on a continuous domain or fail to detect the discreteness that objectively exists. Nevertheless, a characterization of the domain can tell us a good deal about the input that is available to the child and the complexity of the task that is being undertaken.

Russell comes to the conclusion that the assumptions that have dominated our thinking about the psychology of emotion may need to be discarded when we turn to study the process of understanding in the child. Two key assumptions have been the notion of a set of discrete emotion events, each tied to a universally recognizable facial expression, and the related assumption that the child must construct a set of discrete categories tied to such discrete events. Russell argues that these notions should not guide our thinking about the child's understanding for several reasons. First, he presents intriguing data to show that toddlers initially classify facial expressions not in terms of discrete categories but rather in terms of two continuous dimensions, those of pleasure and arousal. Second, he points out that the cross-linguistic study of emotion terms shows that cultures differ in the emotions they identify. The difference is not simply one of greater or lesser specificity. Cultures pick out quite different emotional states. Russell's solution to these problems is to argue that the child starts off from a pancultural base – he or she applies the two dimensions of pleasure and arousal – and then gradually distinguishes emotions located at similar points within that two-dimensional space in terms of the particular script that is associated with each particular emotion. The script for a given emotion can be learned by observing – or being told about – the way in which particular situations, expressive signals, and actions tend to occur in a predictable sequence.

Gordon identifies another widespread assumption. Developmental psychologists looking at the child's developing knowledge of emotion have often adopted a Piagetian perspective: They have assumed that there is a more or less universal timetable to the child's understanding, which reflects the way the child constructs an increasingly adequate understanding of a set of phenomena that are ''out there,'' invariant across culture and fixed by our biological endowment. As a sociologist, Gordon is sympathetic to the constructivist approach, but he adopts a more radical version than the average developmental psychologist. Like other contributors, he postulates a system of emotion components such as subjective experience, expressive behavior, situational appraisal, and so forth. Gordon argues, however, that it is social experience within a particular cultural milieu that teaches the child the linkages among these assorted components. In terms of his social constructionist viewpoint, the creation of such linkages occurs predominantly in interpersonal transactions, which occur during socialization. Such transactions are influenced by social structural variables such as the demographic composition of the cultural group, its economic basis, and its historical context. They are also influenced by more obviously cultural variables: the ethnopsychology of the group and its associated expectations of emotional competence. Finally, even where societies operate with the same emotions or emotion scripts, there may be structural and cultural variations among those societies in the extent to which they expose children to those emotions. Children may or may not be protected from expressions of anger, lust, and grief. More generally, Gordon's chapter gives a systematic overview of the ways in which the emotional reality that the child is exposed to will vary from society to society, so that we should think, not in terms of a universal but of a culture-specific timetable for the child's understanding of emotion.

Lewis, like Gordon, assumes that inbuilt links between particular situations and particular emotions play only a small role in the child's emotional development. Rather, it is socialization practices that determine the emotion displayed in a given situation. If socialization practices are important in creating emotional scripts, the script that is adopted at different ages and in different cultures for a particular situation may sometimes vary markedly. Lewis argues, therefore, that investigations of script knowledge would benefit from the inclusion of a cross-cultural comparison – because respondents in different cultures may adopt a different script – and also from the inclusion of adult respondents – because their judgments may coincide neither with those of younger or older children nor with those of the experimenter. He describes an exploratory study that includes both of these design features. The results show that children (at least beyond the age of 3 years) and adults in different cultures (U.S. and Japan) do agree on the emotion likely to be produced in certain situations. For example, they agree that a birthday party will elicit happiness, whereas a lost pet will elicit sadness. On the other hand, some situations lead to much greater disagreement. For example, American mothers, unlike their children, and unlike Japanese mothers, believe that a child lost in a store would display fear rather than sadness.

Finally, it is worth underlining an important implication of the claims made by Russell, Gordon, and Lewis in part IV. For many situations, the emotion that children display may depend upon their acquisition of a culturally appropriate emotion script. This dependency is important because it reverses the conventional relationship between knowledge and behavior. It is tempting to assume that emotional behavior always precedes emotional knowledge; children initially exhibit particular emotions and only subsequently come to consciously articulate the script they have followed. However, the developmental sequence may go in the reverse direction: Children may learn an explicit script first and only subsequently display the emotion called for in that script. In such cases, we may need to study children's understanding of emotion in order to explain the particular emotion that they exhibit.

A changing theory of emotion

We turn finally to consider one general issue that cross-cuts various chapters in the volume. Harris and Olthof (1982) reviewed various developmental changes in children's understanding of the identification of emotion, strategies for hiding or changing emotion, and the effects and time-course of emotion. They concluded that 6-year-olds adopt an S–R theory of emotion: They think of situations and overt responses as being linked together with little mental mediation. By contrast, older children of 10 and 11 years adopt a mentalistic theory; they acknowledge that a particular situation may elicit various emotional reactions depending on the mental perspective of the person who encounters it.

How does this model stand up in relation to the findings presented in this volume? Two major weaknesses are apparent. First, Harris and Olthof (1982) explained developmental change from 6 years onward more or less exclusively in terms of the increased weight given to mental processes by the older child. The chapters by Harter and Whitesell and by Thompson, in particular, show that this is too narrow an explanation. Over and above any increased sensitivity to mental components, older children also come to invest the situation facing the protagonist with more causal depth. They penetrate further back in time, to consider not just the situation that confronts the protagonist but the causes of that situation.

The second weakness is highlighted in the chapters by Gnepp and by Stein and Trabasso. They point out that even preschoolers lend some weight to mental components: They take goals and preferences into account, and this is inconsistent with Harris and Olthof's model. More recent evidence shows that many 6-year-olds and some 5-year-olds can appreciate that a person's emotion will be jointly determined by the beliefs and the desires that the person brings to a situation, even when those beliefs are known to be false (Harris, 1987). In certain respects, young children clearly adopt a mentalistic concept of emotion.

Nevertheless, some data continue to fit quite easily into the framework advanced by Harris and Olthof (1982). The chapter by Gnepp suggests that it takes several years before school-aged children take idiosyncratic appraisals into account when these must be inferred from the history of an individual and applied to new situations. The chapter by Harter and Whitesell describes marked changes between 5 and 11 years in the ability to appreciate that the same situation can be appraised in two quite different ways, so that two conflicting emotions are aroused. The chapter by Strayer shows that within the same age period there are also marked changes in the way that children explain feelings they share with someone they are observing; younger children attribute the match to situational factors alone, whereas older children given more attention to the individual perspective that the person being observed might adopt.

Thus, we need to explain why preschoolers can take beliefs and desires into account, whereas the impact of other types of mental appraisal is often ignored until well into the school years. The explanation we favor turns on a distinction between the conscious products of mental processing and the more or less unconscious processes that yield such products. In the course of everyday activities, we are fully conscious as adults of what we intend, what we want, and what we believe. For example, in going to retrieve an object, we know which object we want to find, we know where we believe it was last put, and we know where we intend to look. It seems likely that children enjoy the same self-consciousness: They know their own mind in the sense that they can report what they want and what they take to be the case, and they can even appreciate that their desires and beliefs may not be shared by others. To the extent that the correct attribution of emotion depends on an acknowledgment of such conscious mental states, young children successfully adopt a mentalistic theory of emotion.

Other mental processes operate in a less conscious fashion. For example, the acknowledgment of mixed feelings appears to depend on the ability to become aware of the way that distinct aspects of a given situation can be concurrently appraised. Although the child may well engage in such concurrent appraisal – and express mixed feelings as a result – it seems reasonable to suppose that the limited capacity of consciousness makes it hard for the child to focus, at any given moment, on more than one aspect of the situation – and its accompanying appraisal – at a time. Thus, the young child has little or no conscious experience of mixed or conflicting emotions, even though his or her overt behavior may reveal such feelings. At best, the child has an awareness of emotions that shift back and forth, as one aspect and then another of a total situation enters awareness.

In conclusion, we would now maintain that even preschool children can be credited with a mentalistic understanding of emotion. They appreciate that the emotional impact of a given situation depends on the beliefs and desires that are brought to that situation. Nevertheless, their understanding is limited in two important respects. Whether they analyze the situation or the mental states that are brought to it, their analysis lacks depth. So far as the situation is concerned they often – although not always – neglect the causal antecedents that have led up to it, particularly when issues of personal responsibility are at stake. So far as mental states are concerned, they focus on the more immediate and conscious states of belief, desire, and intention. Mental states that lie beneath the threshold of consciousness or are a function of someone's personal history are more rarely taken into account. If this account is correct, we should think of the older child as achieving greater penetration in his or her causal understanding of emotion, but not as introducing any fundamentally new causal elements.

References

Astington, J. W., Harris, P. L., & Olson, D. R. (1988). *Developing theories of mind*. New York: Cambridge University Press.

Bretherton, I., Fritz, J., Zahn-Waxler, C., & Ridgeway, D. (1986). Learning to talk about emotions: A functionalist perspective. *Child Development, 57*, 529–548.

Campos, J. J., Barrett, K. C., Lamb, M. E., Goldsmith, H. H., & Stenberg, C. (1983). Socio-emotional development. In P. Mussen (Ed.), *Handbook of child psychology: Vol. II, Infancy and developmental psychobiology* (M. M. Haith & J. J. Campos, Vol. Eds.) (pp. 783–915). New York: Wiley.

Cummings, E. M. (1987). Coping with background anger in early childhood. *Child Development, 58*, 976–984.

Cummings, E. M., Iannotti, R. J., & Zahn-Waxler, C. (1985). Influence of conflict between adults on the emotions and aggression of young children. *Developmental Psychology, 21,* 495–507.

Donaldson, S. K., & Westerman, M. A. (1986). Development of children's understanding of ambivalence and causal theories of emotions. *Developmental Psychology, 22,* 655–662.

Dunn, J. (1988). *The beginnings of social understanding.* Oxford: Blackwell.

Eisenberg, N. (1986). *Altruistic emotion, cognition, and behavior.* Hillsdale, NJ: Erlbaum.

Eisenberg, N., & Strayer, J. (Eds.) (1987). *Empathy and its development.* New York: Cambridge University Press.

Ekman, P. (1973). *Darwin and facial expression: A century of research in review.* New York: Academic Press.

Flavell, J. (1971). First discussant's comments: What is memory development the development of? *Human Development, 14,* 272–278.

Gordon, R. M. (1987). *The structure of emotion.* New York: Cambridge University Press.

Graham, S., & Weiner, B. (1986). From an attributional theory of emotion to developmental psychology: A round-trip ticket? *Social Cognition, 4,* 152–179.

Harris, P. L. (1983a). Infant cognition. In P. Mussen (Ed.), *Handbook of child psychology: Vol II, Infancy and developmental psychobiology.* (M. M. Haith & J. J. Campos, Vol. Eds.), (pp. 689–782). New York: Wiley.

Harris, P. L. (1983b). Children's understanding of the link between situation and emotion. *Journal of Experimental Child Psychology, 36,* 490–509.

Harris, P. L. (1987). *Children's understanding of the causal links between belief, desire and emotion.* Paper presented at the annual meeting of the developmental section of the British Psychological Society, York.

Harris, P. L., & Gross, D. (1988). Children's understanding of real and apparent emotion. In J. W. Astington, P. L. Harris, & D. R. Olson (Eds.), *Developing theories of mind.* New York: Cambridge University Press.

Harris, P. L., & Olthof, T. (1982). The child's concept of emotion. In G. E. Butterworth & P. Light (Eds.), *Social cognition,* (pp. 188–209). Brighton, U.K.: Harvester.

Harris, P. L., Olthof, T., Meerum Terwogt, M., & Hardman, C. E. (1987). Children's knowledge of the situations that provoke emotion. *International Journal of Behavioral Development, 10,* 319–344.

Heelas, P., & Lock, A. (1981). *Indigenous psychologies.* London: Academic Press.

Hochschild, A. (1983). *The managed heart.* Berkeley: University of California Press.

Izard, C. E. (1971). *The face of emotion.* New York: Appleton-Century-Crofts.

Izard, C. E., & Malatesta, C. Z. (1987). Perspectives on emotional development I: Differential emotions theory of early emotional development. In J. D. Osofsky (Ed.), *Handbook of infant development* (pp. 494–554). New York: Wiley.

Lutz, C. (1987). Goals, events, and understanding in Ifaluk emotion theory. In D. Holland & N. Quinn (Eds.), *Cultural models in language and thought* (pp. 290–312). Cambridge: Cambridge University Press.

Murphy, L. B. (1937). *Social behavior and child personality.* New York: Columbia University Press.

Nelson, C. A. (1987). The recognition of facial expression in the first two years of life: Mechanisms of development. *Child Development, 58,* 889–909.

Premack, D., & Woodruff, G. (1978). Does the chimpanzee have a theory of mind? *Behavioral and Brain Sciences, 1,* 515–526.

Radke-Yarrow, M., Zahn-Waxler, C., & Chapman, M. (1983). Children's prosocial dispositions and behavior. In P. Mussen (Ed.), *Handbook of child psychology: Vol. IV,* Socialization, personality, and social development (E. M. Hetherington, Vol. Ed.) pp. 469–546). New York: Wiley.

Rosaldo, M. Z. (1980). *Knowledge and passion*. Cambridge: Cambridge University Press.

Schacter, S., & Singer, J. (1962). Cognitive, social and physiological determinants of emotional state. *Psychological Review, 69*, 379–399.

Smith, E. E., & Medin, D. L. (1981). *Categories and concepts*. Cambridge, MA: Harvard University Press.

Younger, B. A., & Cohen, L. B. (1985). How infants form categories. In G. Bower (Ed.), *The psychology of learning and motivation: Advances in research and theory* (Vol. 19, pp. 211–247). New York: Academic Press.

Zahn-Waxler, C., & Radke-Yarrow, M. (1982). The development of altruism: Alternative research strategies. In N. Eisenberg (Ed.), *The development of prosocial behavior,* (pp. 109–137). New York: Academic Press.

Part II

Early understanding of emotion

2 Young children's acquisition of emotion concepts

Patricia Smiley and Janellen Huttenlocher

The present chapter is concerned with the emergence of emotion categories in children. Emotion categories are one of a larger set which we will call person categories. These have as an essential feature some internal state – a feature directly accessible only for instances involving the self. Of course, there are observable cues for instances involving other persons and these can be used to infer internal states. For emotion, facial expressions and bodily movements as well as the nature of surrounding situations may enable an observer to identify another person's emotion. Adults understand not only that expressive behaviors are usually a reflection of inner emotional states and that certain situations are strongly associated with certain emotional states, but also that a wide variety of situations can evoke similar emotions. Adults also understand that all these relations are the same for both self and other.

Our examination of the development of adultlike emotion categories in children draws on our earlier work on the development of another set of person categories – namely, intentional action categories. Action categories, like emotion categories, have as an essential feature a particular internal state – namely, an intention. It can be seen that intention is an essential feature by considering those pairs of actions that are behaviorally identical and can be differentiated only on the basis of intention; for example, for killing versus murdering, the distinction lies not in the observable movements, but in the perpetrator's intent. Our studies provided support for a particular model of the development of person categories in which the child's categories initially cover only internal states of self, then, observable features of others' behavior, and, finally, inferred internal states of others. In the present chapter we examine the development of emotion categories and then consider whether there are parallels with the development of

This chapter was prepared with support from NICHHD Training Grant No. T32–HD–07205 to the Department of Psychology at the University of Illinois, Urbana-Champaign, to the first author and with support from The Spencer Foundation to the second author. We thank Carol Dweck for her helpful comments on the manuscript.

27

action categories. If there are parallels, they will provide evidence for a more general model of the development of person categories.

Our approach to studying the development of both person and action categories is to examine the acquisition of word meanings – the range of instances to which words are applied. The word meanings children acquire are potentially a product, not just of concept development, but also of parents' use of words for concept instances (see Huttenlocher, Smiley, & Ratner, 1983). Thus, suppose one found a pattern of lexical acquisition that conformed to a plausible model of conceptual development. If the nature of parent word use to the child were to correspond precisely with that pattern of lexical acquisition, it would be unclear whether child word meanings reflected conceptual development or parent speech. To assess the development of action categories, therefore, we examined both child word meanings and adult usage to the child.

Our data on children's verb meanings provided evidence that intentional action is categorized at first only for the self (Huttenlocher, Smiley, & Charney, 1983). First, we found that when children acquire verbs, they initially apply them only to instances where their own goals are involved. Second, when children first apply verbs to the actions of others, they apply only a subset of the verbs that they applied to the self, namely those that encode perceptually simple acts. We argued that these actions can be categorized on the basis of directly observable features. Only later are verbs learned for others' actions which seem to be based on inferences of intentions.

These early verb meanings differ from adult verb meanings, which cover intentional actions of both self and other, in that they apply only to the self at first. This pattern of lexical acquisition would seem to reflect both the accessibility of intentions to the self and the conceptual problem of inferring them in others. However, because there might also have been a bias in parent use of verbs toward instances of child action, we also examined the nature of input and found no such restrictions in parent usage. Thus, the pattern of acquisition most likely reflects conceptual development.

In this chapter we examine existing data and our own data on child word meanings and parent speech in order to explore the child's developing concepts of emotions, especially in other persons. The data allow us to sketch the course of development of emotion categories in the preschool years. To anticipate our conclusions: We find that the emergence of emotion categories parallels the emergence of action categories, lending support to a more general model of the development of person categories.

Words and the nature of emotion categories

We begin by examining the use of words for emotion categories in the adult language. As indicated above, these categories apply only to persons. Hence, they include two distinct sorts of instances: those involving the self and those involving other persons. Instances involving the self consist centrally in a set of internal states, including feelings of pleasant or unpleasant arousal in reaction to or in anticipation of certain events. These internal states are not directly observable in others. What is observable in others is a set of external indicators, including facial expression, vocal intonation, bodily movements, and situations. Adults are capable of inferring others' internal states from perceptually available information. However, it is not always necessary to engage in an inferential process in order to use emotion words. Consider two cases where inferences of others' internal states might not be made and yet emotion words could be used appropriately.

First, in certain situations the self and other may have an identical point of view; this is likely to happen in situations evoking fear or surprise. In such cases, an observer would be confronted with the same stimuli as the observed other, and emotion words might be applied to other people when in fact only the internal experience of the self has been categorized.

In the second case, there may be consistencies in the perceptually available information across instances in which emotion words have been used; if so, this information could itself be categorized and labeled without inferring an internal state. This is likely to be true especially for expressive behaviors because these have distinctive perceptual characteristics that are reliably associated with certain emotions. Thus, for example, facial expressions like smiling, vocal expressions like crying, and bodily movements like stomping around are habitual associates of happiness, sadness, and anger, respectively. Such behaviors could be categorized as visual, sound, or movement patterns, and might easily be labeled without inferring a corresponding internal state.

Certain situational cues may also be habitually associated with the presence of certain emotions and paired with emotion words. For example, receiving a gift is often associated with happiness and parting from family with sadness. In such cases, people may store their knowledge of the relations between situations and emotions either as events with sets of recurring perceptual features or as scripts. Across such instances, the representations of the situations would be very similar. Observing others in these contexts, one might categorize the recurring events or use scripted knowledge and appropriately apply emotion labels without inferring the accompanying internal state.

The habitual associations between expressive behaviors or situations and particular emotions would frequently permit successful categorization of emotions. There are at least two cases, however, where attempts to categorize emotion on the basis of observables would result either in no categorization of emotion or in an incorrect one. First, consider that the variety of situations that might evoke particular emotions is immense. In fact, the situations one observes may be unique. The external features of such disparate events would not group easily as instances of a certain type already encountered and an observer would not be able to use perceptual information directly to categorize emotions. Because unique or unusual situations are perceptually variable across instances, they could not be included in a perceptually based category but only in one where an internal state is an essential feature.

Further, situations can have different meanings for different persons. As argued by Stein and colleagues (Stein & Jewett, 1986; Stein & Levine, 1987), the particular emotion experienced depends on a person's initial goal with respect to a situation and also on the aspects of the unfolding situation focused on. Thus, having a goal blocked may lead to anger if the blocking agent is focused on, but to sadness if the resultant deprivation is focused on. Presumably the more an observer knows about the variability due to a person's goals and likely focus of attention in situations (i.e., some version of a person's history) and about the particular expressive bodily cues the person uses for display, the more precise will be that observer's inference of the other's internal state. If words were used across such perceptually variable instances they could be taken to refer to the inferred internal states.

In a second case, errors will arise when habitual associates of emotions – bodily expressions or situations – are present but are not accompanied by the usual internal state. So, for example, a person with a pleased expression might well be masking a feeling of sadness and a person leaving family members might be glad. Indeed, the fact that adults realize that a person could be unhappy although smiling or happy although departing indicates that, for them, emotion words encode categories of internal state, not just of observable cues or scripts. Moreover, even if people on occasion do not actively infer others' emotions when they use emotion words, their emotion categories are still categories of internal state.

The development of emotion categories

The acquisition of mature emotion categories would seem to depend on the ability to conceptualize both self and other as experiencers of particular kinds of internal states. There are a number of conceivable patterns of acquisition. Because the experiences of emotion in self and other are so different in important ways, a partial concept covering just self or just others might emerge first. Because emotional states are directly accessible only to the child her- or himself, the child's first categories of emotion might be categories of internal state only for the self. If the child used words only for the self and in situations when he or she apparently felt particular emotions, this would support such a view. Alternatively, categories based on observable cues habitually associated with others' experiences of emotion might be the first to emerge because it might be easier for parent and child to focus jointly on such instances than on internal states of self. After all, when parents label child states, they make inferences, not direct observations, and these may not always be accurate. If the child used words just for others and these uses included only instances where habitual cues were available, this would support such a view.

Another possibility is that the child's category covers instances of both self and other, but nevertheless constitutes a nonadultlike category. Thus, the category might initially include instances of internal states for the self and habitually associated expressions (e.g., crying) or situations (e.g., swinging) for others. Alternatively, the child's category might cover habitual associates for both self and other. That is, even for the self, certain situations might always have been present when parents used emotion words. If this were the case, the child might learn to regard those situations, not certain internal states, as the instances to which emotion words refer. Note that for the self the instances would include only aspects of situations and some bodily movements but not facial expressions because these would be unavailable to the self. If the child used words for either internal states of self and habitual associates for others or habitual associates for both self and others, there would be support for initial categories of these kinds. Word meanings that are partial or in other ways nonadultlike are, however, not unequivocal evidence that the notion of persons as possessors of inner states is lacking. The child might have this notion but experience difficulty linking the idea of person to the range of perceptual cues that permit one to infer the presence of particular internal states.

Finally, an idea of persons (i.e., both self and others) as entities with internal states might be available from the outset or emerge at a certain point in time (due to maturation or experience). There would be evidence that adultlike emotion concepts were available from the beginning of use of emotion words if the referential range of the child's emotion words included both self and others, and included even cases where habitual perceptual cues were unavailable.

In general, evidence that children possess adult categories of emotion should include, first, uses of words for instances where subjective states of the self are clearly encoded because, if the child does not categorize internal states for the self, it would be unlikely that the child has a concept of those states in others. Second, words should also be applied across situations involving others where very different external cues are displayed. That is, to conclude that the child understands that others have emotions, one would expect appropriate usage of emotion words in many different situations where emotions are felt regardless of the vicissitudes in emotion expression or external circumstances.

As stated in the introduction to this chapter, we proposed a model of the development of action categories wherein the child's categories initially cover only internal states of the self, then observable features of others' behavior, and finally inferred internal states of others (Huttenlocher, Smiley, & Charney, 1983). This model is based on evidence that children at first use verbs only as they themselves start to act or in requests for others to produce changes they desire. (At the same time, they rarely produce and comprehend only a subset of verbs for others' actions.) We argued that this pattern of usage reflects the child's categorization of goals of the self. Our evidence for the transition from categorizing observable aspects to inferred intentions of others' actions is based on an analysis of the nature of actions. Some actions are characterized by perceptually similar movement patterns (e.g., bouncing, hitting, pulling), whereas others consist of a series of less predictable movements (e.g., getting, making). We argued that for actions not characterized by regular movement patterns, categorization would depend on inferring an actor's internal state or goal. Our data showed that in learning to apply verbs to others' actions, children first categorized actions with simple movement patterns and then actions where such patterns were absent, probably only after they were able to infer goals.

In subsequent work (Smiley, 1987), we found that when specifically asked about the intentional states of observed actors (e.g., "Why did she hit him?"), only children who understood verbs for the more perceptually variable actions like building, fixing, and so forth, understood the purpose or desire states underlying all types of actions. That is, they knew both that people *pulled* on dogs (a perceptually simple act) because they wanted them and that they *fixed* tape recorders (a perceptually variable act) because friends wanted to use them. These children were 30 months old on average. This finding substantiated our earlier tentative conclusion that the correct categorization of perceptually variable actions depends on understanding what actors want to accomplish by their movements. Moreover, children's later acquisition of verbs for such actions of other people was not due to parents' failure to use these words or to use them in relation to other people's actions. At 16 months, these verbs were among parents' most frequent and 40 percent of uses were in relation to acts of other people (Huttenlocher, Smiley, & Ratner, 1983).

Through our discussion of the literature and our data on emotion words we will propose a model of the development of emotion concepts that parallels the model for the development of action concepts. To this end, we examine how children apply emotion words to the self and others. In particular, we determine when the child applies emotion words to instances where he or she genuinely feels emotion. We also determine when the child applies words to others' experiences, and whether the instances labeled involve perceptually stable external signs – including vocal expressions like crying or habitual contexts – or a variety of expressive cues and contexts. Similarly, for parent use of words, we determine whether both the child's and other people's experiences are labeled and, for others, whether the instances involve only certain expressive cues or contexts or are more variable. As elaborated in the next section, these data allow us to draw conclusions about the nature of the child's emotion concepts.

Parent use of emotion words

In our examination of the child's emotion concepts, we use word meanings as an index. However, the word meanings the child acquires are the product of both conceptual development and language input. Hence, any restrictions or peculiarities in word meanings might be traceable either to the child's conceptual development or to the nature of input. In order to determine whether children's word meanings are a good index of their concepts, we start by examining the nature of input. We examine two aspects of parents' use of emotion words, namely frequency of use and the nature of instances labeled.

First, consider the frequency of use of words. If emotion words are very frequent (and also in salient positions in utterances) in parent speech, yet children do not acquire word meanings, this would indicate they have not established these concepts. In contrast, if parents only rarely use emotion words, children may not even have sufficient exposure to form word meanings. However, if children form word meanings despite low frequency of exposure, this would indicate not only that they have acquired certain concepts but that these concepts are salient ones in their conceptual scheme.

Second, consider the range of instances named by parents. If parents name instances of internal states across behavioral displays and situations for both self and other, yet the child acquires no meaning for the words or only partial meanings (e.g., certain habitual contexts for self, certain expressive behaviors for others), one could conclude that the child has no or only limited categories of emotional experience. However, if input is restricted and full meanings are nevertheless acquired, this would show that the child's emotion concepts are not only adultlike but salient.

In the remaining scenario, if language input is restricted to or biased toward certain instances (e.g., internal states just for self, just crying for others), and the child develops partial word meanings that reflect that bias, one could not conclude without reservation that the child has partial concepts. It *might* be the case that naming practices control concept development. However, it might also be the case that naming practices control the acquisition of word meanings but not concepts; that is, the child might possess other subconcepts of emotion for which he or she lacks words. Indeed, parents' restricted input may be controlled by conceptual development. That is, the child might selectively attend to aspects of the environment that the parent then names. This particular possibility would be supported if the course of acquisition of word meanings conformed with a plausible model of conceptual development such as the one proposed here for person concepts.

According to earlier research, mother speech to 1- to 2½-year-olds contains a fair number of references to a wide variety of internal states, including perception, physiology, affect, moral judgment, cognition, and volition/ability (Beeghly, Bretherton, & Mervis, 1986; Dunn, Bretherton, & Munn, 1987). Estimates of the percentage of mother utterances that contain internal state words range from 5% to 7% of utterances when only the first three types are included (Dunn et al., 1987) to 22% to 59% (increasing with age) when all word types are included (Beeghly et al., 1986). However, these investigators each counted both words referring to behavior (e.g., *cry, have fun*) and words referring to state (e.g., *sad, happy*) as internal state terms on the assumption that behavior words may also refer to the internal states that no doubt are present when the words are used. However, such behavior terms do not explicitly refer to internal states but rather to observable aspects of those states, which, as we have argued, may be relatively easy for the child to categorize. Because the relative frequencies of word types (i.e., behavior versus state) are not given in these studies, it is not possible to tell how often emotion words are used.

In our work, where we counted only emotion words per se, we found very low overall frequency for these words. We observed 11 mother–child pairs longitudinally, making one 5-hour visit every other month. Pairs were observed at home or outside the home in the course of their normal daily activities. Examining parent speech at 16 months and 24 months, respectively, we found an average of only 3 and 4 uses per mother in these 5-hour samples.

When we calculated the frequencies of particular words, at both 16 and 24 months, we found that a word for pleasure (*happy*) was most frequent, followed by words for displeasure (*sad, unhappy*) (Huttenlocher, Smiley, & Prohaska, 1988). Dunn et al. (1987) analyzed the relative frequencies of types of utterance content in their sample and found that utterances dealing with distress were the most frequent; one quarter of all utterances focused on someone's distress. In their corpus, utterances about pleasure were fourth in frequency, after utterances about two physiological states (pain and sleep). The discrepancy between these data and ours concerning the predominance of words for distress in mother speech probably arises from counting both emotion and behavior words versus counting just emotion words. In our data, *cry* (only one of Dunn et al.'s several behavior words for distress) is two times more frequent than *sad* and *unhappy* at 16 months and three times more frequent at 24 months. Thus, internal state words for distress may be no more frequent in Dunn et al.'s data than in ours.

According to the above studies (Beeghly et al., 1986; Dunn et al., 1987), the majority of state and behavior words refer to the child's experience. However, this bias decreases from around 80% at 18 months to around 50% at 30 months. By 30 months, about 20% of uses refer to toys, and the remainder to the mother or sibling. That is, according to these reports, a substantial percentage of utterances refer to behavior or internal experiences of other human beings. (Note, however, that if certain words have a low overall frequency, there may be few or no uses for other people.)

In our data, where we consider only words for emotions, among our few uses we find a referential bias toward entities other than the child. At 16 months, of the 34 total uses, 12 were for the child and 18 were for other entities; at 24 months, of the 46 total uses, 11 were for the child and 23 were for other entities. (The remainder at both ages were idiomatic uses; e.g., "I'm afraid I made a mistake.") Thus, other classes of animates (other people, animals) or their representations (dolls, book characters) were often the focus of parents' utterances.

Despite the raw frequency bias against child instances, the proportion of child instances that involved actual emotional states was greater than for nonchild instances. At 16 months, 11 of 12 uses and at 24 months, 8 of 11 uses for the child involved actual states. In contrast, only 5 of 18 and 4 of 23 of the nonchild uses at 16 and 24 months involved present states in real people. These nine nonchild uses for internal states represent the total usage across all 11 mothers at 16 and 24 months. Further, 5 of these 9 instances involved crying or ceasing crying and one was in a habitual context. The majority of nonchild uses (i.e., 26 of the total of 41) were for book characters; in such cases, emotion words are likely to be habitually associated with one or two fixed contexts. In any case, parent usage of emotion words for pretend internal states of book characters or stuffed animals would only be meaningful instances for children if they already had a notion of others with internal states.

In sum, based on our data, parent use of emotion terms is very infrequent and, based on previous data and our data, usage for present states is biased toward the child. When instances involving other people are labeled, our data show that the majority are of one sort – namely, crying. The low overall frequency in parent speech may prevent acquisition of these words by 2-year-olds. On the other hand, if emotion concepts are especially salient for the child, word meanings might still be acquired. The bias in input toward child states and others' crying behavior may lead the child to apply words only to these instances even if emotion concepts include other people's inner states. Thus, if child word meanings do not cover others' internal states, this would not be conclusive evidence that the child lacks a concept of emotion that covers all persons. However, as we pointed out above, early application of emotion words to states of the self but only to expressive behaviors or strongly associated situations for others would conform to the model of development already supported for another person category, intentional actions. Moreover, recall that for actions, the partial word meanings acquired were *not* attributable to input restrictions.

Children's use of emotion words

In our treatment of children's emotion concepts, we next examine the nature of the instances to which children apply emotion words – that is, whether the instances involve both self and other, and the kinds of experiences covered for each. Previous research has focused on three types of instances: naturally occurring events involving self and other, experimental stimuli showing others' facial expressions, and experimental stimuli showing others in situations. After we examine each of these in turn, we draw some conclusions about the nature of children's emotion concepts based on these findings and the nature of parent language input.

Naturally occurring situations

In studies of use of words in relation to events occurring in the home, Bretherton and colleagues (Bretherton & Beeghly, 1982; Bretherton, McNew, & Beeghly-Smith, 1981) report mothers' recollections of their children's uses of emotion words. Even at 20 months, according to Bretherton et al. (1981), a few children used some emotion words. Most of these were for the self – 5 of 30 children used *happy* when they apparently were happy, and 2 used *scared* when they felt scared. There were also uses of *happy* and *sad* for others when they were observed smiling or crying. By 28 months widespread use is reported (Bretherton & Beeghly, 1982). Each of the four words in the basic vocabulary for positive and negative affective states – *happy, sad, mad,* and *scared* – is used at least once by about two-thirds of children for instances involving the self and by a third to half of children for instances involving another person or entity (e.g., dolls, book characters) or a nonpresent experience of the self or other. Because the latter two categories (i.e., other person or entity and nonpresent experience of self or other) are combined, it is not possible to estimate how many children actually use words for other people at 28 months. Further, the nature of instances (for self or other) is not discussed.

Dunn et al. (1987) report the relative productivity of words used during emotion episodes versus episodes involving other kinds of internal states. At 24 months, children with infant siblings talk primarily about distress; pleasure is the fourth most frequent topic, after two physiological states. For older first borns (32 months), pleasure and distress are also among the four most frequent topics. Just as for the mothers, in tabulating usage, both behavior and state words are counted, so it is not possible to tell how frequently emotion words per se are used. Neither are contexts specified for individual words, so the referents and nature of instances cannot be determined. For example, one cannot tell whether when *sad* is produced it is used for self or other, nor whether crying is always present or a variety of different expressive cues and situations is present.

Bretherton et al. (1981) also reviewed uses reported in diary studies through 36 months. Here the specific contexts of use are given so we can examine the nature of the instances labeled. The majority of uses for all emotion words are for the self. In addition, these instances – for *sad, mad,* and *scared* – are ones where some relevant precipitating event just occurred (e.g., balloon popped, food not ready, scary object presented). The contexts of use for *happy* are not elaborated, although one child's early uses (at 21 months) were in a habitual context, namely, after he stopped crying. In contrast, early uses of *sad, happy,* and *mad* for others involved, not observed event contexts, but crying, smiling, and "acting mad," respectively – instances that might be categorized on the basis of the observable features of these emotion expressions. Only the few uses for others by children over 30 months involved observations of precipitating events. The fact that emotion words are at first used for others' behavior is supported by data showing that, when asked to identify facial expressions, children (2½ to 4 years) understood behavior words (*laughing, crying*) before emotion words (*happy, sad*) (Honkavaara, 1961). (This is despite the fact that, at least in our data, *happy* is much more frequent in parent speech than *laugh*.)

In our work, we observed 21 children in the normal course of their daily activities in two longitudinal studies starting when the children were 13 months old (Huttenlocher et al., 1988). Perhaps because we do not have mothers as informants, we find much less widespread use of emotion words. Nevertheless, we observed uses of *happy, afraid, mad,* or *sad* by a few children when they were 22 to 26 months. *Happy* and *afraid* were used by twice as many children as were the other words. And, as for Bretherton's subjects, some of the uses for self occurred in quite convincing contexts. For example, one child kicked sand at his playmate, was reprimanded, and then said, "I'm mad." Another child closed herself inside a cardboard box, started to cry, and said "I afraid." However, we observed only one use for another person. This child said, "Mommy's sad" as she watched her mother cry. Just as in the Bretherton report on 20-month-olds and the diary data, where instances are described, we find no uses for others by children up to 26 months except where distinctive modes of expressing emotion are present.

These studies rely on children's spontaneous use of words for assessing word meanings. In another study (Smiley, 1987), we elicited use of emotion words in response to videotape recordings of naturally occurring events between peers. We elicited attributions of emotion because children may not have a reason to comment spontaneously on others' emotions. We filmed familiar interactions that were not habitual in that a range of settings (the child's, a playmate's, and other children's homes), a range of objects (the children's own and experimenter toys), and a range of emotional expressions were present. That is, for example, when angry, children sometimes kicked but did not scream, screamed but did not hit, ran out of the room, etc. Interactions leading to happiness, sadness, and anger were chosen from 35 hour-long sessions of peer play.

To explore children's understanding of emotions, an interview procedure was used in which children were asked how the participants felt. Children were first asked an open-ended emotion question, for example, "How does Sara feel?," and if they did not respond, a pair of yes/no comprehension questions was posed. In addition, questions were routinely asked about the actions performed (e.g., "What did Adam do?") and the reasons for actions (e.g., "Why did he take the doll?"). Children's understanding of action goals was assessed because in many cases emotions are felt in situations where goals are affected (facilitated or thwarted) by events. In such cases, the child might have to infer the actor's goal in order to assess his emotional reaction.

We tested 35 children between 21 and 39 months of age. None of the three children under 25 months made any correct responses to emotion questions. For the others, there was no difference in accuracy for children above and below the median age of 30 months. There was, however, considerable variability in the correct application of emotion words to events in this age range. Only 56% of the children responded with 75% or greater accuracy on one or more emotions. Twice as many were highly accurate for *happy* as for *sad* or *mad*. Thus, when children are shown events that vary in their observable cues to emotion – a condition where they may have to infer internal states rather than simply categorize kinds of external cues – about half the 2- to 3-year-olds can apply *happy* and about a quarter *sad* and *mad*.

Although age is not highly related to the application of emotion words, the ability to infer the purposes of others' actions is. That is, only 30% of the children who could not make attributions of others' goals were highly accurate on one or more emotions, whereas 68% of children who could make such attributions were highly accurate on emotions. This suggests that a general ability to infer internal states begins to emerge on the average at around 2½ years, and that in some cases inferring people's emotions may depend on inferring their goals.

Thus, in all the studies where naturally occurring events are the instances covered by word meanings, by about 2 years at least half the children include their own emotional states of at least one sort. At around 2 years, however, probably only a few children include instances concerning other people, and these appear to involve habitual behavioral expressions of emotion – crying, smiling, and stomping around. As reported in the diary studies, a few children over 30 months spontaneously used some words appropriately and, as found in our elicitation study, a quarter to half of the children 25 to 39 months used some words appropriately for instances involving other people across a set of novel contexts. Thus, children's word meanings at first cover internal states of the self and some observable aspects of others' experiences. By six months to a year later, children begin to use words, not just for observable aspects of others' experiences, but apparently for their internal states as well.

Facial expressions

Facial expressions are external cues to the emotions of other people. They vary little from instance to instance and thus, at least for adults, facial expressions can be good predictors of a person's emotional state. Further, there are many cases where no other external cues are available – when an observer does not witness a precipitating event or when that event is internal, when there are no other behavioral expressions, or when a mood state is ongoing – so the ability to interpret facial expressions can be crucial. However, the perceptual features of some expressions contrast only subtly with those of other expressions. Thus, the child must learn to discriminate among them in order to benefit from witnessing this powerful cue.

Several studies of children's understanding of emotion words in relation to facial expressions have been carried out, starting with children as young as 2 years. Bretherton and Beeghly (1982) showed 28-month-olds nine pairs of photographs of infants' and children's faces, including exemplars of *happy, sad,* and *mad*. Children responded correctly on average to half the contrasts but it is unclear whether certain expressions were consistently recognized. In contrast, studies with older children (starting at 3½ to 4 years) consistently report a particular order of acquisition. *Happy* is easiest; it is understood by all 4-year-olds (Felleman, Barden, Carlson, Rosenberg, & Masters, 1983; Izard, 1971; Reichenbach & Masters, 1983). Further, in Izard's extensive study, *mad* was just as easy as *happy,* followed by *surprised* and *scared* at 5 years and by *sad* at 7 years. However, Felleman et al. and Reichenbach and Masters found both *mad* and *sad* to be harder than *happy*.

In these studies, facial expressions were presented with no accompanying context. When, in addition to seeing faces, children heard short descriptions of events that would lead a protagonist to feel a particular emotion, 4-year-olds chose the correct facial expressions for all the basic feeling states – happiness, sadness, anger, fear, disgust, and surprise (Camras & Allison, 1985). Green and Ekman (1973), however, found that when the expressions hardest to discriminate from one another were pitted against each other (also presented with a short verbal context), 4-year-olds still had some difficulty distinguishing *sad* from *angry, angry* from *scared,* and *surprised* from both *scared* and *happy.*

This last result prefigured the work of Bullock and Russell (1985; 1986) with younger children (2 to 5 years). When they set up forced choices between each pair of nine expressions, children (and adults) made the most category errors on faces that were most similar on arousal and pleasantness dimensions. For example, *mad* was confused most with *scared* and *disgusted* and least with *happy* and *excited.* The confusion data were not presented for every word, but *mad* and *scared* were well differentiated (at least 70 percent correct choices against all contrasts) by 3 year olds, *sad* by 4 year olds, and *surprised* only by adults. This order of acquisition of the negative emotions is the same as that found by other researchers. In this research, *surprised* was difficult to discriminate, but this was due to a contrast with *excited,* which was not presented to other groups of subjects.

The studies by Bullock and Russell are exceptional in that very young children were tested systematically. The data showed that 3-year-olds discriminated at least two of the common negative facial expressions, but 2-year-olds could not reliably discriminate any of the group of nine expressions. However, using an alternative task, a similarity sort of the nine faces into two, three, and five groups of like expressions, Russell and Bullock (1986) found that 2-year-olds were as sensitive to two broad dimensions of similarity (arousal and pleasantness) among the faces as were 3- and 4-year-olds and adults.

In our work on facial expressions (Huttenlocher & Smiley, in press), we also tested 2-year-olds but used a smaller set of contrasts, including only *happy, sad, mad, surprised,* and *scared.* In addition, we used stimuli that we felt were more realistic than the black and white photos used in previous studies; we produced a set of color movies of actors whose faces change from neutral expressions to full emotion expressions over a 5-second period. These facial expressions were presented in pairs, contrasting each expression with each of the other four, to 75 children, aged 2½ to 5 years. In the experimental procedure, both expressions were named and subjects were asked to point to one of the expressions. Our criterion for comprehension of each expression was 100 percent correct identification of all 4 pairs.

Our data show that the majority of 2½- to 3-year-olds discriminate *happy* from the other four expressions and that 3- to 3½-year-olds also discriminate both *mad* and *scared.* By 3½ to 4 years, the majority of children understood all five words for faces. Thus, using these movie stimuli and no additional contextual input, the majority of 2-year-olds correctly identified one facial expression, and the majority of older 3-year-olds discriminated all five faces. Although we presented only three potentially confusable negative expressions and two positive ones, these particular facial expressions and their respective labels are rapidly differentiated from one another in the fourth year of life.

As we discussed in the introduction to this chapter, children might learn to decipher facial expressions of various sorts and to apply emotion words to them, yet not make inferences of corresponding internal states. To conclude that the child categorizes, not just the perceptual features of facial expressions, but also (potentially) the felt states of the observed person, one would first want evidence that the child has a notion of emotional states at all. As we saw, by 2 or 2½ years many children do encode some of their own emotional states. Stronger evidence that the child has the ability to categorize internal states in others would consist of a demonstrated ability to categorize instances of emotion where external cues varied across instances. As we saw in the previous section, a majority of 2- to 3-year-olds do categorize perceptually variable instances of happiness in others. In the next section we discuss studies that evaluate the child's application of words to a broader range of emotion situations.

Experimentally produced situations

Certain situations have perceptual characteristics that vary less from instance to instance than others. These commonalities may make them relatively easy to categorize on the basis of observables alone. In these cases even adults may not make inferences about internal states. We included among these cases situations habitually associated with experiences of emotion (e.g., swinging with happiness) and situations evoking fear and surprise, which are scary and surprising to observers as well as to experiencers. For other types of situations, categorizing instances on the basis of perceptually available cues does not seem possible. That is, to categorize a range of situations that differ in their external features as evocative of the same emotion, it is likely the child must make an inference about an *underlying* commonality in internal state.

Experimental studies of the application of emotion words to situations usually involve the verbal and/or visual presentation of two or more vignettes for each emotion. They depict people not personally known to the child in a variety of circumstances. In studies of words used for events in the child's environment, the range of events involving others might be more limited (albeit salient), and application of words to these situations might even be habitual. In some sense then, to evaluate emotion word use at home is to evaluate the *emergence* of the child's ability to categorize emotions in other people. In contrast, experimental studies may assess a further *consolidation* of the child's ability to categorize emotion.

In earlier studies, subjects were asked either to match a facial expression to a situation or to choose the emotion word that describes a protagonist's feeling. (Some studies require spontaneous labeling but these would seem to make greater demands on the child's verbal fluency.) In general, these studies show that *happy* is accurately used as a descriptor of others' emotions by the majority of 3- to 5-year-olds (Borke, 1973; Eisenberg-Berg & Lennon, 1980; Reichenbach & Masters, 1983), and *scared* by 4- to 8-year-olds (Borke, 1971, 1973; Gnepp, 1983).

There is less agreement on *sad* and *mad*. Using slides and a detailed narrative, Eisenberg-Berg and Lennon (1980) found that 4- and 5-year-olds correctly match *sad* faces to incidents of a bike accident and a lost dog. Using only stories, Borke (1971) found that 5-year-olds (but not younger children) understood *sad* situations, whereas both Reichenbach and Masters (1983) and Gnepp (1983) found that 6½- to 8-year-olds (but not 5-year-olds) understood *sad* stories.

Stories about anger also are not accurately matched with expressions or words until over 5 years (Borke, 1971, 1973; Reichenbach & Masters, 1983). The variability in age of understanding of *sad* and *mad* reactions to situations may reflect the notion that a variety of reactions is appropriate in such situations. Indeed, in one study where the degree of consensus among responses to situation types was explicitly measured, there was significant agreement from 5-, 8-, and 11-year-olds that experiences of success and nurturance produced happiness, as well as significant agreement that a threat of punishment led to *either* sadness, anger, or fear and that aggression from another person led to anger *or* sadness (Barden, Zilko, Duncan, & Masters, 1980). As we noted above, Stein and colleagues (Stein & Jewett, 1986; Stein & Levine, 1987) argue that the aspects of situations on which a person focuses (e.g., the intentional aggressor versus the irreplaceability of the attendant loss) determines the emotion felt or inferred (i.e., anger versus sadness).

In our work on situations (Huttenlocher & Smiley, in press), we systematically tested five emotion words with children younger than those in most other studies. (They were the same children, aged 2½ to 5 years, who viewed the facial expression movies.) As for the facial expressions, we produced a set of short color movies with no soundtrack. In the movies, events appropriate for particular emotions were shown, but the child experiencing the emotion did not display bodily movements that might be diagnostic of particular emotions. That is, the child's face was averted and the child did not make angry gestures or adopt a posture of fear or sadness. Our aim was to construct stimuli where only the cues that are more perceptually variable across instances were available.

In contrast to earlier studies, we did not allow responses to vary freely. Rather, we created contrasts, pairing each of five emotions with each other emotion. As in the facial expression task, situations were presented in pairs, each was named, and subjects were asked to point to one. Pairs of situations were similar in most external cues but different in the emotion evoked in the principal actor. For example, in the *happy–surprised* pair, one film showed a girl swinging on a swing and the other showed the same girl on the swing rising up in the air. By presenting forced choices, we constrained the judgments children could make, yet included the crucial contrasts (e.g., between *sad* and *mad*).

The events leading to the various emotions showed young children as experiencers. In addition, the actions shown were among those understood for others by 2½- to 3-year-olds – for example, giving, opening, swinging, taking. Thus, the situations were chosen to be comprehensible to young children. Those meant to evoke happiness included the arrival of pleasing objects (the child gets a gift; sees mother enter the room; feels father hug him) or involvement in a pleasurable activity (swinging). Anger episodes showed frustration (difficulty opening a drawer) or intentional destruction or removal of a valued object by another person (the child's tower is kicked over; ice cream cone is knocked down; gift is pulled away). Events leading to sadness involved losses (the child's mother departs; the child's balloon deflates; ice cream falls off the cone; doll is dropped over a ledge). Surprising episodes involved sudden appearance or unusual events (a birthday cake appears at the top of dark stairs; a tower rebuilds itself; a swing rises in the air; a balloon is discovered in the refrigerator). Finally, scary events included the approach of threatening objects (an ape rising over a ledge; a man lunging at a child; a snake popping out of a drawer) or entering a nonspecifically threatening environment (climbing a dark staircase).

We expected that *scared* and *surprised* might be acquired in relation to situations first since inferences about others' internal states might not be needed to make these category judgments. We also expected, on the basis of other research, that *happy* would be applied to others' experiences before the words for negative emotions. The data showed that, in line with our prediction, *scared* was acquired first (by 3½ to 4 years). *Happy* and *mad* were comprehended by a majority of 4- to 4½-year-olds and *surprised* by 4½- to 5-year-olds. (*Surprised* may be acquired later than *scared* because it is less frequently used by parents.) Finally, *sad* was understood by only a quarter of the oldest group.

Thus, in comparison to facial expressions of emotion where perceptual features are consistent across instances, application of words to situations occurs 6 months to 1½ years later. In comparison to familiar events in the home (for which only *happy* was understood by a sizable number of 2- to 3-year-olds), application of words to unfamiliar situations is at least a year later. The finding that *sad* is understood last for both facial expressions and situations is particularly noteworthy because other researchers (e.g., Dunn et al., 1987) report that distress is the earliest emotional state noticed in other persons. Our situation stimuli showed various kinds of personal losses and no crying. This difference in age of acquisition of words for sadness may reflect the younger child's ability to categorize vocal stimuli (i.e., cries of distress) and the older child's ability to categorize the emotional states that underlie events involving loss of valued objects. In general, then, when instances contain only perceptually variable cues – when there is a greater likelihood that the child makes inferences about underlying internal states of other people – such instances are included in word meanings at 3 to 5 years rather than at 2 to 3 years.

Conclusions

We set out to investigate children's emotion concepts by examining child word meanings and their relation to parent input. We found that children begin to acquire emotion words at an early age – at just around 2 years. Although most words acquired by 2 years are used very frequently by parents (Huttenlocher, Haight, Bryk, Seltzer, & Lyons, 1988), use of emotion words is relatively rare. Thus, the instances to which emotion words refer may be particularly salient for the child at this age. However, as we saw, the instances children include in their word meanings are initially unlike those included in adult meanings. Their word meanings cover only instances of internal states of the self. Whereas words also are used for the expressive behaviors of other people, we argued that the words encode only the behaviors themselves and not the inner states of others. This pattern of acquisition corresponds with the pattern of parent usage, where uses for the child appeared to refer to different kinds of emotional states and uses for others were restricted largely to one expressive behavior (crying). As we noted, such correspondences make it impossible to conclude that word meanings index conceptual development because meanings may instead be solely a reflection of input.

We argued from our earlier empirical work on intentional action categories that person categories in general may follow a developmental course where instances at first involve internal states of the self, then the perceptually available aspects of others' experiences, and finally internal states of other people. In the case of verbs, unlike emotion words, the pattern of acquisition of word meanings did not correspond to the pattern of parent usage. Thus, we were convinced that for verbs the observed pattern of word meaning acquisition reflected conceptual development. Because action and emotion concepts are alike in that an internal state is an essential feature, and because the patterns of acquisition of word meanings are similar in important respects, the acquisition pattern for emotion words probably also reflects conceptual development and not just the pattern of parent speech. Together the data on verbs and emotion words provide support for a general model of the development of person categories.

Related language acquisition research also supports the model. First, there are several domains of experience for which words are applied to internal states of the self before those of other people. These include perception and volition

(Bretherton & Beeghly, 1982), mental states (Shatz, Wellman, & Silber, 1983), and psychological causes of behavior (Hood & Bloom, 1979). Second, there is evidence that words for observable features of behavior are learned before words for the internal states they signify. In the domain of emotion, recall that Honka-vaara (1961) found that children understood words for behavior before they understood words for emotions shown in facial expressions. In the domain of intentional action, there is evidence that children categorize others' actions before they seek to specify reasons for observed actions. That is, children come to realize that actions they can identify might be carried out for a variety of personal purposes. At 2½ to 3 years, they begin spontaneously to inquire about the reasons for others' actions (Cairns & Hsu, 1977; Hood & Bloom, 1979; Smiley, 1987; Tyack & Ingram, 1977).

Nonlanguage evidence. Thus, there is support from the data on action and emotion words and from related investigations for this description of the course of development of person categories. There are three sorts of nonlanguage data, however, that might at first be seen as support for a different view, namely, that emotional states of others are categorized at 1 to 2 years of age. First, researchers have noted that in contexts of uncertainty 12-month-olds seek information from their mothers' faces and respond differentially to the expressions they perceive (Klinnert, 1984; Sorce, Emde, Campos, & Klinnert, 1985). One interpretation of these data is that the child understands the mother's emotions and responds accordingly. We would argue that these data show that preverbal infants categorize only others' expressions, along a positive–negative dimension (see Nelson, 1987). Further, in making these categorizations, the function is not to gather information *about* the other, rather, it is to regulate behavior of the self.

Second, there are reports in the literature that are even more compelling because they concern behaviors directed toward others that seem to reflect inferences of internal states. In a well-known example, Hoffman (1975) suggests that a 15-month-old's offer to his crying friend of, first his own teddy bear, and then his friend's security blanket, reflects awareness of his friend's specific need. Such offers, however, usually are single instances involving habitually associated objects in salient contexts. They do not provide the best evidence that internal states are assessed, because there are such strong contextual elicitors.

Third, there are several reports in the literature (e.g., Dunn et al., 1987; Hoffman, 1975) of young children who, during interactions with parents or siblings, behave in ways that elicit particular emotion-based behaviors from others. For example, Hoffman describes a 20-month-old who had been refused a toy by her sister. She then loudly began to play with her sister's favorite horse. Her sister ran to protect her horse, leaving the desired toy unattended. Such events have been interpreted as evidence that at 2 years or less children not only are aware of particular motivational states of others but also are aware that there is a potential for deliberately creating them in others. It seems to us that, in the absence of other evidence (discussed below) that others are conceptualized as persons, it is more conservative to conclude that young children have knowledge about contingencies between their own and others' behavior related to their own goals, and not necessarily knowledge about others' emotions or goals independent of their own.

Issues in acquisition of concepts of self and other. Although there is substantial evidence for, and little convincing evidence against, the model of development of person categories presented here, the process of category formation is not well understood. We raise two further issues. First, various kinds of evidence indicate that a concept of a self with internal states emerges at 20 to 24 months. That is, as we have discussed, action and emotion words applied to the self emerge at this time. In addition, the primary verb for desire, namely *want,* applied to the self, as well as words denoting the child, including the child's name and the first person pronoun, emerge at this same time (Huttenlocher & Smiley, in press; Huttenlocher, Smiley, & Charney, 1983). The emergence of *want* and the child's name at the same time as emotion words is particularly remarkable because although emotion words are rare in parent speech, *want* and the child's name are among parents' most frequent words to the child for many months prior to their acquisition. Also, although the first person pronoun might present linguistic difficulties for acquisition, the child's name would not, yet they are acquired in either order within one or two months of one another. All of this suggests the possibility that the notion of a self with internal experiences may emerge as a powerful, unitary concept shortly before 2 years, but we know little about the impetus for it.

Second, there is evidence that once internal states are categorized for the self, inferences of internal states in others are not immediate. Consider two possible reasons for the lag in application of internal state words to others. In one case, the child may actively construct an idea of person starting with a notion of a self with internal states. For example, the child may notice parallels in the observable aspects of experiences of self and other and use these as a bridge to draw parallels in internal states. If so, such a process could account for the observed delay. Hoffman (1975) favors such a constructionist view in which only the self is conceptualized at first.

Alternatively, as we noted in the introduction, the concept acquired at 20 to 24 months might be of person rather than of self. Although one might expect that inferences of others' inner states would then be made immediately, there are reasons why they might not be. That is, even if the child had a unitary idea of persons with internal states, this would not obviate the need to form links between observable cues and inner states in others, and this may account for the delay. One probably could not distinguish between these two accounts because in each the child would appear to have an idea only of self at first.

Hoffman, however, provides some anecdotal evidence that the child may indeed initially experience the self, albeit a rudimentary self, as the only seat of emotions. He observes that at 1 to 1½ years, when children observe others crying or looking sad, they often begin to console themselves, as if the unpleasant feeling resided only in the "self." After this initial period, children direct their efforts at the distressed other, but their attempts are identical in content to those they would choose for themselves. Only later are attempts to alleviate distress tailored to the needs of the particular other involved. Thus, at first, even when distress clearly originates with other people, the child apparently experiences an emotional response that is only gradually attributed to those others.

Hoffman claims that empathic reactions occur from early infancy; a prerequisite for understanding that emotions may also reside in others is a cognitive awareness not only of the physical, but also the psychological, separateness of others from the self. There is ample verbal and nonverbal evidence that others are not seen as separate from the self, with different visual perspectives, capable of producing independent goal-directed actions, and possessing desires of their own, until around 2½ years. Thus, at this time children acquire pronouns denoting others (e.g., Loveland, 1984), use dolls as agents (e.g., Lowe, 1975; Watson & Fischer, 1977, 1980), and acknowledge the desires of others by offering them requested objects (Smiley, 1987).

We do not as yet understand how children come to appreciate the point of view of the other. The child may notice parallels between the self and others spontaneously. For example, parallels in behavior may be especially salient for distinctive vocalizations like laughing and crying or for reactions to situations evoking fear or surprise. Alternatively, parallels in both behavior and internal state might be especially salient in playful imitative situations where emotions and goals of the self – salient for the child in their own right – may be substantially identical to those of the other. In addition, parents may verbally note the similarities in behavior, in internal state, or even in behavior–state relations between self and other. Research on the process of reconceptualizing the other is lacking; studies of parent input that are sensitive to the issue of behavior–state relations that we have focused on here might be especially fruitful in this regard.

References

Barden, R., Zilko, F., Duncan, S., & Masters, J. (1980). Children's consensual knowledge about the experiential determinants of emotion. *Journal of Personality and Social Psychology, 39,* 968–976.

Beeghly, M., Bretherton, I., & Mervis, C. (1986). Mothers' internal state language to toddlers. *British Journal of Developmental Psychology, 4,* 247–261.

Borke, H. (1971). Interpersonal perception of young children: egocentrism or empathy? *Developmental Psychology, 5,* 263–269.

Borke, H. (1973). The development of empathy in Chinese and American children between three and six years of age. *Developmental Psychology, 9,* 102–109.

Bretherton, I., & Beeghly, M. (1982). Talking about internal states: the acquisition of an explicit theory of mind. *Developmental Psychology, 18,* 906–921.

Bretherton, I., McNew, S., & Beeghly-Smith, M. (1981). Early person knowledge as expressed in gestural and verbal communication: when do infants acquire a "theory of mind"? In M. E. Lamb & L. R. Sherrod (Eds.), *Infant social cognition.* Hillsdale, NJ: Erlbaum.

Bullock, M., & Russell, J. (1985). Further evidence on preschoolers' interpretation of facial expressions. *International Journal of Behavioral Development, 8,* 15–38.

Bullock, M., & Russell, J. (1986). Concepts of emotion in developmental psychology. In C. E. Izard & P. B. Read (Eds.), *Measuring emotions in infants and children* (Vol. II). Cambridge: Cambridge University Press.

Cairns, H., & Hsu, J. (1977). Who, why, when, and how: a development study. *Journal of Child Language, 5,* 477–488.

Camras, L., & Allison, K. (1985). Children's understanding of emotional facial expressions and verbal labels. *Journal of Nonverbal Behavior, 9,* 84–94.

Dunn, J., Bretherton, I., & Munn, P. (1987). Conversations about feeling states between mothers and their young children. *Developmental Psychology, 23,* 132–139.

Eisenberg-Berg, N., & Lennon, R. (1980). Altruism and the assessment of empathy in the preschool years. *Child Development, 5,* 552–557.

Felleman, E., Barden, R., Carlson, C., Rosenberg, L., & Masters, J. (1983). Children's and adults' recognition of spontaneous and posed emotional expressions in young children. *Developmental Psychology, 19,* 405–413.

Gnepp, J. (1983). Children's social sensitivity: inferring emotions from conflicting cues. *Developmental Psychology, 35,* 805–814.

Green, J., & Ekman, P. (1973). *Age and the recognition of facial expressions of emotion.* Unpublished manuscript.

Hoffman, M. (1975). Developmental synthesis of affect and cognition and its implications for altruistic motivation. *Developmental Psychology, 11,* 607–622.

Honkavaara, S. (1961). The psychology of expression. *British Journal of Psychology Monograph Supplements, 32.*

Hood, L., & Bloom, L. (1979). What, when, and how about why: a longitudinal study of early expressions of causality. *Monographs of the Society for Research in Child Development, 44*(6, Serial No. 181).

Huttenlocher, J., Haight, W., Bryk, A., Seltzer, M., & Lyons, T. (1988). *Early vocabulary growth: relation to language input and gender.* Unpublished manuscript.

Huttenlocher, J., & Smiley, P. (in press). Emerging notions of persons. In N. Stein, B. Leventhal, & T. Trabasso (Eds.), *Biological and psychological approaches to emotion.* Hillsdale, NJ: Erlbaum.

Huttenlocher, J., Smiley, P., & Charney, R. (1983). Emergence of action categories in the child: evidence from verb meanings. *Psychological Review, 90,* 72–93.

Huttenlocher, J., Smiley, P., & Prohaska, V. (1988). *Origins of the category of person: evidence from speech.* Unpublished manuscript.

Huttenlocher, J., Smiley, P., & Ratner, H. (1983). What do word meanings reveal about conceptual development? In Th. B. Seiler & W. Wannenmacher (Eds.), *Conceptual development and the development of word meaning.* Berlin: Springer-Verlag.

Izard, C. (1971). *The face of emotion.* New York: Appleton-Century-Crofts.

Klinnert, M. (1984). The regulation of infant behavior by maternal facial expression. *Infant Behavior and Development, 7*, 447–465.

Loveland, K. (1984). Learning about points of view: spatial perspective and the acquisition of "I/you." *Journal of Child Language, 11*, 535–556.

Lowe, M. (1975). Trends in the development of representational play in infants from one to three years – an observational study. *Journal of Child Psychology and Psychiatry, 16*, 33–47.

Nelson, C. (1987). The recognition of facial expressions in the first two years of life: mechanisms of development. *Child Development, 58*, 889–909.

Reichenbach, L., & Masters, J. (1983). Children's use of expressive and contextual cues in judgments of emotion. *Child Development, 54*, 993–1004.

Russell, J., & Bullock, M. (1986). On the dimensions preschoolers use to interpret facial expressions of emotion. *Developmental Psychology, 22*, 96–102.

Shatz, M., Wellman, H., & Silber, S. (1983). The acquisition of mental verbs: a systematic investigation of the first reference to mental state. *Cognition, 14*, 301–321.

Smiley, P. (1987). *The development of a concept of person: the young child's view of the other in action and in interaction*. Unpublished doctoral dissertation, University of Chicago.

Sorce, J., Emde, R., Campos, J., & Klinnert, M. (1985). Maternal emotional signaling: its effects on the visual cliff behavior of 1-year-olds. *Developmental Psychology, 21*, 195–200.

Stein, N., & Jewett, J. (1986). A conceptual analysis of the meaning of negative emotions: implications for a theory of development. In C. Izard & P. Read (Eds.), *Measuring emotions in infants and children* (Vol. II). Cambridge: Cambridge University Press.

Stein, N., & Levine, L. (1987). Thinking about feelings: the development and organization of emotional knowledge. In R. Snow & M. Farr (Eds.), *Aptitude, learning, and instruction* (Vol. 3). Hillsdale, NJ: Lawrence Erlbaum.

Tyack, D., & Ingram, D. (1977). Children's production and comprehension of questions. *Journal of Child Language, 4*, 211–224.

Watson, M., & Fischer, K. (1977). A developmental sequence of agent use in late infancy. *Child Development, 48*, 828–836.

Watson, M., & Fischer, K. (1980). Development of social roles in elicited and spontaneous behavior during the preschool years. *Developmental Psychology, 16*, 483–494.

3   Children's understanding of changing emotional states

Nancy L. Stein and Tom Trabasso

Introduction

The purposes of this chapter are threefold. First, we wish to assess children's understanding of those events that lead to and follow from different emotional reactions. Second, we are interested in determining whether children as young as five can represent and understand the conditions that lead to changes in emotional responses. Finally, we are interested in children's skill at understanding the concept of ambivalence.

In our effort to understand how children represent events leading to emotional reactions, we first investigate whether or not children understand that both an external event and a motivational state are necessary for emotions to occur. We also evaluate whether or not children understand that attaining a valued goal leads to a positive emotion whereas failing to attain such a goal leads to a negative emotion. In exploring this issue, we inquire as to whether children understand that goal success may occur on one occasion and that goal failure may occur at a later time. Thus, we wish to determine if children understand (1) that changes can occur in maintaining important goals and (2) that changes in goal states produce changes in emotional reactions.

Because the achievement and failure of personal goals are often caused by the same person, we are interested in whether children understand that another person can cause them to feel both good and bad. Moreover, we seek to determine whether children acknowledge the relationship between how they feel about a person and that person's role in facilitating or blocking important goals. In discussing the expression of multiple feelings toward others, we examine the concept of ambivalence. In particular, two issues are important. The first focuses on children's ability to integrate knowledge about another person such that they remember and use positive and negative information to make moral judgments

This research was supported by the National Institute of Public Health and Human Development grant HD 17431, U.S. Public Health Service to T. Trabasso. We wish to thank Susan Eulau for her assistance in collecting and analyzing the data.

and preference decisions about that person. Constructing a representation of a person's good and bad behavior is an essential component in understanding the concept of ambivalence. Second, we consider whether or not the nature of ambivalence is defined by the simultaneous expression of positive and negative feeling states. In order to address this issue, we make a distinction between knowing that two opposing feeling states can be experienced toward another person and actually feeling two opposing emotions at the same time.

Both young children and adults can understand that they can feel different emotions toward a person depending upon the situation that evokes the emotion. Moreover, children can remember quite accurately sequences of events where another person first helps them attain a goal and later blocks the same goal. They can then integrate this type of information so that they acknowledge that they feel neither entirely good nor entirely bad about a person. Whether or not good and bad feeling states are experienced in relation to accessing this knowledge is open to question. Moreover, asserting that ambivalence is defined by the simultaneous expression of positive and negative emotions is also open to criticism. Knowing that two polar-opposite emotions can be expressed toward a person does not tell us much about the actual subjective experience of ambivalence. Are multiple feeling states experienced simultaneously or is the consideration of ambivalent feelings associated with an anxiety response or a more intense negative reaction?

In our discussion section, we discuss different theoretical approaches to the study of ambivalence and attempt to describe how children might develop knowledge about positive and negative characteristics of people. We then bring to bear certain research findings and theoretical frameworks to advance a more detailed analysis of ambivalence per se.

In order to consider each of these issues, we briefly discuss a model of emotional understanding that describes the types of knowledge people acquire about emotion. The model specifies the general conditions under which emotions occur and the conditions that evoke specific emotional reactions. Moreover, the wishes and plans that cause and result from an emotional reaction are discussed. Empirical data is then presented on children's understanding of changing emotional states, their awareness and ability to represent multiple emotional reactions to a specific person, and their skill at integrating positive and negative person information to make moral and emotional judgments about other people.

Stein and Levine's model of emotional understanding

According to Stein and Levine (1987), a central component of emotional understanding lies in the evaluation of the *changes* that occur in the status of valued goals, because an assessment of these changes gives rise to inferences about emotion (Lazarus & Folkman, 1984; Folkman & Lazarus, in press; Lazarus, in press; Stein & Jewett, 1986; Stein & Levine, 1987).

In order to understand and predict emotional reactions, several types of information must be available to the comprehender. First, one must have knowledge about the antecedent conditions that precede an emotional response. Of specific importance is knowledge about what goal is being pursued, how valuable or important the goal is, and the prior expectations about the possibility of achieving or maintaining the particular goal. An awareness of ongoing emotional states and activities prior to the change in the status of a goal is also critical, for an understanding of these dimensions allows a better assessment of how important the current goal change will become.

Events that cause emotional reactions have certain properties. Some aspect of the event must be perceived as novel or unexpected. Information that is not easily assimilated into existing knowledge stores is, by definition, novel or discrepant from what is known. When incoming information cannot be rapidly incorporated into existing knowledge stores, an interruption of ongoing thinking processes occurs. Attention then shifts to a more detailed processing of the new information as an attempt is made to incorporate it into current knowledge stores. At this point, an individual evaluates whether or not the novel information signals a change in the status of valued goals (i.e., whether certain goals are being maintained, attained, or blocked). If such changes in the status of goals are perceived, an emotional reaction occurs.

Once a change in a goal's status has occurred, the individual assesses the causes and the implications of the change for other valued goal states, objects, and activities. Although the recognition of a change in a goal's status is enough to arouse different emotions (e.g., positive or negative), an assessment of the causes and consequences of change leads to further specification as to which emotion is experienced. Further, it is in the assessment of the causes and consequences of a precipitating event that plans for future action are developed.

Given that knowledge about the causal structure of different emotional reactions can be specified, we can begin to evaluate the Stein and Levine (1987) model in terms of its accuracy in predicting the reasoning and thinking processes that accompany emotional understanding. Focusing on children provides a window into the development of emotional knowledge such that we can assess the significant changes that occur in representing emotional knowledge.

Developmental hypotheses

From the above account, in order to understand emotional reactions, children have to know the value of a goal and how they (or others) feel about a goal *before* a change in the status of the goal occurs. Moreover, they must have some idea about the past probability of attaining such a goal. As a precipitating event occurs, children also must have a means of understanding exactly how the event has changed a goal's status and what the relationship is between success or failure of a goal and positive or negative feelings. In essence, this means that even young children need to have some means of constructing successive representations of emotions, goal outcomes, and their associated plans.

In our first study, children's ability to understand and remember successive emotion episodes was investigated. Information concerning a change in the status of a goal was varied over two episodes so that a person underwent two emotional reactions. In the first episode, success or failure at attaining a valued goal was varied. By choosing this variation, we could evaluate what type of inferences children made about different emotional states based upon outcomes of success or failure. For example, we could evaluate how much children wanted to achieve a goal, what emotion was felt, how intense their emotional reaction was when they failed or succeeded, what their explanation was for a particular emotional response, what kind of wish they entertained when a success or a failure occurred, and which plan of action they would carry out once they had a particular reaction.

Having established that children could understand and predict with accuracy the initial emotional reaction in the first episode, a second set of changes in the goal's status was introduced. Here, children were asked to infer the new emotion's valence (either positive or negative), its name, its intensity, its causes, and its consequences, all associated with a second success or a second failure. A study of the changes in the pattern of inferences and the requirement to recall these changes throughout the emotional episode should allow an assessment of children's ability to construct and to compare successive representations.

The ability to infer emotional reactions to recurring goal success (or failure) also plays a role in the comprehension and representation of stories. Basically, stories relate the way in which people go about solving interpersonal and personal problems. Thus, at the beginning of a story episode, an event occurs that challenges a protagonist by creating a set of conditions that signals a change of state with respect to important goals (Stein, 1988; Stein & Glenn, 1979; Stein & Jewett, 1986; Trabasso, van den Broek, & Suh, in press). As a result of an initiating event, the protagonist experiences a lack or loss state accompanied by an emotional reaction. A series of attempts is then carried out to remedy the lack state, and the protagonist again experiences another emotional reaction, either to success or failure at attaining a valued goal. Most stories are structured such that a series of goal failures and successes must be experienced before the protagonist is able to attain a highly valued goal, for *many* conditions must be met and maintained if important goal states are to endure.

Success and failure of goals also determine basic emotional reactions in the plot structure theory of Lehnert (1982). In her system, the character in a story is motivated by goal states; emotional reactions occur when success or failure results with respect to these states. Thus, information on the child's ability to infer emotional reactions from a series of goal success or goal failure episodes not only tells us about children's understanding of real life experiences, but also enriches our knowledge of how children understand narrative events. For narratives draw on and reflect the structure and value inherent in social interaction.

Because, in our studies, the child is required to interpret and to represent internal states and changes in states, the resulting data are also relevant to current issues concerning the child's theory of mind and memory for successive representations (Astington & Gopnik, 1988; Wellman, 1988). Understanding and representing internal state information reflects the development of children's theory of mind. Of particular interest here is the coherent representation of internal states and actions that are organized around emotions. Knowledge of one's or another's emotional reactions, goals, thoughts, and plans and its application to specific episodes reveals how coherent the child's theory of mind is with respect to internal states. Hence, this chapter focuses on children's competence to infer and to remember internal states when these representations change over time.

In a similar vein, our research is relevant to questions about whether or not the child's ability to infer emotional states is regulated by knowledge of external or internal events (Harris, 1983; Harris & Olthof, 1982) and whether or not the child can represent more than one emotional state at a time (Harter, 1979; Harter & Whitesell, this volume). If children can take into account a person's goal and the changes that occur in the goal's status when inferring an emotion, we will have evidence that inferences about emotional states are regulated by knowledge about both internal and external factors and that more than one goal state and emotional state can be represented and compared in memory (e.g., the goal and emotion state before and after a precipitating event). Moreover, if children can retain and integrate information about both good and bad aspects of people, we will also have evidence that the 5-year-old has the basic representational structures to understand and use concepts of ambivalence.

To this end, a series of three data sets are presented. The first pertains to children's skill at representing and remembering successive changes in goal states and their associated emotions; the second pertains to children's ability to talk about those situations where they have felt both good and bad about a particular person; and the third focuses on moral judgments children have made about how they feel about a person who has acted in both a helpful and harmful manner toward another person. We will also use data from our other studies to support our arguments about children's knowledge of ambivalence and the development of emotional understanding.

Data Set 1: Understanding successive changes in emotion states

Method

Subjects. The subjects were 36 kindergarten children from a middle-class school in suburban Chicago. Half of the children were female and half were male. The age range was from 5 years 7 months to 6 years 8 months, with the mean age equal to 6 years.

Stimulus materials. Twelve episodes of two parts each were constructed. The first part of each episode introduced success in attaining a goal (such as a child being allowed to paint) or failure in attaining a goal (such as not being allowed to hear a story). The second part either succeeded in attaining or failed to maintain the same goal. This resulted in six combinations of goal success or failure. In the first three combinations, goal success occurred in the beginning of the episode. Combination 1 continued the success by repeating the same successful set of events. Combination 2 continued the initial success but also augmented the success by enabling more goals to be achieved in the second goal outcome. In combination 3, goal failure was introduced after the initial goal success.

In the subsequent combinations, goal failure occurred in the first part of each episode. In combination 4, the failure was continued by repeating the initial goal outcome. In combination 5, the failure was augmented by having more goal failure, in addition to the initial goal. In combination 6, success followed the initial goal failure.

In order to examine the generality of the results, two different sets of materials were constructed for each of the six combinations. For the combinations with an initial goal success (1–3), the participating child was asked to pretend that he or she was engaged in the activity either of playing with a favorite toy or painting a picture. Continued success involved another opportunity to participate in the activity. Augmented success involved being allowed to take the toy home or having one's painting hung up for all to see. Goal failure involved having another child take away the toy or having the teacher forget to bring the paints.

For the next three combinations, the initial failure involved the child's being denied the opportunity either to be read a bedtime story or to own a puppy. Continued failure involved another opportunity to be denied the same goal. Augmented failure involved either having no bedtime story and being sent to bed early or being denied a puppy and not being able to play with one's friends. Goal success involved getting someone to read a bedtime story or being able to get a puppy.

Examples of the six episodes for one set of goals are:

(1) Continued success

Part 1: Every week, your teacher brings a new toy to class. Everyone takes turns playing with the toy, including you. Everyone gets an hour to play with the toy.

Part 2: This week, your teacher brings a new toy to class for everyone to play with. Again, she says that everyone will take turns playing with the toy and will get to play with it for an hour.

(2) Augmented success

Part 1: Same as (1) above.

Part 2: One time, as you are beginning to play with the toy, your teacher comes over and tells you that you can keep the toy and take it home with you after school. She tells you that she brought two toys, so that she'll have one left for the class. She says that she knows that you will like the toy very much.

(3) Failure following success

Part 1: Same as (1) above.

Part 2: One time, when you are just beginning to play with the toy, a boy/girl comes over and grabs the toy away from you. You have only had the toy for a short time and have not had a full hour to play with it. It is not the boy's/girl's turn.

(4) Continued failure

Part 1: One of the things you like best is to have a story read to you each night before bedtime. Lately, however, nobody has been willing to read you stories. Your mom and dad have had chores to do around the house at your bedtime, so you have had to go to bed without any storytelling for a long time.

Part 2: Tonight at bedtime, you still have to go to bed without anyone reading you a story. Your mom and dad still have chores to do.

(5) Augmented failure

Part 1: Same as (4).

Part 2: Tonight, your mom tells you that she still cannot read you a story before bedtime. And what's more, you have to go to bed an hour early because your mom and dad are having a party and they need quiet.

(6) Success following failure

Part 1: Same as (4).

Part 2: One evening, your mom comes in and tells you that she is going to try and get more things done during the day so that at bedtime she will have time to read you a story from beginning to end.

Three sets of questions were constructed in order to test hypotheses concerning knowledge about emotional states changes. One set occurred immediately after the child heard the first part of the episode. The second set was given after the child heard the second part. The third set was given after the child had heard and was asked to retell the whole episode.

In each part, the questions assessed whether or not children were aware of what the central goal was, how desirable (value) the goal was, the emotion children would feel upon attaining or failing to attain a particular goal, the intensity of the emotional response, the reason for the emotional response, and the wish and plan of action that would result as a function of feeling a particular way and having succeeded or failed at attaining a goal.

Taxonomic scoring of answers to questions. The answers to the questions on reasons for emotional reactions were open-ended and required a taxonomic scoring system. Five categories were used. The first three pertained to (1) wanting, (2) having, or (3) both wanting and having the goal object, activity, or state. The fourth category included consequences of success or failure, usually in terms of what would happen to other goal objects, activities, or states. The fifth category included evaluations of the events as violations of social norms; for example, one was supposed to bring materials or one should not take away toys.

The children's responses to the questions pertaining to the wishes and plans were organized into the following categories: (1) goal achievement or enhancement of existing goals; (2) gratitude toward another for helping to achieve the goal; (3) reinstatement of a denied or lost goal: (4) substitution of another goal or activity; (5) forfeiture or giving up a lost or denied goal; (6) seeking revenge on an agent who caused goal failure; (7) expressing emotion or focusing on feelings generated by success or failure.

Design. Each child heard the stories in two of the six conditions as follows: for the Continued Success and Continued Failure episodes (1 and 4), for the Augmented Success and Augmented Failure episodes (2 and 5), and for the Failure following Success and Success following Failure episodes (3 and 6). Twelve children were randomly assigned to each of these three conditions. The children were distributed equally by sex across the conditions. The order in which they heard the stories for each condition and the order of story versions within each condition was counterbalanced across subjects.

Procedure. Children were interviewed individually, and all responses were tape recorded. The interview with each child was structured as follows: The child heard the first part of the episode and was asked the first set of questions. Then, the second part of the episode was read and the child was asked the second set of questions. Following this, the child was asked to retell as much of the story he or she could remember. After the retelling, the child was asked the third set of questions. The same procedure was used for the second episode in the session.

Results

The results of this study are presented in three parts. The first part focuses on the inferences reported after each part of the emotion episode was presented. These results are similar to *immediate recall,* and for the purposes of this paper will be labeled as such. The second part is concerned with those inferences made after the entire emotion episode was presented and recalled. These results will be labeled *delayed recall.* The third section focuses on the specific content of the explanations, wishes, and plans generated for positive versus negative emotions.

Immediate recall of initial success outcomes. Children reported that the initial success outcomes were highly desirable: Almost all children (99%) said that they would like to experience such an outcome, and almost all (95%) said they would feel very happy about it. Moreover, all children (100%) could accurately identify the goal motivating the story character to value such an outcome. The mean intensity associated with happiness averaged 4.34 on a five point scale.

In explaining happy responses, the majority (55%) of children asserted that they really liked and valued the focal activity (e.g., I'm happy because I really like to paint), whereas the remainder (45%) expressed their happiness by referring to the completed successful outcome (e.g., I'm happy because I got to paint). The most frequent plan associated with happiness was one of goal enjoyment, given by almost all (93%) of the children. This plan involved participating in the valued activity and getting (or maintaining) pleasure from doing so (e.g., I would draw pretty pictures; I would play with my puppy all day).

Immediate recall of initial failure outcomes. All children (100%) could identify what the initial goal was. The clear majority (81%) reported that experiencing failed outcomes would be highly undesirable: They did not want such an outcome to happen to them. The predominant emotion the children associated with goal failure was sadness (64%); the remainder of the children expressed anger as a reaction to failure (36%). The mean intensity associated with these emotions was high – 3.85 on a five point scale.

In explaining sadness or anger, more children (59%) referred to the actual failed outcome (i.e., I didn't get to paint; I didn't get the puppy) than to the desire to attain the goal (41%; i.e., I really wanted to paint, I really love puppies). However, this difference was not significant.

The plans associated with a failed outcome were: substituting a new goal, 49% (e.g., I would play with my kitty instead), reinstating the failed goal, 19% (e.g., I would try to get a puppy again), forfeiting the failed goal, 16% (e.g., I would just give up and not paint), or focusing on a nonverbal expression of emotion, 16% (e.g., I would stamp my feet really loud). The plans for failed outcomes did not overlap with the plans for successful outcomes.

In summary, for both initial success and failed outcomes, 6-year-old children were able to indicate what the appropriate goal activity was, whether or not they valued the goal activity, and the appropriate emotion associated with failure or success. A high intensity score was associated with their emotional responses. Clear differences in the content of explanations and plans were found as a function of successful versus failed outcomes. When children succeeded, explanations focused on *getting* something they wanted. When children failed, they focused on *not having* something they wanted. The desire to maintain or enjoy a

Table 3.1. *Answers to questions for second outcome of episodes*

	Continued success	Augmented success	Failure after success	Continued failure	Augmented failure	Success after failure
Emotional reaction						
happy	.96	.96	.00	.04	.04	.98
sad/angry	.04	.04	1.00	.96	.96	.02
Shift from positive to negative emotion	.04	.00	.96	.00	.00	.96
Explanations that include a new goal or outcome	.00	.67	.92	.00	.79	1.00
Plans that contain a new goal or outcome	.00	.79	.92	.50	.75	1.00

goal followed success. For failure, the desire to reinstate, substitute, or forfeit the goal was the prototypical response.

Immediate recall of the second outcome: continued success, augmented success, or success–failure. As the left half of Table 3.1 indicates, children responded to continued or augmented success with very strong happy responses and did not change emotion states. However, when an initial success was followed by a failed outcome, 96% of all children shift from a positive to a negative emotional response. The probability of shifting emotional valence was compared across the three conditions and was found to be significant (Chi-square $= 42.26$, $df = 2$, $p < .01$).

Two other dimensions were also found to differentiate among the three conditions. When the specific content of emotion explanations and plans were examined, significant differences were found in the *augmented success* and the *success–failure* conditions when compared to continued success (explanations: Chi-square $= 22.4$, $df = 2$, $p < .01$; plans: Chi-square $= 16.24$, $df = 2$, $p < .01$). In particular, these differences focused on reference to the new outcome or to the new goal mentioned in the second half of the emotion episode. For example, when success was augmented, children shifted the focus of their explanations for happiness from liking a particular toy to getting to keep the toy. When success turned to failure children shifted from their happy explanation of liking a toy to a sad or angry explanation of having the toy taken away from them. Similar shifts occurred when children generated *plans* to adapt to the new outcomes presented in augmented success or success–failure conditions.

Immediate recall after second outcome: continued failure, augmented failure, or failure–success. As the right half of Table 3.1 indicates, when failure was continued or augmented, almost all children continued to report negative emotions. However, when a successful outcome followed a failed outcome, 96% of the children shifted from a negative to a positive emotion (Chi-square $= 38.74$, $df = 2$, $p < .01$).

Although continued and augmented failure almost always guaranteed a negative emotional response, the specific emotion given to the second failed outcome was often different from the emotional response given to the first failed outcome. When failure was continued, 21% of the children shifted from sad to mad or from mad to sad. When failure was augmented, 29% made similar shifts. The proportion of children reporting an emotional shift in these two conditions did not differ from one another, although they did differ from the proportion shifting emotions in the failure–success condition (Chi-square $= 16.68$, $df = 2$, $p < .01$).

Significant differences among the three conditions were found in the content of explanations and plans generated for the second half of the emotion episode. When failure was maintained, children did not shift the focus of their explanations. However, when failure was augmented or when success occurred after failure, children did incorporate the new goal/outcome information into their explanations (Chi-square $= 15.97$; $df = 2$, $p < .01$). Differences also were found among the three conditions in the frequency of shifting the focus of a plan to adapt to a new outcome. However, the proportion of children who shifted the focus of their plans in the augmented failure (75%) and failure–success (100%) conditions did not differ significantly from the proportion who shifted plans in the continued failure condition (50%).

The shift in plans for the continuing failure condition is not surprising in retrospect. When failure continues to accrue, one of two things happens: (1) Children generate a new strategy to deal with continuing loss (e.g., instead of just forfeiting the goal and doing nothing, children may begin to substitute other goals that are more realistic) or (2) rather than deal with the loss per se, children begin to attack the agent who caused the loss. These plan changes indeed characterized the plan shifts of children presented with repeated failure. The data strongly suggest that, even though the failed outcome remains the same from time one to time two, children begin to make new inferences each time an event is recoded. Thus, the focus of attention, in terms of the dimensions considered important to the child, begin to shift. The fact that many children change their emotional responses (e.g., from mad to sad or from sad to mad) under conditions of repeated failure also supports this argument.

In summary, when changes occur in opportunities to attain or maintain a goal, a specific pattern of inferences occurs with respect to success versus failure. Overall, children show a high degree of sensitivity to changes in goal success or failure, and they have little difficulty associating success with happiness, goal enjoyment, and liking the activity. Moreover, when success was augmented, children immediately understood that new goals were being achieved and shifted their attention to deal with the new information.

Similarly, when goal failure occurred, the emotions of anger and sadness were always given, the plans were ones of goal substitution, forfeiture, reinstatement, and revenge, and explanations for emotions focused on the failure or outcome. When goal failure was augmented, children again responded appropriately by focusing on the new goals that were denied and by formulating plans of actions to cope with the augmented failure.

The most sensitive types of understanding occurred when successful outcomes followed failed outcomes or when failed outcomes followed successful outcomes. The shifts in emotions, explanations, and plans were almost total, with children giving completely appropriate responses.

These immediate recall data are important because they strongly suggest that children are attuned to shifts in goal attainment, the causes of such shifts, and the appropriate plans for dealing with shifts. Memory for shifting sequences of goal failures and successes are also at the root of the notion of ambivalence: In order to feel both good and bad about an event or person, the child must understand that both goal failure and goal success can be associated with the focal person or event. That is, one day a teacher can let a child paint, and the next day the teacher can deny or prohibit the activity. Thus, if children's delayed recall for such shifts in goal success and/or failure sequences is accurate then it is likely that children have the knowledge base from which to experience ambivalent reactions. The next section focuses on the child's ability to recall emotional changes after the presentation of the entire episode.

Delayed recall. Following the presentation of both parts of the emotion episode, children retold the entire sequence and were then asked how they felt at the beginning and how they felt at the end of the episode. They were also asked if they perceived any change in their feelings during the presentation of the two parts of the emotion episode. The results indicated that children were highly accurate in their recall of appropriate emotions for continued and augmented success, as well as for failure after success. Children preserved the valence of their emotion response in the two success conditions (96%) and changed the valence (96%) for success–failure (Chi-square = 42.26; df = 2, p < .01). Likewise, children accurately recalled the specific emotion label reported at each location of the episode: for continued and augmented success, the emotion of happiness was recalled both times. For failure after success, the emotion of happiness was recalled first and then sadness or anger. Thus, the probability of reporting the same emotion state versus a different emotion state across recall conditions was significant (Chi-square = 38.98; df = 2, p < .01).

Children also perceived changes in their emotional states in differing degrees across the three conditions. The degree of perceived change reported was 25, 54, and 96 percent for the continued success, augmented success, and failure after success conditions, respectively (Chi-square = 10.43, df = 2, p < .01).

The data for the initial failure groups were similar to those for groups that had initial successes. When failure either continued or was augmented, the reported valence remained the same for each part of the episode. When success occurred after failure, children reported a significant change in valence (Chi-square = 15.16, df = 2, p < .01). Children also reported specific emotional state changes in each of the three groups (e.g., shifts from sad to mad or from sad to happy). In the continued and augmented failure groups, approximately half of the children reported shifting emotional states during the two-part episode. In the success after failure condition, almost all children reported emotional state changes.

As we previously showed, about a quarter of the children in the continued and augmented failure conditions actually changed their negative emotion states from the first to the second outcome (e.g., from mad to sad or from sad to mad). Thus, the perception of change for these children would be highly accurate. Additionally, children in these two conditions often shifted the focus of their explanations and plans to cope with continued or augmented failure. Thus, subjects could well be reporting changes in intensity of feeling a specific emotion, given that a plan of explanation changed during the episode. The important finding here is that children were highly accurate in recalling valence shifts from negative to positive emotion states and very accurate in recalling specific emotion states within the domain of negative feelings.

Overall, the delayed recall data indicated that 6-year-old children can represent a sequence of emotion states and that they can accurately remember shifts in their feeling states and the reasons for these shifts. The failure–success and success–failure conditions were the ones that presented the least difficulty for children, indicating that children's memory for situations that may give rise to ambivalent feelings is quite good at this young age.

Content analysis of explanations. An analysis of explanations to the second outcome in each episode showed differences as a function of whether success or failure occurred. Differences were also found in failure explanations as a func-

Table 3.2. *Specific types of wishes and plans generated to cope with the different emotional reactions*

	Wishes: emotion			Plans: emotion		
	Happy	Sad	Mad	Happy	Sad	Angry
1. Goal achievement or enhancement	.69	.03	.00	.67	.03	.00
2. Gratitude toward another	.04	.00	.00	.12	.00	.00
3. Goal reinstatement	.00	.42	.24	.00	.11	.21
4. Goal substitution	.11	.50	.45	.10	.50	.59
5. Goal forfeiture	.00	.00	.00	.00	.14	.00
6. Revenge toward agent	.00	.00	.24	.00	.06	.20
7. Express emotion or focus on feeling	.05	.03	.03	.05	.14	.00

tion of feeling angry versus sad. When success occurred, reference was more frequent to the motivating goal (58%) than to the outcome (36%). Conversely, failure in the second episode generated more reference to the failed outcome (48%) than to the motivating goal (29%). These data were similar to the explanatory data gathered in response to initial success or failure. However, experiencing success or failure in the second part of the episode showed a significant difference in the frequencies of referring to outcomes versus motivating goal.

The content of failure explanations was then categorized as a function of the negative emotion expressed. When children expressed anger rather than sadness, they were more likely to include reference to the agent or event that *caused* the failure (54% versus 21%) and they were more likely to cite the violation of a social norm (38% versus 5%). However, when children expressed sadness rather than anger, they were more likely to refer to the *consequences* of goal failure (28% versus 4%).

Wishes and plans. Table 3.2 contains the wishes and plans generated to successful or failed outcomes. The wishes and plans are listed according to the emotion reported rather than by the outcome experienced. Clearly happy wishes and plans were associated with successful outcomes, whereas angry and sad wishes and plans followed failed outcomes. The emotion reported rather than the outcome experienced (e.g., augmented success versus continued success, etc.) was the more predictive variable in understanding the nature of wishes and plans. The most frequent wishes given for happiness were ones involving goal maintenance or goal enjoyment. For anger and sadness, goal reinstatement and goal substitution were the most frequent. Little overlap in the wishes generated for positive versus negative emotion was found.

The marked difference in wishes for positive and negative emotions generalized to the overt plans used to cope with success or failure. Again, goal maintenance and enjoyment were most frequently associated with happiness, whereas goal substitution was most frequently associated with sadness or anger.

Two interesting findings characterized the wishes and plans associated with sadness and anger. First, only sadness was associated with forfeiting the goal or with an overt expression of emotional feeling, whereas only anger was associated with revenge. Second, changes in strategies from wishes to plans was more marked for sadness than for anger.

In particular, for sadness, 50% of the children wished for goal substitution and 42% wished to reinstate the original goal. Virtually none of the children said they wanted to forfeit the goal. When it came to generating a real plan that would be carried out to cope with sadness, the desire to reinstate the goal dropped to 11%. Rather, children chose to forfeit the goal (14%) or to express the emotion either by crying or by talking about how sad they were (14%). These data indicate a differential understanding of the nature of wishes versus plans. Children realize that, although goal reinstatement may be desired, it may not be possible to achieve it. Therefore, their plans include few attempts to reinstate the goal.

For anger, wishes and plans were similar. Goal substitution was the most frequently used strategy, with revenge and goal reinstatement the second strategies of choice.

Data Set 2: Understanding and talking about ambivalent feelings

At the end of the study, children were asked whether or not they had ever felt good and bad at the same time. They were also asked if they had ever liked and disliked someone at the same time. Harter (1979) has claimed that young elementary school children cannot accept the possibility that an individual can feel two different emotions at the same time, whether toward an object or event (feeling good and bad) or toward a person (liking and disliking). Overall, 51% of the children believed that they had felt good and bad at the same time and 42% said they had liked and disliked someone at the same time. When asked what had happened to make them feel good and bad at the same time, almost all of the children (98%) gave valid responses. Goal conflict situations such as the following were cited: "My mom said I couldn't go outside and play but my big brother said he was going to give me a present," and "At my ice-skating competition I had a solo. I fell down right in the middle of it, but I still got a ribbon." These children are focusing on different aspects of the same situation, and seem to understand that, although one goal has been blocked and makes them feel bad, another, perhaps unexpected, goal has been added, making them feel good.

When children were asked the circumstances under which they liked and disliked someone at the same time, 80% said it was during altercations with family members or friends. One child said, "I fight with my brother all the time. I don't like him when we're fighting, but I really still love him." Another said, "The boys at school fight over me. They pull at my arms in different directions. They're my friends and I like them, but I don't like them when they pull my arms."

Data Set 3: Recognizing ambivalent feelings

The data just presented indicate that at least half of 6-year-old children understand and spontaneously talk about situations that elicit both good and bad feelings. As such, the results suggest that concepts of ambivalence may develop earlier than Harter and Whitesell (this volume) suggest. However, the procedures used in the above-mentioned study relied upon children's ability to *recall* instances of ambivalence in instances where multiple feelings existed.

Classically, recall is not the most sensitive measure of comprehension. Rather, recognition and judgment about the presence of ambivalence would provide a more accurate assessment of children's developing knowledge. Thus, in the two data sets presented in this section, we discuss results from two separate judgment studies. In both studies, positive and negative attributes or actions of story characters had to be taken into consideration, and moral judgments had to be made. Moreover, comprehension or recall data were collected.

Study 1. In this study, reported in Stein and Trabasso (1985), the main task set out for 5- and 8-year-old children was as follows. They were told stories about a protagonist, where three pieces of information were provided:

1. a description of a story character's habitual trait classification in terms of being mean or kind;
2. an event that could call for mean or kind behavior to be expressed; and
3. the response of the story character in terms of whether mean or kind behavior was expressed.

For the purpose of the present chapter, the situations of interest are those where a *conflict* exists between the story character's trait description, the appropriate behavior that should be expressed given a particular event, and the actual response of the story character. In particular, those situations where the character was described as kind but expressed behavior that was mean (and vice-versa) are of interest.

After the children heard each story, performance on several tasks was required. The tasks of interest are the following: First, children were asked whether they accepted the trait description of the character offered in the story. That is, did they believe that John was either mean or kind? This is an important question because we tend to assume that subjects interpret text information at face value, and in fact they may not. Information presented in a text is often discounted and deemed inaccurate given the presence of other information. In the present study, discounting was indeed the case when both kindergarten and third grade children were presented with certain types of inconsistent information and acceptance the norm when presented with other inconsistencies. In particular, when the context in which a character acted was inconsistent with both trait and action descriptions, children accepted the accuracy of the trait description 96% of the time. When the context and action were both inconsistent with the trait, children accepted the trait description only 28% of the time.

Examples of trait acceptance are given in the following accounts. Essentially, when John is presented as *kind* and Sally does some harm to him, the expectations might be that John should not act mean but should not attempt to help Sally either, despite his tendency to be kind. When John acts in a kindly fashion and helps Sally, despite Sally's hurtful behavior, children believe that John is *really kind*. When John chooses to act in a revengeful manner, however, 42% of the children no longer accept the fact that John is kind, despite Sally's hurtful action. Thus, for half of the children, being kind means displaying consistency of action, despite the situation provoking action inconsistent with the trait. When John is portrayed as kind and the situation calls for kindness, the expectation should clearly be that John will act in a kindly manner. When John does not do so, 72% of the children refuse to accept the characterization of John as kind.

These data speak to two issues. First, when positive and negative trait information is presented in a story, this information is not necessarily perceived as being entirely accurate. Rather, children assess the trait depending upon their expectations and beliefs about what behaviors are appropriate for a given conflict situation and a particular type of person. So even though the ideal situation would be to have children believe an actual "inconsistency" exists, many of them tend to discount the discrepant information. Thus, uncertainty is set up regarding how a story protagonist is to be characterized, in terms of being perceived as mean or nice all of the time.

The second task children were asked to complete was a moral judgment task. Children rated a story character on a seven point scale, where 1 was considered very bad and 7 was considered very good. If the story character was described in negative trait terms and carried out a negative action, the mean scale rating was 1.44. For negative traits and positive actions, or for positive traits and negative actions, the mean rating was 4.0. For positive traits and positive actions, the mean rating was 6.94. These data show that when positive and negative information is presented about a character, children make inferences that the character is neither good nor bad but somewhere in between.

When children were asked to give an explanation for why a story character carried out an action, given a particular trait description, the data revealed that children were indeed using context information to understand changes in behavior. That is, when the context was harmful to a character, children could understand and use context information to explain divergence from a trait description. But, in doing so, their estimation of the moral character of a protagonist *changed*. They now had information about both the good and the bad dimension of a character. Similarly, if a story character displayed an action incongruent with a trait and context description, children's explanations for action referred to the context, but evaluation of the moral goodness of the character also changed. Children showed awareness that the character was not entirely good or bad but somewhere in between.

Study 2. A second study, reported in Stein and Trabasso (1982), can also be used to examine children's ability to both recognize and use contradictory person information in making moral judgments about a person. In this study, 5- and 8-year-old children were presented with stories where one of two children had to lie or commit a moral transgression in order to achieve a positive goal. For example, in one scenario Peter asked Mary to play with him in the afternoon. Mary knew that it was Peter's birthday and she wanted to surprise him with a present, so she had to go shopping in secret. To do this she had to lie to Peter and tell him she was sick. Then she went shopping and bought him a birthday present.

The control condition for the same scenario was presented in the same way except that Mary lies to Peter because she wants to go shopping for herself. That is, she has no intention of carrying out a set of positively oriented behaviors toward Peter. Thus, in the experimental condition we have a character who has good intentions and carries out positive actions, but in so doing commits a moral transgression by lying. In the control version, we have a character who has bad intentions, carries out actions congruent with those intentions, and commits a moral transgression.

Our data showed that children in the experimental condition always produced more mixed-polarity moral judgments than children in the control condition. The mean moral judgment score for the experimental group was 3.54 (little bad, little good) and 1.71 (very bad) for the control group, supporting the hypothesis that children considered both positive and negative actions in the experimental stories before arriving at a decision about moral character.

The justifications for moral judgment ratings in the experimental condition changed with age. Although both 5- and 8-year-old children gave mixed polarity judgments, third graders gave more justifications that made reference to both positive and negative personality characteristics (46% for third graders, 28% for kindergarten children). The younger children referred more to only negative traits than third graders (50% versus 30%) in justifying their mid-value scale scores. Thus, although older children's scale judgments are similar to younger children's, they mention both positive and negative character actions as justifications more frequently that kindergarten children.

Additional probe questions were used to ascertain whether or not a full understanding of both positive and negative information resulted. In almost all cases (96%), kindergarten children were as aware of using both positive and negative information as third graders. When probed directly and explicitly about whether or not both tyes of information were considered in their moral judgments, the overwhelming majority of the younger children (77%) in the experimental condition agreed. As a comparison, children in the control condition stated that only negative information was considered (and the story presented only negative information). Thus, we have a good example of complex judgments being made by 5-year-olds, where they recognize and use both positive and negative information. When asked to verbalize about their reasons for judgments, however, many of them give only part of the information used to arrive at a decision.

General discussion

Several conclusions can be drawn from our data. First, it is evident that 5- and 6-year-old children evaluate and explain events that elicit emotions in terms of underlying goal-outcome structures. From one of our recent studies (Stein & Levine, 1986), 3-year-old children also appear quite able to do the same. As we previously illustrated, explanations for emotion focus primarily on two dimensions: the goals that drive the desire to maintain a particular state and the outcome that reflects the current status of goal attainment or failure.

Children's sensitivity to goals was also evident in their wishes and plans. First and foremost, children's wishes contained information that focused on the desire to reinstate failed goals or on the desire to maintain achieved goals. These findings also hold for 3-year-old children, as reported by Stein and Levine (1986). As new successes or failures were introduced, attention in planning immediately shifted to the new goals associated with the outcome. Thus, wishes and plans in response to a new success incorporated the desire to maintain the new goal as well as the old one. Wishes and plans in response to augmented failure incorporated the desire to reinstate both the augmented and the original goal.

The degree to which goals versus outcomes were targeted to explain emotional reactions was significantly influenced by the nature of the outcome. When failure occurred, the outcome was referenced more than the goal. When success occurred, the goal was mentioned more than the outcome. Despite the uneven distribution of referencing goals, it should be noted that ongoing desires are mentioned as reasons for emotional reactions more than half of the time. We have shown this to hold for 3-year-olds (Stein & Levine, 1986) as well as for older children and adults.

These data appear to be inconsistent with earlier claims of Harris (1983) and Harris and Olthof (1982), who argued that young children fail to understand that internal states, as well as external events, regulate emotional reactions. The fact that young children refer to external events as causes of emotional reactions does not negate their understanding of the important role that goals play in regulating emotions.

A critical test of whether children understand that preferences and desires are necessary prerequisites for emotional reactions can be carried out by using a method of counterfactual questioning. If children are asked to reason about the possibility of having a negative emotional reaction to goal failure given that they *did not want* to achieve the goal in the first place, they should assert that they would not feel sad, mad, and so forth. Similarly, if children are asked about the possibility of feeling happy, given that they achieved a goal that they *didn't really want to attain,* their reply should negate the feeling of happiness.

This is exactly what happened in our first study (Data Set 1). When children were asked the following: "If you didn't like your toys and if you didn't want to play with them, would you be sad or angry if you lost them?" almost all (97%) responded by saying no. When asked why they wouldn't feel sad or angry, they responded by saying that they didn't like their toys, so they didn't care if the toys got lost. In fact, the majority of children (57%) said they would be glad if they could get rid of the toys. Similar responses were given when children were asked to reason about the conditions under which positive emotions occur. They were well aware of the necessity of valuing and wanting something in order to feel happy about achieving a particular goal (97%). In fact, most of the children (67%) said they would feel sad if they attained something that they really didn't want to have. Thus, the relationships between desires, outcomes, and emotional reactions are quite clear to young children.

One reason for focusing on outcomes in emotion explanations may be that outcomes carry information about the *certainty* of a change in the status of a goal. That is, reference to the outcome signifies that certain conditions with respect to current goal attainment have *changed.* Thus, the outcome contains information about changing conditions. The goal, on the other hand, normally refers to those conditions that remain constant. Thus, the outcome may be seen as a more direct *cause* of the emotion than the prevailing goal. In fact, Stein and Levine (1986) found that adults include reference to outcomes more frequently than do children.

The fact that differential weights were given to outcomes and goals as a function of success or failure is somewhat puzzling. It should be remembered that this effect was present only in the explanations for the *second* emotional reaction in each episode. No significant differences in the frequency of mentioning of goals versus outcomes were found in explanations for emotional reactions to the first success or failure. Here we consider why this might be so.

The differential focus on goals versus outcomes in explaining emotion may correspond to the focus of attention and processing strategies used to understand goal failure versus goal success. When failure occurs, the first assessment of the situation may be to ascertain the *reality* of the failure and the permanence of the conditions that led to failure. Mentioning the outcome as the source of failure may be useful as a reminding strategy to assess both the reality and permanence of the failure. Given that reinstatement is the primary wish associated with failure, an assessment of the permanence of the failure is critical.

Under conditions of success, focusing on the outcome may be less important because the goal has already been achieved. The more important feature of goal success may be to think about how the original goal is important in determining the maintenance of other goals. Thus, focusing on the goal as an explanation for success may serve as a reminding strategy to evaluate how important the current goal is in achieving other goals. Success may initially allow a faster consideration of the role that one goal plays in maintaining other goals.

Our data also indicate that emotion knowledge is organized into rather discrete categories, depending upon the positive or negative valence of the emotions. Not only did the content of explanations differ for happiness versus anger and sadness, but the types of wishes and plans also differed significantly. The primary wish and plan associated with happiness was one of maintaining the goal or enjoying the valued activity. The primary wishes and plans for sadness and anger were ones of goal reinstatement and goal substitution.

For the two negative emotions of sadness and anger, further differentiations were made. Children who responded with anger were more likely to want and to seek revenge than children who expressed sadness. Children who expressed sadness were more likely to want to reinstate the original goal. The plans generated to cope with sadness were directed more toward goal forfeiture and overt expression of emotion (usually crying).

In our previous studies (Stein & Jewett, 1986; Stein & Levine, 1986, 1987; Trabasso, Stein, & Johnson, 1981), we have also argued for the discreteness of basic emotion categories such as happiness, sadness, fear, and anger. Our position is different from the one adopted by Shaver, Schwartz, O'Connor, and Kirson (in press) and Russell (this volume) who argue that emotion categories are prototypical in nature. Our data do not support the basic tenets of prototype theory for the following reasons.

First, prototype theory would predict that for each emotion category, a family resemblance principle regulates membership. Thus, the dimensions of the evaluation and planning process that lead to a particular emotion need not share any features in common with other instances of the same emotion as long as each instance has one or two dimensions in common with the most prototypical instance of the emotion category. Thus, explanations for a particular emotion, as well as the plans associated with it, can vary in terms of those dimensions included and not necessarily overlap with one another.

Our data thus far do not support this assertion. Explanations for happiness always included reference to the fact that a valued goal was attained or can be attained with a high degree of certainty. The negative emotions of anger and sadness are always associated with goals that have failed. These dimensions always occur in explanations, and no overlap exists between positive and negative emotions on these specific dimensions. Fear is also distinct from anger and sadness (Stein & Levine, 1987). Whereas anger and sadness occur under conditions of certain goal failure, fear is expressed when goal failure has not yet occurred, but where the conditions are highly probable that failure will occur. Thus, when explanations for fear are given, an acknowledgment that goal failure *will* occur is always given. Moreover, the dimensions associated with the causes of fear do not overlap those associated with anger and sadness.

The two emotions that do have features in common are anger and sadness. Both occur as a function of goal failure. However, the conceptual knowledge that enables the identification of anger is unique and distinct from the knowledge of sadness. Anger occurs when attention focuses on the cause of goal failure such that a plan is constructed to remove the obstacle preventing success. Thus, the conditions leading to failure and the plan of reinstating the goal or *altering* the original conditions leading to failure are necessary components of anger.

These conditions are *not necessary* components of sadness. Unlike anger, sadness is associated with the evaluation of the consequences of loss plus a realization that the goal cannot be reinstated (or at least easily reinstated). Thus the plan associated with sadness is one of goal abandonment or substitution. Even though sadness shares certain features with anger, it is still conceptually distinct and nonoverlapping.

Prototype theory would predict that instances of anger should arise where attention has not been shifted to the cause or where no plan is available to alter the conditions leading to failure. In our studies, almost all instances of anger show an attention to the causal conditions, and most wishes associated with anger aim at reinstating the goal. Thus, the dimensions of goal failure *and* an analysis of the causal conditions leading to failure generalize over all instances of anger.

Orientation toward the implications of loss and goal abandonment characterize most instances of sadness and never characterize instances of anger. The only dimensions that consistently overlap for the two emotions are goal failure and the wishes associated with each emotion. The wish to reinstate the original goal is just as strong for sad reactions as it is for anger reactions. Apparently, the reality of goal failure does not affect the longing for goal reinstatement.

Despite the overlap in the wishes generated in response to the two emotions, each still retains unique features shared by all instances of each emotion category. Thus, we could argue that the conceptual knowledge structures that are used to understand emotions have distinct boundaries and specific features that characterize all instances.

Much of the confusion about the structure of emotion categories results from an analysis of the causes and consequences of emotion. Many investigators attempt to describe emotion categories by analyzing the events that precipitate emotions. Although the data from these studies suggest that some emotions are more distinct than others (see Trabasso, Stein, & Johnson, 1981, for an analysis of different emotions), attempting to distinguish emotions by only the events that cause them or the consequences that ensue from them presents serious problems.

Theoretically we could conceive of one event generating all three negative emotions. The crux of the issue, however, is not whether the same event generates three different emotions. The question is whether the dimensions that are *inferred* about a precipitating event are common to each of the three emotions. In our theory (Stein & Levine, 1986, 1987), the dimensions that regulate the experience of each emotion are distinct from one another, and each emotion has a set of necessary dimensions that span all instances. Thus, it is the analysis of the underlying concept structure of the event, and not the event itself, that accounts for the dimensions unique to each emotion.

In terms of understanding and representing changes in emotional states, children evidenced sensitivity to the following types of change: First, they could recall changes in valence with a high degree of accuracy; second, they could recall shifting from one negative emotion to another; and third, they were sensitive to shifts of intensity within an emotion category. That is, children could accurately report a perception of change in a happy situation when a goal was augmented. Similarly, they were sensitive to changes that led to a denial of another goal. Thus, when children are presented with two events and have a chance to respond to each emotionally, they are able to represent and recall these events.

The moral judgment data support our assertion that 5- and 6-year-olds understand that they can feel more than one way about a person or an event. About half of our 6-year-olds could actually generate situations and contexts where they felt both good and bad about an event and where they had both liked and disliked a person. In explaining their ambivalence, children referred to those situations where a person, most often a sibling, had helped them achieve an important goal but also had blocked important goals.

Our judgment data showed unambiguously that all 5-year-old children were able to take into consideration both good and bad characteristics of a person in making moral judgments. The end result of observing both good and bad behavior in a person was to judge them as neither bad nor good but somewhere in between. Although 5-year-old children had more difficulty verbalizing both the positive and negative dimensions underlying their moral judgments, they had no difficulty giving accurate nonverbal judgments about the moral character of a person displaying good and bad traits. Moreover, they were able to answer probe questions accurately.

These data suggest that the origins of ambivalence may be represented serially rather than simultaneously. We submit that children first develop one set of feelings toward a person, either good or bad, along with definite expectations about how that person will act in various situations. When a child then observes a person acting counter to expectations, a new feeling is expressed and the original expectations are called into question. A comparison process then results between the differing feelings expressed and the different expectations that result from knowing that a person is capable of good behavior in some situations and harm in others.

In the process of integrating disparate information and acquiring a concept of ambivalence, children may experience the positive and negative feelings that are associated with the original situations. It is unclear, however, whether children – or adults, for that matter – feel good and bad at the same time. Knowing that someone can make you feel good and bad or knowing that you both like and dislike someone is different from experiencing good and bad feelings simultaneously.

We would argue that to experience an emotional reaction the appraisal process surrounding an event must be activated. Subjects must attend to those aspects that made them feel good and bad. Two possible outcomes should result as a function of reviewing discrepant knowledge about a person. First, the good and bad feelings can be reinstated. However, these emotions should occur in sequence, especially if the reminding process involves a full retrieval of the original eliciting event. It should be remembered that events eliciting emotional reactions do so as a function of an appraisal process, and this process involves an attempt to understand and incorporate some type of novel information about the original event. Remembering that a person made you feel the opposite way may initiate a shift in emotional state such that the opposite feeling is reinstated, but only as a function of reappraising the original event. Thus, good and bad feelings may alternate as a function of a reappraisal of past events.

A second possibility may occur. As children become more aware that an individual can be both harmful and helpful, a more integrated knowledge representation should be formed such that lists of both good and bad characteristics can be retrieved quickly, along with the situations that enabled these inferences to be made. The feeling state associated with this knowledge, however, should be one of *anxiety* or discomfort, rather than the original positive and negative feeling states.

We adhere to this position, although ambivalence necessitates the retrieval of knowledge about good and bad behavior, because the activation of this knowledge carries with it high degrees of uncertainty. When we know that a person can be both harmful and helpful, even though we know the situations in which these behaviors occurred, it becomes more difficult to predict when that person will display positive or negative behavior. Thus, our trust or expectation that a person will act consistently is weakened. We can no longer predict with certainty that good or bad things will occur. Under these conditions, discomfort, anxiety, or even fear results.

Thus, our model and description of ambivalence is distinctly different from Harter and Whitesell's (this volume). First, we submit that the concept of ambivalence carries two components: a knowledge component and a feeling state component. The knowledge component includes an awareness that a person is capable of both harmful and beneficial action and that different feeling states result as a function of each class of action. The feeling component associated with ambivalence should be one of discomfort and anxiety or one of an alternation between positive and negative feeling states, due to the uncertainty and lack of predictability that comes with an attempt to understand a person's future behavior.

The fact that Harter and Whitesell report that older children and adults are more prone to true experiences of ambivalence with simultaneous rather than sequential experience of positive versus negative emotion is more a function of how they report their data than the actual feeling of polar opposite emotion states. Using verbal report data, such as "I feel happy and sad about . . ." or "I felt good and bad about . . . ," to ascertain simultaneity does not ensure that both emotion states have been experienced. What these data imply is that Harter and Whitesell's subjects have a well integrated representation of the situations that cause ambivalence and that rapid access to feeling state terms may be associated with coherent representations of ambivalence. Whether simultaneous good and bad feeling states are experienced is another question.

To date, we know of no studies that focus on the feeling states that accompany talk about ambivalence. We would predict that if a concurrent record were kept of the facial expressions, gestures, vocalizations, and talk that accompanies ambivalence, certain types of sequences would prevail. First, hesitation and uncertainty would occur, with an associated facial expression of anxiety or discomfort (distress). Knowing that a person cannot be predictably beneficial or harmful sets the stage for the emotional reaction and accompanying gestures of anxiety. A fear expression may even occur. According to our findings (Stein & Levine, 1987), fear and anxiety result when a threat to a valued goal is present. Fear occurs when the threat is well defined and relatively certain. Anxiety occurs when the threat is somewhat less but still possible. Positive and/or negative emotion may then be expressed as the events that caused the ambivalent reaction are reviewed. Subjects should then begin to reevaluate and reassess the eliciting events with respect to their judgments about the predictability and causes of both harmful and beneficial behaviors.

If a particular feeling state is reinstated, this implies that subjects never fully incorporated the novel aspect of the situation into a coherent representation. For example, being reminded of how mean or bad a person is sometimes carries with it an almost permanent disbelief about the negative behavior, given that the same person is known to be capable of extremely positive behavior. We believe that failure to build a coherent representation of the negative situations comes from a lack of knowledge about the full range of conditions that produce both positive and negative behavior.

Finally, consideration of positive and negative aspects of a person may lead to a more permanent state of sadness or happiness. Ambivalence carries with it a high degree of uncertainty, thus putting an individual into an unstable state. In situations of high uncertainty the tendency is to reduce the uncertainty by assessing whether or not an individual's behavior can be more readily controlled and explained. If a judgment is made about the impossibility of controlling negative behavior of another, then an individual may wish to withdraw from a relationship, causing loss and subsequent sadness. If a judgment is made about the possibility of controlling the negative behaviors, then happiness should result.

Given our model of ambivalence, future studies will need to focus on the feeling states that children *experience* when they are reminded of both good and bad attributes of another person. Critical questions revolve around the sequence of emotion states observed as well as the thinking and reasoning associated with each state. Moreover, since ambivalence implies an unstable state with regard to the feeling states toward another, the *resolution* of ambivalent feelings becomes important also.

Three questions remain. Does knowledge of dual feeling states lead to the simultaneous experience and expression of these states? Can children younger than 5 experience ambivalence? And, are young children from the ages of 3 to 5 capable of understanding multiple and changing representations of emotion situations? The last question is important because of the recent controversies arising from research focused on exploring the young child's concept of mind (Astington & Gopnik, 1988; Wellman, 1988).

On the one hand, some researchers (Astington & Gopnik, 1988) believe that 3- and 4-year-old children cannot encode multiple or changing representations of an event, object, or person. On the other, other researchers (Wellman, 1988) predict that even 3-year-old children are capable of acquiring and using such representations. Our own data (Stein & Levine, 1986) suggests that 3-year-olds can remember changing emotion states and make the correct inferences about the causes of emotions. Moreover, these children distinguish their own emotional reactions and beliefs from those of other people. Thus, the ability to understand changes in internal states is present quite early.

We contend that what changes as function of development is children's knowledge of the conditions that elicit both positive and negative behavior, their knowledge about other people and themselves, and their knowledge about the plans and actions that lead to successful adaptation to situations. Future research will be necessary to specify the exact nature of this knowledge development and the role that learning and socialization play in the acquisition of emotion concepts.

References

Astington, J. W., & Gopnik, A. 1988. Knowing you've changed your mind: children's understanding of representation change. In J. W. Astington, P. C. Holms, & D. R. Olson (Eds.), *Developing theories of mind*. Cambridge: Cambridge University Press.

Borke, H. (1972). Interpersonal perceptions of young children: egocentrism or empathy? *Developmental Psychology, 7,* 104–106.

Demos, E. V. (1974). Children's understanding and use of affect terms. Unpublished doctoral dissertation, Harvard University.

Emde, R. (1980). Levels of meaning in infant development. In W. A. Collins (Ed.), *Minnesota symposium on child psychology* (Vol. 13). Hillsdale, NJ: Erlbaum.

Folkman, S., & Lazarus, R. S. (in press). Coping and emotion. In N. L. Stein, B. Leventhal, and T. Trabasso (Eds.), *Psychological and biological approaches to emotion*. Hillsdale, NJ: Erlbaum.

Harris, P. L.. (1983). Children's understanding of the link between situation and emotion. *Journal of Experimental Child Psychology, 36,* 490–509.

Harris, P. L.. (1985). What children know about the situations that provoke emotions. In M. Lewis & C. Saarni (Eds.), *The socialization of emotions*. New York: Plenum.

Harris, P. L.. & Olthof, T. (1982). The child's concept of emotion. In G. Butterworth & P. Light (Eds.), *Social cognition*. London: Harvester.

Harter, S. (1979). *Children's understanding of multiple emotions: a cognitive–developmental approach*. Address given at the Ninth Annual Piaget Society Meetings, Philadelphia.

Lazarus, R. S. (1984). On the primacy of cognition. *American Psychologist, 39,* No. 2, 124–129.

Lazarus, R. S. (in press). Constructs of the mind in adaptation. In N. L. Stein, B. Leventhal, and T. Trabasso (Eds.), *Psychological and biological approaches to emotion*. Hillsdale, NJ: Erlbaum.

Lazarus, R. S., & Folkman, S. (1984). *Stress, appraisal, and coping.* New York: Springer-Verlag.

Lehnert, W. (1982). Plot units: a narrative summarization strategy. In W. G. Lehnert & M. H. Ringle (Eds.), *Strategies for natural language processing.* Hillsdale, NJ: Erlbaum.

Mandler, G. (1975). *Mind and emotion.* New York: Wiley.

Mandler, G. (1984). *Mind and body: a psychological theory of emotion.* New York: Norton.

Mandler, G. (in press). A constructivist theory of emotion. In N. L. Stein, B. Leventhal, & T. Trabasso (Eds.), *Psychological and biological approaches to emotion.* Hillsdale, NJ: Erlbaum.

Shaver, P., Schwartz, J., O'Connor, C., & Kirson, D. (in press). Emotion knowledge: further explanations of a prototype approach. *Journal of Personality and Social Psychology.*

Stein, N. L. (1988). The development of storytelling skill. In M. B. Franklin & S. Barten (Eds.), *Child language: a book of readings.* New York: Cambridge University Press.

Stein, N. L., & Glenn, C. G. (1979). An analysis of story comprehension in elementary school children. In R. O. Freedle (Ed.), *New directions in discourse processing* (Vol. 2): *advances in discourse processing.* Norwood, NJ: Ablex.

Stein, N. L., & Jewett, J. (1985). A conceptual analysis of the meaning of anger, fear, and sadness. Paper presented at the Society for Research in Child Development, Toronto, April.

Stein, N. L., & Jewett, J. (1986). A conceptual analysis of the meaning of negative emotions: Implication for a theory of development. In C. E. Izard & P. Read (Eds.), *Measurement of emotion in infants and children.* New York: Cambridge University Press.

Stein, N. L., & Levine, L. (1986). *Causal organization of emotion knowledge.* Paper presented at the Psychonomic Society Meetings, New Orleans.

Stein, N. L., & Levine, L. (1987). Thinking about feelings: the development and organization of emotional knowledge. In R. E. Snow & M. Farr (Eds.), *Aptitude, learning, and instruction* (Vol. 3): *Cognition, conation, and affect.* Hillsdale, NJ: Erlbaum.

Stein, N. L., & Levine, L. (in press). Making sense out of emotional experience: the representation and use of goal-directed knowledge. In N. L. Stein, B. Leventhal, & T. Trabasso (Eds.), *Psychological and biological approaches to emotion.* Hillsdale, NJ: Erlbaum.

Stein, N. L., & Trabasso, T. (1982). Children's understanding of stories: a basis for moral judgment and dilemma resolution. In C. J. Brainerd & M. Pressley (Eds.), *Verbal processes in children.* New York: Springer-Verlag.

Stein, N. L., & Trabasso, T. (1985). The search after meaning: comprehension and comprehension monitoring. In F. J. Morrison, C. Lord, & D. Keating (Eds.), *Applied developmental psychology,* Vol. 2. New York: Academic Press.

Trabasso, T., Stein, N. L., & Johnson, L. R. (1981). Children's knowledge of events: a causal analysis of story structure. In G. Bower (Ed.), *Learning and motivation* (Vol. 15). New York: Academic Press.

Trabasso, T., van den Broek, P., & Suh, S. (in press). Logical necessity and transitivity of causal relations in stories. *Discourse Processes.*

Wellman, H. (1988). First steps in the young child's theorizing about the mind. In J. W. Astington, P. L. Harris, & D. R. Olson. (Eds.), *Developing theories of mind.* Cambridge: Cambridge University Press.

Part III

Developmental changes in understanding emotion

4 Developmental changes in children's understanding of single, multiple, and blended emotion concepts

Susan Harter and Nancy Rumbaugh Whitesell

Introduction

The field of psychology is witnessing a growing interest in emotional expression and the understanding of emotion concepts, particularly from a developmental perspective. The present chapter will focus on children's understanding of selected emotion concepts, exploring how the child's cognitive–developmental level influences his or her *theory* of emotions. We have been particularly interested in the child's cognitive construction or reconstruction, as it were, of his or her emotional experience, rather than emotional expression per se. In this chapter we will not only describe a number of developmental sequences in children's understanding of emotion concepts, but also attempt to provide a theoretical interpretation of these findings, drawing upon current theories of cognition and emotion.

Our initial approach to the development of emotion concepts was largely empirical. We sought to document a number of naturally occurring developmental sequences that emerged based on our content analysis of children's spontaneous responses to relatively open-ended questions. We subsequently designed specific tasks to provide a more systematic description of these sequences. Most recently, we have directed our attention to the theoretical interpretation of the sequences we have documented. In so doing, we have focused primarily upon the cognitive–developmental underpinnings of children's emotion concepts. However, our findings have also revealed the need to speak to the potential role of certain socialization experiences in shaping children's emerging understanding of their emotions.

We will adopt such a developmental framework in dealing with several specific topics. First, we will review our work on children's understanding of the simultaneity of emotions, presenting a developmental sequence that can be interpreted within a framework that draws heavily upon Fischer's (1980) skill theory. Our most recent work has addressed the issue of whether simultaneous emotions such as happiness and anger necessarily provoke an experience of *conflict*.

81

We will also explore the emergence of the understanding of *self-affects*, specifically pride and shame. Our findings have documented an interesting developmental sequence that requires an interpretation drawing upon both cognitive level and the socialization experiences of the child. In addition, one particular emotion, depression, will be examined from the standpoint of multiple emotions as well as self-affects. Does depression represent a combination of emotions, for example, sadness plus anger? Moreover, if anger is a component of the emotion blend, does it represent a self-affect, that is, anger directed toward the self, or is the anger directed toward another person, namely an external target?

Finally, we will extend our developmental analysis to an examination of the ages at which children understand such basic emotions as happy, sad, mad, and scared, as well as more differentiated emotions. In so doing, we will draw upon recent emotion prototype theory (Shaver, Schwartz, Kirson, & O'Connor, 1987) that articulates a hierarchy of emotion concepts among adults. Prototype theory also speaks to the commonly understood *causes* of the basic emotions among adults. Thus, we will be examining the applicability of such causal categories to explanations generated by children at different developmental levels, documenting similarities as well as differences between children and adults in their understanding of those factors provoking the basic emotions.

Children's understanding of simultaneous emotions

A growing body of evidence reveals that young children are incapable of appreciating the fact that they can experience seemingly opposing emotional reactions simultaneously. Our own sensitivity to this issue began with the clinical observations of the first author followed by normative-developmental research designed to document, and interpret, the sequence through which such an understanding emerges. Within a play therapy context, it was observed that young clients had particular difficulty in acknowledging the co-occurrence of positive and negative emotions (Harter, 1977). These children would typically deny the simultaneous experience of two emotions, asserting that they could have but one feeling at a time.

This dichotomous thinking was particularly evident in regard to emotional reactions to significant others. For example, a child would be consumed with anger toward a parent, sibling, or friend, staunchly denying any feelings of affection or love. With regard to issues of loss, he or she would be pervasively sad over the departure of a loved one, totally unable to acknowledge the positive emotions they undoubtedly also felt for the individual. Although one may be tempted to conclude that such difficulties are primarily a function of the presenting problems that brought the child client to therapy, our own work has revealed that such phenomena have a normative, cognitive–developmental, basis, although they may well be exacerbated in clinic populations.

Our initial findings are quite consistent with a number of studies in the literature that reveal a general three-stage sequence in children's understanding of simultaneous emotions (Carroll & Steward, 1984; Donaldson & Westerman, 1986; Gnepp, McKee, & Domanic, 1987; Harris, 1983a, 1983b; Harris, Olthof, & Meerum Terwogt, 1981; Harter, 1982; 1986a; Harter & Buddin, 1987; Meerum Terwogt, 1984; Reissland, 1985; Selman, 1980). These studies document a sequence in which the youngest children deny the coexistence of two feelings. At the next stage, children acknowledge that two feelings can co-occur in temporal order, in sequence, although they cannot occur simultaneously. At the third stage, the oldest children acknowledge that two feelings can occur simultaneously.

Our most recent normative research (see Harter, 1986b; Harter & Buddin, 1987) has focused specifically on the issue of simultaneity. We have now documented a systematic acquisition sequence that described the emergence of the understanding of simultaneous emotions. We have identified two dimensions that govern this sequence. One is the *valence* of the two emotions, whether they are of the *same* valence (i.e., both positive, such as happy and glad, or both negative, such as mad and sad) or whether they are of *opposite* valence (one positive and one negative, e.g., happy and mad, or glad and sad). The second dimension involves the *number of targets* toward which the emotions are directed, namely *one* target as the focus of the two feelings or *two* targets, where one of the emotions is directed toward one target and the second emotion is directed toward a different target.

Our strategy was to design a task that would systematically tap children's understanding of the four combinations of valence and target, namely: (1) Same valence, same target, (2) Same valence, different targets, (3) Different valence, different targets, (4) Different valence, same target. In this manner, we could determine whether a scalable acquisition sequence might be demonstrated (see Harter & Buddin, 1987, for procedural details).

Moreover, we sought a post-hoc theoretical interpretation of the lawful progression that our findings revealed. In so doing, we have focused primarily on the underlying cognitive-structural changes that may be related to developmental differences in children's understanding of simultaneous emotions. In addressing the cognitive-structural changes involved, we have relied heavily on Fischer's (1980) skill theory. This theory builds upon Piaget's work and has much in common with other contemporary theories of cognitive development (see Case, 1985; Higgins, 1981; Pascual-Leone, 1970).

A complete description of Fischer's theory is beyond the scope of this chapter. However, a basic underlying structural dimension involves the number of representations that a child can cognitively control, coordinate, or integrate simultaneously. Thus, we have applied this type of analysis to the levels of emotional understanding that were empirically demonstrated. A detailed description of the application of Fischer's theoretical levels to our empirically determined levels is presented elsewhere (Harter, 1986a). Here we describe each of our five levels and interpret them according to the principles of Fischer's theory. Although we did not utilize this theory to make a priori predictions about the particular sequence of levels, nevertheless it provides a useful framework for systematically describing the structures of the levels obtained. Because other theories may offer equally compelling explanations of this sequence, future work should focus on the differential predictions suggested by theoretical alternatives, and should test these directly.

Level 0. The youngest children (mean age, 5.2) simply deny that two feelings can simultaneously coexist. Although they may acknowledge that two feelings can be experienced sequentially, they are adamant in their belief that it is impossible for two emotions to occur together. That they are firmly entrenched in a theory that precludes the simultaneous experience of two feelings is clear from many of their comments: "There is no way two feelings could ever go together at the same time"; "You can't have two feelings at the same time because you only have one mind"; "I could be happy that I was watching TV and then sad that I had to go to bed, but I couldn't feel both of those at the same time."

Applying Fischer's theoretical principles, the level 0 child has developed single representations for separate emotions (e.g., happy, glad, sad, mad, scared). However, at any point in time, only one emotional representation can be applied to a given event. The child can deal with emotions that occur in temporal order, because this involves only one emotion at a time. Yet the child denies that he or she can have two feelings at the same time because he or she cannot simultaneously relate, integrate, or coordinate two representations that refer to different emotions, no matter how similar they appear to be. Thus, the child cannot relate "happy" to "glad" or "sad" to "mad" simultaneously.

Level 1. These children (mean age, 7.3) show the first appreciation for the simultaneous experience of two emotions, but this understanding is restricted to combinations in which emotions of the *same* valence are directed toward a *single* target, for example, "If your brother hit you, would you be both mad and sad"; "I was happy and glad that I got a new puppy for Christmas." Children at this level report that two feelings cannot be directed toward two different targets simultaneously, nor can opposite valence feelings co-occur.

According to our theoretical analysis, at Level 1 the child is beginning to develop *representational sets* for feelings of the same valence, constructing separate emotion categories, one for positive emotions and one for negative emotions. Thus, feelings within each category are becoming somewhat differentiated from one another (e.g., happy versus glad within the positive representational set, mad versus sad within the negative set). Thus, the child has some ability to cognitively control variations *within* each emotional set, that is, be both happy and glad over one event or mad and sad about one target. However, the emotions within a given set are not yet sufficiently differentiated to allow the child to direct them toward different targets simultaneously. That is, the child cannot yet simultaneously control variations within a given emotional set or variations in targets in order to relate the two variations to each other. This is the first cognitive limitation of Level 1. The second limitation is that the child cannot yet integrate the sets of positive and negative emotions, sets that are viewed as conceptually distinct and therefore incompatible. Thus, emotions of opposite valence cannot be experienced as simultaneous.

Level 2. At this level (mean age, 8.7), children can bring two *same*-valence feelings to bear on different targets simultaneously, for example, "I'd be mad if she broke my toy and sad that she went home"; "I was excited I went to Mexico and glad to see my grandparents." However, these children deny the simultaneity of opposite-valence feelings, for example, "I couldn't feel happy and scared at the same time; I would have to be two people at once!"

At Level 2, the child overcomes the first cognitive limitation of Level 1 by developing *representational mappings* that permit one to control and relate variations within a same-valence emotional set to variations within a set of targets. Thus, the child can map one emotion onto one target – "mad that she broke my toy" – and attach the second same-valence emotion to a different target – "sad that she went home." However, the child has not yet overcome the second cognitive limitation of the previous level, since he or she cannot yet integrate the sets of positive and negative emotions. This limitation precludes the possibility that one can acknowledge a positive and a negative emotion simultaneously.

Level 3. The child (mean age, 10.1) demonstrates a major conceptual advance in that he or she can now appreciate simultaneous *opposite* valence feelings. However, these emotions can only be brought to bear on different targets. Thus, the negative emotion is directed toward a negative event ("I was mad at my brother for hitting me") and the positive emotion is directed toward a different, positive aspect of the situation ("but at the same time, I was really happy that my father gave me permission to hit him back"). In other cases the two targets are even more discrete, for example, "I was sitting in school feeling worried about all of the responsibilities of a new pet but I was happy that I had gotten straight A's on my report card."

At Level 3, the child advances to what Fischer terms "representational systems" in that he or she can now integrate the representational sets for positive and negative emotions. This allows the child to acknowledge positive and negative emotions simultaneously. However, the child cannot yet bring two opposite valence feelings to bear on a single target. Rather, he or she exemplifies what Fischer terms a "shift of focus," directing the positive feeling to a positive target or event and then cognitively shifting the focus of the negative feeling to a negative event. The concept that the very same target can simultaneously have both positive and negative aspects is not yet cognitively accessible to the child.

Level 4. Here, children (mean age of 11.3) become able to describe how opposite-valence feelings can be provoked by the *same* target, for example, "I was happy that I got a present but mad that it wasn't exactly what I wanted"; "If a stranger offered you candy you'd be eager for the candy but also doubtful if it was OK"; "I was happy I was joining the new club but also a little worried because I didn't know anyone in it."

At this level the child overcomes the limitations of the previous period in that he or she can now acknowledge that the same target can provoke both a positive and negative emotion. The cognitive advance would appear to be the child's new-found capacity to differentiate one target into positive and negative aspects and then coordinate these aspects with the corresponding positive and negative emotions, simultaneously. Thus, each of the levels in this analysis involves developmental change with regard to the number and type of representations that the child can simultaneouly control, coordinate, or integrate. The levels examined place increasingly greater cognitive demands on the child, thereby resulting in the systematic, age-related progression that we have documented.

It should be emphasized that this sequence defines children's *understanding* or acknowledgment of the simultaneity of two emotions and not their direct experience per se. That is, observations reveal that children manifest multiple emotions behaviorally at ages much younger than those reported for the levels just described, although our findings suggest that they are not cognitively aware of these emotion combinations, as assessed through self-report techniques. It should also be noted that the ages at which metacognitions about multiple emotions are achieved in our studies are higher than those reported by other investigators (see Stein & Trabasso, this volume). There would appear to be several reasons for this discrepancy. First, in our procedure we have required subjects to *generate* examples of the co-occurrence of two emotions, whereas others have merely asked subjects to respond to hypothetical situations that commonly elicit such emotion combinations in children. Second, we have emphasized simultaneity in that subjects are repeatedly told to provide examples in which the emotions occurred *at the very same time*. In other studies, the focus has been on how the same situation can provoke two emotions, although they need not occur at precisely the same moment in time. Finally, our scoring criteria have been quite stringent (see Harter & Buddin, 1987), particularly at the highest levels, where children must give a highly integrated description of how the two emotions can co-occur simultaneously. When these considerations are taken into account, the findings from different laboratories are not contradictory.

To pursue the issue of temporal simultaneity, one may well question whether children or even adults can actually experience two emotions, particularly those of opposite valence, at the very same time. Introspection would suggest that although the same event may well provoke two different emotional reactions, they are experienced as rapidly oscillating, as one cognitively shifts one's focus from one aspect of the causal event to another. We have begun to explore this issue with children, asking them at the end of our formal procedures whether they really felt the two emotions at exactly the same time or whether it felt like one was followed very quickly by the other. The majority of our sample of 9- to 12-year-olds who had previously generated examples of simultaneous opposite-valence emotions reported that it felt more like one was quickly followed by the other. Thus, in future studies it will be interesting to link these perceptions more directly to potential cognitive shifts of focus, as well as to determine whether certain emotion pairs are more difficult to experience at precisely the same time.

Another refinement in extending our findings involves the distinction between two emotions directed toward elements of a given *situation* and two emotions directed toward one *person*. As an exploratory effort, we have asked subjects to indicate how one person could cause them to have both a positive and negative feeling at the same time. Only about half of our Level 4 subjects could give a compelling example. Conceptually, this task requires that one realize that al-though attributes or behaviors of a person are integrated within that individual, they must be sufficiently differentiated such that one's positive feeling is attached to a positive characteristic or action at the same time that one's negative feeling is attached to a negative characteristic of the person. The differentiated percep-tions of both self and other must all be simultaneously coordinated in order to perform this task successfully. A few of our oldest children were able to give a reasonably convincing response, for example, ``My dad made me happy and mad at the same time. I was happy that he brought me a gift but mad at him because he made me wait until I finished my homework before I could open it.'' Given that other people are such powerful sources or causes of one's emotions, it will be important to pursue this issue, since it has important developmental as well as clinical implications.

Clinical implications

As noted above, this particular sequence is not only of interest from a developmental perspective but has clinical applications as well. From a clinical perspective, it is critical that this normative acquisition sequence be appreciated as a backdrop against which to assess a given child's ability to deal with multiple emotions. Based on our findings, it will not be until late childhood that one would expect a child to thoughtfully conclude that he or she is indeed feeling both positive and negative emotions toward a significant other. Thus, an appreciation for these age norms may aid us in guarding against the temptation to overinterpret the difficulty a child client may have in verbally acknowledging the simultaneity of two emotions. That is, we should not rush to the assumption that a child's inability to express love for a parent toward whom he or she might be feeling angry at the moment is a pathological index of splitting or denial.

Our age norms can also be used in the diagnostic process. For example, if a child is at an age-appropriate level of emotional understanding in one domain (e.g., emotions related to school performance) but at a lower level in our sequence in another domain (e.g., peer relationships), this type of unevenness or decalage may well be of diagnostic significance. One may well suspect certain psychological problems in the latter domain, where the child is at a lower level of understanding with regard to the simultaneity of emotions. Difficulties in this domain may well have precluded the development of more age-appropriate emotion concepts. Thus, one can utilize a child's manifest level of understanding across the different domains of his or her life as a barometer of potential adjustment problems, if not more severe pathology, depending on how developmentally delayed the child appears to be.

An awareness of the ages at which these developmental milestones are achieved may also have an impact on therapeutic interventions. A goal for certain psychodynamically oriented therapists is for the child to develop insight into the mixed emotions that he or she experiences in relation to the significant others and events in one's life. Often the clinician will *infer* that the child is experiencing opposite-valence emotions toward a family member, for example, and as a therapeutic goal will expect the child to acknowledge these feelings. However, our normative-developmental findings reveal that the acknowledgment of simultaneous opposite valence feelings toward one person is the most difficult acquisition in the sequence. Thus, one would not expect a child to appreciate such mixed emotions until later childhood, and therefore it may be difficult if not impossible for the child to gain insight into such an issue.

Do opposite-valence feelings necessarily cause conflict?

An issue of both theoretical and clinical interest is whether opposite-valence feelings necessarily cause an experience of intrapsychic conflict. A number of theorists, ourselves included, have implied that if opposite-valence emotions are simultaneously experienced, they necessarily provoke intrapsychic conflict or ambivalence (Harris, Olthof, & Meerum Terwogt, 1981; Harter, 1977; Selman, 1980). However, we cannot merely assume that because one feels happy and mad simultaneously, for example, these feelings are experienced as conflictual. In certain instances, conflict may be experienced, whereas in other instances seemingly opposite-valence emotions may harmoniously coexist. Thus, it behooves us to determine whether there is conflict or harmony, rather than merely to assume that there is conflict when in fact it may not exist. One study in the literature (Donaldson & Westerman, 1986) reports that it is not until late childhood that one comes to appreciate the fact that opposite-valence feelings can interact with one another to produce a feeling of ambivalence. Children at their higher highest level report that opposite-valence feelings toward the same target (a pet in hypothetical situations they presented) can be experienced as mixed up, confusing, or in conflict.

In our own work, we have focused primarily on the experience of intrapsychic conflict, namely the degree to which children experience opposite-valence feelings toward significant people in their life as clashing with each other. We have selected the 9 to 12 age range because most children at this age appreciate the fact that they can have opposite-valence feelings at the same time. We selected two opposite-valence emotion pairs to pursue, happy versus mad and happy versus sad, because our previous research has demonstrated that these are the most commonly mentioned opposite-valence pairs that children spontaneously describe. The primary question, therefore, is whether the co-occurrence of these opposite-valence feelings produces an experience of conflict or whether such feelings can coexist harmoniously.

The methodological challenge for us was to design a procedure whereby we could communicate the *concept* of conflict between two emotions, in order that children would understand what we were asking, yet be able to deny conflict if it did not match with their experience. Toward this end, we used magnets as props. We mounted nickel-size magnets on the ends of dowel sticks such that in one case the pair of magnets repel each other, symbolizing that the two emotions are clashing, fighting, struggling, at war, or not getting along with each other. These descriptive phrases accompanied the presentation of this pair of magnets. The second pair of magnets were mounted on the dowel sticks so that they attracted one another, symbolizing that the two feelings were getting along or were in harmony with each other. We discovered that children within the 9 to 12 age range find the magnets quite compelling as an analogue of conflicting as well as of harmonious emotion pairs.

Our procedure involves asking children about the simultaneity of happy and sad feelings, as well as happy and mad feelings, where in one case the target of the emotion is a peer and in another case a parent (see Whitesell, 1987, Whitesell & Harter, in press, for methodological details). Children generate their own examples of what particular events could cause the simultaneous co-occurrence of these emotion pairs. We then inquire about whether the two emotions in each pair are fighting or clashing or whether they get along with each other, such that the child does not experience any internal conflict. Subjects are asked to select the magnet pair that best portrays their own experience of the two feelings, and then provide a description of the reasons for their choice.

Interestingly, the findings reveal that within the age range we selected, conflict is experienced in only about 50 percent of the situations generated by our subjects. In the other half of the responses, children indicate that the feelings get along or are in harmony. That children understand the distinction between fighting or conflict and getting along or harmony is clear from their their verbal descriptions (that is, we have not relied solely on their choice of magnet pairs).

Among those who indicate that the feelings are in conflict, the large majority of children convincingly describe an *internal struggle,* typically personifying the feelings. Sample descriptions are: "Sometimes the two feelings make you feel like your head is throbbing or it might be like two people fighting and getting pushed against the side or something"; "The feelings are fighting, each one is trying to jump over on top of the other one and smash it"; "The mad feeling wants to take over like the Russians and the U.S., the Russians want to take over but the U.S. is like the happy feeling that wants to keep peace."

The descriptions of *harmony* between feelings or lack of conflict are equally convincing. Most children describe the absence of an internal struggle. Sample descriptions are: "There is no controversy inside you, you don't feel mixed up"; "If I am really happy, the mad feeling just sort of fades and gets covered up by the happy"; "They both kind of agree with each other, the feelings don't have emotions, they just agree to keep it cool"; "Both feelings are there, but they mix really easy"; "I'm just mostly happy. The sad feeling is there, but it's not really controlling how I feel. I think because I want to feel happy, I don't want to feel sad."

The interesting question becomes just what factors are responsible for whether opposing emotions do or do not cause conflict. We have some insights into this issue because we asked children to rate the *intensity* of each emotion in the pair, as well how *similar or different* the two emotions appeared to be. The intensity dimension actually represented the emotional balance of the two emotions. That is, subjects were presented with an array of five circles or "pies" for each emotion pair, one array for happy/mad and one for happy/sad. These circles depicted combinations of the two emotions ranging from one feeling taking up most of the circle, for example, mostly happy (with one small "slice" of mad), at one extreme, to a circle depicted mostly mad (with one small "slice" of happy) at the other extreme. The middle circle is bifurcated such that each feeling occupies half of the area. Thus, we were interested in whether the particular strength or intensity of each emotion in the pair might have an impact on the degree to which conflict was experienced. One hypothesis is that if the two feelings are of equal strength or intensity, they may be more likely to do battle, that is, they would be more likely to be experienced as in conflict.

Children were also asked to rate the *similarity/dissimilarity* of the two emotions on a five-point scale. The five possible descriptions from which they could select were: (1) sort of alike, (2) sort of alike and sort of different, (3) sort of different, (4) really different, and (5) opposites. Given that we were inquiring about potentially opposite-valence feelings only (happy–mad and happy–sad), there were more choices reflecting differences between the feelings. We predicted that the more different the feelings were perceived to be, the more conflict would be reported.

The findings revealed that the dimension of intensity or emotional balance between the two feelings as well as the dimension of perceived similarity or difference contributed to the level of conflict reported. Moreover, these two dimensions appeared to be relatively independent of each other, such that each made independent contributions to the experience of conflict. With regard to the intensity dimension, the greatest conflict is reported when either the positive and negative emotions are equal in strength or when the negative emotion is somewhat greater in strength than the positive emotion. Conflict is rarely experienced if the positive emotion is greater in intensity than the negative emotion.

With regard to the similarity dimension, there is more experience of conflict the more dissimilar the two feelings. Thus, if happy and mad are perceived to be opposites, there is a maximum experience of conflict, whereas if these two feelings are perceived as less different, or in fact even somewhat similar, conflict is much less likely to be reported. We view this particular measure as quite critical because it cautions us against making the assumption that the emotion pairs we have *labeled* as opposing are necessarily perceived as opposites; they may be experienced along a number of points in the continuum from opposites to similar.

The additive nature of these two dimensions in predicting conflict can be observed in Figure 4.1. It can be seen that if the emotions are perceived as different and if the emotional balance is such that the intensity of the negative emotion is either equal to or greater than the positive emotion, then close to 80 percent of the responses represent conflict between the two emotions. If the emotions are perceived as different, but the emotional balance is such that the positive emotion is more intense than the negative emotion, then there is considerably less conflict. Similarly, if the emotions are perceived as similar, but the negative feeling is equal to, or greater in strength, than the positive, there is less conflict. The least conflict is reported when the emotions are perceived as similar and the strength or intensity of the positive emotion is greater than the negative emotion.

These findings illuminate two critical dimensions that control the extent to

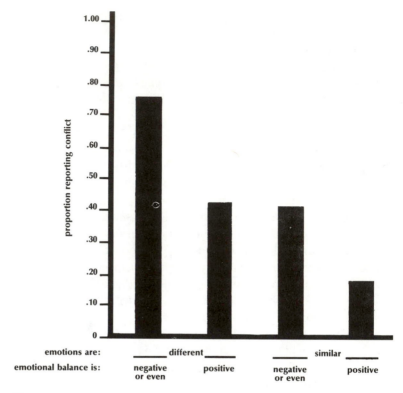

Figure 4.1. Proportion of children reporting conflict, by perceived similarity and emotional balance.

which emotions of seemingly opposite valence produce the experience of intrapsychic conflict between the two feelings. Emotion pairs in which the negative emotion is either equal in strength to or more intense than the positive emotion, and in which the two emotions are quite different if not opposite, produce the greatest experience of conflict. Although these findings are interesting, they do not tell the entire story. Rather, they shift the level of inquiry by raising the question of why some events – for example, the specific actions of peers and parents – lead to negative feelings of greater intensity than positive feelings and to the perception that the negative and positive feelings are quite different. We have a few clues from our most recent pilot work. A negative feeling is more likely to be perceived as very intense, dominating the positive emotion, if it occurs in the context of a relationship that is important to the child and if the action of the other (either peer or parent) violates an expectancy. For example, a friend and supposed confidant who tells one's secrets to another violates the implicit rules governing a friendship, leading one to be very angry, such that the anger at least temporarily overpowers the positive feelings of happiness or affection for one's friend. To take another example, the parent who forgets an important occasion in the life of the child may cause feelings of anger or sadness to predominate over the more typical happiness over the parents' actions.

Children reporting such events also indicate that not only do these experiences provoke conflict between the two emotions but that they cause them to spend a great deal of time thinking about the event. Moreover, in situations where conflict is experienced, children claim that it is extremely difficult to make the negative feeling go away. We are pursuing these themes in our present research, attempting to relate the causes of each emotion to the degree to which two affects are perceived as dissimilar and to the intensity of the negative and positive emotions. Although there is still much to be learned about the specific causes of emotional reactions that may or may not produce conflict, our findings clearly indicate that we should not assume that seemingly opposite valence-feelings necessarily provoke an internal experience of conflict. In normative as well as clinical samples, it behooves us to demonstrate the dynamics of conflict or its absence rather than merely assume that conflict is operative.

The developmental emergence of self-affects: pride and shame

In the preceding sections, we dealt with children's understanding of simultaneous emotions, focusing primarily on the cognitive-developmental factors that govern their acquisition. A related topic involves the emergence of certain more complex single emotions that would appear to represent emotion blends. We have been particularly interested in the emergence of an understanding of pride and shame because not only do they require underlying cognitive advances but they are heavily dependent upon certain socialization experiences. From a cognitive perspective, pride and shame require more than the single representations that are sufficient for such basic emotions as happy, sad, mad, and scared. An understanding of pride or shame requires the differentiation and integration of several features. For example, pride combines joy over the mastery of a particular skill as well as happiness because the accomplishment was appreciated by others. Shame typically combines some sense of sadness or regret, as well as anger toward the self, for committing a transgression.

However, an analysis of the development of an understanding of the concepts of pride and shame must also take into account those socialization experiences necessary for their emergence. This has been the primary focus of our own research. Paradoxically, perhaps, pride and shame have been described as ''self-affects'' – namely, affects that one can experience with regard to the self, in the *absence* of others. That is, one can engage in events that provoke the feeling that one is proud of oneself, or ashamed of oneself, when these events have not been directly witnessed by other people. As we shall see, however, the ability to experience these self-affects is highly dependent upon one's socialization history.

Cooley (1902), a well known scholar of the self, was one of the first to devote thoughtful attention to the emotions of pride and shame and their relationship to the social origins of the self. For Cooley, the self was a social construction, the incorporation of the attitudes a person believes significant others hold toward the self. Thus, one adopts the reflected appraisals of these others in the form of what Cooley metaphorically called the looking-glass self. However, the self, so constructed, does not merely represent a cognitive appraisal of one's attributes, imagined in the eyes of significant others, but a *self-feeling,* namely an affective reaction to this appraisal. In describing the reactions of the adult self, Cooley singled out the emotions of pride and shame, in particular, and in so doing set the stage for a developmental analysis of how these emotions might emerge.

Although pride and shame could clearly be experienced by adults in the absence of others, Cooley noted that "The thing that moves us to pride and shame is not the merely mechanical reflection of ourselves, but an imputed sentiment, the imagined effect of this reflection upon another's mind" (1902, p. 153). Cooley was clear on the point that this sentiment is social in nature, based upon social custom and opinion, though it becomes somewhat removed from these sources through an implied internalization process. Cooley wrote that the adult is

not *immediately* dependent upon what others think; he has worked over his reflected self in his mind until it is a steadfast portion of his thought, an idea and conviction apart, in some measure, from its external origin. Hence this sentiment requires time for its development and flourishes in mature age rather than in the open and growing period of youth. (1902, p. 199)

Cooley further laid the groundwork for a developmental analysis of shame and pride when he wrote:

The reference to other persons involved in the sense of self may be distinct and particular, as when a boy is ashamed to have his mother catch him at something she has forbidden, or it may be vague and general, as when one is ashamed to do something which only his conscience, expressing his sense of social responsibility, detects and disapproves; but it is always there. There is no sense of ''I,'' as in pride or shame, without its correlative sense of you, he, or they. (1902, p. 153)

These themes have been echoed in more contemporary treatments of shame and pride, in which the initial role of external evaluation of socializing agents appears paramount (Erikson, 1963; Harter, 1983, 1986b; Lewis & Brooks, 1978; Piers & Singer, 1953; Rogers, 1951; Stipek, 1983). These authors have argued that the ability to experience the emotions of pride and shame requires the internalization of parental values in the form of an ego ideal, a standard, against which one comes to compare one's performance. Thus, pride and shame are socially derived emotions that also have direct implications for one's feelings of worth, given their origins in parental evaluations of the self (see Harter, 1986b; Stipek, 1983). As these latter theorists have suggested, this type of analysis leads to the expectation that the young child would require an actual audience that witnesses, and reacts to, behaviors that are shameful or, alternatively, worthy of pride. However, the need for such a social audience would decline, developmentally, as one internalized the value or standards of significant others, because children could then apply these standards directly in order to feel either proud or ashamed of oneself in the absence of observation.

Until recently, this kind of analysis, although very plausible, has been largely speculative. In our work, we have begun to document the emergence of the understanding of the emotions of pride and shame, utilizing a socialization framework. The first findings were rather serendipitous, resulting from an openended interview in which we simply asked children ages 4 to 11 to describe the feelings of pride and shame, and to provide a cause for each. We discovered that our youngest subjects, typically the 4- to 5-year-olds, could not provide a compelling description or a very plausible cause, although most were aware of the valence of the two feelings, namely that pride is a good feeling and shame is a bad feeling.

Interestingly, among our 6- and 7-year-olds, who had some intuitions about these feelings, many of the responses involved descriptions of how parents would be proud or ashamed of them for their actions, that is, significant *others* were proud or ashamed of the *self*. Examples of pride included: "Dad would be proud of me if I took out the trash"; "Mom would be proud if I cleaned my room"; "My parents would be proud if I won something"; "Dad was proud of me when I made a goal." Examples of shame included: "Mom would be ashamed of me if I did something bad or got into trouble"; "Dad was really ashamed of me when I broke the window"; "Mom was ashamed of me when I got into her stuff after she told me not to"; "My parents get ashamed when I do something naughty."

Typically it was not until about the age of 8 that children gave examples of how they could be ashamed or proud of *themselves*. In these spontaneous accounts, children would report such examples as: "I was really ashamed that I broke my friend's bike and didn't tell him": "I hit my brother for no real reason and felt ashamed of myself"; "I took something of my sister's without asking"; "I hurt my friend's feelings and really felt ashamed." For pride, typical examples were: "I dived off the high diving board"; "I got all A's on my report card"; "I did a good deed and got a medal"; "When I did something the best."

Although these latter responses did not *specify* whether an audience was or was not present, we became curious about this dimension. That is, our openended responses did not allow us to determine whether the experience of being proud of oneself or ashamed of oneself required the observation of another or whether one could experience these self-affects in the absence of others. We had some clues, however, from the responses of certain subjects. For example, in pursuing one 9-year-old's description of an experience in which he had felt ashamed of himself, we asked whether he could feel ashamed when he was all alone, or whether someone had to watch what he had done. His thoughtful reply was quite illuminating: "Well I *might* be able to be ashamed of myself if my parents didn't know, but it would sure help me to be ashamed if they were there!"

These preliminary findings suggested the fruitfulness of studying the developmental course of the concepts of pride and shame more systematically, particularly with regard to the role of the audience. In so doing, our focus was on the development of children's *understanding* of pride and shame, on their ability to *conceptualize the causes* of these emotions, rather than upon the very first expressions of these emotions in early childhood. In particular, we were interested in the substages that appeared to be precursors of the child's emerging ability to appreciate the fact that one could be proud or ashamed of the self in the absence of any observation by others.

Prior to the design of a procedure in which we systematically tested the emergence of the concepts of pride and shame, we felt the need to perform a content analysis of the *causes* of pride and shame generated by children in our exploratory interview study. That is, we wanted to select events that were representative or prototypical of both pride and shame across most subjects. Among our earlier sample, we identified 40 subjects between the ages of 7 and 11 who appeared to understand the concepts of both shame and pride, as evidenced by the causes they generated.

Our content analysis of the causes of shame revealed that the vast majority of responses fell into two categories: (a) damage to someone else's property, and (b) harm, either physical or psychological, to another person. Examples in the first category (which accounted for 62% of the responses) involved breaking something that belonged to someone else, getting into someone else's things without their permission, and taking something of someone else's, often when it had explicitly been forbidden. Examples in the second category (which accounted for 31% of the responses) involved physical harm – hitting, kicking, or beating someone up – and psychological harm – being mean to someone or hurting their feelings. Thus, these two categories alone accounted for 94% of the responses, and both involved active transgressions against others, often prefaced by comments about doing something you shouldn't or aren't supposed to do, getting into trouble, or doing something naughty. Thus, the large majority of perceived causes of shame within this age range seem to represent forbidden acts, violations against others – sins of commission, as it were, that involve one's conduct. The remaining responses involved not doing something that one should have (4%) and lack of competence (2%, or 1 response out of 40).

Our findings are of interest given some controversy in the literature over whether the causes of shame primarily involve transgressions or whether they also involve lack of competence or accomplishment. The spontaneous responses of children within the age range of seven to eleven suggest that the most salient actions provoking their experience of shame involve transgressions against others. This is not to say that other events are irrelevant to the experience of shame nor that lack of competence may not become a factor in later development. The causes of shame may well change with age. However, children's responses did suggest that selection of a transgression might be the most fruitful avenue to pursue in addressing the more systematic description of a developmental sequence of the understanding of shame.

We also performed a content analysis of children's responses to our initial open-ended questions about pride. This analysis revealed four categories, three of which involved the display of *competence* or an accomplishment that involved some outcome or product. The three subcategories of competence/accomplishment involved (a) performing an athletic feat, which comprised 41% of the responses (e.g., winning a race, performing a gymnastic maneuver, making a goal); (b) demonstration of *academic* competence, which comprised 12% of the responses (e.g., getting all A's, doing well on a test, getting a good report card); and (c) other, more idiosyncratic, accomplishments, 24% (e.g., singing on stage, showing animals, drawing pictures, making shelves, baby-sitting). Seventy-seven percent of the responses occurred in these first three categories denoting competence or a personal accomplishment.

The fourth category (23%) seemed qualitatively different and was typically offered by the youngest subjects: (d) doing a chore at home that was requested by the parents (e.g., taking out the trash, cleaning my room, mowing the lawn, helping my mom vacuum, cleaning out the basement, helping to straighten up).

These findings suggest that the causes of shame and pride during this age period reflect different domains of performance. Shame is provoked by transgressions, primarily actions in violation of others, whereas pride typically involves the demonstration of a competent act, an accomplishment credited to the self. Based on these findings, we opted, in a follow-up study, to focus on a transgression as a prototypical cause of shame, and on an athletic feat as a cause of pride. The goal was to demonstrate a scalable developmental sequence.

Given our framework, focusing on the *socialization* component of both pride and shame, we devised a procedure that would be sensitive to the role of the observing parent. That is, we sought to determine whether parents were required to "support" the reported experience of pride and shame. Toward this end we designed two sets of vignettes. To assess shame, we constructed a pictorial vignette with four frames and a brief story line to accompany the pictures. The story concerns a situation in which the parents have forbidden the child to take any money from a very large jar of coins in the parents' bedroom. However, the child transgresses and takes a few coins.

There were two separate story sequences. In one sequence, no one observes the act and no one ever finds out (an outcome we attempted to insure by describing the money jar as very large and the child as taking only a few coins). In the second sequence, the parent catches the child in the act. The primary dependent measures included the child's description of the emotions that the child would feel in the first sequence (where the act is not detected) and a description of the emotions that both child and parent would feel in the second situation where the parent catches the child in the act. To aid in the child's identification of emotions, a series of pictures and accompanying labels of both child emotions and parent emotions was provided, because we wanted to give children every opportunity to select the emotions of pride and shame if they could demonstrate such an understanding (see Harter, Wright, & Bresnick, 1987, for details).

To assess an understanding of *pride,* we selected a gymnastic feat as the demonstration of competence. In the first sequence, the child goes to the playground on a Saturday when no one else is there and tries out a flip on the bars, one that he or she has been working on at school. The child attempts a flip that he or she has never been able to perform successfully before and does it really well. In the first sequence, the child leaves the bars, knowing that no one else was at the playground and thus no one observed the flip. The child is then asked what feeling he or she would have at that time.

In the second pride sequence, the parent accompanies the child to the playground and observes the child successfully performing the flip for the first time. The child is asked how he or she would feel as well as how the observing parent would feel having watched the child doing the flip. Here again, pictorial aids in the form of photographs of facial expressions of these emotions by a child, for the first sequence, and by a child as well as by a parent, for the second sequence, were presented to the child.

The results for both pride and shame revealed a parallel three-stage sequence that is interpretable within our socialization framework. At *Level 0,* there is no mention of either pride or shame on the part of child or parent in either sequence, whether the child is observed or not observed. Children at this age level are the youngest in the sample, with a mean age of approximately 5 years. Subjects give very clear responses about their potential emotional reactions to these situations, reactions that are quite telling. In the transgression situation where they are not observed by the parents, they report that the child character (with whom they are encouraged to identify) would feel bad, scared, or worried about the possibility of detection. When they are caught by the parent, they also feel extremely scared or worried about the likelihood of punishment. However, there is no acknowledgment of pride or shame.

Level 0 subjects in the pride sequences of stories report that they would feel happy, glad, or excited in the situation where their gymnastic feat is not observed by the parent. In the story where the parent witnesses their performance, they also report that both they and the parent would feel happy, glad, excited. That is, there is no mention of pride, either on the part of the parent or the self.

At *Level 1*, children (between the ages of 6 and 7) report that in the situation where the act has been observed, parents will be ashamed, or proud, of the child, and most children report that they, too, will feel ashamed or proud, seemingly in response to the parental reaction. However, what also places children at this level is the fact that they do *not* report any feelings of shame or pride in the story sequence where the child is *not* observed. Thus, this seems to be the transitional level in our socialization formulation: The act must be observed, in the case of both a transgression (to experience shame) and the demonstration of competence (to experience pride). In the absence of parental observation, no such potential self-affects are acknowledged.

The hallmark of *Level 2* (age 8 and older) is that in the absence of parental observation children spontaneously acknowledge that they will feel ashamed of themselves or proud of themselves. It should be noted that the stories in which the child was *not* observed were always presented first, so that any response of shame or pride on the part of the child was not simply a generalization from the sequence in which they were observed. Thus, at Level 2, children appear to have internalized the standards by which shame and pride can be experienced in the absence of direct, parental observation. Interestingly, the large majority of children at this level do not merely report the emotions of shame and pride, but specifically indicate that "I would feel ashamed, or proud, of *myself.*" Thus, they appear to be at the stage where these affects do function as self-affects, in the sense that one is truly ashamed or proud of the self.

Definition of pride and shame

In a separate part of the interview, we asked children to define pride and shame, in order to obtain a secondary, and separate, measure of their understanding of these emotions. We devised scoring criteria for these responses that tapped the highest level of understanding of these emotional concepts as self-affects. That is, we wanted to assess children's understanding of pride and shame independently and relate this understanding to their level as determined by the responses to the pictorial vignettes.

Based upon our theoretical framework, we established criteria by which we judged these definitions, examples of definitions that met these criteria, and examples of these descriptions that were unacceptable. For both emotions, subjects had to indicate clearly that they would feel proud or ashamed of the *self* (and not merely proud or ashamed). There were also content criteria: For shame, the subject had to indicate sadness, sorrow, or regret over a transgression that went beyond mere concern over negative consequences for the self (e.g., fear of punishment). For pride, they had to specify an act of competence or a personal accomplishment.

Examples of good definitions are: "I'd be ashamed of myself if I hit my brother, I'd be sorry that I did it''; "You feel sorry when you do something bad, and you are ashamed of yourself, mad at yourself, and sad that you did it''; "You're proud of yourself cause you did something, happy at yourself because you did something right''; "It's being proud of yourself because of something you did, like getting straight A's on your report card.''

Examples of definitions that did *not* meet the criteria are: "You didn't tell the truth of something and you feel ashamed and scared inside because you might get a spanking''; "You did something bad and your mom's mad at you, you're ashamed of what you did, and scared about what your mom might do''; "You did something good and you were shocked and happy''; "You're proud when something good happens like you ran a race or got a new puppy.''

An analysis by level revealed that Level 0 subjects did not have a conceptual understanding of either pride or shame, that is, they could not define these emotions satisfactorily. At Level 1, children had a limited ability to define these emotions. They may have mentioned that they felt ashamed or proud, but they did not acknowledge that this affect was directed toward the self. Typically, shame involved a transgression but children were more concerned about the parental reaction than they were about their own regret. Pride typically involved competence-related acts, although often the accompanying positive affects did not clearly specify pride in the self. Thus, many of these Level 1 responses seemed like affective scripts, in that they had certain elements of the appropriate causes of shame and pride, but they were not convincing in their description of affects clearly directed toward the self.

At Level 2, not only was the content of the definitions appropriate, but children more clearly described how they felt ashamed and proud *of the self*. Thus, these findings converge with those on the emotional responses children gave to the stories at each of the three levels, further documenting the developmental emergence of an understanding of pride and shame.

When not observed, would children want to tell someone about their actions?

The fact that these affects have social origins, that is, they must first be supported by the observations and reactions of others, raises an interesting question with regard to what children opt to do when an act is not observed. Does one conjure up an imaginary audience of significant others or does one actually tell these others about the event? We have data on the second issue because we specifically asked children to indicate, in the condition where the story child was *not* observed, whether they would tell anyone or not. We asked this both about the gymnastic feat and about the transgression of taking pennies from the jar in the parents' bedroom.

The patterns were different for pride and shame. For pride, there were virtually no developmental differences. The vast majority of children at each level indicated that they would relate their triumph to others, typically the parents. The percentages of children that would tell about the gymnastic feat were 71% at Level 0, 91% at Level 1, and 93% at Level 2. (Those that would not tell reported rather idiosyncratic reasons, e.g., "They wouldn't let me go back to the playground on a Saturday"; "They might try to do it and hurt themselves"; "They'd be mad that they didn't see it, I just want to keep it a secret.")

The descriptions of the vast majority who would tell someone about their accomplishments indicated that telling would enhance their own positive affective response to the event – happiness for the youngest children and pride for the older children. Thus, although pride can come to be internalized developmentally, the socialized component of this self-affect would appear to persist in the form of a strong need or desire to share an unobserved display of competence with significant others.

For shame, the pattern is somewhat different in that the percentage of children who would tell someone (typically the parents) about their transgression increases systematically with their level. The percentage of those that would tell were only 10% at level 0, 68% at Level 1, and 85% at Level 2. The particular reasons why they would or would not tell illuminate this pattern. Of the 90% at Level 0 who would not tell, the typical reason was fear of punishment, for example, "I'd be too scared about what mom would do"; "They'd be really mad"; "I'd be afraid I'd get in trouble." These reasons are consistent with children's reported emotional reactions to the initial stories; at Level 0 the child in the transgression scenario is worried or scared and sees the parents as angry.

There is a dramatic shift between Level 0 and Level 1 in that 68% of the Level 1 subjects indicate that they *would* tell about what they had done. Most commented that they would "feel better" having told. Thus, to the extent that social agents are the initial source of shame, confessing to them helps alleviate the negative affective reaction they experience when they commit an unobserved transgression. Thus, the parental reaction is still very relevant, in this case not only to promote one's feelings of shame but as the vehicle through which one can atone, as it were, for one's misbehavior.

The Level 2 children (85% of whom said they would tell) provide an even more sophisticated version of this attitude. Their responses suggest that they have internalized the capacity to feel ashamed of themselves, but that relief from this feeling can only occur if they confess to the external source (the parents) who were initially responsible for instilling the standards to be internalized. Typical examples were : "If I confess, then the awful feeling wouldn't be inside of me, I'd be relieved to get rid of it"; "It would make me feel better to get it off my mind"; "You would get it off your conscience"; "It's better to tell the truth and get it off your mind"; "I'd feel a lot better being honest and just telling them"; "If you tell, then you wouldn't have a guilty conscience and that feeling would go away." The confession to significant others, therefore, would appear to play a powerful role in alleviating the internal feeling associated with feeling ashamed, further bolstering our analysis of the manner in which shame is socialized.

In summary, the findings converge on a theoretically meaningful account of the social origins and developmental course of pride and shame. At Level 0, children do not acknowledge the affective reactions of pride and shame, nor can they define these affective labels. Rather, they focus on the fear they experience in anticipation of parental anger and possible punishment. These responses appear to be important precursors of the ability to gradually internalize the parental reactions in the form of anger directed toward the self. At Level 1, children offer descriptions in which they feel ashamed and proud, but only when the parents have witnessed the child's behavior and also feel ashamed or proud of the child. Their definitions suggest that their understanding is organized as affective scripts that require the support of the parental reactions in the form of either shame or pride directed toward the child. These children have not yet internalized these affective reactions and thus cannot acknowledge them in the absence of the parents' direct response to their actions. At Level 2, the internalization process has proceeded to a point at which the child can experience feeling ashamed and proud of the self in the absence of parental surveillance or observation. However, the strong need to tell the parents about one's accomplishments when one is proud of oneself – in order to reinforce the feeling of pride – or to tell the parents about one's transgressions when one is ashamed of the self – in order to relieve oneself of the feeling of shame – suggests that the imagined audience is also internalized, as Cooley initially hypothesized.

It should be emphasized that these findings document an age-related developmental sequence of children's *understanding* of the emotional *concepts* of pride and shame. They do not speak to the earlier emergence of the expression and display of pride and shame in the second year of life. As has been suggested by other investigators (see Stipek, 1983), one would expect to find a similar sequence in that the first manifestations of pride and shame would need to be supported by parental reactions in which they manifest their pride or shame about the child. Further research should be directed toward examining such a sequence in very young children, as well as probing the individual differences in parental reactions to children's behavior that may well produce individual differences in children's capacity to experience and internalize pride and shame as self-affects.

Is depression a mix of feelings and does it involve self-affects?

In our studies of more complex, yet single, affects, we have also been intrigued by the emotional experience of depression in children. First, we have been interested in whether depression in children is primarily a more intense version of sadness or represents a blend of feelings. The clinical literature suggests that, for adults, depression often constitutes a mix of sadness and anger. Thus, we were interested in determining if older children shared these perceptions. Secondly, if depression does represent a blend of these two feelings, are these affects self-directed or more externally directed? In particular, we were curious about whether children would acknowledge anger as a component of depression and, if so, was this anger directed toward others or toward the self?

Recently we have begun to explore these questions in a pilot study in which we interviewed 10 sixth and seventh graders, identified as depressed, from our larger pool of middle-school students. These particular children were selected on the basis of their self-reported depressed affect on a subscale of our depression instrument (see Harter & Nowakowski, 1987a, 1987b) tapping mood/affect along the dimension of cheerful or happy to sad or depressed. Thus, these were children who had indicated that they were extremely sad or depressed. Of interest to us in the interview was whether any other emotions were experienced in conjunction with sadness when they were depressed – that is, whether depression represented a combination or blend of affects more typically regarded as discrete. As suggested above, we were curious about whether children of this age would spontaneously mention anger when asked about the feelings that comprise depression. Among those reporting anger, we were further interested in the target of this anger, namely whether it was directed toward *others* or toward the *self*.

The reports of these 10 subjects were quite clear with regard to whether depression involves a blend of emotions. Eight of the 10 specifically volunteered that depression involved a combination of sadness and anger, the 9th reported a mix of sadness and frustration, and the 10th indicated that it was feeling sad and "not really mad," although her further explanation documented the anger component that she had tentatively tried to deny. Thus, these exploratory interviews revealed that, among a small group of children reporting depressed affect, the emotional experiences clearly involved sadness coupled with anger.

The next question of interest involved the target of this anger: Was it directed toward the self or toward someone else? Across the 10 children, 13 different examples were generated. Of these 13 responses, 54% were directed toward the self and 46% were directed toward another person. Among those directed toward the self, children were quite explicit in stating that "I get mad at myself." The two causes for this anger involved feeling responsible for not getting good grades and feeling mad at the self for treating other people badly, for example, being mean, being harsh, or putting others down.

The causes of anger toward others were also quite clear. All 46% of these anger responses involved descriptions of how peers teased them, put them down, were mean to them, made fun of them, or ganged up on them. The common feature of these responses is that others were causing psychological harm to the child, putting her or him down as a person.

These preliminary findings suggest that the experience of depression among children reporting depressed affect or mood does involve a blend of two emotions: sadness and anger. However, they also reveal that the target of the anger varies depending on the individual or situation. For certain children, other people are the cause of anger, whereas for other children the anger is directed toward the self. These findings have clinical implications in that they suggest that the causes of depression, as well as the manner in which it is experienced, vary across children. These findings are reminiscent of the distinction, first introduced by Freud (1917/1957), between mourning and melancholia. For Freud, the depressive reaction among those in mourning involved anger toward another responsible for the loss and hurt, whereas the melancholic experienced anger toward the self in the form of self-blame, low self-esteem, and low energy level.

We have pursued this distinction in a larger study, asking middle-school children to indicate which emotions are involved in their experience of depression (Harter & Renouf, 1987). The vast majority of these young adolescents reported a combination of anger and sadness. Among this group, we also inquired about whether the anger was directed toward others or toward the self. The finding revealed that approximately 60% of middle-school children reported anger toward others, whereas the remaining 40% reported anger directed at the self. We further determined that those describing anger toward the self also reported (a) more depressed affect, (b) lower self-worth, and (c) greater self-blame (three separate subscales on our Dimensions of Depression Profile for Children and Adolescents; see Harter & Nowakowski, 1987a). Thus, it would appear that when anger toward the self is acknowledged in the context of depression, it is accompanied by relatively intense depressed affect as well as negative self-attitudes. (Although our initial procedure required that children select one primary target of their anger – self or others – in our current research, we are investigating the possibility that children of this age may acknowledge anger toward the self as well as anger toward others, assessing the strength with which each is experienced. Because adults, when depressed, often report a vacillation of sadness and anger, it will be instructive to determine whether older children have similar perceptions.)

The results of our pilot study are also intriguing in that they illuminate the causes of both sadness and anger within the context of depressive reactions. The primary causes of sadness involved not getting something one wanted (typically good grades) or the loss of friendship. The primary causes of anger toward others entailed psychological harm inflicted on the self by others that entailed a perceived violation of the self. The major cause of anger toward the self involved the perception that one was falling short of one's goals, violating one's own self-standards. As we shall see in the next section, these causes are consistent with those theoretical and empirical efforts that have attempted to identify prototypical causes of discrete emotions. We turn to this final topic next, exploring the applicability of prototype theory to the emotional responses of children.

Does children's understanding of the causes of emotion conform to adult prototypes?

In recent years, there have been a number of studies empirically investigating children's understanding of the causes of the basic emotions of happiness, sadness, anger, and fear. These studies have demonstrated that even very young children have an understanding of certain plausible antecedent events that provoke these emotions (see Borke, 1971; Bretherton & Beeghley, 1982; Harris, 1983a, 1983b; Harris, Olthof, & Meerum Terwoft, 1981; Stein & Levine, 1987; Trabasso, Stein, & Johnson, 1981). With few exceptions (see Stein & Levine, 1987), however, studies of children's understanding of emotional causation have not been guided by a unifying theoretical framework.

More theoretical attention to issues involving the structure, causes, and course of emotions can be found in the literature on adult affective responses (see Roseman, 1984; Shaver, Schwartz, Kirson, & O'Connor, 1987). We find the framework of Shaver et al. particularly compelling in its attention to the structure of adults' hierarchy of emotion concepts as well as to an analysis of the prototypical causes of the basic emotions across adult subjects.

From a structural perspective, Shaver et al. build upon Rosch's (1978) work in identifying a hierarchy of emotion concepts that include superordinate, basic, and subordinate levels. Applying this to emotional understanding, Shaver et al. have demonstrated that the most superordinate distinction made by adults is between positive and negative emotions. At the next level, designated as basic, six emotions emerge, representing differentiations within the classes of positive and negative emotions. These six are happiness, love, surprise, sadness, anger, and fear.

The more subordinate tier of emotions concepts consists of further differentiations of these basic emotions. For example, more differentiated forms of anger include annoyance, rage, frustration, outrage, scorn, and envy, to name a few. Happiness can be differentiated into cheerfulness, exhilaration, pride, contentment, and so forth. Sadness can be broken down into such emotions as agony, despair, grief, dismay, humiliation, pity, and so forth. The more differentiated forms of fear include fright, horror, anxiety, nervousness, apprehension, and so forth.

In our work we have not yet addressed the entire hierarchical network of emotion concepts in children. However, we have demonstrated that by as young as 4, children can sort facial photographs of the six basic emotions into the superordinate categories of good feelings and bad feelings. In addition, responses to open-ended questions asking them to give examples of five of the basic emotions (happy, sad, mad, loving, scared – we did not include surprise) reveal that across the age range of 4 through 11, 100% of the children were able to give a compelling description and example of happy, sad, mad, and loving, and 95% provided such a description of scared. Thus, it would appear that although the Shaver et al. hierarchy has been posited as a structural analysis of adult emotion concepts, it has developmental implications in that, as young as 4, children understand both the superordinate structure and the basic emotions.

A second goal of the prototype approach is to provide an analysis of the *experience* of the basic emotions with regard to three components: (1) the perceived causes or antecedents of each emotion; (b) the behavioral and physiological reactions to each emotion; and (c) for negative emotions, attempts at emotional and behavioral control. The goal of Shaver et al.'s analysis is to identify common or prototypical causes as well as reaction across subjects through an examination of college students' descriptions of how they experience the basic emotions.

In our own work, we have obtained data on children's descriptions of the first component, the causes of four of the basic emotions: happy, sad, mad, scared. Thus we can determine whether the prototypical antecedents identified for adults are also obtained in the open-ended responses of children ages 4 through 11. This issue was examined with regard to three specific questions: (a) Do the *categories* of prototypical causes identified for adults exist in the descriptions of children? (b) If so, do they occur with the same *frequency* across the age levels sampled, and do these frequencies in any way correspond to the levels at which adults report similar causes? (c) Are the *specific examples* of what causes each emotion similar or different for children at different age levels as well as for children compared to adults?

In order to answer these questions, it was first necessary to perform a content analysis on the open-ended responses of our child subjects. In so doing we were guided by the categories in Shaver et al., but we did not impose their categories on the children's descriptions. We will discuss each of the four basic emotions of happy, mad, sad, and scared, with regard to the adult prototype and the extent to which children's responses do or do not correspond in terms of the three questions raised above.

For happiness or *joy,* Shaver et al. identify a number of prototypical causes including, in order of frequency: *Getting what was wanted,* a desirable outcome; *Experiencing task success* or an achievement; *Being accepted, belonging, receiving love, like affection;* and *Experiencing highly pleasurable stimuli* or sensations. All four of these causal categories appeared in the descriptions of our child subjects. *Getting something wanted or desired* accounted for approximately 70% of the responses and thus was the most frequent cause of happiness for children, as it was for adults (the Shaver et al. subcategory of receiving a surprise was also coded in this category, because many of the children referred to the receipt of presents or gifts, where it was not clear just how much of a surprise element there was). *Task success or accomplishments* (approximately 10% across the entire child sample) involved descriptions of competencies, positive attributes, and specific achievements. The analogue of *Being accepted, belonging, and so forth* (approximately 10% of the responses) appeared in descriptions of visiting others and having others do nice things for oneself, namely positive social interaction with friends or family. *Experiencing pleasurable stimuli* (approximately 10%) occurred in the records of children primarily as playing and having fun. (One adult category, *Reality exceeding expectations,* or *Things being better than expected,* did not appear in the records of children. It should be noted that this was also one of the less frequent causes in the adult protocols.)

The findings for happiness or joy, therefore, indicate that with regard to our first question concerning whether similar categories existed in the accounts of children, the answer is a definite "yes." Children acknowledge the same types of causes as do adults. In terms of our second question, whether these antecedents are generated with the same frequency, it would appear that among both adults and children, *Getting something wanted or desired* is the most common cause of happiness and occurs in the vast majority of accounts. Children would appear to differ from adults, however, in the extent to which *task success or personal accomplishments* produce an experience of joy, as this appears to be more common in the descriptions of adults. *Being accepted, belonging* and *Experiencing pleasurable stimuli* are among the less common causes in the records of both adults and children.

Interestingly, for our child subjects, there were no age differences in the frequency with which the most common category, *Getting something wanted or desired,* was mentioned. At all three age levels examined, 3–5, 6–8, and 9–11, the percentage hovered around 70%. Slight age trends were observed, however, for two other categories. *Experiencing pleasurable stimuli* decreased systematically with age from approximately 20% among the youngest subjects to about 2% for the oldest group. In addition, *Task success/accomplishments* increased with age from about 2% among the youngest children to 18% among the oldest group.

Although children as young as 3 and 4 would appear to understand the proto-type for the causes of their own happiness, as might be expected, the *specific examples* provided by children at the different ages reflect age-appropriate inter-ests and desires that would not be contained in the reports of adults. These joyful accounts included playing with dolls, being tickled, getting new pets, visiting grandparents, going to the zoo, visiting the fire station to see the trucks, going to slumber parties, getting a new toy, going to MacDonald's to eat french fries, and so forth. However, if one merely did an analysis of the manifest content of these causes without a structural analysis of the *features* of these antecedents, one would erroneously conclude that children's understanding of the causes of happiness was quite different from that of adults, whereas in fact it is quite analogous.

The *anger* prototype for adults, as described by Shaver et al., involves two primary causes: *Physical or psychological pain,* a violation of the self, often including loss of power, status or respect, and insult; and a slightly less common cause involving *Things not working out as expected,* where there is the violation of an expectation and/or the frustration/interruption of a goal-directed activity. Moreover, in the adult prototype, these events are characterized by a judgment that the situation was unfair, wrong, illegitimate, or contrary to what ought to be.

Our content analysis of the children's reports of the causes of anger indicated that 97% of the responses fell into the primary two categories, *Physical or psy-chological pain* (e.g., being hit, being yelled at, having others be mean to you, having your feelings hurt), which accounted for 62% of the responses, and *Things not working out as expected* (either not getting something that one wanted or having something happen that one did not desire; e.g., being grounded, not being able to play, getting punished, having my sister come in my room), which ac-counted for 35% of the responses. Although most of the children did not explic-itly explain that such actions represented violations or were unfair, this feature was certainly implied by the nature of the causes they offered. Unfortunately, our interview procedure did not encourage them to expand on this possible di-mension, an issue that should receive attention in future research.

Interestingly, there were no developmental differences in the frequency with which these categories were utilized across our three ages. Thus, it would appear that the anger prototype emerges very early in the development with regard to perceived antecedents of anger for the self. As noted above, however, this con-clusion needs to be tempered by the fact that we have *inferred* some sense of unfairness in these responses. To the extent that concepts of fairness and morality pursue a developmental course, it may well be that although the types of actions (e.g., violations against the self) are present in the accounts of the youngest children, the judgment that they are unfair may not emerge until somewhat later in development.

As with the causes of happiness, the specific examples of events that provoke anger are age-appropriate and thus the content of these responses differed from that of adults. Thus, children encountered such aggravations as being poked in the eye by your brother, having to clean your room when you don't want to, having a friend lose your Star Wars toy, finding that a friend has put gum in your hair, having to go to bed earlier than you want, being teased by other kids, having your block tower knocked down, having to eat liver, being bitten by your younger brother, being sent to your room, having someone take your piggy bank, having people call you a braceface, getting stepped on by someone at recess, having your train set wrecked by your little brother, and so forth. Nevertheless, the analogues to the adult causes of anger are clear, justifying the prototype approach.

The *sadness* prototype for adults includes the following categories, according to the findings of Shaver et al. (1987): *Loss of a valued relationship* either through death or separation, the most common cause; *An undesirable outcome,* either getting something not wanted or not getting what was wanted or wished for, including reality falling short of one's expectations; *Psychological harm,* being rejected, excluded, or disapproved of by another; *Feeling powerless or helpless;* and *Empathy for the distress of others.*

Four of these five categories could clearly be identified in the descriptions of children. The *harm* category in children's responses, however, included examples of physical harm (being hit, yelled at, bitten), harm to one's property (having one's toys broken, having someone mess with your things) as well as psychological harm (being left alone, having someone hurt your feelings, being teased). *Loss of relationship was also exemplified by the death of family members, loss of friendships, and people moving away. Undesirable outcomes* in these child accounts typically involved not getting something one wanted, e.g., not getting to go to your friend's house, not getting a present you wanted, not getting to play baseball, not getting bunk beds, getting a bike that was too small. *Feeling powerless or helpless* often involved incompetence or negative attributes, e.g., striking out, not being about to jump off the slide, losing in basketball, flunking a test.

With regard to the category of *Empathy for the distress of others,* it was difficult, given our procedure, to determine the extent to which certain responses involving illness or death to others involved an empathic response. Thus, we did not code these as a separate category, despite responses where such empathy might well be inferred. The descriptions that were the most problematic in this regard involved the many responses concerning pets. The accounts are replete with stories of pets who have been injured, lost, or put to sleep, or who have died. Fully 28% of the causes of sadness among the oldest age group involved something that had happened to a pet. However, the verbal responses obtained did not allow us to determine whether these responses should be scored as empathy, as the loss of a relationship, or as harm to the self by extension, in that pets were often viewed as a possession. Thus, this interesting issue requires further study, in terms of why negative events befalling a pet cause sadness, as well as just what function pets play in the emotional lives of children.

Unlike the pattern of causes generated by children for happiness and anger, where little developmental change was observed, there were interesting age differences for sadness in two categories, *Harm to the self* and *Loss of relationship*. In the harm category, there was a dramatic decrease with age, in that the percentage shifted from 62% of all responses among the youngest children to 35% for the middle age group, to 17% among the oldest age group. The opposite shift was observed for the category of loss of relationship, which accounted for only 14% of the causes of sadness among the youngest group, but shifted to 47% for both the middle and the older age groups.

These age differences are interpretable in light of the developing ability of children to establish meaningful relationships that also have some stability, such that loss is cognitively interpreted as a cause for sadness rather than anger. The theorizing of Selman (1980), Kohlberg (1976), and Loevinger and Wessler (1970), provides a framework for such an interpretation in that the earliest stages of development represent a more egocentric view of relationships where one attempts to satisfy one's own hedonistic needs. It is only in middle childhood and beyond, according to these formulations, that one is capable of appreciating such psychological dimensions as the reciprocal nature of relationships, characterized by concern for the other as well as mutual trust. With this cognitive-developmental advance, the dissolution of such a relationship would more likely be cause for sadness over the loss than at earlier ages. The developmental differences revealed for the causes of sadness, therefore, indicate that it is not until later childhood that one observes the adult prototype in the sense that loss of a valued relationship is the primary cause of sadness.

Our content analysis of the causes of sadness reveals the same child-centered concerns that we have identified for the preceding emotions at the level of the specific examples generated. Causes for sadness include falling off your bike, being spanked by your mom, having to play alone in your sandbox, being bitten by your baby sister, scraping your knee, somebody taking money from your piggy bank, not being able to find your dolly, having your bunny die, not having anyone to play with, not getting invited to a birthday party, falling down and hurting yourself, having your grandfather die, having to put your dog to sleep, having your dad not take you to the zoo after he promised, having your science teacher retire. However, with the exception of the ambiguities surrounding the many misfortunes involving pets, the vast majority of responses could be coded in terms of categories based on adult prototype research.

The adult prototype for *fear* is captured by three themes or categories: *Threat of harm or death,* the most common; *Being in a novel, unfamiliar situation* that may include being alone or being in the dark; and *Threat of social rejection,* which may be linked to failure, loss of control, or loss of competence. These three categories were identified in the children's descriptions, in the same order of frequency. *Threat of harm,* the most frequent response, included descriptions of someone following you, beating up on you, thinking someone might kill you, being afraid of getting lost, and so forth. Fear of a *novel, unfamiliar situation,* the next most common category in children's accounts, included descriptions of being afraid in the dark, being scared of strange noises, being scared of going into haunted houses, and so forth. *Threat of social rejection,* although infrequent, was represented by a few responses focusing on the fear of what adults might do in the face of incompetence or a transgression, for example, I'd be scared if I forgot my homework; scared that my mom will get mad, because I did something I shouldn't have, and punish me.

Two developmental trends were noteworthy. Responses in the category of *Threat of harm* decreased with age from 73% (ages 3–5) to 55% (6–8) to 40% (9–11). Conversely, responses in the category of *Novel, unfamiliar situation* increased from 25% to 43% to 49% for the three age groups, respectively. Although responses concerning *Threat of social rejection* were infrequent, there was nevertheless a slight age tendency for these to increase with age (1% to 2% to 11%, across the three age groups).

The greater fear of harm among the youngest subjects may well be due to their greater sense of vulnerability as well as to their inadequacy in being able to protect themselves. In addition, the younger children also made numerous references to their fear of mystical or fairy tale figures, e.g., monsters, dragons and ghosts. The increase with age for the category of unfamiliar or novel situations seemed due to the wider range of potentially fearful novel situations in which older children may find themselves, as exemplified by responses involving walking home at night, being in a dark alley, going to junior high school, being in a scary movie without your parents, etc. Roller coasters were also common among the descriptions of the older children, although these responses are qualitatively different in that they seem to represent thrill-seeking designed to produce fright rather than fear of the unknown per se.

As with the other emotions described, the content of children's concerns contributed to these age differences and also provided contrasts with adult responses, with regard to the specific events that provoke fear. Thus, children report being scared of being gobbled up by monsters, of ghosts, of robots, of falling out of bed, of lightning, of scary dreams, of noises in the basement at night, of cars when crossing the street, of being poisoned by witches, of the dark when the lights are out, of getting lost in the mountains, of someone sneaking up behind me and saying "Boo," and of hearing a strange noise when one is babysitting. However, each of these concerns represents one of the prototypic categories identified above.

In summary, the prototype approach, applied to the causes that children generate for these four basic emotions, would appear to have considerable merit. The adult *categories* were clearly represented in the responses of children, although the specific examples given by children differed in that they referred to age-appropriate content. Moreover the rank order of the frequency with which causal themes were generated was quite similar, particularly for the emotions of happy and mad, where age differences were minimal.

The largest developmental differences were obtained for sad and scared. For sad, responses in the *loss of relationship* category were rare among the youngest children. Sadness at this age level was much more likely to be provoked by *harm to the self.* However, among the oldest children, as among adults, the most common category involved relationship loss. For fear, there was an age-related increase in descriptions of *unfamiliar* situations that provoked fright, coupled with a decrease in accounts of events that directly involved harm. The overall frequencies, however, revealed a pattern similar to that found for adults.

The demonstration that even very young children understand the prototypic causes of the basic emotions is of interest developmentally, although it also raises a number of critical questions concerning the origins of this knowledge. It should be noted here that the findings bear on children's *understanding* of the causes of happy, sad, mad, scared, as assessed through their spontaneous accounts of events that provoke each emotion in their own lives. By the age of four, children generate descriptions that demonstrate their awareness of many of the features captured by the adult prototypes. Thus, it would appear that through some combination of their emotional experiences as well as the socialization of emotion concepts, certain essential features of these prototypes are mastered at a very early age.

We are assuming, at this point, that children have mastered basic critical features that lead to such cognitive generalizations about causes, rather than having merely learned lists of discrete situations that may provoke emotions. The fact that they are able to respond appropriately to novel situations that capture the essence of prototypical causes is one indirect source of evidence. However, future research should examine these issues more closely. Moreover, the extent to which these features are learned through significant others labeling children's emotions and their causes, through significant others labeling the causes of their own emotions, or other forms of cultural transmission, such as books, television, and/or peer and school experiences, is another interesting issue for further study.

Not all features of each prototype are necessarily in place among younger children, however. Those features that may require more experience or more advanced levels of cognitive development will emerge at a later age or stage. It was noted that for the causes of anger, although one might *infer* that children's examples represented violations of the self that implied unfairness, it may well be that judgments about the unjustness of the event do not emerge until middle childhood or beyond. In addition, a major cause of sadness, in the adult proto-type – namely relationship loss – does not appear to emerge full-blown until middle childhood, with the development of a more mature understanding of re-lationships. It should also be noted that young children do not yet understand most of the more differentiated emotions that represent the subordinate tier in the Shaver et al. hierarchy, as we demonstrated earlier in regard to pride and shame. Additional findings (see Harter & Buddin, 1987) reveal that it is not until middle childhood that certain of these more differentiated emotions – for example, joy-ful, excited, proud, disappointed, depressed, disgusted, worried, frustrated, ashamed, and guilty – are generated and understood. It would be of interest, therefore, to more systematically determine when the broad range of subordinate emotion concepts emerge developmentally. An application of prototype theory, therefore, will allow one to detect many similarities across developmental level, as well as certain differences. It is this overall pattern that must be appreciated, and that remains to be more fully explained.

Summary and conclusions

We have attempted, in the present chapter, to describe the development of a number of emotion concepts in children. We first presented findings reveal-ing that the emergence of children's ability to understand that two emotions can co-occur undergoes a five-stage developmental sequence that can be interpreted with regard to the underlying cognitive structures required at each level. We further demonstrated that at the highest level, where two feelings of opposite valence (e.g., happy and mad) are simultaneously experienced, they do not nec-essarily cause phenomenological conflict. We identified certain features that are correlated wtih the experience of conflict, for example, the intensity and the similarity of emotions in the pair, although further research is necessary to delin-eate the causal factors producing these features.

We also described a developmental sequence governing the emergence of an understanding of more complex single emotions that come to be directed at the self, namely pride and shame. Specifically, we investigated the extent to which this sequence can be related to socialization experiences, although an under-standing of these emotions also depends upon cognitive-developmental level.

The very youngest children do not comprehend the concepts of pride and shame; they cannot define them, nor do they mention them in situations where an acknowledgment of these feelings would be appropriate. At the next level, children describe experiences of pride and shame, but only within contexts in which parents directly observe the child's acts and manifest their own pride or shame in the child. At the most advanced level, children report the experience of pride and shame even when the act is not observed by the parents, that is, they can experience pride and shame *in the self* without the social scaffolding required at earlier stages.

We also raised the issue of whether in later childhood one particular affect, depression, represented a blend of two emotions experienced simultaneously. The findings revealed that a small sample of depressed children clearly view depression as a combination of sadness and anger. Given our interest in affects directed toward the self, we were also curious about whether the anger component of depression represented a self-affect or an affect directed more externally, toward others. We discovered that in approximately half of the descriptions children reported that they were mad at the self, whereas the remaining accounts provided examples of anger directed outward, toward others. The clinical importance of identifying the particular target of the depressed child's anger was emphasized, along with a number of correlates of each orientation, for example, self-worth and self-blame.

Finally, we sought to determine whether an application of emotion prototype theory, initially formulated to explain the structure of emotion concepts in adults, would illuminate our findings on children's understanding of emotions. Here, we discovered that not only do very young children have an appreciation for the basic emotions identified in prototype theory, but that children's understanding of the causes of the basic emotions have many features in common with adult prototypes. Overall, the evidence presented on these topics underscores the need not only to identify developmental *differences* in children's emotional understanding, but to investigate developmental *similarities* and their origins as well. In so doing, we must turn our attention to a combination of both cognitive-developmental and socialization theory to provide the most complete and convincing interpretation of these patterns.

References

Borke, H. (1971). Interpersonal perception of young children: egocentrism or empathy. *Developmental Psychology, 5*, 263–269.

Bretherton, I., & Beeghly, M. (1982). Talking about internal states: the acquisition of an explicit theory of mind. *Developmental Psychology, 18*, 906–912.

Carroll, J. J., & Steward, M. S. (1984). The role of cognitive development in children's understandings of their own feelings. *Child Development, 55,* 1486–1492.

Case, R. (1985). *Intellectual development: a systematic reinterpretation.* New York: Academic Press.

Cooley, C. H. (1902). *Human nature and the social order.* New York: Scribner's, 1902.

Donaldson, S. K., & Westerman, M. A. (1986). Development of children's understanding of ambivalence and causal theories of emotion. *Developmental Psychology, 22,* 655–662.

Erikson, E. (1963). *Childhood and society.* New York: Norton.

Fischer, K. (1980). A theory of cognitive development: the control and construction of hierarchies of skills. *Psychological Review, 87,* 477–531.

Freud, S. (1917/1957). *Mourning and Melancholia, standard edition,* 14:243–258. London: Hogarth Press.

Gnepp, J., McKee, E., & Domanic, J. A. (1987). Children's use of situational information to infer emotion: understanding emotionally equivocal situations. *Developmental Psychology, 23,* 114–123.

Harris, P. L. (1983a). Children's understanding of the link between situation and emotion. *Journal of Experimental Child Psychology, 36,* 490–509.

Harris, P. L. (1983b). What children know about the situations that provoke emotion. In M. Lewis & C. Saarni (Eds.), *The socialization of affect.* New York: Plenum.

Harris, P. L., Olthof, T., & Meerum Terwogt, M. (1981). Children's knowledge of emotion. *Journal of Child Psychology and Psychiatry, 45,* 247–261.

Harter, S. (1977). A cognitive-developmental approach to children's expression of conflicting feelings and a technique to facilitate such expression in play therapy. *Journal of Consulting and Clinical Psychology, 45,* 417–432.

Harter, S. (1982). Children's understanding of multiple emotions: a cognitive-developmental approach. In W. F. Overton (Ed.), *The relationship between social and cognitive development.* Hillsdale, NJ: Erlbaum.

Harter, S. (1983). A cognitive-developmental approach to children's understanding of affect and trait labels. In F. C. Serafica (Ed.), *Social-cognitive development in context.* New York: Guilford.

Harter, S. (1986a). Cognitive-developmental processes in the integration of concepts about emotions and the self. *Social Cognition, 4,* 119–151.

Harter, S. (1986b). Processes underlying the construction, maintenance, and enhancement of the self-concept. In J. Suls & A. Greenwald (Eds.), *Psychological perspectives on the self* (Vol. 3). Hillsdale, NJ: Erlbaum.

Harter, S., & Buddin, B. J. (1987). Children's understanding of the simultaneity of two emotions: a five-stage developmental acquisition sequence. *Developmental Psychology, 23,* 388–399.

Harter, S., & Nowakowski, M. (1987a). The dimensions of depression profile for children and adolescents: unpublished manual. University of Denver.

Harter, S., & Nowakowski, M. (1987b). The relationship between self-worth and affect in children: implications for childhood depression. SRCD presentation, Baltimore, MD.

Harter, S., & Renouf, A. (1987). Children's understanding of depression. Unpublished manuscript, University of Denver.

Harter, S., Wright, K., & Bresnick, S. (1987). A developmental sequence of the understanding of pride and shame. Paper presented at the Society for Research in Child Development meetings, Baltimore, April.

Higgins, E. T. (1981). Role taking and social judgment: alternative developmental perspectives and processes. In J. H. Flavell & L. Ross (Eds.), *Social cognitive development.* New York: Cambridge University Press.

Kohlberg, L. (1976). Moral stages and moralization. In T. Lickona (Ed.), *Moral development and behavior.* New York: Holt.

Lewis, M., & Brooks, J. (1978). Self-knowledge and emotional development. In M. Lewis & L. Rosenblum (Eds.), *The development of affect*. New York: Plenum.

Loevinger, J., & Wessler, R. (1970) *Measuring ego development* (Vol. 1). San Francisco: Jossey-Bass.

Meerum Terwogt, M. (1984). *Emotional development in middle childhood: a cognitive view*. Unpublished doctoral dissertation, Vrije Universiteit te Amsterdam, Amsterdam.

Pascual-Leone, J. (1970). A mathematical model for the transition rule in Piaget's developmental stages. *Acta Psychologica, 32*, 301–345.

Piers, E., & Singer, P. (1953). *Shame and guilt*. Springfield, IL: Thomas.

Reissland, N. (1985). The development of concepts of simultaneity in children's understanding of emotions. *Journal of Child Psychology and Psychiatry, 26*, 811–824.

Rogers, C. (1951). *Client-centered therapy*. Boston: Houghton Mifflin.

Rosch, E. (1978). Principles of categorization. In E. Rosch & B. B. Lloyd (Eds.), *Cognition and categorization*. Hillsdale, NJ: Erlbaum.

Roseman, I. (1984). Cognitive determinants of emotions: a structural theory. In P. Shaver (Ed.), *Review of personality and social psychology* (Vol. 5). Beverly Hills, CA: Sage.

Selman, R. L. (1980). *The growth of interpersonal understanding*. New York: Academic Press.

Shaver, P., Schwartz, J., Kirson, D. & O'Connor, C. (1987). Emotion knowledge: further explanation of a prototype approach. *Journal of Personality and Social Psychology, 52*, 1016–1086.

Stein, N. L., & Levine, L. J. (1987). Thinking about feelings: the development and organization of emotion knowledge. In R. E. Snow and M. Farr (Eds.), *Aptitude, learning, and instruction* (Vol. 3): *Cognition, conation, and affect*. Hillsdale, NJ: Erlbaum.

Stipek, D. (1983). A developmental analysis of pride and shame. *Human Development, 26*, 42–54.

Trabasso, T., Stein, N. L., & Johnson, L. R. (1981). Children's knowledge of events: a causal analysis of story structure. In G. Bower (Ed.), *Advances in learning and motivation* (Vol. 15). New York: Academic Press.

Whitesell, N. R. (1987). Children's experiences of conflict between opposite valence emotions. Poster presented at the biennial meetings of the Society for Research in Child Development, Baltimore, April.

Whitesell, N. R., & Harter, S. (in press), Children's reports of conflict between simultaneous opposite-valence emotions, *Child Development*.

5 Causal attributions and children's emotional understanding

Ross A. Thompson

Emotions are an important part of a child's everyday experience, and thus emotional understanding contributes to knowledge about others and oneself. Students of social-cognitive development have begun to appreciate this, and their research has revealed that important aspects of emotional understanding emerge early and grow in sophistication and scope throughout the childhood years (see Masters & Carlson, 1984, for a review). For example, several researchers (Bretherton & Beeghly, 1982; Bretherton, Fritz, Zahn-Waxler, & Ridgeway, 1986; Bretherton, McNew, & Beeghly-Smith, 1981; Dunn & Kendrick, 1982a, 1982b) have documented that, after the age of 2, toddlers spontaneously comment on the intentions, feelings, and desires experienced by themselves and others. These spontaneous utterances reflect not just an appreciation that others can evince diverse kinds of internal experiences, but that these feelings can differ significantly from the child's own. By the age of 3½, children can accurately identify situations that elicit simple emotional reactions like happiness, sadness, anger, and fear (Borke, 1971; Harter, 1982; Mood, Johnson, & Shantz, 1978), and by the early grade-school years their emotional lexicon has expanded to include concepts of pride, shame, guilt, surprise, gratitude, and other complex emotional states (Harter, 1982; Russell & Ridgeway, 1983; Schwartz & Trabasso, 1984; Weiner, Kun, & Benesh-Weiner, 1980). Children also learn to accurately label prototypical facial expressions of emotion at roughly the same ages (Izard, 1971; Odom & Lemond, 1972).

Children also better appreciate the psychological complexity of emotional experience with increasing age. For example, by age 11 they are more likely to attribute emotional arousal to internal causes rather than to external events (Wol-

My research on emotional inferencing reported in this chapter benefited from the valuable guidance of Scott Paris throughout all phases of the work. Preparation of this chapter also benefited from the comments and suggestions of a number of colleagues, including Richard Dienstbier, Bernard Weiner, Sandra Graham, Carolyn Saarni, and Paul Harris. I am very grateful for their contributions. Tables 5.1, 5.3, and 5.4 are copyrighted (1987) by the American Psychological Association, and are reprinted by permission of the publisher.

117

man, Lewis, & King, 1971), they increasingly appreciate how emotional display rules function (Harris & Olthof, 1982; Harris, Olthof, & Meerum Terwogt, 1981; Saaarni, 1979), they better understand that emotional states can be internally redirected (e.g., thinking happy thoughts in a sad situation) (Harris et al., 1981), and their appreciation of ambivalent feelings and of the simultaneous experience of multiple emotions increases (Donaldson & Westerman, 1986; Harter, 1982; see also Carroll & Steward, 1984). When a story character's facial expression is inconsistent with the emotion that would be expected from contextual cues (e.g., a happy face on a child holding a broken toy), younger children primarily rely on facial cues, whereas older children draw increasingly on contextual information and also offer reasons for the inconsistency that include consideration of display rules and other psychological factors (Gnepp, 1983; Iannotti, 1978; Kurdek & Rodgon, 1975; Reichenbach & Masters, 1983; see, however, Burns & Cavey, 1957, and Greenspan, Barenboim, & Chandler, 1976). Because of children's early use of facial cues, it is unsurprising that Gnepp, Klayman, and Trabasso (1982) found that preschoolers as well as adults emphasized personal information over situational and normative information when drawing conclusions about a story character's emotional experiences.

Thus, with increasing age, children not only develop a broader range of emotional concepts, but also increasingly appreciate the psychological dimensions of emotional experience. This growth in emotional knowledge is important for at least three reasons. First, it helps children interpret their own emotional experiences in more sophisticated ways. For example, an awareness that one can experience more than one emotion simultaneously may help children better interpret their feelings in situations that foster ambivalent or conflicting reactions (such as when parents argue). Second, it fosters more acute interpretations of the direct emotional displays of others. When children master an understanding of display rules, for example, they can appreciate that another's manifest display of emotion may mask different underlying feelings.

The growth of emotional knowledge is also important for a third reason: It increases children's competence at *inferring* emotion in others when direct cues are lacking. This chapter is concerned with developmental changes in children's emotional inferences, especially from the standpoint of attribution theory. In many everyday situations, of course, children must estimate or predict others' emotional reactions without being able to directly observe their facial or vocal expressions. In peer relations, for example, children often make predictive inferences of how other children will feel in competitive or conflictual situations. Estimates of the emotional reactions of parents or teachers are important in children's self-evaluations related to moral behavior or achievement successes or failures. In disciplinary encounters when a parent asks the child how the victim of her actions felt, this often requires a rather sophisticated inference of the victim's emotions. A child's emotional inferences are thus likely to influence a variety of socioemotional and personality processes. If there are developmental changes in children's emotional inferencing skills, they are likely to have important influences on many other aspects of social-cognitive understanding.

Consider the following study. Several years ago, Martin Hoffman and I (Thompson & Hoffman, 1980) examined the role of empathy in children's guilt responses to everyday forms of wrongdoing. Children of various ages were presented with short stories describing a wrongful act committed by one child against another (e.g., taking another's prized toy), and were subsequently asked to imagine they were the wrongdoer and to describe how they would feel and act afterward. Before this role-playing, however, half the children at each age were asked to think about and describe the *victim's* feelings at the story conclusion (these feelings were not explicitly described in either the story narrative or in the accompanying pictures). We found, as expected, that children who had been encouraged to empathize with the victim later reported feeling greater guilt after assuming the wrongdoer's role, compared to those who had not. Unexpectedly, however, children in the empathy-induction condition varied in the kinds of emotional reactions they inferred in the victim at each age. Whereas the majority of the youngest children perceived the victim as feeling sad, all of the oldest children attributed anger to the victim. Thus, although *all* children viewed the victim as being upset, they varied significantly in the *kind* of distress they inferred in this story character. These findings have since been replicated in a second, independent study (Thompson, in press).

Although we found no evidence in these small samples that these varying inferences of emotion systematically affected children's guilt responses, emotional inferences are likely to make a difference in similar situations. Children who attribute anger to someone they have wronged are likely to worry about retaliation more than children who infer sadness in the victim, and this may affect not only their experience of guilt, but also their ability to view the victim sympathetically and to respond accordingly. In a similar manner, helping another person in distress may be affected by the kinds of emotion children attribute to that distressed individual. In short, the kinds of emotional inferences made by children as they are reacting to another individual may affect many aspects of their subsequent reactions to that person.

How do children's inferences of emotion change with age? The purpose of this chapter is to explore this question. In particular, I will describe one approach to understanding emotional inferences that has been offered recently by Bernard Weiner, Sandra Graham, and their students (Graham & Weiner, 1986; Weiner, 1985a; Weiner & Graham, 1984), in which the development of emotional inferencing skills is linked to the growth of causal understanding and attributions in childhood. This perspective will be outlined, and research deriving from this theoretical model will be summarized and then critically evaluated. A new study based on this emotion-attribution model will also be presented, and its implications for further study of the development of children's emotional inferences will be offered in the concluding section of this chapter.

The attribution-emotion model

Like other attribution theorists, Weiner, Graham, and their colleagues argue that people devote considerable effort to understanding the causes underlying their own experiences and those of others. Although this causal search is especially salient when these experiences are unexpected or undesirable (e.g., failing an exam for which one has studied), there is nevertheless a strong tendency to ascertain causal influences in many situations. There is a broad range of possible causes to which outcomes can be attributed: They may relate to intrinsic factors (such as one's ability, effort, or background), the intervention of other people, the nature of the situation or task itself (e.g., "This was an exam anybody would fail"), perceptions of good or bad luck, or other factors.

The answers obtained from this causal search influence three important reactions: (a) one's expectation that such an event will recur, (b) one's perception of the conditions fostering its recurrence, and (c) one's affective responses to this event. With respect to one's expectation that an event will recur, causal attributions vary on a dimension of *stability*, which relates to their likelihood of recurring. Stable causes include, for example, one's underlying ability, aptitude, and enduring features of a situation or task; unstable causes include luck, mood, and changing task parameters. When one attributes the cause for an event to a stable agent, that event is thought to be more likely to occur again than when the agent is perceived as changing or unstable. For example, if exam failure is attributed to perceptions of one's ability (e.g., lacking competence in math) or consistent feature of the task (e.g., "This instructor always writes difficult exams"), it is reasonable to expect that failure will recur on subsequent exams. On the other hand, if failure is attributed to unstable causes such as bad luck, one can be more optimistic about success in the future. The stability of causal attributions can be used to predict not only the likelihood that academic successes or failures will recur, but also the probability of social success (e.g., "How likely is he to accept my second invitation to dinner?"), professional and financial experiences (e.g., "Why can't I get a raise?"), and moral compliance (e.g., resisting temptations to cheat or steal). There is thus considerable flexibility to these attributional processes.

With respect to the second prediction – that is, identifying the conditions fostering the recurrence of an event – causal attributions also vary on two additional dimensions: *locus* and *controllability*. Causal agents with an internal locus include personal ability, aptitude, and effort; those with an external locus include the intervention of others and situational or task features. Moreover, some of these agents are personally controllable (e.g., effort), whereas others are not (e.g., aptitude or luck). Thus causal agents that vary in their causal locus and controllability provide important information about whether an event may be fostered (or inhibited) in the future, and how. For example, when preparing for an exam, it is helpful to believe that performance is strongly influenced by one's effort (e.g., studying), which is an internal and controllable causal agent. On the other hand, students who believe that the bases for their academic success are largely external and/or uncontrollable (e.g., luck or the teacher's biases) may experience considerable helplessness in such situations or use much different strategies to promote success (such as second-guessing the teacher). Again, such attributions may also be relevant to determining how to increase one's social desirability, earning power, moral stature, or other nonacademic concerns. In general, then, causal attributions provide useful knowledge that can shape expectations of future events.

Causal attributions also provide important information guiding emotional reactions to these events. Here the concern is not with using attributions to predict future events, but with how they influence our feelings about events that have already occurred. As the foregoing examples may suggest, salient and (at times) powerful feelings may accompany our causal analysis of everyday experiences. A student, for example, who attributes unexpected failure on an exam to the teacher's unrealistically high expectations may not only derive important inferences concerning future success in this course, but also experience strong feelings of anger related to these inferences. An employer who recognizes and rewards the performance of employees not only fosters the perception that personal effort increases productivity, but also feelings of pride and competence. When a child's misbehavior results in harm to another, the parent's admonitions not only shape the child's attributions for misbehavior, but may also induce guilty feelings as a result. Thus, causal attributions not only provide predictive information related to the recurrence of events, but also influence emotional reactions to these events. In this manner, they help to shape the motivational bases for later behavior.

Weiner (1985a) and Graham (Graham & Weiner, 1986; Weiner & Graham, 1984) argue that such emotional reactions occur in a two-step sequence. The first step consists simply of an outcome evaluation: Was I successful or did I fail? The result of this "primary appraisal" is a global positive or negative emotional reaction, resulting in one or more of a variety of *outcome-dependent, (causal) attribution-independent* affects. These include emotional reactions like happy, sad, upset, frustrated, and glad. They are determined by one's success or failure in attaining a desired goal, regardless of the cause for that outcome. Thus a student may experience happiness when receiving a high score on an exam, regardless of whether the grade was due to diligent studying, the help of another, or luck.

Following this, a second step may occur in which one initiates a causal search to explain that outcome. This more complex appraisal process ("secondary appraisal") may refine or modify the initial, outcome-determined emotional reaction. More specifically, it may lead to one or more *(causal) attribution-dependent* emotional reactions like pride, guilt, surprise, anger, and gratitude. These emotional reactions rely not only on perceptions of the outcome of an event, but also on conclusions concerning its causes. Thus if a student's high grade was attributed to diligent studying, pride would be the natural reaction; if the achievement was instead attributed to another's assistance (e.g., a tutor), gratitude instead of pride would be expected. Attribution-dependent emotional reactions are cognitively more complex than are outcome-dependent emotions, because they rely on consideration not only of whether success or failure has occurred, but also of its underlying cause. In other words, attribution-dependent reactions require a "secondary appraisal" of the situation.

Weiner and Graham have identified a simple taxonomy of attribution-dependent emotional responses based on the various causes to which situational outcomes can be attributed (see Weiner, 1985a; Weiner & Graham, 1984; see also Weiner, Russell, & Lerman, 1978, 1979). When success can be attributed to ability, feelings of confidence or competence are the result. When it is due to long-term effort, relaxation ensues. Both ability and effort, as internal causes, also elicit pride. When success is attributed to the intervention of another, on the other hand, gratitude is expected. Turning to failure outcomes, when such outcomes can be attributed to one's (lack of) ability, feelings of incompetence and shame ensue (and may elicit pity or sympathy from others). When failure is due to (lack of) effort, guilt results (and this may evoke anger from observers). And when failure is thought to result from another's intervention, anger toward that person is the expected emotional response. It is interesting that when luck is the causal agent, surprise is the expected response whether the outcome is success or failure.

These researchers also note that these attributionally derived emotional responses often have broader implications for one's affective life. For example, when success or failure is attributed to internal causes (such as ability or effort), emotional responses like pride, competence, guilt, or shame are especially important because they are esteem-related emotions, and thus play an important role in self-evaluation. This is not true for emotional reactions resulting from attributions to extrinsic agents (e.g., the intervention of another or luck). The causal dimension of internal or external locus is not the only one with broader emotional implications. Causal stability is also important, giving rise to emotions such as hopelessness or resignation (in the case of failure due to stable causes), and hopefulness (when succcess is attributed to stable causes). Emotional reactions like these assume a motivational role in one's efforts to change or maintain current conditions. Finally, the dimension of controllability is also significant for affective life because it concerns the degree of personal responsibility for events, and is thus related to interpersonally evaluative emotions such as gratitude (in the case of success) and anger and pity (in the case of failure). Thus the causal dimensions of locus, stability and controllability, which provide important predictive information related to the recurrence of events, are also related to the broader emotional ramifications of these events. In particular, they can assume an important role in self-esteem and in the sense of hope or helplessness experienced in efforts to alter one's current circumstances.

Taken together, it is apparent that diverse emotions may arise from the two-step process outlined by Weiner and Graham: an initial emotional reaction derived from a simple evaluation of one's success or failure, and a more complex emotional response directly linked to one's causal analysis. Thus, initial emotional reactions are refined and modified in the course of a successively more complex cognitive evaluation of the causes underlying events. Weiner and Graham have not only provided another important perspective on how cognition undergirds and shapes emotional experience, but have specified how this occurs through attributions of causality for events.

This analysis of attribution-emotion linkages is not only applicable to how individuals respond to personal experiences, but also to their inferences of the emotional reactions of others, given knowledge of others' situational conditions. That is, the association of certain causal attributions with emotional reactions is relevant to understanding or predicting the emotional behavior of others as well as of oneself. Moreover, given the ways in which emotional reactions are predicated on successively more complex cognitive appraisals of events, one would expect to find developmental changes in emotional understanding as children's appraisals of emotion-eliciting situations become more sophisiticated and broader in scope. This attribution-emotional model may therefore provide useful insights into the development of emotional inferencing skills in childhood. What follows is a review of this developmental literature.

Developmental considerations

Although the attribution-emotion model is not an explicitly developmental formulation, it has important implications for researchers concerned with the development of emotional understanding. First, insofar as the arousal of emotions like pride, guilt, pity, gratitude, anger, and surprise is lawfully related to certain causal attributions,[1] this should be apparent when these emotional concepts have been acquired developmentally. That is, children's experience of these emotions should be consistently linked to predictable antecedent causal conditions, and their understanding of these experiences in others should be similarly informed by an appreciation of their causal antecedents. Second, this model argues that such attribution-emotion linkages should apply to a variety of situations (e.g., achievement, social-conventional, moral, etc.), and should have predictable consequences when they are understood by children. In other words, causal ascriptions should not only provoke specific emotional reactions, but should have direct implications for self-esteem and motivation to succeed, as predicted by the model.

Third, but perhaps most important, the attribution-emotion model suggests that young children may initially generate primarily outcome-dependent emotions in interpreting their experiences and those of others, but at later ages make greater use of attribution-dependent emotions. This change would be expected not just because of age-related growth in the emotional lexicon. Instead, younger children may rely on outcome-dependent emotions because they require a less complex appraisal of the situation; essentially, they require only an assessment of success or failure (i.e., "primary appraisal"). In contrast, attribution-dependent emotional reactions require an analysis of both outcomes and their agents, which is a cognitively more demanding enterprise (i.e., "secondary appraisal"). Furthermore, outcomes are salient and easily understood sources of emotional arousal in others, and are frequently-used bases for moral judgment and conventional understanding by young children (Shantz, 1983). In contrast, most causal agents are neither as salient nor as self-evident to young children as is success or failure, and this further complicates their causal analysis. To be sure, researchers have demonstrated that preschoolers can accurately identify causal agents in simple situations (e.g., short story narratives), so their capacity to engage in a directed causal analysis of familiar situations should not be doubted (see Green, 1977, and Trabasso, Stein, & Johnson, 1981). However, there are good reasons for uncertainty concerning the ability of young children to engage in *spontaneous* causal research, especially in the context of generating emotional inferences. Taken together, the attribution-emotion model suggests that children will exhibit an initial tendency to rely on the cognitively less complex outcome-dependent emotions in interpreting their own experiences and those of others. With increased causal understanding (including a growing appreciation of the psychological complexity of emotional experiences) at later ages, children are more likely to generate more sophisticated attribution-dependent emotional inferences.

Previous research

Weiner, Graham, and their colleagues have designed a number of studies to test these and other developmental formulations deriving from their attribution-emotion model (see Graham & Weiner, 1986, for a review). Consistent with the educational applications of their model, much of their research has focused on children's emotional inferences in the context of academic achievement. An important aspect of this research is their effort to demonstrate reciprocal relations between causal ascriptions and emotional inferences – that is, that certain attributions may not only foster derivative emotional reactions, but that knowledge of another's emotions may imply causal ascriptions made by that person.

An initial investigation by Weiner, Graham, Stern, and Lawson (1982) illustrates this reciprocity. Children at ages 5, 7, and 9 were shown illustrated stories describing a student who failed a test, to which the teacher responded with either anger or pity (i.e., "felt sorry") toward the student. In each case, children were asked to rate the extent to which the student's failure was due to low ability or poor effort. A previous investigation had demonstrated that, under similar conditions, adults and older children reliably inferred that the teacher's pity was due to ascribing the student's failure to low ability (i.e., an intrinsic, but uncontrollable causal agent), but that teacher anger was aroused when failure was attributed to poor effort (i.e., intrinsic, but more controllable). Would younger children derive the same causal inferences from the teacher's emotional reaction?

They did, but developmental changes in these inferences were also apparent. Concerning the teacher's anger, children at all ages concluded that the student's failure was due to a lack of effort, although the 5-year-olds were significantly weaker in this inference than were the 7- and 9-year-olds. Concerning the teacher's pity, only the 9-year-olds reliably concluded that the student's low ability was the cause of failure. Thus, although children at all ages could use emotional reactions to infer underlying causal ascriptions to some extent, developmental changes indicated considerable growth in this understanding in middle childhood, and these changes occurred in patterns specific to different attributions, rather than more globally. Weiner and his colleagues interpreted these findings to reflect developmental changes in children's understanding of ability and effort as causal factors in academic success (Nicholls, 1978). That is, the association of teacher pity with student ability develops, in their view, as children begin to appreciate that low ability can be a stable cause for academic failure.

The findings from a second investigation gave credence to this view. Graham, Doubleday, and Guarino (1984) asked children between the ages of 6 and 11 to recall situations in which they felt guilty ("ashamed") about their own behavior, or anger or pity ("felt sorry") for another. In addition, for each situation, they were asked to rate the extent to which the emotion was provoked by circumstances that were controllable by oneself (in the case of guilt) or by the other person who was the target of the emotion (in the case of pity and anger). Graham and her colleagues found that for children at all ages, pity was evoked by conditions that could not be controlled by another, whereas anger was elicited by circumstances over which another could, in fact, exercise some control. There were no developmental changes in responses to these emotions, perhaps because (contrary to Weiner et al., 1982) children were responding to self-generated and thus familiar emotion-eliciting situations. With respect to guilt, however, developmental changes were apparent: the youngest children (ages 6–7) reported feeling guilty in circumstances that were largely *un*controllable, whereas older children reported guilt in conditions involving personal control (and thus responsibility). Younger children evidently did not link guilty feelings to failure for which one is personally responsible; their experience of guilt was a more global, less discriminating response. In this respect, it is noteworthy that guilt was the only self-directed emotion studied in this investigation, and also falls under considerable socialization pressure in middle childhood. In sum, consistent with the previous investigation, even young children grasped meaningful linkages between attributions and emotions, although developmental changes were paramount.

Children's understanding of guilt was further investigated in a third, unpublished study by Graham (1985), reported by Graham and Weiner (1986). This study also explored developing concepts of pride and gratitude. For each emotion, a pair of short story narratives was created that varied on a causal dimension relevant to that emotion. For guilt, the dimension related to personal controllability or responsibility; for pride, the dimension was locus of control (internal or external); for gratitude, the dimension concerned whether the other person's act was volitional. These dimensions were chosen, of course, because they are fundamental to the kind of attributional analysis giving rise to the emotion of interest. Thus, for example, the two stories concerning gratitude both described a story character who was new to the school being chosen for a baseball team. In one version, the captain did so voluntarily. In the other version, the act was required by the rules. For each story, children between the ages of 5 and 11 were asked to describe the intensity of the target emotion (guilt, pride, or gratitude) experienced by the story character at the conclusion.

Graham found that with increasing age, children's inferences of emotion in the story character became more differentiated according to the causal dimension underlying the pair of stories for that emotion. For example, older children attributed guilt to a story character who was responsible for wrongdoing, but did not do so when wrongdoing was unavoidable. In contrast, younger children differentiated less between controllable and uncontrollable circumstances when inferring the amount of guilt in the story character. In a similar manner, with increasing age, inferences of pride were differentiated depending on whether the locus of success was intrinsic or extrinsic, and inferences of gratitude varied more according to whether another's assistance was genuinely voluntary or not. In sum, children appeared to develop more specific and discriminating emotional concepts with increasing age, and in ways consistent with the attribution-emotion model. Guilt was increasingly and discriminatingly related to failures owing to personal responsibility, pride to success deriving from intrinsic causes, and gratitude to another's freely offered assistance.

The behavioral consequences of certain attribution-emotion linkages were also explored in two studies. In the first, Weiner and Handel (1985) presented children between the ages of 5 and 12 with two sets of short story narratives. The first set consisted of eight variations of a story concerning social rejection (i.e., one child refusing to play with another), with each variation providing a different reason for the rejection. In four of the stories, the reason was intrinsic to the rejected child (e.g., the child was not good at games), and in the remaining four stories, the reason was extrinsic (e.g., it was hard to get to the child's house). After each story, children were asked how likely they would be to divulge the real reason for rejection and, if the real reason was known, how hurt the rejected child would be. A similar procedure was used with the second set of stories, which involved a broken social agreement that occurred for reasons either personally controllable or uncontrollable. For this second set, children were again asked whether they would reveal the true reason for the broken agreement and, if it was revealed, how angry the other person would be.

Perhaps the most striking finding from this study was that there were no age-related changes in children's perceptions of how hurt or angry the other child would be in these stories. Children at all ages consistently predicted that the victim would be more hurt if intrinsic rather than extrinsic reasons were divulged, and more angry if controllable rather than uncontrollable reasons were revealed. In a similar manner, children at all ages were more inclined to conceal intrinsic/controllable rather than extrinsic/uncontrollable reasons from the victim. Thus, from a remarkably early age (5 years), children recognized that angry or hurt feelings are more likely to rise in others when they are rejected for personal reasons, consistent with the attribution-emotion model. Furthermore, this awareness evidently inclined even young children to conceal the real reasons for rejection to spare the other person's feelings (i.e., to use deception).

Another study investigated the motivational consequences of emotional cues in academic situations, and is in many ways the most ingenious of the studies reviewed here in its efforts to simulate achievement experiences rather than relying on hypothetical story narratives. Graham (1984) presented sixth-graders with a set of puzzles to complete in timed trials. After children completed the first puzzle successfully, failure was induced in the next four trials by the use of more difficult puzzles. Following each failure, the experimenter used both nonverbal and verbal cues to convey either anger or sympathy with the child's performance, or provided no explicit emotional reaction at all (a control condition). A variety of dependent measures were gathered throughout these trials and after they were completed. Graham found that children in each of the three affect conditions (experimenter anger, experimenter sympathy, or control) derived the predicted causal ascriptions from the experimenter's response. Children in the anger condition reported that the experimenter thought they did not try hard enough, whereas children in the sympathy condition perceived the experimenter as doubting that they were good at puzzles. These findings are consistent with those from the earlier study by Weiner and colleagues (1982) described earlier.

More important, Graham found that the experimenter's emotional reactions affected children's expectancies for future performance. By the fifth trial, children in the sympathy condition were predicting significantly poorer performance on future trials compared to children in the other two conditions. Thus the adult's emotional messages not only influenced perceptions of *her* causal ascriptions for the child's failure, but also shaped the child's *own* expectancies for future success. However, there were no associations between experimenter emotion and more global indicators of the child's perceived competence and persistence in a later, untimed puzzle task. In other words, these affective cues were used by children in a situation-specific manner, and did not seem to be more broadly generalized to other achievement tasks.

Evaluation

Taken together, this series of studies by Weiner, Graham, and their colleagues provides important information concerning the development of children's understanding of attribution-emotion linkages. They highlight the fact that from a remarkably early age children are aware that certain emotional responses are linked to an observer's causal analysis of situations, and that emotional reactions in others may imply causal ascriptions as well as the reverse. The development of this understanding seems to proceed in attribution-specific ways rather than occurring in a more global, generalized fashion. For example, children appreciate that an observer's anger may be linked to situations involving another's failure due to lack of effort *before* they are aware that guilt results from personal failure for the same reason. The explanation for this disparity in attribution-emotion knowledge is not entirely clear. Finally, these studies also indicate that as their understanding of attribution-emotion linkages increases, children respond in other ways that are consistent with the model proposed by Weiner and Graham. That is, they modify their expectancies for achievement success and report that they would engage in social deception in ways consistent with their causal analysis of events. In sum, the findings from this ambitious set of studies provide important empirical support for the attribution-emotion model.

There are, however, some issues that must be addressed in interpreting these findings, especially those concerning developmental changes in children's emotional inferences. The results of these studies indicate that considerable growth occurs in children's understanding of the meaning of certain attribution-dependent emotions, especially in their recognition that distinct associations exist between certain causal attributions and derivative emotional experiences. It is not clear whether this developmental growth is primarily conceptual or semantic. That is, it is sometimes difficult to determine whether children's basic understanding of emotions like guilt and gratitude is changing, or whether changes are occurring primarily in children's application of these semantic labels to emotional experiences that are already reasonably well understood by the child. For example, I have found that even very young children understand the emotional reactions associated with receiving help from another, although they often confuse the meaning of the relevant semantic label "gratitude" (some, for example, report that the help-giver experiences gratitude, rather than the help-receiver). In short, because a conceptual understanding of emotion can develop well in advance of semantic understanding (especially in young children), it is sometimes uncertain whether these studies document developmental changes in semantic or conceptual comprehension of emotional experience.

Part of the problem, of course, is that some of the research in this area relies on children's use of emotion labels without careful procedural checks to ensure children's accurate use of these labels. When children are asked to recall experiences in which they felt guilty or ashamed, for example, are younger children inclined to think of embarrassing episodes, whereas older children more appropriately recall instances of wrongdoing? A content analysis of the vignettes they produce would help to answer this question. If so, this could explain the association of guilt with uncontrollable as well as controllable experiences in young children (cf. Graham, 1985, and Graham et al., 1984). Because the use of complex emotion labels may be problematic, in the future alternative research strategies should be used that better tap children's conceptual understandings of emotional experiences that are unconfounded with semantic development. For example, children could be presented with a story narrative that describes experiences leading to feelings of pride in the story character (without the specific label being used). Children could then be asked to choose between two (or more) short stories in which the story character felt "the same way," and in which the circumstances of the test stories led to different feelings in the story character (e.g., one story resulting in feelings of gratitude, another in feelings of pride, and so forth).[2] The use of procedures such as these would reduce the existing confound between developmental changes in children's conceptual comprehension of emotion and their semantic use of emotion terms, and would contribute to a clearer appreciation of age-related changes in emotional understanding.

Another methodological issue concerns differences in the use of experimenter-generated versus self-generated vignettes in assessing children's emotional understanding. There is some evidence from the studies reviewed above that children exhibit more acute understanding of emotion-attribution linkages when reflecting on their own experiences as compared to hypothetical story situations (e.g., compare understandings of pity for Weiner et al., 1982, and for Graham et al., 1984). This difference merits further exploration in order to elucidate whether children are capable of more sophisticated emotional understanding when reflecting on personal experiences than when inferring emotion in others. There is considerable reason to expect this to be so, because children are likely to be more sensitive to the motivational underpinnings of their own emotional reactions and thus to derive more meaningful attribution-emotion linkages from personal experiences as compared to hypothetical ones. If this is true, however, it remains risky to generalize across these different situations in drawing conclusions about the development of emotional understanding in children. Indeed, different sequences of growth (as well as common patterns) may be evident in the development of an understanding of emotion in oneself compared with the understanding of emotion in others.

In sum, the ambitious research studies conducted by Weiner, Graham, and their colleagues offer considerable evidence in support of their attribution-emotion model. Although there are interpretational problems concerning the locus of developmental change and the potentially different bases of emotional understanding in self and other, these studies provide a strong foundation for future work on this perspective.

Unanswered questions. However, other important questions still remain in evaluating this formulation. First, from a developmental standpoint, do children initially focus on situational outcomes when deriving inferences about others' emotional reactions and only later integrate outcome information with causal ascriptions, as predicted by the model? Is this reflected in the quality of their emotional inferences (i.e., outcome-dependent or attribution-dependent)? Will it be evident also in their *reasons* for generating these inferences (i.e., focusing on causal agents rather than the story outcome alone)? Although the preceding research indicates considerable age-related growth in children's understanding of attribution-emotion linkages, most of this evidence appears in research situations in which children are faced with highly explicit emotional and/or attributional cues to guide their analysis (see also Weiner et al., 1980). In contrast, further research is required using less directed conditions to explore children's spontaneous emotional inferences in response to different situations, as well as the reasoning underlying them, to elucidate whether the theoretically predicted developmental transition from outcome-dependent to attribution-dependent emotional inferences is clearly apparent.

Second, do these attribution-emotion linkages generalize to the broad range of different situations eliciting emotion in children and adults? Because of its educational applications, much of the research deriving from this model has focused on experiences related to academic achievement, although supportive findings have also emerged from studies using nonacademic scenarios. However, it would be useful to systematically compare the kinds of inferences generated by children in situational domains that are much different – such as comparing achievement situations with moral dilemmas or with scenarios involving social-conventional issues. Doing so would enable students of social-cognitive development to determine whether there is sufficient generality in children's emotional inferences across these diverse situational or content domains despite important variability in other aspects of children's thinking about these domains (Shantz, 1983).

Third, does the experience of success or failure have a systematic effect on children's causal analyses of situations, and the kinds of emotional inferences that result? This question is important because whether or not children combine this outcome information with a causal analysis in inferring emotion in others, the experience of success or failure itself may guide their causal analysis in systematic ways. In this regard, it is important to test developmentally the attributional view that unexpected or undesirable experiences – which are more likely to be associated with failure experiences – precipitate a more salient or systematic causal analysis compared to anticipated or desirable experiences (see Weiner, 1985b; Wong & Weiner, 1981). If this is so, does this affect the emotional inferences that result?

Fourth, and finally, further research is needed to assess developmentally children's understanding of a broader range of attributional cues and the emotional reactions with which they are associated. Because the attribution-emotion model has such important educational applications, much of the research reviewed above has focused on causal ascriptions related to ability and effort. Although these are important (and the focus of significant early socialization experiences), they do not exhaust the range of meaningful causal conditions that give rise to diverse emotional reactions in children and adults. The attribution-emotion model predicts that specific emotional reactions should accompany causal attributions to the intervention of another, luck, and other causal agents. Studying the emotional consequences of luck ascriptions would be especially valuable because children are not often encouraged to attribute their success and failure experiences to good or bad luck, and thus may not have a sophisticated appreciation of the emotional ramifications of luck attributions.

A new developmental study. To summarize, four questions remain to be addressed in further evaluating the attribution-emotion formulation. First, can the theoretically predicted developmental transition from outcome-dependent to attribution-dependent emotional inferences be confirmed, and is it reflected in both the *kinds* of inferences children generate as well as the *reasons* offered for them? Second, are these inferencing processes broadly generalizable across different content domains (e.g., achievement versus moral situations)? Third, do success or failure outcomes have a systematic effect on children's emotional inferences, perhaps through the kinds of causal analyses they elicit? Fourth, would developmental research using a broader range of attributional cues (e.g., to personal effort, another's intervention, luck), confirm the predicted attribution-emotion linkages?

With these questions in mind, I designed another developmental investigation to examine these aspects of the attribution-emotion formulation (Thompson, 1987). In particular, I was interested in determining whether the quality of children's emotional inferences – and the explanations they offered for them – varied systematically according to three factors. These were (1) the attributional cues provided the child (personal effort, the intervention of another, or luck[3]). (2) the outcome of the story (success or failure), and (3) the content domain of the story (achievement or moral) presented to children in short narratives. This study used a within-subjects design to provide a more powerful test of these influences.

In addition, methodological safeguards were used to ensure that observed developmental differences in children's emotional inferences could not be attributed to confounding influences. For example, both open-ended (i.e., free-response) and forced-choice response measures were included to control for age-related differences in verbal production ability. To facilitate understanding, the forced-choice options included simple line drawings of pertinent facial expressions accompanying each of the emotion response options, and these options were discussed at the beginning of the study and periodically reviewed throughout the testing to ensure that young children maintained adequate understanding of these options. Furthermore, the range of options was simple (happy, sad, proud, guilty [feeling "bad about yourself"], angry, grateful, surprised, and neutral ["nothing"]), and were fully within the emotional lexicon of even the youngest children in this study (see Schwartz & Trabasso, 1984). Finally, a memory check was conducted with an independent sample of second graders (the youngest age included in this sample) to ascertain adequate retention of critical elements of the story narrative, especially concerning causal information related to the story outcome. In these ways, the study was designed to ensure that observed developmental differences could not be attributed to verbal production deficiencies, inadequate comprehension of the emotion options, or forgetting important aspects of the narrative.

Second graders, fifth graders, and college students were read 12 paragraph-length stories, each describing a sequence of events leading to an outcome for the story character and were subsequently asked to describe how the story character felt at the conclusion and why. The stories used in this study were designed to ensure that they were consistent on all content dimensions except those that were specifically varied for research purposes (see Thompson, 1987). Each participant in the study was read one story for each of 12 story conditions resulting from a factorial design involving two content domains (achievement and moral), two outcomes (success or failure), and three causes for the story outcome (personal effort, another's intervention, or luck). Because a large number of stories in achievement and moral domains (with systematic variations in outcome and causal agent) were initially developed, the 12 stories heard by each participant involved different characters and different situations (in contrast to repeating the same story in several versions, which is often the case in previous research). After hearing each story, they were asked to describe in their own words the story character's feeling at the story conclusion, and to explain why the character felt this way. Following this, they were again asked to indicate the story character's feelings by means of the forced-choice response array (8 line drawings with emotion labels underneath).

Results

Each participant's responses to the open-ended and forced-choice response measures were coded in dichotomous fashion to reflect either the presence or absence of the theoretically expected attribution-dependent emotional inference for each story condition. Thus, consistent with the attribution-emotion model, stories with success outcomes attributed to personal effort were expected to yield inferences of pride in the story character; attributions to another's intervention should elicit inferences of gratitude; and attributions to luck should evoke surprise inferences. For stories with failure outcomes, attributions to (lack of) effort should yield inferences of guilt; attributions to another's intervention were expected to yield inferences of anger, and attributions to luck should again evoke surprise inferences. The same predictions were made for studies concerning achievement and moral content domains.[4] When a response included these inferences of emotion in the story character, that response was deemed to reflect the predicted attribution-dependent emotion. For example, in a story with a positive outcome due to the story character's effort, a child who responded, ''I think the boy would feel happy and proud,'' was rated as having provided the expected attribution-dependent emotion. A child who indicated only that the character felt happy would not.

Finally, each transcription of the explanation offered by each participant for each emotional inference was coded dichotomously to indicate whether the reason included consideration of the relevant cause underlying the story outcome, or focused on outcome information alone. A child who said, ''she felt that way because she won the race'' was rated as relying on outcome information alone;

another who indicated that the character felt as she did "because she practiced hard to win the race" was rated as including causal factors in her explanation.

I first examined the kinds of emotional inferences offered by children and adults. The findings for the forced-choice measure are presented in Table 5.1. As expected, there was a significant main effect for age: On both forced-choice and open-ended response measures, adults and fifth graders provided more of the predicted attribution-dependent emotional inferences than did second graders, who instead tended to offer a larger proportion of outcome-dependent inferences like happy or sad.

Another way of understanding these findings is to examine the modal inference offered by participants (i.e., the response provided by a plurality) at each age. These findings are presented in Table 5.2. It is apparent that in many story conditions, second graders provided predominantly outcome-dependent inferences like happy or sad. Contrary to expectations, they did, however, also infer the emotions of pride and guilt quite frequently in the story character, and in both predicted and unpredicted conditions. In contrast, in every story condition except those involving luck attributions, the inferences of fifth graders and adults were consistently the predicted attribution-dependent emotions. These findings are generally consistent with the predictions of the attribution-emotion model, and provide some support for the expected developmental transition from outcome-dependent to attribution-dependent emotional inferences. However, they also indicate that even young children have a grasp of some attribution-dependent emotions (i.e., pride and guilt), although they overextend their applications.

One other aspect of these findings merits note. In addition to a significant main effect for age, there was also a very significant main effect for causal attributional condition revealed in the analyses of both forced-choice and open-ended response measures. For both measures, participants of all ages provided a higher proportion of expected attribution-dependent inferences for stories entailing effort attributions (i.e., inferences of pride and guilt), and the smallest proportion of such inferences for stories entailing luck attributions (i.e., inferences of surprise or neutral affect). In other words, as Tables 5.1 and 5.2 indicate, stories involving the character's personal effort (or lack of effort) more reliably evoked the predicted inferences of pride or guilt at *all* ages. Stories involving good or bad luck, by contrast, seldom elicited the expected inferences even among adults. I shall comment on this unexpected finding later.

Because the youngest children tended to offer a greater proportion of outcome-dependent emotional inferences than older children and adults, did their *explanations* for these inferences focus largely on the story outcome? This would be expected, according to the attribution-emotion formulation, because outcome-dependent inferences are thought to rely on an exclusive analysis of situational outcomes regardless of causal analysis (i.e., "primary appraisal"). In general,

Table 5.1. *Mean proportion of predicted attribution-dependent emotional inferences by age and story characteristics*

	Story characteristics: achievement domain						Story characteristics: moral domain					
	Positive outcome			Negative outcome			Positive outcome			Negative outcome		
Age level	Effort	Others	Luck	Effort	Others	Luck	Effort	Others	Luck	Effort	Others	Luck
Second grade	.42	.12	.17	.33	.46	.08	.38	.21	.21	.79	.25	.08
Fifth grade	.50	.38	.08	.38	.38	.04	.46	.42	.38	.79	.54	.12
Adults	.67	.38	.17	.58	.71	.12	.71	.42	.33	.71	.46	.17

Note: Data based on responses to forced-choice measure.

Table 5.2. *Modal emotional inference by age and story characteristics*

	Story characteristics: achievement domain						Story characteristics: moral domain					
	Positive outcome			Negative outcome			Positive outcome			Negative outcome		
Age level	Effort	Others	Luck	Effort	Others	Luck	Effort	Others	Luck	Effort	Others	Luck
Target expected	Proud	Grateful	Surprised/ neutral	Guilty	Angry	Surprised/ neutral	Proud	Grateful	Surprised/ neutral	Guilty	Angry	Surprised/ neutral
Second grade	Proud	Proud	Proud	Sad	Sad	Sad	Proud	Happy	Happy	Guilty	Sad	Guilty
Fifth grade	Proud	Grateful	Happy	Guilty/ sad	Angry/ sad	Sad	Proud	Grateful	Surprised	Guilty	Angry	Sad
Adults	Proud	Grateful/ happy	Happy	Guilty	Angry	Sad	Proud	Grateful	Neutral	Guilty	Angry	Sad

Note: Data based on responses to forced-choice measure.

the analyses of the justifications provided by children and adults for their inferences of emotion indicated that they did (see Table 5.3). A significant main effect for age indicated that, when explaining their emotional inferences, adults and fifth graders more often cited the causal elements in the story narrative, whereas the second graders relied more frequently on outcome information alone. It is important to remember, however, that this was not due to recall deficiencies in the youngest children, because an independent memory check revealed that second graders recalled all the important elements of the story narrative (including causal agents) with near-perfect accuracy. Instead, it appears that when considering how a story character feels, the youngest children were primarily considering that person's success or failure, regardless of its causal antecedents. These findings are thus also consistent with the predictions of the attribution-emotion model.

Further analyses of these data indicated two other important main effects. First, there was again a significant main effect for causal attributional condition: When the story outcome was attributed to another's intervention, participants at all ages were more likely to include causal considerations in their reasons for their inferences. On the other hand, such considerations were least likely to occur when the story outcome was attributed to luck. This finding may be related to the relative salience of different causal agents (i.e., another's intervention is more visible and self-evident than luck, and is thus easier to consider as an explanation for emotional behavior), and this possibility will be explored further below. Second, there was a significant main effect for story outcome: At all ages, participants were most likely to include causal considerations in their reasons for their emotional inferences when the outcome was failure, rather than success. Thus the outcome of the story was important to causal analysis: Failure provoked a more intensive search for causal considerations for individuals of all ages in this study.

Thus far, it is apparent that when examining both the *kinds* of emotional inferences offered by children and adults, as well as the *explanations* provided for these inferences, developmental changes accord well with the predictions of the attribution-emotion model. Children at younger ages tended to provide a greater proportion of outcome-dependent emotional inferences that were justified with reference to a story character's success or failure alone. In contrast, older children and adults relied to a greater degree on attribution-dependent inferences, and these were explained in terms of causal elements in the story narrative.

Of course, these changes in inferences and the explanations offered for them could be parallel developmental trends, with no necessary association between them. For this reason, the final analyses concerned the *linkage* between emotional inferences and their justifications *within each age*. That is, when children and adults used attribution-dependent emotions in their judgments of the story

Table 5.3. *Mean proportion of inference justifications entailing causal considerations by age and story characteristics*

| | Story characteristics: achievement domain | | | | | | Story characteristics: moral domain | | | | | |
| | Positive outcome | | | Negative outcome | | | Positive outcome | | | Negative outcome | | |
Age level	Effort	Others	Luck	Effort	Others	Luck	Effort	Others	Luck	Effort	Others	Luck
Second grade	.29	.38	.12	.67	.62	.42	.21	.46	.29	.38	.67	.62
Fifth grade	.54	.50	.50	.67	.83	.58	.50	.46	.21	.46	.83	.58
Adults	.54	.71	.50	.58	.79	.54	.67	.25	.54	.46	.67	.67

Note: Data based on responses to the open-ended measure.

Table 5.4. *Proportion of justifications entailing outcome considerations or causal considerations for each kind of emotional inference*

Emotional inference	Quality of reason offered					
	Second grade		Fifth grade		Adult	
	Outcome-oriented	Causal-oriented	Outcome-oriented	Causal-oriented	Outcome-oriented	Causal-oriented
Happy	.79	.21	.69	.31	.51	.49
Sad	.44	.56	.49	.51	.47	.53
Proud	.82	.18	.50	.50	.42	.58
Guilty	.49	.51	.43	.57	.36	.64
Grateful	.31	.69	.12	.88	.15	.85
Angry	.33	.67	.06	.93	.25	.75
Surprised or neutral	.65	.35	.43	.57	.46	.54
All others	.36	.64	.65	.35	.68	.32

character's feelings, were these justified with reference to causal elements in the story narrative? This question is crucial to the attribution-emotion formulation, because attribution-dependent emotions are thought to rely conceptually on antecedent cognitions related to causal attributions (i.e., ''secondary appraisal''). It was thus important to determine whether the use of attribution-dependent inferences by children and adults reflected this kind of causal analysis in the justifications offered for them.

The findings related to attribution-emotion linkages are presented in Table 5.4 according to the age of the respondent, and thus reflect some of the developmental changes noted earlier. These data also indicate, however, that the linkage between specific attribution-dependent inferences and the kind of explanations provided for them varied according to the emotion in question. For inferences such as grateful and angry, children and adults at all ages reliably justified them with reference to causal elements in the story narrative (i.e., the intervention of another), as predicted. When these emotions were used, in other words, they were frequently accompanied by explanations referring to the causal agent in the story. For emotions such as proud and guilty, the link to causally oriented rationales increased progressively over the age span studied. For the remaining emotions, there were weaker developmental changes and little evidence of a consistent or progressive attribution-emotion linkage in participants' responses. Thus, although there were clear developmental changes in both the *kinds* of emotional inferences and the *reasons* given for them (as predicted), these parallel developmental trends were *linked* in different ways depending on the emotion in question. In short, not all attribution-dependent inferences were necessarily on causal reasoning, at least as reflected in the justifications offered for them.

Implications

In general, the findings from this study are consistent with the formulations of the attribution-emotion model, but they indicate that a more expanded framework for viewing the growth of children's emotional inferencing skills is warranted. In particular, they suggest to me that the development of emotional understanding may be shaped by socialization processes that are likely to interact with the growth of attributional understanding in childhood, and thus offer important new directions for further research.

Consider, for example, children's developing understandings of pride and guilt, which are theoretically linked to situations in which one's effort (or lack of it) is the causal agent. It was apparent in this study that even young children had a remarkably acute appreciation of the kinds of situations that evoke these feelings in a story character. They reliably inferred pride or guilt in conditions warranting these inferences. What can account for this early understanding? One explanation is that children are taught achievement and moral values with regular reference to the child's own actions and their consequences, and thus teachers and parents provide important early information about when it is appropriate to experience self-evaluative emotions in these domains. As a result, children in this study had a good grasp of the conditions that warrant feelings of pride or guilt in achievement or moral situations.

But despite this understanding, young children were not very *discriminating* in linking these feelings to particular attributional cues. Instead, pride and guilt were inferred in both expected and unexpected conditions, indicating that considerable ambiguity remains in their understanding of these emotions. For example, they not only considered pride an appropriate response when success was due to effort, but in virtually *any* situation involving achievement success (see Table 5.2). Similarly, guilt was evoked not only by moral failure for which one is responsible, but also by situations for which one is not responsible (e.g., bad luck). Thus, despite the fact that second graders in this study had a good grasp of the appropriate conditions for feeling proud and guilty, they were not discriminating in linking these feelings to specific causal cues, and consequently inferred pride and guilt in inappropriate situations as well. Similar findings have been reported by Graham et al. (1984) and by Graham (1985), as described above. It is clear, therefore, that early understandings of pride and guilt are not as distinctly linked to particular causal attributions as they are for adults, and may be more globally associated with situations in which one has succeeded or failed. Whether this is due to exaggerated perceptions of personal responsibility imposed by social-cognitive limitations (Stipek, 1983), from confusion concerning the nature of intentionality, from early social experiences (e.g., children are often encouraged by authority figures to feel responsible for situations for which they may, in fact, not be the cause), or from some combination of these, remains for future research to elucidate.

How does a more discriminating conception of these emotions emerge in middle childhood? It is reasonable to assume that with further experience in the effort-oriented reward structure of the school (Dweck & Elliot, 1983) and the emergence of conformity-based conventional moral reasoning that emphasizes good intentions (Kohlberg, 1976), the salience of personal effort per se as a prerequisite for feelings of pride and guilt is likely to increase. This is surely facilitated by the growth of social-comparison processes (Ruble, 1983) over the same period. Thus, it is unsurprising to find the fifth graders in this study displaying a much more discriminating appreciation of the appropriate attributional conditions for inferring pride and guilt in the story character. In sum, the progressive linkage of feelings of pride and guilt with the relevant causal attributions may be an outcome, in part, of children's developing mastery of achievement and moral value systems, together with allied changes in their social-cognitive understanding.

This suggests, however, that the developmental changes that occur in children's understanding of this attribution-emotion likage may be more complex than initially considered. That is, children may not simply change from an exclusive reliance on outcome information ("primary appraisal") to causal information ("secondary appraisal") in formulating emotional inferences. Rather, even young children may engage in a serious causal analysis of situational events, but a causal analysis that at times is qualitatively different from that employed by older children and adults, based on more limited social-cognitive abilities and a different experiential history. When faced with success due to personal effort, younger children, like older ones, seem to perform the relevant causal analysis and derive the expected emotional response (i.e., pride). When faced with failure due to bad luck, however, it seems likely that young children are also searching for causes, but perform a different causal analysis compared to that of older children (i.e., they assume they are personally responsible), and a different emotional inference results. Thus, the most important developmental changes that have been observed in these studies may concern changes in secondary appraisal processes with increasing age, rather than the transition from primary to secondary appraisal processes. Unfortunately, the analysis of the explanations offered by children of different ages for their emotional inferences was not sufficiently sensitive to identify developmental changes of this kind, and this issue remains for future research.

Now consider, by contrast, the emotions of anger and gratitude. It was apparent in this study that when children inferred these emotions in the story character, they had the relevant causal analysis clearly in mind (i.e., that another person had intervened to create the story character's success or failure), and this analysis was similar to that used by older children and adults. Why? It is likely that an early understanding of this attribution-emotion linkage derives from the relative salience of this attributional cue to young children, especially compared with more complex and invisible attributional cues like effort, ability, and luck. When another person is the causal agent, in other words, one's causal analysis is facilitated by the salience and visibility of the agent. Thus, this attribution-emotion linkage is clear and early emerging, in part because it requires less cognitive work.

Finally, consider the emotion of surprise and its attributional cue relating to good or bad luck. The evidence from this investigation, as well as others, indicates that this attribution-emotion linkage is not well-established even by the adult years. In this sample, adults were more likely to infer the relevant outcome-dependent emotion (i.e., either happy or sad) than to infer surprise or even neutral affect in a story character whose success or failure was due to luck. Similar findings have been reported in Weiner's research (see Weiner, Russell, & Lerman, 1978, 1979). (It is important to remember here that it is not that an outcome-dependent emotional response is wrong in these situations [or in other situations involving different attributional cues]. Rather, the question is whether this initial outcome-dependent response is supplemented by an attribution-dependent reaction thought to reflect a deeper causal analysis of the situation.)

Why do adults as well as children fail to infer surprise (or neutral affect) when luck is the causal agent, contrary to theoretical predictions? Several explanations may be proposed. First, the problem may be with perceptions of luck as a causal agent. In Western industrialized societies, luck is often minimized as a potential causal agent in favor of other, more controllable agents (e.g., "bad luck" is really due to one's carelessness or lack of effort, "good luck" derives from careful planning, etc.). These kinds of culture-specific attributional biases may thus have caused participants in this study, and others, to derive a different kind of causal analysis from the stories presented to them. Second, the problem may be with the derivative emotions: surprise or neutral affect. There is some evidence that adults and children tend to misattribute anhedonic emotions like surprise or neutral affect, largely because people generally expect others to be in a positively or negatively valenced emotional state most of the time (i.e., *not* neutral) (see Felleman, Barden, Carlson, Rosenberg, & Masters, 1983; Reichenbach & Masters, 1983). If this kind of inferential bias concerning others' emotions is true, it could explain why children and adults in this study tended to infer the relevant outcome-dependent emotions in story characters experiencing good or bad luck, rather than inferring anhedonic emotions like surprise or neutral affect.

Third, it is important to note that surprise (or "nothing") is a more transient emotional state than are other attribution-dependent emotions. Thus, if participants considered how the story character felt in a more enduring sense, they may have inferred the relevant outcome-dependent emotion rather than attributing surprise. In sum, multiple explanations can be offered for the failure of these findings (and others) to confirm the theoretically expected linkage between luck attributions and emotional inferences of surprise or neutral affect. Each merits further empirical exploration, in part because each has important implications for the kind of attributional analysis outlined in this chapter.

To summarize, it seems that a broadened attribution-emotion formulation is required to encompass the developmental findings reported here and in other studies. Such a broadened view must take into consideration a host of socialization influences as well as social-cognitive processes that are likely to interact complexly with the growth of attributional understanding in childhood. These include the ways in which emotion knowledge is transmitted to children by important socialization agents (and, quite simply, the broadened ecological contexts in which such knowledge is provided), the nature of culture-specific attributional tendencies and biases, children's growing mastery of the psychological complexity of emotional experiences in others, the salience of different attributional cues as these are affected by social learning as well as by their cognitive demands, and the emergence of self-reflection as an avenue of emotional understanding (Selman, 1980). These influences suggest that important developmental changes are occurring in the nature of secondary appraisal itself – that is, in how children are assessing in progressively more sophisticated ways the causal determinants of situations they encounter. Many of these influences on the development of emotional understanding remain poorly understood, and thus there is a substantial research agenda here. However, such an agenda must be taken seriously by students of the attribution-emotion model in order to construct a thoroughgoing *developmental* analysis of the growth of emotional inferencing skills in childhood.

Finally, in view of the research questions motivating this investigation, three additional comments on the findings are necessary. First, it is noteworthy that there were no consistent main effects for the content domain of the stories (i.e., achievement or moral) in the analyses of emotional inferences or the explanations offered for them. This suggests that, despite the important conceptual differences between these domains of reasoning, children's thinking concerning emotional behavior may be highly comparable. This is important news to students of social cognition who may wish to exploit this commonality to explore other areas of similarity in thinking about these situational domains. Second, although the story outcome did not have a systematic influence on the kinds of emotional inferences offered by children and adults, it did affect the explanations offered for these inferences. When failure occurred, there was a greater proportion of explanations focusing on causal considerations in the story narrative, suggesting greater depth to the causal analysis of children and adults. This finding, together with a similar report by Trabasso and colleagues (1981), suggests that failure may indeed heighten the salience of causal circumstances for children as well as adults, perhaps because of an increased motivation to account for the lack of success (e.g., Wong & Weiner, 1981). Third, and finally, there were no sex differences reported in any of the studies reviewed in this chapter. This rather consistent finding suggests that the kinds of emotional inferencing processes outlined here are not substantially affected by gender-related socialization processes bearing on emotional understanding in children and adults. This is a provocative conclusion – partly because gender differences have been found in other aspects of attributional understanding – and warrants further examination by students of gender socialization.

General conclusions

The research reported in this chapter concerning the attribution-emotion model suggests that children may proceed through three rough steps in the construction of attribution-emotion linkages. In their earliest understandings of emotion in themselves and others, young children are likely to rely on cognitively uncomplicated outcome-dependent emotions such as happy and sad, which are not only early elements of a child's emotional lexicon but can also be easily understood due to their reliance on a straightforward assessment of success or failure (i.e., "primary appraisal"). Not long afterward, however, children begin mastering more complex emotion concepts that are deemed "attribution-dependent" according to this formulation. At this second step in the development of emotional understanding, however, it appears that children's earliest usages of these concepts are nondiscriminating: They are likely to be predictably related to the kinds of eliciting conditions identified by attribution theorists, but also to a variety of other situations as well. Like many linguistic concepts, in other words, it appears that these earliest usages of attribution-dependent emotions are "bootstrapped" onto the specific socialization experiences through which these concepts are initially encountered. Thus, children at this step of understanding often do not reliably demonstrate an appreciation of the linkage of these emotion concepts to specific attributional cues. However, they may still engage in a "secondary analysis" of emotionally arousing situations in their efforts to understand the causal antecedents of these situations. There is reason to believe, however, that the quality of their secondary analysis may differ qualitatively from that of older children and adults in many situations, in part because of existing limitations on cognate areas of social-cognitive understanding.

Finally, a third step in the development of emotional understanding is achieved when children begin to master – in part through broadened causal understanding – the specific attributional cues related to these emotions. At this point, earlier understandings of these emotion concepts become more refined and discriminatingly linked to particular causal conditions as their causal analysis of such situations becomes more sophisiticated. It should be emphasized, however, that this three-step sequence does not approximate a stagelike model: Several studies indicate, for example, that children's construction of specific attribution-emotion linkages does not occur in parallel fashion for different emotions, but occurs at different ages and at distinct acquisition rates. For example, children master the linkage between the intervention of another and the emotions of gratitude and anger long before they demonstrate an understanding of the personal effort–pride–guilt association. Thus, a developmental analysis must focus on specific kinds of attribution-emotion linkages, rather than looking at the development of global attributional skills.

Throughout, I have emphasized that a thoroughgoing developmental analysis of emotional understanding must entail a broadening of the attribution-emotion framework initially proposed by Weiner and Graham, taking into consideration a range of allied socialization and social-cognitive processes that also have important influences on the growth of emotional knowledge. The paragraphs above outline an ambitious agenda for researchers who are interested in developing such a broadened formulation. Several other issues, not outlined above, also merit further attention.

First, it will become increasingly important for attribution-emotion theorists to consider the generality of their model, especially in light of the rapidly burgeoning research literature on the development of emotion and emotional understanding. For example, because emotional experiences are complex and multi-determined, how reliable is the link between specific causal antecedents and derivative emotional reactions? Weiner (1985a) has recently indicated that an emotion may be experienced in the absence of its linked antecedent and, conversely, a linked emotion does not necessarily follow from a specific causal ascription. Given this, can researchers identify the boundary conditions of this formulation: the conditions, in other words, that better define when specific attribution-emotion linkages can be expected to occur and when they may not? Does the attribution-emotion model help us to understand emotional blends, for example, which may be a more frequently occurring experience than singular emotional arousal? Can it provide a useful understanding of ambivalent or conflicting emotions experienced simultaneously? Most of the children in my research identified more than one emotion in the story character – what does this indicate for their understanding of emotion in others and the causal analysis that precedes it? And how is the applicability of the attribution-emotion model influenced by culture-specific attributional biases, such as those outlined above with respect to luck? Serious consideration of these questions will help to specify more precisely the potential contributions of this approach.

Second, it will be equally important for researchers to consider the nature of developmental changes in children's causal analysis as a corollary issue to the development of emotional understanding. As I have indicated above, it is likely that many of the developmental changes in emotional inferences identified thus far in the literature derive not from a developmental transition from primary to secondary appraisal processes, but rather from a growing sophistication in the *kind* of causal search in which children spontaneously engage. What is needed here is to proceed beyond a distinction between "primary appraisal" and "secondary appraisal," and to consider developmental changes in the nature of "secondary appraisal" itself. How does the causal search of children change with development: Do they recognize a broader range of causal agents? develop a more discriminating analysis of the causes underlying different situations? acquire a more differentiated comprehension of causal agents that are longstanding elements of a child's causal lexicon? In addition, as noted above, it seems likely that the quality of causal search that children use in responding to personal experiences of emotional arousal is different from the search they use in appraising the experiences of others, and this merits further study. For example, Miller and Green (1985) have described the kinds of coping processes ("secondary appraisal") used by children in situations giving rise to threat and frustration, which are doubtless different from how children appraise similar experiences of others. Does self-understanding of emotional arousal and its antecedents, in this sense, act as the vanguard for other-understanding? Are there situations in which this relation is reversed?

It is important that in a recent review of the literature on "spontaneous" causal analyses, Weiner (1985b) found a very small number of studies examining the kinds of causal searches used by children, and this is an important shortcoming in our knowledge. Connell (1985), for example, has noted that in achievement situations, children become more sure of what causes them to succeed and fail with increasing age, although "unknown" causes remain an important part of their attributional analysis throughout the school years. What is also unknown is what implications this may have for the growth of emotional inferencing skills.

Third, the nature of individual differences in causal analysis and its emotional implications has received very little exploration thus far. It seems reasonable to expect that children develop different attributional "styles" as a consequence of parent child-rearing practices (e.g., disciplinary procedures), their experiences in the broader ecology of development (e.g., inner-city versus middle-class settings), and perhaps also with their range of prior emotional experiences and temperamental style (see Dienstbier, 1979). The developmental study of individual differences promises to provide additional light on attribution-emotion linkages by highlighting normative influences that lead to idiosyncratic modes of causal analysis in children of different ages.

Fourth, and finally, new methodologies must be employed by researchers in this area to better grasp the natural conditions eliciting emotion in children of different ages. Many of the prevailing methodologies in this literature present children with highly salient and specific attributional or emotional cues in abstract stimulus conditions, or seek to evoke personal recollections of experiences within well-defined scenarios. Under rather stereotyped emotion-eliciting conditions, children can demonstrate the predicted patterns of attribution-emotion understanding at remarkably young ages. What remains to be demonstrated is how this is relevant to children's emotional responses in common, everyday situations that are meaningful to them, and how an attributional analysis can inform our appreciation of naturally occurring emotion in children. This could profitably begin at a descriptive level in order to document how emotional understanding is gradually constructed by children as they grow up. Furthermore, as noted earlier, greater use of methodologies that rely less on children's understanding of semantic emotion labels will help us to distinguish the development of children's conceptual understanding of emotion from their ability to use linguistic labels appropriately.

In a seminal article, Graham and Weiner (1986) argued that attribution theory has much to offer the field of developmental psychology, but confessed "bafflement" concerning what developmental psychology could offer attribution theory. It should be clear that a wide-ranging developmental analysis of the growth of attribution-emotion linkages in childhood promises to provide important insights into how these linkages are gradually constructed by children and the meanings they have for children as well as adults. In this manner, developmental research promises to inform attribution theory also.

Notes

1. For example, Weiner and Graham (1984) have suggested that some attribution-emotion linkages may have a genetic basis.
2. I am grateful to Paul Harris for suggesting this idea.
3. There were no causal attributions to the story character's ability because the emotional inferences likely to be generated by ability attributions are not easily distinguished from those associated with effort attributions, especially in view of the limited vocabulary of the young children interviewed in this study.
4. Pretesting indicated that causes involving luck often have a "discounting effect" on emotional experience, with subjects reporting that they would feel nothing because the outcome was capricious. For this reason, "neutral" was included (in addition to "surprise") as a predicted attribution-dependent inference in story conditions involving luck as a cause. The results of this study would have been little affected, however, if inferences of surprise had been considered alone.

References

Borke, H. (1971). Interpersonal perception of young children: egocentrism or empathy? *Developmental Psychology, 5,* 263–269.

Bretherton, I., & Beeghly, M. (1982). Talking about internal states: the acquisition of an explicit theory of mind. *Developmental Psychology, 18,* 906–921.

Bretherton, I., McNew, S., & Beeghly-Smith, M. (1981). Early person knowledge as expressed in gestural and verbal communication: when do infants acquire a "theory of mind"? In M. E. Lamb & L. R. Sherrod (Eds.), *Infant social cognition* (pp. 333–373). Hillsdale, NJ: Erlbaum.

Bretherton, I., Fritz, J., Zahn-Waxler, C., & Ridgeway, D. (1986). Learning to talk about emotions: a functionalist perspective. *Child Development, 57,* 529–548.

Burns, N., & Cavey, L. (1957). Age differences in empathic ability among children. *Canadian Journal of Psychology, 11,* 227–230.

Carroll, J. J., & Steward, M. S. (1984). The role of cognitive development in children's understandings of their own feelings. *Child Development, 55,* 1486–1492.

Connell, J. P. (1985). A new multidimensional measure of children's perceptions of control. *Child Development, 56,* 1018–1041.

Dienstbier, R. A. (1979). Emotion-attribution theory: establishing roots and exploring future perspectives. In H. E. Howe, Jr., & R. A. Dienstbier (Eds.), *Nebraska symposium on motivation,* Vol. 26 (pp. 237–306). Lincoln: University of Nebraska Press.

Donaldson, S. K., & Westerman, M. A. (1986). Development of children's understanding of ambivalence and causal theories of emotion. *Developmental Psychology, 22,* 655–662.

Dunn, J., & Kendrick, C. (1982a). Siblings and their mothers: developing relationships within the family. In M. E. Lamb & B. Sutton-Smith (Eds.), *Sibling relationships* (pp. 39–60). Hillsdale, NJ: Erlbaum.

Dunn, J., & Kendrick, C. (1982b). *Siblings: love, envy, and understanding.* Cambridge: Harvard University Press.

Dweck, C. S., & Elliot, E. S. (1983). Achievement motivation. In P. H. Mussen (Ed.), *Handbook of child psychology.* Vol. IV. *Socialization, personality, and social development* (E. Mavis Hetherington, Vol. Ed.) (pp. 643–691). New York: Wiley.

Felleman, E. S., Barden, R. C., Carlson, C. R., Rosenberg, K., & Masters, J. C. (1983). Children's and adult's recognition of spontaneous and posed emotional expressions in young children. *Developmental Psychology, 19,* 405–413.

Gnepp, J. (1983). Children's social sensitivity: inferring emotions from conflicting cues. *Developmental Psychology, 19,* 805–814.

Gnepp, J., Klayman, J., & Trabasso, T. (1982). A hierarchy of information sources for inferring emotional reactions. *Journal of Experimental Child Psychology, 33,* 111–123.

Graham, S. (1984). Communicating sympathy and anger to black and white children: The cognitive (attributional) consequences of affective cues. *Journal of Personality and Social Psychology, 47,* 40–54.

Graham, S. (1985). *The developing influence of affect on social behavior.* Unpublished manuscript, University of California at Los Angeles.

Graham, S., Doubleday, C., & Guarino, P. A. (1984). The development of relations between perceived controllability and the emotions of pity, anger, and guilt. *Child Development, 55,* 561–565.

Graham, S., & Weiner, B. (1986). From an attributional theory of emotion to developmental psychology: a round-trip ticket? *Social Cognition, 4,* 152–179.

Green, S. K. (1977). Causal attribution of emotion in kindergarten children. *Developmental Psychology, 13,* 533–534.

Greenspan, S., Barenboim, C., & Chandler, M. J. (1976). Empathy and pseudo-empathy: the affective judgments of first- and third-graders. *Journal of Genetic Psychology, 129,* 77–88.

Harris, P. L., & Olthof, T. (1982). The child's concept of emotion. In G. Butterworth & P. Light (Eds.), *Social cognition: studies in the development of understanding* (pp. 188–209). Chicago: University of Chicago Press.

Harris, P. L., Olthof, T., & Meerum Terwogt, M. (1981). Children's knowledge of emotion. *Journal of Child Psychology and Psychiatry, 22,* 247–261.

Harter, S. (1982) A cognitive-developmental approach to children's understanding of affect and trait labels. In F. C. Serafica (Ed.), *Social-cognitive development in context* (pp. 27–61). New York: Guilford.

Iannotti, R. (1978). Effect of role-taking experiences on role taking, empathy, altruism, and aggression. *Developmental Psychology, 14,* 119–124.

Izard, C. (1971). *The face of emotion.* New York: Appleton-Century-Crofts.

Kohlberg, L. (1976). Moral stages and moralization: the cognitive-developmental approach. In T. Lickona (Ed.), *Moral development and behavior* (pp. 31–53). New York: Holt, Rinehart & Winston.

Kurdek, L. A., & Rodgon, M. M. (1975). Perceptual, cognitive, and affective perspective-taking in kindergarten through sixth-grade children. *Developmental Psychology, 11,* 643–650.

Masters, J. C., & Carlson, C. R. (1984). Children's and adults' understanding of the causes and consequences of emotional states. In C. Izard, J. Kagan, & R. Zajonc (Eds.), *Emotions, cognition and behavior* (pp. 438–463). New York: Cambridge University Press.

Miller, S. M., & Green, M. L. (1985). Coping with stress and frustration: origins, nature, and development. In M. Lewis & C. Saarni (Eds.), *The socialization of emotions* (pp. 263–314). New York: Plenum.

Mood, D. W., Johnson, J. E., & Shantz, C. U. (1978). Social comprehension and affect-matching in young children. *Merrill-Palmer Quarterly, 24,* 63–66.

Nicholls, J. G. (1978). The development of the concepts of effort and ability, perception of academic attainment, and the understanding that difficult tasks require more ability. *Child Development, 49,* 800–814.

Odom, R. D., & Lemond, C. M. (1972). Developmental differences in the perception and production of facial expressions. *Child Development, 43,* 359–369.

Reichenbach, L., & Masters, J. C. (1983). Children's use of expressive and contextual cues in judgments of emotion. *Child Development, 54,* 993–1004.

Ruble, D. N. (1983). The development of social-comparison processes and their role in achievement-related self-socialization. In E. T. Higgins, D. N. Ruble, & W. W. Hartup (Eds.) *Social cognition and social development* (pp. 134–157). Cambridge: Cambridge University Press.

Russell, J. A., & Ridgeway, D. (1983). Dimensions underlying children's emotion concepts. *Developmental Psychology, 19,* 795–804.

Saarni, C. (1979). Children's understanding of display rules for expressive behavior. *Developmental Psychology, 15,* 424–429.

Schwartz, R. M., & Trabasso, T. (1984). Children's understanding of emotions. In C. Izard, J. Kagan, & R. Zajonc (Eds.), *Emotions, cognition, and behavior* (pp. 409–437). New York: Cambridge University Press.

Selman, R. L. (1980). *The growth of interpersonal understanding.* New York: Academic Press.

Shantz, C. U. (1983). Social cognition. In P. H. Mussen (Ed.), *Handbook of child psychology: Vol. III. Cognitive development* (J. H. Flavell & E. M. Markman, Vol. Eds.) (pp. 495–555). New York: Wiley.

Stipek, D. J. (1983). A developmental analysis of pride and shame. *Human Development, 26,* 42–54.

Thompson, R. A. (in press). Empathy and emotional understanding: the role of empathic distress in children's experience of guilt. *Cognition and Emotion, 3.*

Thompson, R. A. (1987). Development of children's inferences of the emotions of others. *Developmental Psychology, 23,* 124–131.

Thompson, R. A., & Hoffman, M. L. (1980). Empathy and the development of guilt in children. *Developmental Psychology, 16,* 155–156.

Trabasso, T., Stein, N. L., & Johnson, L. R. (1981). Children's knowledge of events: a causal analysis of story structure. In G. H. Bower (Ed.), *The psychology of learning and motivation* (pp. 237–282). New York: Academic Press.

Weiner, B. (1985a). An attributional theory of achievement motivation and emotion. *Psychological Review, 92,* 548–573.

Weiner, B. (1985b). "Spontaneous" causal thinking. *Psychological Bulletin, 97,* 74–84.

Weiner, B., & Graham, S. (1984). An attributional approach to emotional development. In C. Izard, J. Kagan, & R. Zajonc (Eds.), *Emotions, cognition, and behavior* (pp. 167–191). New York: Cambridge University Press.

Weiner, B., Graham, S., Stern, P., & Lawson, M. E. (1982). Using affective cues to infer causal thoughts. *Developmental Psychology, 18,* 278–286.

Weiner, B., & Handel, S. J. (1985). A cognition–emotion–action sequence: anticipated emotional consequences of causal attributions and reported communication strategy. *Developmental Psychology, 21,* 102–107.

Weiner, B., Kun, A., & Benesh-Weiner, M. (1980). The development of mastery, emotions, and morality from an attributional perspective. In W. A. Collins (Ed.), *Development of cognition, affect, and social relations. Minnesota Symposium on Child Psychology* (Vol. 13, pp. 103–129). Hillsdale, NJ: Erlbaum.

Weiner, B., Russell, D., & Lerman, D. (1978). Affective consequences of causal ascriptions. In J. H. Harvey, W. Ickes, & R. F. Kidd (Eds.), *New directions in attribution research* (Vol. 2, pp. 59–90). Hillsdale, NJ: Erlbaum.

Weiner, B., Russell, D., & Lerman, D. (1979). The cognition–emotion process in achievement-related contexts. *Journal of Personality and Social Psychology, 37,* 1211–1220.

Wolman, R. N., Lewis, W. C., & King, M. (1971). The development of the language of emotions: conditions of emotional arousal. *Child Development, 42,* 1288–1293.

Wong, P., & Weiner, B. (1981). When people ask "why" questions and the heuristics of attributional search. *Journal of Personality and Social Psychology, 40,* 650–663.

6   Children's use of personal information to understand other people's feelings

Jackie Gnepp

The development of children's understanding of other people's feelings has been given much attention in recent years. How do children of different ages figure out what other people feel, and how do they anticipate what others are likely to feel given certain events? In many cases, other people's emotional reactions can be predicted from their physical or social situations because situational factors exert a strong influence over our feelings. In some cases, however, an understanding of other people's feelings can only be achieved by considering factors that lead to individual differences in people's perspectives on similar situations. For example, we might make different inferences about the emotional reactions of a single woman who learns that she is pregnant if we knew that she had traditional middle-class values than if we knew that she had been fretting about her biological clock. A good example with children comes from a study by Chandler (1973). In one of the cartoon sequences he used, a boy is saddened by seeing his father off at the airport. Later, the boy receives a toy airplane in the mail and begins to cry. Only by recognizing that the toy airplane reminds the boy of the departure of his father can we understand why the toy makes him feel sad instead of happy. In this example, we have person-specific information about the boy. We would not wish to generalize from this boy's reaction upon receiving a toy airplane to other children's reactions. In contrast, the adult example illustrated a somewhat broader type of personal information[1]: There are current social norms and sociopolitical viewpoints that differentially influence the reactions of different categories of women to the situation described. In both cases, though, an accurate understanding or prediction requires the use of information that differentiates the individual in question from other people.

For children to understand that there may be group differences and individual

Preparation of this chapter was supported by National Institute of Child Health and Human Development Grant HD18774, which also funded several of the studies described in this chapter. Some of these ideas were presented at a symposium on Children's Understanding of Emotion conducted at the meeting of the Society for Research in Child Development, Toronto, April 1985. I wish to thank Joshua Klayman and Paul Harris for helpful comments on an earlier version of this chapter.

151

differences in people's emotional reactions to events, they must understand that there are psychological as well as situational determinants of other people's feelings. They must distinguish between people likely to share their cognitive interpretations and evaluations of events and people who are unlikely to do so. Such discrimination would require consideration of the nature of the situation (i.e., do people tend to vary in their reactions to this situation or does this situation elicit the same reaction from almost everyone?) and a comparison of the personal characteristics of the other person with those of the self (i.e., does this other person differ from me on a dimension that is relevant to understanding his or her feelings in this situation?). Personal characteristics relevant to understanding another individual's emotional reactions vary in generality. Some apply to broad classes of people (e.g., demographic characteristics, such as age and gender), some apply to a smaller segment of people (e.g., dispositional factors, such as abilities, personality traits, and ideologies), and some are person-specific (e.g., an individual's prior experiences, prior behaviors, and previous emotional reactions).

Among the questions I will consider in this chapter are: What types of personal information can children use when it is available? When do children come to recognize the situations in which personal information is necessary to figure out how another person feels? Are children able to seek such information if it is not readily apparent?

A model of the use of personal information

To begin, I will present a three-phase model for the use of personal information. This is a rational model; that is, it describes how people might logically use personal information to make more sensitive inferences about other people's feelings. When adults are motivated to understand another person's inner experiences, they may use a process somewhat like this one. The extent to which children's behavior appears to conform to this model at different ages will be considered later.

The model starts with the observation of a person in a situation. People's emotions can only be understood in the context of the situations that evoke them because emotions are determined by the individual's evaluation or "appraisal" of the situation (Arnold, 1970; Lazarus, Averill, & Opton, 1970; Levanthal, 1980; Mandler, 1975; Schacter, 1964). Thus, to understand another person's emotional reaction, one must understand that person's perspective on the eliciting events. As Smither (1977) expressed it,

To empathize, the child must understand how the other person feels in regard to a particular situation, and how the other perceives the situation. That is, the child must understand the other's appraisals and evaluations about the situation . . . the observer must conceive of some motivational relation between perceived actions, interactions, and events involving the empathee and his resulting feeling-states. (p. 271)

Sometimes, of course, our understanding of another person's feelings comes not through direct observation of an emotion-arousing situation, but through verbal explanation. Verbal depiction allows us to understand other people's feelings about either private experiences or situations in the past and tends to provide information about the person's appraisals as well as about the situation itself (Smither, 1977). For our purposes, then, observing a person in a situation is taken to include learning this information through verbal re-creation of the original event as well as observing the person in the situation first-hand.

At this point, it would be helpful to define a "situation." Clearly, situational contexts surround us at all times, are multifaceted and constantly changing, and move in and out of our conscious awareness. For our purposes, however, a situation is defined as a single, observable event or episode that may take less than a second (e.g., a bolt of lightning) or may last weeks (e.g., having the flu). Situations are not defined by time, but by our perception of them as unitary elicitors of our reactions. In this definition, concurrent situations (e.g., a lightning storm occurring while you have the flu) are treated as multiple situations that would occasion multiple passes through the three-phase model. Similarly, compound situations (e.g., opening a gift that your little brother then snatches away) are treated as separate situations that would be analyzed individually. This is not to deny that the emotional effects of one situational component can interact with those of other situational components (Harris, 1983). Indeed, interactive effects can occur with completely separate situations as well (Thaler, 1985). Rather, it is to suggest that determining people's reactions to compound situations requires us to proceed through the three-phase model more than once, each time beginning with the person in one of the component situations.

Why not begin the model with the observation of a person and his or her expressions of emotion (facial, vocal, postural, or behavioral)? There are two related reasons for not doing so. Each has to do with the idea that emotions are defined by cognitive aspects. One is that the recognition and labeling of an emotional expression is not the same as the understanding of an individual's inner experience. To understand an individual's inner experience one must understand something about what the individual is reacting to and what leads her or him to react in that way. The second reason is that emotions often cannot be correctly identified on the basis of overt expressive behavior alone. Rather, emotions identified in this way may be confused with other emotions having different cognitive referents, but similar behavioral components (Frijda, 1969). For example, feelings of regret, hurt pride, loneliness, and sympathy for another's pain, although very different emotions, might all involve similarly sad facial expressions, postures, and so forth. Research with children has tended to focus on the simplest emotions – namely, happy, sad, angry, and afraid. These are the emotions most clearly associated with discrete facial expressions and characteristic behaviors. Admittedly, when working with children, the emotion researcher must study those emotions that children understand. However, it has been argued that the focus on these emotions has restricted the study of the processes involved in understanding other people's feelings by drawing attention away from the many emotions that can only be recognized and understood with reference to contextual meanings and to the individual's motives (Harris, Olthof, Meerum, Terwogt, & Hardman, 1987; Smither, 1977). Thus, the three-phase model for the use of personal information to understand emotion begins with the observation of a person in a situation and treats emotional expression as just one more cue to the individual's appraisal.

The first phase of this three-phase model involves determining whether or not the use of personal information is called for (see Figure 6.1). As indicated earlier, people's feelings can often be inferred from situational information alone, based on knowledge of typical human reactions to events. However, different people sometimes have different emotional reactions to the same event because they evaluate the situation differently. Therefore, the first step (1A) is to determine whether the situation is associated with a single emotional reaction or with more than one emotional reaction. If the situation commonly elicits different emotions in different people, then we should recognize that personal information is needed to infer an individual's reaction (step 1C). If, however, the situation is strongly associated with a single emotion, then it may be reasonable and efficient to infer that the other person's reaction is the typical emotional reaction (step 1A to 1B to 3A). Relying on the usual emotional association to a situation is appropriate if there is no other information available, or if other information is consistent with the emotion typically associated with the situation. However, if other information suggests that the person may not be experiencing the usual emotional reaction (step 1B), then we should again recognize that personal information about the individual is needed (step 1C).

The second phase of the three-phase process involves seeking personal information, if that information is judged necessary. Seeking personal information might involve asking questions about the particular individual, or it might involve reviewing one's knowledge of the individual to see if pertinent information is already available. The information obtained (steps 2A and 2B) can then be used to reach an understanding of the individual's emotional reaction.

Phase 3 of the emotion-inference process involves predicting and/or explaining the other person's feelings. In the simplest cases we can do this by inferring that the individual feels the way most people do in that situation (step 3A). However, when we have qualifying personal information available, a more sophisticated approach requires the coordination of the personal and situational

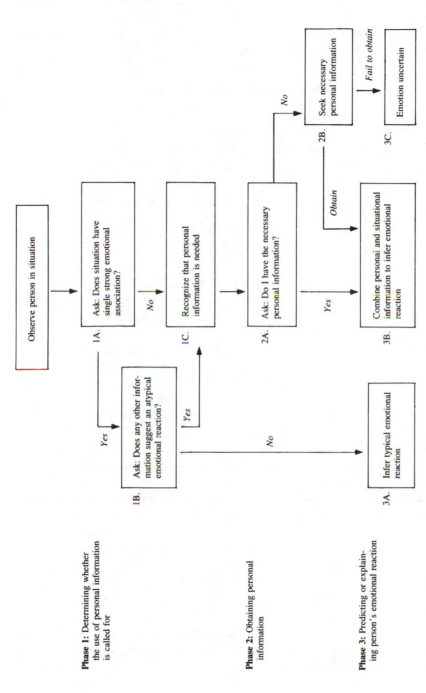

Phase 1: Determining whether the use of personal information is called for

1A. Ask: Does situation have single strong emotional association?

1B. Ask: Does any other information suggest an atypical emotional reaction?

1C. Recognize that personal information is needed

Phase 2: Obtaining personal information

2A. Ask: Do I have the necessary personal information?

2B. Seek necessary personal information

Phase 3: Predicting or explaining person's emotional reaction

3A. Infer typical emotional reaction

3B. Combine personal and situational information to infer emotional reaction

3C. Emotion uncertain

Observe person in situation

Figure 6.1. Three-phase model for the use of personal information to understand other people's feelings.

information (step 3B). There are also cases in which we remain unsure that we have understood another person (step 3C). This happens when we recognize a need for personal information but are unable to obtain the relevant information to let us decide among the alternatives.

Research on children's emotional inferences

Most of the research on children's affective inferences has focused on the final Phase 3 judgments without analyzing the intervening processes; that is, most studies have examined children's judgments of other people's feelings given a limited amount of information about the person and the situational context. As a result, we know relatively little about the changes in these component processes that underly the changes in children's ability to understand other people's feelings.

Inferring emotions from situations

In the simplest case (following the model down the left-hand side), a situational inference is sufficient to infer another person's feelings. Imagine that a child is sitting by her dog and the dog is very ill. At step 1A, we realize that the person's situation has a single, strong emotional association; in this case, sadness. This leads to step 1B, where we find no additional information to suggest that this person is experiencing an atypical emotional reaction. Thus, we would infer the emotional reaction that is typically associated with this situation. Research has consistently shown that young children can make such emotional inferences successfully if the situations described are simple and familiar (Barden, Zelko, Duncan, & Masters, 1980; Borke, 1971, 1973; Gnepp, 1983; Gnepp, Klayman, & Trabasso, 1982; Mood, Johnson, & Shantz, 1978; Reichenbach & Masters, 1983), and if the emotions implied are simple and familiar (Brody & Harrison, 1987; Wiggers & van Lieshout, 1985).

Two methods have been proposed by which children infer emotions from situations. One method involves attributing to the other person the feelings one imagines for oneself in that situation. This method of inferring other people's feelings has been termed "projection" by some (Chandler & Greenspan, 1972; Dymond, 1950; Hastorf & Bender, 1952) because the subject projects his or her own imagined feelings onto the other person. Inferring other people's feelings by reference to the self is an effective method primarily when the situation is a familiar one and when the other person is similar to oneself. Hughes, Tingle, and Sawin (1981), for example, reported that kindergarten children show increased understanding of other children's feelings following reflection on their own emotional reactions to similar situations.

The second method by which children might infer emotions from situations involves generalizing across all people to determine what feelings people in general would have in response to those circumstances. In other words, the child attributes to the other person the most common emotional reaction to the situation. This method has been termed "stereotypy" or "stereotypic accuracy" (Chandler & Greenspan, 1972; Cronbach, 1955; Gage & Cronbach, 1955). The effectiveness of inferring another person's emotions by thinking about people in general depends on one's knowledge of the relative frequency of various emotional reactions to the situation.

When only situational cues to emotion are provided, it is difficult to know if children are inferring the other person's emotion by imagining how they themselves would feel in that situation, or by thinking about how people in general feel in such situations. Both processes are likely to lead to the same response because children as young as 4 years of age show a high degree of consensus about their anticipated emotional reactions to a variety of emotional situations (Barden et al., 1980; Silverman & Drabman, 1983). Thus, although different in principle, projection and thinking about people in general are, in practice, likely to lead to the same inferences.

Recognizing equivocal situations

Thus far we have been discussing situations that have a single strong emotional association. In such cases, judging other people's feelings from the situational context is usually sufficient because people commonly share their appraisals of those affect-laden events. However, there are many cases in which an emotional reaction cannot be inferred from the situation alone with any confidence. As indicated in steps 1A and 1B of the model, this is the case when the situation itself lacks a single predominant emotional implication, or when there is information available suggesting that the usual implication does not apply in the present case. Thus, the first step toward sophisticated emotional reasoning is the ability to recognize when the acquisition and use of personal information is called for.

To begin, consider step 1A of the model. Despite the pervasive commonalities among people, there are many situations that are associated with quite a bit of variation in how people react. Consider the example of a person whose job change requires a move from a rural to an urban setting. Some people prefer rural living, whereas others prefer an urban lifestyle. Thus, it would not be possible to judge this person's emotional reaction to the move on the basis of the situational information alone. Rather, we would need to know something about this person's tastes and preferences. Similarly, for situations in which mixed feelings are possible, we would need personal information to determine whether the individual experienced more than one emotion and, if so, the relative strengths of each emotion.

When a situation is emotionally equivocal (associated with more than one emotion), it is inappropriate to judge another person's feelings from the situational context alone. Instead, observing a person in such a situation should cue us to recognize that personal information is needed before we can predict the person's feelings with any confidence (steps 1A and 1C).

Before learning how to make emotional inferences in equivocal situations, children must develop the understanding that situations *can be* equivocal, that is, that situations can evoke different reactions in different people. The earliest recognition that situations evoke different feelings in different people probably occurs with regard to situations in which reactions vary according to broad groups of people. For example, there are situations that take on different meaning for older versus younger people or for males versus females. Whereas a 3-year-old girl might infer that her older brother or her mother would be happy to receive a doll as a gift, children rarely make such egocentric inferences by age 6 (Flavell, Botkin, Fry, Wright, & Jarvis, 1968; Zahn-Waxler, Radke-Yarrow, & Brady-Smith, 1977). Similarly, when asked what would make parents feel various emotions, only preschoolers give child-appropriate responses such as, "Mommy would be sad if she couldn't go out and play" (Harter, 1982). By early school age, then, children have some understanding that situations can be emotionally equivocal, at least in cases where broad cultural stereotypes such as age and gender apply.

Children also need to be aware of the existence of individual differences that cannot be inferred from cultural norms. For example, some children are fond of dogs and will play with any who seem willing, whereas others are wary of dogs and will avoid even the friendliest of them. Gnepp, McKee, and Domanic (1987) did a series of studies to find out whether children recognize that some situations commonly elicit different emotional reactions in different people, and that they cannot be certain how a person will feel in such equivocal situations. Gnepp et al. presented children with a set of scenarios describing different situations. Some scenarios described unequivocal situations (situations where the base rate for one particular emotion is high) and some described equivocal situations (situations "that commonly elicit positive emotional reactions in some people and negative reactions in others," p. 115). For each scenario, children from kindergarten through third grade were asked to say they were thinking of one feeling if they were *sure* how the story character felt, but to say they were thinking of two feelings if maybe the person felt one way or maybe felt a different way. In a second experiment, the children were asked to say if almost everyone feels the same way about these situations or if some kids like them and some kids don't like them.

The results indicated that even kindergarten children are aware that almost everyone feels the same way about unequivocal situations (e.g., they like getting a new toy; they don't like losing a race; they are scared to be alone in the dark) and that different people feel differently about emotionally equivocal situations (e.g., some kids like dogs and some kids don't; some kids like egg salad sandwiches and some kids don't). However, when asked to think about the emotional reaction of an individual, children often failed to acknowledge that the person might feel one way or might feel a different way, even in situations that elicited the response "some kids like it and some don't." The 5- and 6-year-olds felt sure that they understood the emotional reaction of an individual in an equivocal situation and they tended to say they were thinking of only one feeling for both the equivocal and unequivocal situations. Older children were more likely to say they were thinking of both positive and negative emotional reactions for the equivocal situations while continuing to think of only one feeling for the unequivocal situations. These children explained their choices of two feelings primarily by referring to the person's appraisal of the situation (e.g., "maybe he likes dogs, or maybe he thinks the dog might bite him"). However, about half the time, even the 8-year-olds reported thinking of only one possible feeling for a person in an emotionally equivocal situation. These results suggest the possibility that children understand the uncertainty of the link between equivocal situations and emotions when thinking about groups of people, but lose sight of this relationship when thinking about individuals.

A study by Gove and Keating (1979) also provides evidence about children's understanding that different people feel differently about emotionally equivocal situations. They presented preschoolers with stories and pictures describing events involving two story characters. In two of the stories the outcome was the same for each character (e.g., receiving a dog), but the facial expressions of each character differed (for the dog story, happy versus scared). Some of the children were able to provide explanations, either psychological, physiological, or situational, to account for the differing facial expressions in the presence of seemingly identical situations. Five-year-olds accounted for the different facial expressions by suggesting "psychological differences" (e.g., she likes dogs; he's afraid of dogs) slightly more than half the time, whereas 3-year-olds did so less than a third of the time. Children who were unable to provide these psychological explanations tended to reconstruct the situation (e.g., one dog has teeth and the other does not) or, less commonly, appeal to physical health. Gove and Keating considered these latter responses to be failures of explanation because they do not demonstrate an understanding that the *same* situation may give rise to different feelings in different people.

When a situation is equivocal, it is usually because people can have different appraisals of that situation, and a person's reaction is determined by his or her appraisal. The appraisal may depend on the specific situational aspect to which the individual attends (e.g., the fun and affection of a puppy versus its need to be housebroken and taken for early morning walks) or on some personal characteristic of the individual (e.g., previous negative experiences with dogs). Multiple appraisals can occur not only across individuals, as described above, but also within individuals. That is, one individual may have multiple appraisals of an event (e.g., this medicine will make me feel better, but it sure tastes awful; or it's fun to go to summer camp, but I might get homesick). Consequently, it is possible for an individual to experience more than one emotion in response to an event.

Harter (1982) has found that during the early school years, children deny the possibility of a person's experiencing more than one emotion in response to a single situation. Not until about age 9, on average, do children understand that a person may experience multiple emotions simultaneously (see also Harris, 1983). Thus, children must learn two things about emotionally equivocal situations. One is that different people react differently to such situations and, as a consequence, an individual's reaction to emotionally equivocal situations cannot be inferred from the situational context alone. The other is that it is possible for a person to experience more than one emotional reaction to such equivocal situations as a result of multiple appraisals of the same situation.

When information suggests an atypical reaction

As indicated in the model, personal information should be considered not only when the situation is equivocal, but also when there is information to suggest that the individual may not be experiencing the typical reaction to an event. The suggestion of an atypical emotional reaction (step 1B) should lead us to recognize that personal information is needed (step 1C), and to consider whether or not we have the necessary personal information (step 2A). Consider, for example, cases in which a person exhibits expressive cues that seem incongruent with the situational context. Several studies have presented children with just such conflicting cues to emotion (Burns & Cavey, 1957; Denham, 1986; Deutsch, 1974; Gnepp, 1983; Greenspan, Barenboim, & Chandler, 1976; Hoffner & Badzinski, 1987; Iannotti, 1978; Kurdek & Rodgon, 1975; Reichenbach & Masters, 1983; Urberg & Docherty, 1976; Wiggers & van Lieshout, 1985). In most of these studies, children are asked to judge another person's feelings given facial expressive cues that suggest one emotion and situational cues that suggest a different emotion (e.g., a frowning child at a birthday party).

Several researchers assumed that the character's expressive cues were sufficient personal information. Thus, they reasoned that a mature (or empathic) response would be to infer that the character's true feelings were those suggested by the expressive cues (Burns & Cavey, 1957; Iannotti, 1978; Kurdek & Rodgon, 1975). Contrary to expectations, preschoolers and kindergartners were found to make their emotional judgments primarily on the basis of facial expressions, whereas older children increasingly relied on the situational cues in making their judgments (see also Gnepp, 1983; Hoffner & Badzinski, 1987; Reichenbach & Masters, 1983).

Other investigators took the position that expressive cues alone did not provide sufficient personal information to understand an individual's feelings. For example, Greenspan et al. (1976) suggested that a mature response to the conflicting cues they presented would be to express uncertainty about the character's emotions. They showed children a videotape in which a man looks amused after losing at arm wrestling. Emotional understanding, according to Greenspan et al., consisted in accurately reporting the incongruous facial expression and indicating uncertainty about the character's feelings. Similarly, Smither (1977) argued that "if the situation and action cues are incongruent, then we cannot empathize because we cannot make sense of the other's reactions" (p. 258). From this point of view, we would follow the path down the right-hand side of the three-phase model (step 2A through step 2B to step 3C) and conclude that the other person's emotion is uncertain to us.

In natural contexts, however, we can often do more than choose one cue over another, or merely remain uncertain. Rather, when there are conflicting cues to another person's feelings, we consider all the information and attempt to arrive at an understanding that integrates all of the various cues. A study by Gnepp (1983) provides evidence about the extent to which, and the ways in which, children of different ages integrate conflicting cues to emotion. In that study, children were asked to tell stories about six different pictures that portrayed conflicting facial and situational cues to emotion. One such picture is shown in Figure 6.2. Preschool children ages 3 and 4 were able to reconcile the conflicting cues so as to form a coherent conception of the other person's circumstances and reactions 46% of the time. Children ages 6 and 7 were able to do so 65% of the time, and those aged 11 and 12, 80%.

There were also interesting developmental changes in *how* the cues were reconciled. These changes can be illustrated with the stories told by children in response to the picture shown in Figure 6.2 (Gnepp, 1982). When asked to tell a story about a child with a happy facial expression who was about to be inoculated by a doctor, 70% of the preschoolers who integrated the conflicting cues did so by attributing an idiosyncratic perspective to the character (e.g., "He's happy because the doctor's going to shoot him; because he likes shots"). Such attribution of idiosyncracy probably represents an early precursor of the ability to understand the psychological causes of people's reactions to situations. These responses resemble later psychological explanations in their use of words that imply mental appraisals and goals – words such as *like, want,* and *try* – but they provide no explanation for *why* the person might have that reaction. Such expla-

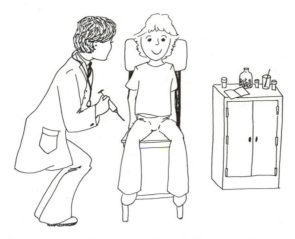

Figure 6.2. Example of a conflicting cues picture (Gnepp, 1982, 1983).

nations might involve elaborating on the situation (i.e., introducing new events or aspects of the situation that would change the character's view of the situation), or suggesting that the character was actually reacting to a different situation. The remaining 30% of the 3- and 4-year-olds who integrated the conflicting cues did so by providing such explanations.

In contrast, 88% of the 6- and 7-year-olds who reconciled the conflicting cues did so by elaborating on the situation (e.g., "This girl had to get her appendix taken out and she was happy because they hurt her so much when they were in"). The majority of 11- and 12-year-olds (61%) also integrated the conflicting cues by elaborating on the situation. However, another 35% of them told stories in which the character masked the expression of emotion (e.g., "She's about to get the shot, so she's like hanging onto the chair, smiling, trying to hide her fear from the doctor"). Data from the full set of stories (Gnepp, 1983) indicate that children of all ages were likely to reconstruct the situation, but the tendency to suggest that the other person has an idiosyncratic opinion all but disappears by age 6, as children's ability to elaborate on the situation improves. New ways of understanding conflicting cues also develop later in childhood, especially as children learn the social functions served by display rules (see Gnepp & Hess, 1986; Saarni, 1979).

Seeking personal information

Generally speaking, children who participate in experiments like those described above are not given the opportunity to ask questions about, or otherwise obtain, personal information about the people whose emotions they are to judge. Of course, children do bring their understanding of emotions and considerable world knowledge to bear in judging other people's probable reactions. If they are unable to obtain the additional information necessary to figure out precisely how the other person feels, they can at least generate some reasonable hypotheses, as described above. However, in natural contexts, when children feel uncertain about how another person is reacting or will react to a situation, they may attempt to seek further information. Little is known about children's ability to seek needed personal information or about their proclivity to do so. Although even toddlers will occasionally ask for situational information (e.g., "You sad Mommy. What Daddy do?"; Bretherton & Beeghly, 1982), there is little evidence of children's asking for personal information except inadvertently through "why" questions.

Children's ability to seek information to help them make emotional inferences was investigated in two studies (Gould, 1984; Gnepp & Johnson, 1989). In the study by Gould, children ranging in age from 5 to 11 were instructed to ask questions to help them figure out how other children would react to emotionally equivocal situations. In analyzing their questions, Gould found that older children were more likely than younger ones to ask about the story characters' preferences (e.g., "Does Chris like cauliflower?"), even though children at all ages could use that information to infer the characters' feelings if it was provided. Gould also reported that the 5- and 6-year-old children found it difficult to ask questions at all.

Gnepp and Johnson (1989) studied the types of information requested by children aged 9, 11, and 13 who were presented with emotionally equivocal scenarios. Requests for information about the story characters' cognitive appraisals, past experiences, or past behaviors were classified as questions seeking personal information. Other questions were categorized as either requests for information about the characters' concurrent thoughts, feelings, and behavior, or as requests for situational information. The tendency to request personal information increased with age, but also was influenced by story content. In a follow-up study, an independent sample of children of the same ages ranked sets of questions in terms of their usefulness for inferring the characters' feelings. Interestingly, children at all the ages studied selected the personal information as most helpful, although story content again had a strong effect on children's information preferences. Thus, it appears that children demonstrate a preference for having personal information before they are reliably able to formulate requests for that information.

The studies by Gould and by Gnepp and Johnson are unusual in allowing children to seek additional information beyond the limited amount provided in most studies. It is clear that more research is required before we can understand the development of the ability to obtain the personal information needed for inferring emotion.

Varieties of personal information

When we bring our knowledge about people to bear on our inferences about people's emotional reactions to situations, there are several levels at which we can do so. Assuming that everyone feels the same way about a situation and that we can use ourselves as a standard is the most general. Recognizing cases in which we differ from most other people, and using our understanding of the primary consensus for reactions to a situation, is somewhat more specific. More discriminating than that may be using our knowledge of cultural stereotypes (e.g., how boys differ from girls in their reactions to situations). We can also use more specific norms – for example, the reactions of people from a specific social group (e.g., the Laotian immigrant girls in a particular neighborhood). At a more specific level, we may consider the reactions of people with particular personality traits (e.g., timid children may feel differently about a situation from brave ones, or shy children may feel differently from gregarious ones). And at the most specific level, we may consider person-specific information, that is, information about an individual's unique characteristics (e.g., her or his prior experiences). Thus, recognition of the need for personal information may lead us to seek (Phase 2) and to use (Phase 3) a wide variety of different sources of information about the individual. A number of studies have examined children's understanding of various kinds of personal information. In terms of the three-phase model, such studies follow the center path from step 2A, where we determine that we have the necessary personal information, to step 3B, where we combine this information with the situational information to predict or explain the individual's emotional reaction.

Using knowledge of cultural stereotypes. Although some work on children's social role taking has explored children's ability to take age and gender stereotypes into account, the influence of such broad stereotypes has not been studied much in the area of children's affective perspective taking. Most studies of children's understanding of emotion only require that children make inferences about other children of their own age and gender. A few experimenters have endeavored to minimize children's use of projection by making the target characters dissimilar from the subjects and the target situations ones outside the personal experience of the subjects. For example, both Rothenberg (1970) and Deutsch (1974) used dramatic skits involving adult characters in adult situations. However, such an approach can be problematic when studying children's emotion judgments developmentally because children become increasingly familiar with the adult world as they get older.

Using specific normative information. Gnepp et al. (1982) provide one of the few studies of children's ability to take into account information about the dispositions of people in a particular social group. Subjects were told brief stories about children "who lived in different places." The stories contained normative information about the habitual behavior of children where the story character lives. For example, one of the eight stories was about a girl named Sarah. "She lives in Green Valley. In Green Valley, the people are friendly with tigers and play games with them all the time [normative information]. One day, Sarah was walking along and she saw a tiger." Subjects in this study indicated how they thought the protagonist felt by choosing from among facial expressions representing happy, afraid, or sad/mad. Preschool children (ages 4 and 5), as well as older children (ages 6 and 7) and adults, used the normative information to modify their emotional inferences. For example, given the above information, the children judged Sarah to be happy, whereas children not given that information judged Sarah to feel scared. These results indicate that even preschool children can set aside their use of projection and their thinking about people in general when contradictory normative information is provided.

Using personality traits. Another form of personal information that differentiates categories of people is information about personality. Knowledge of other people's personality characteristics is an especially powerful form of personal information because it may influence people's reactions to a large variety of events; that is, it not only suggests stability across time, but also some consistency across situations. Developmentalists have begun to explore children's ability to infer personality traits and to use these inferred traits to predict future behavior (e.g., Heller & Berndt, 1981; Rholes & Ruble, 1984). However, little attention has been given to children's ability to predict a person's emotional reaction based on an understanding of his or her personality.

To study this, Gnepp and Chilamkurti (1988) constructed six stories, each dealing with a different personality trait: three positive traits (honest, clown, and helpful) and three negative traits (cruel, shy, and selfish). To illustrate the traits, stories presented in the *trait* condition described the protagonist's past behavior in three different situations. (See Figure 6.3 for an example of one story.) This was followed by a description of a new event involving the protagonist. Stories told in the *event-only* condition only described the new event. Subjects in both conditions were asked to predict and explain the protagonist's emotional reaction to the new event. Then subjects in the trait condition were questioned about the kind of person the protagonist was, to make sure that they had made the intended personality attribution. Indeed, subjects recognized the traits implied more than 95% of the time.

Subjects in this study included children ages 6, 8, and 10 and adults. A comparison of the trait and event-only conditions indicated that subjects of all ages were influenced by the protagonist's personality in making their predictions, but the oldest children and adults were more influenced by this knowledge than were

This is a story about a boy named Jerry. Jerry always makes his friends laugh.

During recess, he makes silly noises and weird faces.

When his teacher is not looking, Jerry copies her and everybody laughs.

One day, Jerry walked into class and took off his boots. When the class saw he was wearing one black shoe and one white shoe, they all started laughing. Do you think Jerry felt happy or sad when they laughed?

Figure 6.3. Sample story assessing the use of personality information for inferring later emotional reactions (Gnepp & Chilamkurti, 1988).

younger children. Similarly, older children and adults were much more likely than younger children to explain the protagonist's emotional reaction in terms of his or her personality. For example, one boy said that Jerry would feel happy "because he got all this fun and attention. . . . He gets wound up and does funny things. He wants people to laugh at him."

Use of person-specific information. Most types of personal information involve generalizing across people as well as differentiating among them, in that the information applies to categories of people (e.g., old people, shy people, people who live in Manhattan). However, some personal information applies primarily to a specific individual, rather than to any recognized category of people. Such person-specific information involves the greatest degree of differentiation and is most directly related to understanding a particular individual's emotional reactions. Such information is likely to be privileged information, that is, information about an individual that is not readily apparent in the way cultural or normative information might be, but rather must be gained verbally or through experience with the individual. Person-specific information may also be situation-specific and time-specific, or it may be much more general in the way personality characteristics are.

Consider a study by Deutsch (1974) in which 3- and 4-year-old children were shown filmed episodes involving conflicting expressive and situational cues to emotion. In one scenario, for example, a woman is working at a desk when someone enters and offers her a cup of coffee. The woman reacts angrily, saying, "I know you meant well, but I can't put up with this, this morning. I really did not want to be disturbed and you walk in and offer me coffee" (Deutsch, 1974, 1973). Thus, the woman's remarks explain her otherwise incongruous emotional reaction. The children were asked to describe what happened. Although they could accurately label the characters' emotions and behaviors, only the brightest children were able to provide reasons for the characters' reactions in view of the interpersonal behavior with the second actor. Several aspects of this task make it difficult for young children, most notably its strong reliance on verbal ability and the use of adult situations that may not be fully comprehensible to young children. Thus, it is all the more impressive that some children, even at this young age, were able to combine the personal and situational information so as to explain the emotional reactions of these characters.

The Deutsch study provided relatively time-limited person-specific information, but others have attempted to operationalize the concept of personal information in a way that applies across time and that suggests the origins of the other person's feelings. Gnepp et al. (1982) provided person-specific information that described the character's behavioral dispositions. For example, one of the eight stories used was about a boy named Mark who lived in Tree Land. "Mark eats grass whenever he can. It was dinner time and Mark's mother called him to dinner. 'What's for dinner?' Mark asked. 'Grass,' said his mother. 'We're having grass for dinner.' " Here, the situation has a strong negative emotional association, but there is qualifying personal information about Mark's preferences. Four- and 5-year-olds, as well as older children and adults, predicted that Mark would be happy to eat grass for dinner. Of course, subjects who were not provided with the personal information about Mark's behavioral dispositions predicted that Mark would be upset. Thus, even young children are able to combine person-specific information with situational information (step 3B in the model) when the personal information readily suggests the protagonist's mental appraisal of the situation. Children's responses were "personalized" in that they reflected the unique perspective of the protagonist on the situation. Gnepp et al. also found that when children were presented with conflicting normative and person-specific information they preferred to base their emotional inferences on the information that is most directly relevant to the other person's appraisal of the situation. In other words, like adults, children give more weight to information about an individual's dispositions than to information about the dispositions of a group to which the individual belongs.

Past history as a source of person-specific information. In both the Deutsch (1974) and Gnepp et al. (1982) studies, the protagonist's appraisal of the situation can be readily inferred from the person-specific information provided. How well can children infer other people's appraisals when this information is not provided so explicitly, and how well can they use these inferences to understand emotional reactions? These questions were the focus of two studies (Gnepp, in press; Gnepp & Gould, 1985), both of which used person-specific past history information. For example, one of the six stories used by Gnepp and Gould was about a girl named Robin: "One day Robin went to school and her best friend said to her, 'I don't like you anymore!' The next day, Robin saw her best friend on the playground." When asked how Robin felt, some children said that Robin was sad to see her friend because they're not really friends anymore, or because her friend hurt Robin's feelings before. These are personalized responses because they reveal an understanding of the protagonist's perspective the next day in light of her prior experiences. Other children said that Robin was happy because she sees her best friend on the playground and they can play together. Such responses can be termed "situational" because they are based entirely on the second event without regard for the psychological influence of the prior experience.

On average, 5-year-old children made more situational inferences than personalized ones. And, across the six different stories, even 10-year-old children failed to infer the personalized emotional reaction nearly one-third of the time. Interestingly however, the frequency of personalized inferences varied as a function of the emotions portrayed in the different stories. When the character had a negative experience, children were relatively likely to make personalized inferences about its effect on the character's subsequent appraisal of a usually positive event. They were least likely to make personalized inferences when the character had a positive experience with a usually negative event.

Children did better in a condition in which they were *told* the character's atypical emotion and then were asked only to explain it. Thus, it appears that children's difficulties with personalized inferences are due in part to a failure to recognize when the person's past history suggests an atypical emotional reaction (step 1B). Even when told of the emotional reaction, however, kindergartners have difficulty combining the personal and situational information so as to infer the other person's perspective on the final event (step 3B).

Why is it so difficult for children to make personalized inferences from past history information? A recent study (Gnepp, in press) suggests two possible reasons: (1) children have difficulty inferring other people's appraisals of events from knowledge of their personal history, and (2) children have difficulty in applying the inferred appraisals to later events. This study examined two forms of personal history information: prior experiences and prior behaviors. Some of the children in the study heard only a description of the protagonist's behavior or experience in a past situation, and were asked to infer what the protagonist thought of the situation. For example, they were told that on the last family walk, Lee repeatedly asked if they could stop walking and go back to the car (behavior), or that Lee got hot and tired and his feet hurt (experience). Children ages 8 and 11 were more likely than 6-year-olds to infer the protagonists' appraisals accurately (e.g., they were more likely to say that Lee didn't like walking in the park). Still, even the 6-year-olds understood the protagonists' opinions about two-thirds of the time.

Other children heard about the protagonist's behavior or experience in the past situation, followed by a subsequent event. (See Fig. 6.4 for an example.) For each story, an independent group of children had indicated strong agreement about the emotion associated with the event, and that consensus emotion conflicted with the protagonist's prior history. In the example shown, going for a walk in the park with the family is usually considered a happy event, but Lee's past history suggests he will be sad.

Children who heard such stories found it difficult to make personalized inferences of emotion. The 6-year-old children made personalized inferences of emotion less than half the time. Of course, children's ability to infer emotional reactions that reflected the protagonists' prior behaviors or experiences increased with age. Still, the difference between children's ability to infer the characters' appraisals and their ability to infer the characters' later emotional reactions suggests *two* problems in making personalized emotional inferences: determining the other person's perspective and applying this perspective to new situations.

Conclusions

In this chapter I have argued that a proper understanding of people's emotions often requires that we consider information that differentiates one person from another. Such personal information may range from broad generaliza-

1. This is a story about a boy named Lee. One day Lee's family took him for a walk in the park.

2a.
Behavior
After just a few minutes, Lee said, "Can we go back to the car?" Lee's mom said, "But we just started walking." A few minutes later Lee said, "Can we stop walking now and go back to the car?"

or

2b.
Experience
Lee got very hot and tired and his feet started hurting right away. Lee got scratched all over by the bushes.

3. The next week, Lee's mom said, "Let's all go for a walk in the park this afternoon."

Figure 6.4. Sample story assessing the use of past history information in two versions: Behavior (pictures 1, 2a, 3) and Experience (pictures 1, 2b, 3) (Gnepp, in press).

tions about groups of people (e.g., country of origin, gender, age) to knowledge applicable to only one person (e.g., unique life events). The nature of the information we use is a function of what information we believe might be relevant, and our ability to seek such information. When the emotion-eliciting situation is a familiar one and the other person is similar to us, we may simply infer the other person's feelings by imagining our own reaction to the situation. Given a familiar situation and self–other similarity, such "projection" would be an efficient approach with a high probability of leading to the correct inference. When the situation is a familiar one, but we know very little about the other person, then we should base our emotional inference on people in general, that is, on how most people would feel in that situation. In such cases, attempting to differentiate among individuals given inadequate information merely introduces error into the process (Cronbach, 1955; Hoch, 1987).

There are times when inferences based on ourselves or on people in general are not appropriate, however. This is the case when we cannot imagine how we would feel in the other person's position, or when there is no consensus reaction to the situation, or when we perceive the other person to be sufficiently dissimilar from us that we think the other person's feelings are not likely to be the same as those we would have in that situation. We should then recognize the need to incorporate personal information and to seek it if such information is lacking. Inferences that are modified by personal information are especially important when dealing with more complex emotions because most complex emotional reactions are comprehensible only when the individual's interpretation of the situation is understood.

In learning to understand other people's emotions, children face a complex developmental task. Accurate inferences about emotions require knowledge about a multitude of emotion-evoking situations and knowledge about how people's group membership, personal characteristics, and personal history can affect their reactions to events. Furthermore, a degree of cognitive sophistication is required to know when information is needed, which information is relevant, and how to incorporate multiple sources of information into an inference.

What can we conclude, based on the research to date, about the development of the ability to understand other people's feelings? In the preschool years (roughly 3 to 5 years of age), children can infer basic emotions from situations and facial expressions that are simple and familiar. When facial expressions of emotion and situational cues conflict, children of this age are strongly influenced by the facial expression in judging emotion. In the absence of expressions of emotion, these children tend to infer an emotion they associate with the situation, sometimes overlooking obvious social category factors such as parent versus child. However, when provided with personal information in the form of verbal or behavioral expressions of appraisal, these young children are often able to use this information to make personalized emotional inferences and sometimes to explain conflicting cues to emotion. When person-specific information readily suggests the other person's appraisal, emotional inferences are based on this information rather than on conflicting normative or situational information.

In the early school years (roughly 5 to 8 years of age), children expand their repertoire of situations whose emotional significance they comprehend. They also develop a greater awareness of how personal information affects the link between emotions and situations. They understand, for example, that broad cat-

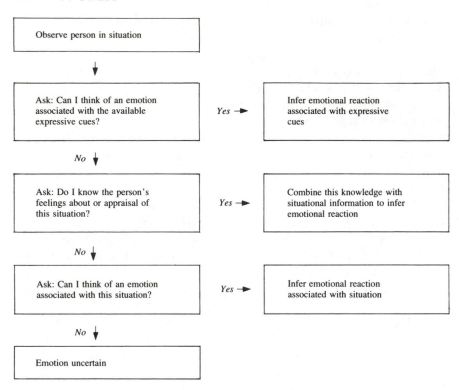

Figure 6.5. Model of emotional inference process for children in the preschool to early school years.

egories such as age and gender influence people's reactions to situations. They also recognize that some situations are emotionally equivocal, and that different people feel different ways in those situations. Children in this age range are still limited in their understanding of the role of appraisals, however. They can explain why two individuals have different emotional reactions to the same event, but they often fail to consider that one person might feel either of two (or more) different ways in response to an equivocal situation. They can infer other people's appraisals from their prior behaviors and experiences, but they have some difficulty in using these inferences to infer emotional reactions to later events.

In later grade school years (roughly ages 8 to 12), children's understanding of complex situations and complex emotions increases. When situational cues and facial cues conflict, children give increased weight to the situational cues in their

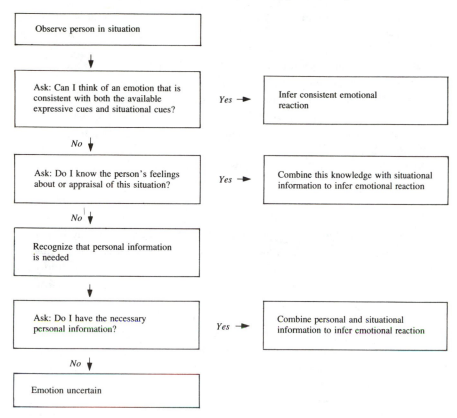

Figure 6.6. Model of emotional inference process for children in the early to middle school years.

judgments of emotion, and they show an increased ability to reconcile the conflicting cues. They understand that an individual might feel one way or might feel a different way in emotionally equivocal situations, and they recognize the possibility of multiple emotions within an individual as well. They demonstrate an awareness that information about the other person's appraisals is necessary to infer her or his emotional reaction to an equivocal situation and they develop the ability to seek such information. Children in this age range can make personalized inferences of appraisals based on other people's behaviors, experiences, and personality traits, and they can use these inferred appraisals to predict and explain people's emotional reactions to later events.

In the preschool to early school years, children's emotional inferences can be described by a model something like the one shown in Figure 6.5. Judgments are arrived at with a minimum of information processing and without the need to coordinate multiple pieces of information. Expressive cues are considered first and are weighted heavily.

In the early to middle school years, children's inferences suggest a somewhat more complex model that gives increased weight to situational information and to other forms of personal information (see Figure 6.6). These children may, on occasion, rely on a simpler process, like the one proposed for younger children, but they are increasingly capable of combining and integrating multiple sources of information.

Older children and adolescents probably become capable of using a more complex inference process, similar to the one described by the three-phase model provided earlier in this chapter. They too may choose to use a simpler, shorthand process at times, especially when dealing with simple, basic emotions. However, these simpler processes will prove inadequate when trying to understand the feelings of people experiencing more complex emotions, so mature judges will attempt to obtain and use personal information in conjunction with their understanding of situations to comprehend other people's feelings more fully.

The development of the basic processes of emotional inference begins quite early, but undergoes a long period of refinement and improvement. This development appears to continue into adulthood, as evidenced by more proficient and consistent performance by adolescents and adults on experimental tasks. Indeed, the fact that adults (even well-meaning ones) are sometimes socially insensitive attests to the complexity of the emotional inferences process, and suggests that learning to understand other people's feelings is an aspect of development that is never quite completed.

Note

1. Throughout this chapter, I use the term "personal information" to refer to any information about the person (in contrast to the situation), including demographic information, the social group to which the person belongs, and unique characteristics of the person. In the past, I have used this term to refer only to unique characteristics of the person, and I specifically differentiated it from "normative information" as well as situational information (see Gnepp, Klayman, & Trabasso, 1982). In the present chapter, however, personal information is conceived of as a broad category that subsumes normative information and "person-specific" information.

References

Arnold, M. B. (1970). Perennial problems in the field of emotion. In M. B. Arnold (Ed.), *Feelings and emotions*. New York: Academic Press.

Barden, R. C., Zelko, F. A., Duncan, S. W., & Masters, J. C. (1980). Children's consensual knowledge about the experiential determinants of emotion. *Journal of Personality and Social Psychology, 39*, 968–976.

Borke, H. (1971). Interpersonal perception of young children: egocentrism or empathy? *Developmental Psychology, 5*, 263–269.

Borke, H. (1973). The development of empathy in Chinese and American children between three and six years of age: a cross-culture study. *Developmental Psychology, 9*, 102–108.

Bretherton, I., & Beeghly, M. (1982). Talking about internal states: the acquisition of an explicit theory of mind. *Developmental Psychology, 18*, 906–921.

Brody, L. R., & Harrison, R. H. (1987). Developmental changes in children's abilities to match and label emotionally laden situations. *Motivation and Emotion, 11*, 347–365.

Burns, N., & Cavey, L. (1957). Age differences in empathic ability among children. *Canadian Journal of Psychology, 11*, 227–230.

Chandler, M. J. (1973). Egocentrism and antisocial behavior: the assessment and training of social perspective-taking skills. *Developmental Psychology, 9*, 326–332.

Chandler, M. J., & Greenspan, S. (1972). Ersatz egocentrism: a reply to H. Borke. *Developmental Psychology, 7*, 104–106.

Cronbach, L. (1955). Processes affecting scores on "understanding of others" and "assumed similarity." *Psychological Bulletin, 52*, 177–193.

Denham, S. A. (1986). Social cognition, prosocial behavior, and emotion in preschoolers: contextual validation. *Child Development, 57*, 194–201.

Deutsch, F. (1973). Cognitive and social determinants of female preschoolers' empathic ability, helping and sharing behavior (Doctoral dissertation, Pennsylvania State University, 1972). *Dissertation Abstracts International, 33*, 6585 A–6586 A.

Deutsch, F. (1974). Female preschoolers' perceptions of affective responses and interpersonal behavior in videotaped episodes. *Developmental Psychology, 10*, 733–740.

Dymond, R. F. (1950). Personality and empathy. *Journal of Consulting Psychology, 14*, 343–350.

Flavell, J. H., Botkin, P. T., Fry, C. L., Wright, J. W., & Jarvis, P. E. (1968). *The development of role-taking and communication skills in children*. New York: Wiley.

Frijda, N. H. (1969). Recognition of emotion. In L. Berkowitz (Ed.), *Advances in experimental social psychology* (Vol. 4, pp. 167–224). New York: Academic Press.

Gage, N. L., & Cronbach, L. (1955). Conceptual and methodological problems in interpersonal perception. *Psychological Review, 62*, 411–422.

Gnepp, J. (1982). *Affective perspective taking: reconciling conflicting affective cues*. Paper presented at the meeting of the American Psychological Association, Washington, D.C., August.

Gnepp, J. (1983). Children's social sensitivity: inferring emotions from conflicting cues. *Developmental Psychology, 19*, 805–814.

Gnepp, J. (in press). Personalized inferences of emotions and appraisals: component processes and correlates. *Developmental Psychology*.

Gnepp, J., & Chilamkurti, C. (1988). Children's use of personality attributions to predict other people's emotional and behavioral reactions. *Child Development, 59*, 743–754.

Gnepp, J., & Gould, M. E. (1985). The development of personalized inferences: understanding other people's emotional reactions in light of their prior experiences. *Child Development, 56*, 1455–1464.

Gnepp, J., & Hess, D. L. R. (1986). Children's understanding of verbal and facial display rules. *Developmental Psychology, 22*, 103–108.

Gnepp, J., & Johnson, L. K. (1989). Children's ability to seek information to make emotional inferences. Manuscript in preparation.

Gnepp, J., Klayman, J., & Trabasso, T. (1982). A hierarchy of information sources for inferring emotional reactions. *Journal of Experimental Child Psychology, 33*, 111–123.

Gnepp, J., McKee, E., & Domanic, J. A. (1987). Children's use of situational information to infer emotion: understanding emotionally equivocal situations. *Developmental Psychology, 23*, 114–123.

Gould, M. E. (1984). *Children's recognition and resolution of ambiguity in making affective judg-*

ments. Paper presented at the meeting of the Midwestern Psychological Association, Chicago, May.

Gove, F. L. & Keating, D. P. (1979). Empathic role-taking precursors. *Developmental Psychology, 15,* 594–600.

Greenspan, S., Barenboim, C., & Chandler, M. J. (1976). Empathy and pseudoempathy: the affective judgments of first- and third-graders. *Journal of Genetic Psychology, 129,* 77–88.

Harris, P. L. (1983). Children's understanding of the link between situation and emotion. *Journal of Experimental Child Psychology, 36,* 490–509.

Harris, P. L., Olthof, T., Meerum Terwogt, M., & Hardman, C. E. (1987). Children's knowledge of the situations that provoke emotion. *International Journal of Behavioral Development, 10,* 319–343.

Harter, S. (1982). A cognitive-developmental approach to children's understanding of affect and trait labels. In F. C. Serafica (Ed.), *Social-cognitive development in context.* New York: Guilford.

Hastorf, A. H., & Bender, I. E. (1952). A caution respecting the measurement of empathic ability. *Journal of Abnormal Social Psychology, 47,* 574–576.

Heller, K. A., & Berndt, T. J. (1981). Developmental changes in the formation and organization of personality attributions. *Child Development, 52,* 683–691.

Hoch, S. J. (1987). Perceived consensus and predictive accuracy: the pros and cons of projection. *Journal of Personality and Social Psychology, 53,* 221–234.

Hoffner, C., & Badzinski, D. M. (1987). *Children's integration of facial and situational cues to emotion.* Paper presented at the meeting of the International Communication Association, Montreal, May.

Hughes, R. Jr., Tingle B. A., & Sawin, D. B. (1981). Development of empathic understanding in children. *Child Development, 52,* 122–128.

Iannotti, R. J. (1978). Effect of role-taking experiences on role taking, empathy, altruism, and aggression. *Developmental Psychology, 14,* 119–124.

Kurdek, L. A., & Rodgon, M. M. (1975). Perceptual, cognitive, and affective perspective taking in kindergarten through sixth-grade children. *Developmental Psychology, 11,* 643–650.

Lazarus, R. S., Averill, J. R., & Opton, E. M. Jr. (1970). Towards a cognitive theory of emotion. In M. B. Arnold (Ed.), *Feelings and emotions* (pp. 207–232). New York: Academic Press.

Levanthal, H. (1980). Toward a comprehensive theory of emotion. In L. Berkowitz (Ed.), *Advances in experimental social psychology* (pp. 139–207). New York: Academic Press.

Mandler, G. (1975). *Mind and emotion.* New York: Wiley.

Mood, D. W., Johnson, J. E., & Shantz, C. U. (1978). Social comprehension and affect-matching in young children. *Merrill-Palmer Quarterly, 24,* 63–66.

Reichenbach, L., & Masters, J. C. (1983). Children's use of expressive and contextual cues in judgments of emotion. *Child Development, 54,* 993–1004.

Rholes, W. S., & Ruble, D. N. (1984). Children's understanding of dispositional characteristics of others. *Child Development, 55,* 550–560.

Rothenberg, B. B. (1970). Children's social sensitivity and the relationship to interpersonal competence, intrapersonal comfort, and intellectual level. *Developmental Psychology, 2,* 335–350.

Saarni, C. (1979). Children's understanding of display rules for expressive behavior. *Developmental Psychology, 15,* 424–429.

Schachter, S. (1964). The interaction of cognitive and physiological determinants of emotional state. In L. Berkowitz (Ed.), *Advances in experimental social psychology* (Vol. 1, pp. 49–80). New York: Academic Press.

Silverman, W. K., & Drabman, R. S. (1983). Affective matching in nine-year-old girls. *Journal of Psychology, 115,* 123–129.

Smither, S. (1977). A reconsideration of the developmental study of empathy. *Human Development, 20,* 253–276.

Thaler, R. H. (1985). Mental accounting and consumer choice. *Marketing Science, 4,* 199–214.

Urberg, K. A., & Docherty, E. M. (1976). Development of role-taking skills in young children. *Developmental Psychology, 12,* 198–203.

Wiggers, M., & van Lieshout, C. F. M. (1985). Development of recognition of emotions: children's reliance on situational and facial expressive cues. *Developmental Psychology, 21,* 338–349.

Zahn-Waxler, C., Radke-Yarrow, M., & Brady-Smith, J. (1977). Perspective-taking and prosocial behavior. *Developmental Psychology, 13,* 87–88.

Part IV

The control of emotion

7   Children's understanding of strategic control of emotional expression in social transactions

Carolyn Saarni

Introduction

• Four-year old Joel turned the wheel of his tricycle too hard and tumbled onto the pavement. His hands smarted only a bit, but then he noticed his mother had looked up from her gardening. He screwed his face into a grimace, let out a moan, and peered with abject agony at his cupped hands. Mother dropped the shovel and ran over to comfort Joel.

• Cynthia, age 7, knew there was going to be trouble when she heard her father shouting outside; he was probably drunk again. She knew she must not let him see her upset or tearful: He had turned on her, hitting her on the side of her head too many times before, just because he could not stand to see anybody upset around him. She stiffened her mouth, blinked hard, and tightened her face and body into a rigid stance. Her father came indoors and ignored her.

• David was new at the junior high. He went to the school cafeteria to buy his lunch and hoped to meet some kids there. As he was eating his hot-dog for lunch and looking around the crowded room, the wiener slipped out of the bun, splattering mustard on his shirt; it then went skittering across the floor. David felt mortified but managed a laugh and announced to a couple of other kids at the table, "I guess *that* dog wanted to go for a walk." Everyone laughed and started joking with him about who would step on the dog's tail first.

These three scenarios capture the kind of emotional and social complexity involved in the management of emotional-expressive behavior. Joel at a young age can intensify or exaggerate his emotional-expressive behavior, whereas Cynthia has learned to mask hers behind a stoic or wooden facade. David substitutes other expressive behavior for what he actually feels. All three children reveal how they cope simultaneously with what they feel and what the social situation consists of. Managing one's emotional-expressive behavior constitutes such coping and thus is a dynamic and multifaceted behavior domain, encompassing muscle coordination, cognitive development, self-concept, motivation, social skills, and perhaps even temperament.

In order to discuss children's understanding of how and why they and others

I wish to thank Jane Weiskopf for her invaluable assistance in the recent research reported in this chapter.

might strategically monitor and "manipulate" their expressive behavior, a theoretical platform needs to be developed. Rather than trying to elaborate each of the six abovementioned facets of emotional-expressive behavior management into such a platform, I shall propose as the more encompassing thesis of this chapter that the social context cannot be separated from the emotional behavior of the individual. In order to support this thesis, the following theoretical statements will be examined with regard to empirical research:

1. Emotional development occurs *because* we exist within interpersonal systems.
2. Emotional-expressive behavior has immediate utility in its adaptive plasticity, particularly within social contexts.
3. Building upon these two ideas, special attention will be paid to the proposition that when children come to realize that what they really feel need not correspond to what they express overtly, they become capable of new and more subtle strategies for interaction with others. These new strategies permit the control of emotional-expressive behavior such that the child can dissimulate her or his feelings in some interpersonal transaction in an adaptive and/or culturally prescribed fashion.

Prior to examining these ideas, I will discuss briefly a curious bias that has been evident in psychological research on children's understanding of emotion – and which the present chapter aspires to avoid. This bias has been discussed by Heider (1984) from an anthropological perspective as a propensity for researchers to interpret emotional experience in a polarized way such that a false dichotomy emerges between emotion as a state system, primarily studied by psychologists (e.g., Ekman, 1984; Izard, 1977) and emotion as interaction (or interpersonal process), primarily studied by sociologists (e.g., Gordon, 1981, this volume; Hochschild, 1983; Kemper, 1978; Shott, 1979), anthropologists (e.g., Lutz, 1985; Rosaldo, 1984), and, interestingly, also by infancy researchers (e.g., Lewis & Michalson, 1983, see also Lewis, this volume; Sroufe, Schork, Motti, Lawroski, & LaFreniere, 1984; Stern, 1974).

Heider contends that a continuum exists both within any given culture and across cultures, which ranges from extreme emphasis on emotion-as-inner-experience (or state) to emotion-as-interaction. He suggests that North American culture is dominated by the assumption that emotion is an inner experience, whereas other cultures are more interaction-oriented. If we unwittingly apply our North American bias of emotion-as-inner-experience to our research on emotional development, our scientific inquiries may be constrained by that bias, thus limiting our understanding of how emotional experience may be "codified" by a given culture, including our own.

Until recently, this possible bias was evident in investigations of children's understanding of emotion, which examined children's comprehension of emotions as something *internally* experienced, albeit connected to situation or expression (e.g., Harris, 1985; Harter, 1982; Saarni, 1979a). The coordination of emotion-as-inner-experience along with emotion-within-interaction as a fundamental feature of children's developing understanding of emotion has been a goal (and only implicitly so) in only a few recent investigations (e.g., Carlson, Felleman, & Masters, 1983; Dunn & Munn, 1985; Gnepp, this volume; Gnepp & Chilamkurti, 1987; McCoy & Masters, 1985; Saarni, 1985a; Strayer, 1985, this volume). It is the explicit goal of the present chapter to explore how children's understanding of emotion is linked with their concomitant understanding of social transactions, and, indeed, it could be argued that the study of one often permits the study of the other. With this perspective aired, I return to the discussion of the above premises.

Emotional development occurs within interpersonal systems

I do not think that one can examine emotions ontogenetically without emphasizing the social context of emotional experience. This social context is complex and may well be so from an early age, judging from what infancy researchers tell us (e.g., Malatesta, 1985; Emde, 1980; Lewis & Michalson, 1983). The social context entails at least the following four features: (a) a relationship with another, (b) the use of emotional-expressive behavior as social information/communication, (c) the response of the other to one's emotional experience, which rapidly leads to *negotiation,* and (d) the appraisal of meaning, a concept drawn from Lazarus (1984),. which is socialized through one's collective social relations over time.

The four features of social context noted above influence children's emotional development. They are also likely to influence a child's understanding of emotions in coordination with whatever level of self-awareness and capacity for self-reflection the child has reached (see Jurkovic & Selman, 1980, for a discussion of the development of psychological insight into the self). An elaboration of these four features of social context relative to understanding emotional experience is as follows: We have implicit or explicit relationships with intimates, acquaintances, or strangers, which impact on how we subjectively interpret our emotional response as well as what we reveal expressively to such individuals. The process of emotion socialization is often reflected in these transactions, and in subsequent interpersonal exchanges we may be influenced to respond on one or two levels: We may actually begin to feel what we think we ought to feel in some specified context (see Hochshild, 1983; also further discussion in this chapter), and/or we are influenced to monitor and manipulate our expressive behavior, which we can dissociate, within some limits, from our actual feelings for the sake of some strategic social goal.

We also make use of others' expressive behavior, even when they appear to be expressing nothing, as social information; this in turn affects our own emotional response to that individual. For example, elsewhere (Saarni, 1982,) I have argued that our nonverbal emotional-expressive behavior often carries metacommunicative information about the relationship between the sender and receiver. (Metacommunication is used here to mean that there can be multilevel messages attached to the literal message being communicated.) Family systems theorists such as Satir (1967) or Watzlawick, Beavin, and Jackson (1967) have long thought that the "command" feature (or metacommunicative message) of a given communication lay in nonverbal behavior and could reflect such relationship features as the distribution of power between individuals (see also Haley, 1963), the sender's attitude about the interpersonal exchange itself, the sender's feelings and attitudes about her or his own self, and the sender's feelings and expectations about the interactant. Thus, our emotional-expressive behavior may carry considerable social information over and beyond the mere expression of some singular emotional state.

This social information *may* be part of what appears in dissembled facial expressions, although such dissemblance may also simply represent a modified expression of the emotion that is genuinely being felt internally. For example, I observed children in a situation contrived to appear "natural" to elementary school children wherein they received an inappropriate gift (e.g., an unimaginative baby toy) from the experimenter for their participation in a task (Saarni, 1984). The experimenter was ostensibly conducting marketing research on academic work books. One set of expressive behaviors that I coded was called "transitional" in that it referred to behaviors that appeared to fall between readily displayed dissembled expressive behavior (e.g., a big smile, appropriate eye contact, and an enthusiastic thank-you) and the display of a genuine emotional-expressive reaction to the disappointing gift (e.g., gaze avoidance, no smile, no thank-you). Among these transitional expressive behaviors were some that also suggested that the child was seeking guidance for how to respond to the market researcher upon receiving the inappropriate gift (they had received candy and money the previous day for doing the same sort of task). Some children would, for example, make eye contact with the experimenter, then look down toward the gift, back to the experimenter, down at the gift, and so forth. Head tilts, suggesting a questioning of what was going on, also occurred and were coded in this category. Anxious behaviors also occurred, e.g., biting the lips, tongue movements outside the mouth, and so forth. These expressive behaviors could be construed as providing social information to the onlooker (i.e., the market researcher), for example, that the child felt there was a need for the adult in the situation to intervene in this awkward situation. Indeed, that was what happened next: The experimenter announced that there must have been a mistake, and an attractive set of felt-tip colored markers was given to the child.

Thus, these "transitional" emotional-expressive behaviors functioned as metacommunicative cues about the social transaction, namely: (a) the child felt less power in the situation relative to the adult (e.g., the anxious behaviors), (b) the child felt awkward about the interpersonal exchange (e.g., the slight smile, abrupt loss of smile, the mumbled thank-you), (c) the child felt unsure of her- or himself (e.g., knit brows while smiling, head tilts), and (d) the child wanted the market researcher to provide guidance in the situation (e.g., frequent gaze shifts, questioning vocalization). To sum up, expressive behavior reflects not only the sender's emotional experience, whether it be genuine or dissembled, but also social information about the nature of the relationship between sender and receiver.

We become involved in a series of what may be extremely rapid and strategic emotional-expressive transactions: A dynamic sequence of reciprocal emotional responding occurs in which we react to the other's expressive behavior, which, in turn, influences the subsequent emotional response from the other, and so forth. I refer to this fluid "dovetailing" process as social-emotional negotiation and discuss it in greater detail below in the section on preinteraction expectancies (see also the chapter in this volume by Gnepp for further illustrations). Finally, we make attributions about what our own and others' emotional experience means (e.g., see both Strayer and Thompson, this volume). We assign causes; we posit temporal constraints to the emotional experience; we may even deny that we feel anything at all.

Research on satisfaction/dissatisfaction in adults' close relationships also illustrates well how relationship information manifests itself in emotional-expressive cues as well as in the causal attributions made by the interactants. A recent review (Bradbury & Fincham, 1987) on affect and cognition in close relationships suggests that relative to satisfied couples, distressed couples viewed occurrences of negative affect and behavior as persistent and global, both in their relationship and as traits in one another. They were also more likely to reciprocate negative affect and behavior in their interactions with one another. Their attributions were more likely to foster ongoing unhappiness, whereas positive affect and behavior were given short shrift and discredited. Bradbury and Fincham develop a complex model in which they describe the interface of both cognitive and affective components that sustain the negativity of such distressed relationships; however, what they are essentially describing is the fluid turn-taking of emotional and expressive behaviors between the spouses or partners in which a remarkably predictable, albeit unhappy, negotiation is effected. This research with adults is also clearly related to the next theme, how emotional-expressive behavior is influenced by interpersonal experience, which I will look at from a socialization standpoint.

Interpersonal influence on emotional-expressive behavior

A basic assumption that characterizes my own research and other studies reviewed here is that children's emotional experience is inseparable from socio-cultural meaning. Beginning with care-givers' differential responses to infants' emotional-expressive behavior (e.g., Malatesta, 1985) and continuing throughout childhood and adolescence, children's expressive behaviors elicit *interpersonal* responses, that may be verbal or nonverbal, active or passive (as in ignoring a child's emotional behavior). Even when the child or adolescent is alone, an imaginary audience may "witness" and "react" to the child's emotional experience (e.g., Breger, 1974). These interpersonal contexts, real or projected, influence the ways that children express and interpret their emotional experience. The mechanisms for this influence may be (a) direct socialization, that is, reinforcement contingencies, (b) of an indirect sort, that is, observing and/or incorporating the experience of others, or (c) according to expectations communicated by others to the child, which are subsequently internalized in the self as personal expectancies. Each of these modalities of influence will be briefly discussed and commented on relative to whether they appear to affect the structuring of actual emotional states or to influence primarily the external expression of emotion.

Direct socialization

An important study by Malatesta and Haviland (1982) illustrates well how direct social influence may be exerted on emotional-expressive behavior, even during early infancy. As expected, they found that mothers revealed positive facial expressions when interacting with their infants (in front of a video camera and experimenter). However, contingent responses by the mothers, which had to appear within a half second for instrumental conditioning to occur, closely followed their infants' facial expressions only when the infant gave a positive display (about 25 percent of the time). The outcome was that by six months of age the proportion of negative facial expressions had significantly declined relative to the positive ones. Overall, the mothers appeared to be "dampening" the intensity of their infants' expressive behavior. Given our culture's emphasis on positive expressive displays and moderation in intensity of display, these mothers appear to influence their infants to modulate their emotional-expressive behavior. However, this is not to say that the mothers had any awareness of what they were doing, nor can we discount the effect of the camera and experimenter on the mother's behavior. It is also possible that these young infants were changing their proportion of negative expressive displays relative to positive ones for reasons other than their mothers' apparently contingent social responding.

Malatesta and Haviland also found an interesting sex difference: Infant boys received more matching expressive behaviors from their mothers than did infant girls, but girls received a greater diversity of expressive behaviors from their mothers. Malatesta and Haviland interpreted this sex difference as one that permitted the mothers to modulate the negative emotions displayed (e.g., irritability) by the boys more attentively, whereas the girls were given the opportunity to acquire exposure to a greater variety of social and expressive interactions with their mothers. With our current methods we cannot tell whether the mothers were specifically modifying the emotional *states* of their infants or affecting the frequency of emotional-expressive displays without altering the corresponding emotional states. I could imagine that the display of mild distress or irritability in the infant might become gradually inhibited or blunted in its expression, even as the distress state persists. On the other hand, Malatesta and Haviland might argue, relative to the sex differences noted above, that mothers were intervening directly in the affective states experienced by their infants such that irritability was soothed or the infant was distracted. The infants' emotional states would then have been replaced by comfort and perhaps by interest, respectively.

Parents also attempt to modify their children's emotional-expressive behavior by using deliberate strategies. (Whether they are effective or not is another matter!) We are all familiar with parents trying to pacify their cranky, crying child in the grocery store through offering sweets or frowning and nudging their child to be less rambunctious in public places.

Direct conditioning of what one genuinely feels – as opposed to merely what one expresses – appears in clinical anecdotes about the acquisition of phobic responses as well as in the behavioral systematic desensitization procedures followed when trying to ameliorate the intense anxiety aroused by the phobic stimulus. As for parents, they may not distinguish between the expression of emotion and its internal state when they try to reinforce positively or through negative sanctions the emotional-expressive behavior of their children.

Indirect influence

By indirect social influence on the development of emotional-expressive behavior, I am referring to processes such as social referencing, identification, and observational or imitative learning. These processes of influence may be thought of as indirect in so far as temporal situational factors may intervene between the initial stimulus and the subsequent emotional-expressive behavior.

Social referencing. Social referencing means looking to another's expressive behavior in an ambiguous situation and responding in accordance with that expression. In a typical experiment, mothers are asked to display a negative facial expression in some new situation facing the baby. The effect of their expression on the baby's behavior is then examined. For example, the infant may be less likely to cross the visual-cliff if it sees its mother appearing frightened (Sorce, Emde, Campos, & Klinnert, 1985). Feinman and Lewis (1983) found that social referencing was also implicated in how infants responded emotionally and expressively to strangers: Mothers' overtly positive greetings to strangers led to more relaxed, even welcoming behavior on the part of their babies. An avoidant, distant response to strangers on the mothers' part was associated with greater wariness and distress on the part of their infant when also approached by the stranger.

Social referencing apparently functions as a source of influence on the infant's emotional state in that it affects the infant's appraisal of an otherwise emotionally ambiguous stimulus situation. The infant's subsequent expressive behavior seems to be in direct correspondence to its internal state. However, it is conceivable that when older children and adults use social referencing in emotionally ambiguous situations, they use others' expressive cues more in an imitative fashion, and their internal state is not necessarily affected. Obviously for infants the capacity to make use of social referencing to figure out what to feel in some unfamiliar and ambiguous situation is a complex development, involving abilities to make comparisons across situations, to imitate, and to comprehend the meaning of others' expressive behavior. Amazingly enough, infants in the second half of the first year begin to demonstrate these skills and thus can learn very rapidly and efficiently the emotional meanings of assorted situations by observing their social environment.

Identification. Identification has its conceptual roots in psychoanalytic theory. Generally speaking, it refers to the unconscious incorporation of the traits, attitudes, feelings, and behaviors of a significant person into one's own emotional and behavioral repertoire. Thus, identification processes presumably influence both the internal emotional states and the expressive behavior *styles* exhibited by an individual. My use of the term *style* as a way to characterize expressive behavior is strictly descriptive. We are all familiar with the person who chronically giggles when anxious, who typically smiles through clenched teeth, or whose other body parts habitually move in a fashion that provides additional cues about what he or she is feeling inside. What we do not know is whether any of these expressive styles have their origin in identification with some significant person in the individual's life. Although I am not aware of any empirical research that directly addresses identification per se in the development of emotional-expressive behavior, a study by Camras, Grow, and Ribordy (1983) is provocative. They examined the ability of physically abused and neglected children to choose the right facial expression to go with a brief situation in which the emotion was also named (e.g., "it is her birthday, and she is happy"). In comparison to normal children, the abused and neglected children were significantly less accurate overall in their choices across the different emotions sampled. They also found a tendency for the abused children to be relatively less accurate in their choice of expressions for "happy" situations in comparison to the normal children, whereas there was less difference in accuracy rates between the abused and normal children for the recognition of sadness and anger.

Identification may be involved in that abused children may incorporate the more negative emotional and expressive behavior of their parent(s), given that the incidence of pleasant and harmonious interaction between abusing parents and their offspring is considerably lower than in nonabusive families (e.g., Burgess & Conger, 1978; Linehan, Paul, & Egan, 1983). This "identification with the aggressor" may interfere with the more typical acquisition of stereotyped beliefs for when happy responses are usually expected; instead, negative responses may be more frequently expected across such situations. (See also Barden, Zelko, Duncan, & Masters, 1980, for a discussion of how by 4 years of age normal children have already typically acquired many consensually shared expectations about situational determinants of emotions.) Lastly, it has been tragically all too often documented that children who were abused tend to repeat the abuse with their own children (e.g., Kempe & Kempe, 1978; Perry, Doran, & Wells, 1983). This repetitive intergenerational cycle suggests that identification is a useful construct for trying to explain how the emotional-expressive behavior of a parent becomes incorporated into and perseveres within a child's own repertoire, despite its being dysfunctional, legally proscribed, and destructive.

Imitation. Imitating the emotional-expressive behavior of another person is a strategy that we have at our disposal throughout our lifetime for figuring out how to modify our self-presentation. We are also reinforced when such imitation proves to be socially efficacious. Most obviously, imitation influences our expressive behavior, and perhaps with long-term repetition of the imitated expressive behavior (and receiving the efficacious social reinforcement), the corresponding internal emotional state is also experienced. This latter development may come about simply because the emotion-eliciting situation is appraised differently: For example, what was formerly viewed as nerve-wracking (but self-presentation was expressively managed so that one appeared confident) is now perceived as a well-rehearsed activity for which one has routinely been commended for one's competence. The former emotional state of tense anxiety has been replaced by a state of ease.

Some of my research in progress seeks to examine how children come to attribute social approval to emotional dissemblance in some situations and disapproval of dissemblance in other situations. My results to date suggest that children focus on the nature of the relationship between the interactants as the primary "pivot" around which social approval or disapproval varies (see also Saarni, in press).

Looking at another powerful source of influence in our culture, namely media, I suspect advertising and many television shows attempt to capitalize on their viewers' propensity to imitate the emotional-expressive behavior of other people, in order to gain social approval, to avoid disapproval, etc. For example, Noble (1983) found among Australian youth that fully 57% reported learning how to act "cool" by watching reruns of an American television show called *Happy Days*. Among that group of young viewers, 35% agreed that they also learned how not to be "square," and 21% discovered what to do when one feels shy. Knowing how to look "cool" and to avoid looking "square" or shy imply considerable management of one's emotional-expressive behavior. Whether the children actually imitated the *Happy Days* characters' expressive behavior is not known, but they certainly were capable of articulating what to do expressively, which shows that for this young adolescent group the *strategic* management of one's emotional-expressive behavior is readily understood and used in order to gain social efficacy.

Hochschild (1983) provides us with a vivid example of adults acquiring the "appropriate" emotional-expressive behavior via imitation. She studied the training provided by Delta Airlines to prospective flight attendants (in this case they were all female). The training program inculcated a sense of belonging with the company, which was reinforced by having the trainees live together in a dormitory and work closely with one another. They were expected to imitate the emotional-expressive displays of their supervisors and to model for one another the "proper" way to display feelings, e.g., to smile agreeably at an aggravating passenger. Hochschild sums up the emotional message from Delta Airlines as "learn to manage your feelings, and learn to attune yourself to feeling rules because doing this will get you places" (p. 159). Managing one's emotional-expressive behavior may not only be socially efficacious but, as suggested by Hochschild, it may also help one to earn more money and realize one's ambitions in the increasingly service-oriented economy that we now live in.

Expectancies

Elsewhere I have discussed in greater detail how people come to anticipate both what they will feel and what they will express in a given situation (Saarni, 1985). This process of expectancy formation depends on social interaction, with one individual communicating to the other that a credible and valid expectation exists for feeling X in some situation. If the second individual, let us say a child, accepts that expectation as indeed being a credible and valid perspective, then the child begins to comply with that viewpoint as a suggestion for how he or she will feel. If the particular situation re-occurs and the child does indeed feel something similar to the suggested emotional response, the suggestion is further validated and begins to become internalized as a personal expectancy. The personal expectancy, once in place, operates as an assimilatory "filter" or belief for what sort of emotional reaction is to be expected in a particular kind of situation.

An example of the above cognitive-communicative process may be found in how children take on some of their parents' fears without ever having had the opportunity to see their parents' reaction to the feared object, animal, insect, roller-coaster, lightning, thunder, earthquake, or whatever. Then, when presented with the particular feared stimulus, even in the absence of their parents, they react with considerable and genuine fear. To illustrate, we took an eight-year-old boy, Dean, on an abalone hunting trip on the Northern California coast. One has to stick one's hands into rocky crevices in tide pools to locate the abalone, and, of course, one does not always know nor see what one is going to touch. Although other accompanying children, a couple even younger than Dean, were eagerly searching under rocks, there was no way that Dean was going to put his hands under a rock where surely a Moray eel would bite him and undoubtedly electrocute him as well! As it turns out, Dean's mother had been badly frightened by a Moray eel while skin-diving in Hawaii some years before and had told her son a vivid story about this terrible flashing green eel that lunged after her as she swam past its rocky crevice. Dean had absorbed a powerful fear about an animal he had never seen, and neither contradictory evidence nor rational explanations would undo this expectancy of danger and fear. In a sense, phobias constitute a similar sort of powerful assimilatory "emotional filter" for a class of stimuli and may also be strengthened through someone's communicated expectation to the individual about how dreadful, incapacitating, and so forth some situation "really" is.

The preceding discussion suggests that the socialization of emotion occurs, in coordination with a biological substrate, according to processes that we only partly understand. Both emotional states and emotional-expressive behavior are affected by socialization, sometimes in tandem, sometimes separately. What adds to our difficulty in investigating aspects of emotion development, such as children's understanding of emotional-expressive behavior, is precisely this interplay of emotion and social interaction: The interdependency of emotional and social development means that both must be studied for valid descriptions of either domain to be obtained.

The utility of emotional-expressive behavior lies in its adaptive plasticity, particularly with respect to social situations

This second premise is complementary to the first: If our emotional development proceeds within interpersonal networks, we need to be flexible in our emotional-expressive behavior, because those networks change throughout our lives. Thus, the definition of adaptive plasticity that I am using here is *not* simply whether cultures *A* and *B* differ from one another by "prescribing" different emotional responses to the same eliciting circumstances (e.g., Harkness & Super, 1985, describe the socialization practices involved in the inhibition of crying among Kipsigis children, which differ from those experienced by American children, with the outcome between the two cultures being rather different views toward children's crying at times of ceremony as well as at times of ordinary frustration). The sort of adaptive plasticity that interests me here is how the same individual can vary his or her emotional response to similar eliciting circumstances, depending on who else is present and/or on how the social context (in which the eliciting circumstance is embedded) may shift. Indeed, many of the studies discussed under the different modalities of socialization of emotion fit within this second premise as well. I will focus on two recent investigations to illustrate how emotional-expressive behavior is adaptive to its socio-cultural context. The first is an ethnographic study of several mother–daughter pairs in South Baltimore (Miller & Sperry, 1987); the second is an interview-based study I conducted with elementary and junior high school children on anticipated parental reaction to genuine displays of emotional-expressive behavior (Saarni, 1987).

Ethnographic study

Miller and Sperry emphasize that culture organizes and elaborates emotional experience. Their focus is on the socialization of anger and aggression, and although their ethnographic methodology incorporated a variety of observational data, what were primarily reported were the oral exchanges between mothers and their young, approximately 2½-year-old daughters. They defend their reliance on language as the means for examining how anger and aggression are used adaptively in this South Baltimore working class community in that emotion words can encode a variety of aspects of emotional experience – for example, the internal emotional state of anger or the expressive behavior of hitting and biting. The relative degree to which a culture or subculture favors some verbal expressions of emotional experience over others may suggest how the culture organizes that emotional experience.

In fact, what Miller and Sperry found was that in this community anger was primarily referred to in the context of interpersonal aggression, and the language was rich in aggressive phrases rather than in emotion state words. (See Smiley & Huttenlocher, this volume, for a different viewpoint that emphasizes use of emotion state words as the key criterion for determining that a child understands the emotional state in question.) Miller and Sperry provide examples from the mothers whereby people "get flattened out," "put in skillets and stripped down to size," "slammed in the head," and so forth. However, all this vividly described aggression is guided by cultural rules. Specifically, one *ought* to retaliate against an instigator who has violated one's rights, but if the violation of rights has not occurred or if the instigator is a parent or parental authority, one may not display one's aggression. Such disapproved aggressive reactions were viewed as self-indulgent, not justifiable, and as indicating "spoiled children."

The adaptive plasticity that I see in their research is that not only did these mothers and their daughters feel angry, but they also had to *cope*. And coping is adapting to the interpersonal demands that elicited the emotional experience of anger – for example, somebody's transgression such that one must retaliate and/ or defend oneself. Thus, a child was encouraged to defend herself aggressively when, for example, another child bit her (considered a legitimate reason for retaliation). Furthermore, in this community the emotion of sadness appeared to be discouraged. Acts of injury and transgression were to be met with retaliative anger and aggression, that are, in a sense, empowering. By contrast, to respond to injury and transgression with sadness, hurt, discouragement, disappointment, or the like would be to leave oneself more open to possible victimization or exploitation. To sum up, in this particular community the differential encouragement of one emotional reaction over other possible emotional reactions to the same eliciting situation facilitated feeling more powerful as well as justified. However, if the social context of the eliciting situation changed – for example, a parent rather than another child slapped the child – then the child's anger-plus-aggression response was inhibited or perhaps displaced onto a safer target, pets, toys, and younger siblings being notorious victims for displaced aggression.

Genuine displays of emotion

The second study that illustrates the adaptive plasticity of emotions in social situations is one I conducted with 7-, 10-, and 13-year-old children (Saarni, 1987). With the aid of cartoon-accompanied vignettes, 85 children were interviewed about the interpersonal consequences of showing genuine displays of emotion in a family situation. Seven different social contexts were given to the children, and for each one the children were asked to choose from among four parental reactions to the child-protagonist's emotional display the one they thought likely to occur. These four parental reactions ranged from most accepting to most controlling or restrictive toward the protagonist's emotional display. For each vignette the children were also asked to provide a justification for why they thought the parent would react that way.

Even the youngest age group (7 years) proved to be very aware of a critical social context variable, namely, who is likely to be made vulnerable by the display of genuine emotion. Of the seven vignettes, four featured another person in the story who might become vulnerable due to the protagonist showing his or her real feelings (e.g., showing one's disgust at Grandma's strange-looking casserole might result in her feelings being hurt). For these four vignettes, a majority of the children chose the more controlling parent reactions.

For two of the three vignettes in which the protagonist rather than another person was potentially vulnerable, older children anticipated more accepting parent reactions to the display of real feelings than did younger children. The themes of these two vignettes were showing one's sadness at having made a mistake during a solo performance and displaying distress at an impending injection; the theme of the vignette in which no age difference occurred was fear at being threatened by a bully (all children anticipated a relatively accepting parental response). These results suggest that children have some awareness of or at least believe that parents have empathy for their children's feelings and may respond with acceptance rather than restrictiveness.

The justifications given by the children were coded into six categories (see Saarni, 1987, for details of coding). For all but one of the vignettes, the justifications offered by the children depended on the parental reaction that they selected. If the child expected a *controlling* parental reaction to the display of the protagonist's genuine feelings, the child justified that expectation by an appeal to convention (e.g., "Don't be rude") or by claiming that the protagonist ought to change his or her feelings and/or behavior (e.g., "She should be serious and not giggle"). The justifications based on convention occurred in the vignettes where a third person was also involved (i.e., grandmother or grandfather, an accident victim, or a funeral party). The justifications based on the belief that the child should change his or her feelings and/or behavior were obtained in the vignettes in which the protagonist was in an emotionally vulnerable position (i.e., getting an injection, being threatened, making a mistake during a solo performance).

In contrast, if the child expected an *accepting* parental reaction to the display of genuine feelings, the child justified the response by emphasizing that the parent was concerned with how the child-protagonist felt and occasionally by how others or the parent might feel. These justifications did not differ as much across the different vignettes, although the proportion justifying the parental reaction by appealing to how the child felt tended to be higher in the vignettes with a vulnerable protagonist.

These intriguing individual differences emphasize again the complex nuances involved in children's understanding of how emotional-expressive behavior influences others. Children in this age span of 7 to 14 years anticipated that the experience of genuine emotion would elicit specific interpersonal consequences from parents. Moreover, they readily justified their expectations about parental reactions. Only a few children came up with tangential or "I don't know" responses to the interview questions used with these cartoon-accompanied vignettes, and even then it was typically only a single vignette that elicited such a response. Thus, even using fictional material, children found the themes meaningful, and they perceived parents as indeed having a reaction to their children's display of emotions. We might infer that with regard to their own personal experience children readily understand that important others, such as parents, react in predictable ways to their display of emotion. Children come to realize that they can influence outcomes of social situations by controlling their emotional displays.

This interview study showed that children are sensitive to *who* would be potentially made vulnerable by the display of genuine feelings – the communicator of the genuine feelings or someone else with whom he or she was interacting. Not that children specifically said, "don't show your real feelings because you or someone else will be negatively affected"; rather, it was their clear-cut choice of different parent reactions to the display of genuine feelings that showed that children distinguished who would potentially be made vulnerable by the display of real feelings. They had gotten the message loud and clear from their parents that if someone else might be adversely affected by their display of genuine feelings about some matter, then they had better modify their emotional-expressive behavior accordingly.

This study left many questions unaddressed, such as how children might anticipate their *own* parents' reactions. It would also be descriptively useful to determine whether children articulate clear distinctions based on gender of parent and to determine whether there is an interaction between gender of parent and gender of child in what sorts of parental responses are anticipated to the display of genuine feelings. In the present study gender of parent did figure in several significant three-way interactions involving either parent reaction choice or justification category, but the sample size was too small to permit meaningful interpretation in most cases.

The same seven vignettes were given to 124 adults who were also parents in order to evaluate whether children's expectations about parental reactions were congruent with what adults themselves believed to be likely parental reactions to children's genuine emotional displays (Saarni, 1988). The adult and child patterns were remarkably similar in terms of which social contexts elicited either controlling or accepting parental reactions. However, child and adult justifications differed: Adults were more likely to justify the parental reaction by appealing to how the parent felt – not surprisingly, the children were more likely to justify parental reactions as stemming from how the child felt. Adults were also more likely to predict more controlling parental reactions to boys than girls when boys displayed genuine emotions in situations in which they were vulnerable. There was no parallel sex difference among the child subjects. A sex difference among the parents also emerged: Mothers tended to give justifications for parental reactions that focused on children, that is, that the child's feelings were the reason for the parent reaction or that the child's behavior should change. Fathers' justifications tended to emphasize an appeal to conventionality or to the parent's own feelings, or else they said "that's what I would do."

Our culture specifies that the strategic control of emotional-expressive behavior needs to take into account what the interpersonal consequences are to the display of feelings, i.e., whether they serve one's own self-interest or that of another person. Sensitivity to those anticipated consequences dictates, in part, how adaptive one is in social transactions. However, this is not to be confused with social approval-seeking; sensitivity to the potential interpersonal consequences of one's expressive display of emotions does not necessarily mean pandering to others' needs or expectations. It is also important to take into account the significance of the felt emotion to one's self (see Saarni, in press, in which the issue of balance between showing one's feelings or not is discussed further).

Dissociation of emotional state and expressive behaviors permits implicit strategies for interaction with others

As children develop the awareness that their internal emotional state does not have to correspond to their external expressive behavior, they have also acquired implicit strategies for interaction with others. An elaboration of this dissociation of state and expressive behavior suggests that these implicit strategies of interaction reflect a two-step process: the anticipation of another person's response is followed by managing one's own emotional-expressive behavior so as to influence the anticipated emotion-mediated response from the other person. Obviously, the other also has anticipations about the interaction and will be similarly regulating her or his self-presentation. The seemingly simple two-step process quickly becomes a complex dance of anticipation and maneuver to influence the stream of interaction (from a social psychological perspective, see also Baumeister, 1982; Darley & Fazio, 1980). This process has been aptly labeled *negotiation* by Dunn and Munn (1985) in their work with young children in family contexts, by Selman and Demorest (1984) in their clinical observation of troubled adolescents, and by Hinde (1985) in his ethological analysis of signaling behavior. A series of studies will be reviewed here in order to tease out how children conceptualize this mutual maneuvering of expressive behavior. My emphasis will be on the expectancies held prior to a specific interpersonal transaction and on how features of the social context affect emotion management.

Appearance versus reality

There are basic cognitive developmental prerequisites to being able to regulate one's emotional-expressive behavior, particularly in advance of some social transaction. As Harris, Donnelly, Guz, and Pitt-Watson (1986) have cogently demonstrated (and replicated with Japanese children as well; Gardner, Harris, Ohmoto, & Hamazaki, 1988), children need to understand appearance–reality distinctions relative to emotional dissimulation (see Flavell, 1986, for a general review of the development of the appearance–reality distinction). In the case of emotional-expressive behavior management, "appearance" quite literally refers to the appearance of the facial expression, which under conditions of dissemblance does not correspond to "reality" – namely, the actual emotion being felt subjectively. Furthermore, children would also presumably need to have some sort of intuitive awareness of what their subjective emotional state actually is if they are to dissimulate their expressive behavior effectively. Although children and adults may dissemble unwittingly, I would speculate that such unconscious dissemblance of emotional-expressive behavior more often represents highly learned and even habitual expressive dissimulation. For example, many American women "automatically" smile when mildly anxious or embarrassed, or we habitually smile upon receiving a gift, even if it is a disappointing one.

Harris et al. determined that children as young as 6 years in both England and Japan understood the appearance–reality distinction as applied to noncorrespondence between facial expression and internal state. Gross and Harris (in press) found that there were also a few 4-year-olds who understood this distinction, but that by age 6 many more children readily comprehended that expressive behavior could dissimulate an emotion not genuinely being felt. Gross and Harris also found that 6-year-olds understood that (a) an onlooker can have a false belief about someone's emotional state, (b) a misleading facial display can lead another person to have a false belief about oneself, and (c) such misleading displays are a consequence of the desire to protect oneself or manipulate a situation to one's advantage.

Further evidence that young children can dissociate expressive behavior from internal state may be found in Cummings's research (1987). He investigated the *behavioral* ramifications of preschool children's reaction to a staged argument between two adults. In subsequent interviews, Cummings found that a majority of the nonresponsive children (4–5 years) said that they wanted to ignore the argument even as they admitted feeling angry about it. He concluded that the children's apparent lack of behavioral response masked angry feelings. Thus, behaviorally children may well enact the appearance–reality distinction for emotion before they can verbally articulate it, a common pattern in cognitive development research.

Preinteraction expectancies

Once children can anticipate that they can mislead an onlooker about their real feelings by modifying their facial display, they can conceivably use this skill in conjunction with taking into account information about their prospective interactant. Gnepp and Chilamkurti (1987; see also Gnepp, this volume) have documented that 6-, 8- and 10-year-old children can take into account personality information about a protagonist and use such information to predict the protagonist's emotional response. They found that even the youngest children could do this to some degree. In addition, Gnepp and Gould (1985) determined that across the grade-school years children increased their skill at accurately interpreting an event from another's perspective, taking into account that individual's prior experience.

I contend that expectancies about anticipated social interaction – or preinteraction expectancies, as they are referred to in social psychological research – are operative at rather young ages (certainly by school entry), may be observed in children's emotional-expressive behavior in social transactions (e.g., Saarni, 1984), and may possibly be evident in their verbal responses to interview questions about how and why they manage their emotional-expressive behavior (e.g., Saarni, 1979a, 1979b, 1985b). However, we lack a clear demonstration of how children come to *conceptualize* their preinteraction expectancies as related to their emotional-expressive behavior management.

Research based on adults (e.g., see a review by Ickes, Patterson, Rajecki, & Tanford, 1982) has suggested that one common type of preinteraction expectancy is based on reciprocity: The interactants anticipate mutually congruent behavior from each other (e.g., approach–approach or avoidance–avoidance). A second common type of preinteraction expectancy is based on compensation: An individual anticipates an undesirable response from another unless he or she compensates in advance. This can take the form of a "pre-emptive strike," appeasement, distraction, or of any self-presentation intended to modify the interaction (see also Swann & Snyder, 1980; Patterson, 1984).

It is not known, for example, when or under what conditions reciprocity or compensation emerge in expectancies held by children, or whether there are developmental precursors to these two modes. Clearly, being able to make appearance–reality distinctions relative to emotional state and expression and being able to take into account personal information about one's prospective interactant would be prerequisites for children to be able to alter strategically their self-presentations to others in order to affect the expected social outcome. Whether children recognize that others may be similarly strategic in their self-presentations due to the preinteraction expectancies that they hold is not known. Although adults may be capable of *recognizing* that such reciprocal strategizing of self-presentations occurs, it is clear that they do not consistently *use* such knowledge in their relationships (e.g., Patterson, 1984).

Social context and emotion management

A few studies have been conducted that permit us to begin to describe children's anticipations about how emotional-expressive behavior will be managed, relative to different age groups and according to different social contexts (e.g., Gnepp & Gould, 1985; Saarni, 1979a). However, it is still unclear as to what it is about the social context that systematically affects the preinteraction expectancies held by children. I will suggest three different features of social contexts that may contribute to preinteraction expectancies and subsequent emotional-expressive behavior management: (a) controllability, (b) status differential, and (c) degree of affiliation. How these three features may affect expectancies and subsequent emotion management are discussed below.

An early descriptive study shed some light on social contexts and expressive behavior management. Six-, 8-, and 10-year-old children were asked to nominate their personal reasons for masking or substituting their feelings of hurt/pain and fear (Saarni, 1979b). Fifty-eight percent of all the reasons mentioned fell in the category of avoidance of derision or embarrassment. Additionally, all three age groups mentioned substitution of expressive behavior as a way of getting attention, for making someone feel sorry for oneself, and for getting help.

Children's responses about when it would be appropriate to show their genuine feelings were also coded in this study. With increasing age, children cited *more* reasons or occasions for the appropriate expression of feelings. Nine categories of reasons were derived for when it would be appropriate to show one's real feelings; in descending order of frequency they were: (a) if the feelings were very intense; (b) if one was sick, injured, or bleeding; (c) if one was with certain people, such as parents or friends; (d) if special or unusual misfortunes occurred, such as being in a fire, falling off a building (!), dropping one's homework in a puddle, or having one's lunch stolen at school; (e) if one was in a special setting or environment (such as an amusement park, in a horror movie, alone watching TV); (f) if one was a young child; (g) if one was being scolded or had been caught doing something wrong; and finally (h) if one had been unjustly accused, one should show how one feels about it.

What is evident from this descriptive study is the common expectation of disapproval (e.g., derision) from others for revealing spontaneous and genuine negative expressive behavior (i.e., pain/hurt and fear) wherein one's vulnerability may be exposed. (Note that anger is not included here.) The fact that the older children were much more likely to provide a variety of reasons and occasions for when it would be appropriate to show one's feelings suggests that they view expressive behavior as indeed being managed or regulated: There are specific times and places when feelings may be directly revealed as well as when they should be inhibited or modified in some way. The pattern of responses suggested that with increasing age there was a concomitant increase in flexibility in the deployment of emotional-expressive behavior, whether modified or genuine in display, a conclusion echoed by Shennum and Bugental (1982).

Controllability. What is also interesting about the nine categories above is that the two most often cited circumstances for when feelings could be revealed imply limited controllability over the feeling states in question (i.e., having very intense feelings, being ill or injured). In addition, the categories about special misfortunes, being a young child, and being mistakenly scolded are also uncontrollable, but more from the standpoint of lack of control over the events giving rise to the feeling states. It is likely that many of the feeling states over which a child experiences relatively little control also occur in situations in which the child perceives herself or himself as having little control over the emotion-eliciting events.

In terms of children's conceptualizations about why and when genuine emotions might be expressed, these descriptive categories suggest that children make attributions along dimensions that bear some resemblance to Weiner and Graham's (1984) dimension of controllability. Weiner and his colleagues have defined controllability in this context as "causes that are perceived as subject to volitional influence" (p. 104; see also Weiner & Handel, 1985). Weiner and Handel's (1985) recent study on when children would reveal the real reasons for possibly hurting another child's feelings also indicated that the dimension of controllability was critical in children's thinking. They were more likely to communicate to the target *un*controllable reasons for a supposed social rejection than controllable reasons or excuses. This kind of reasoning bears some similarity to children's belief that it is "OK" to reveal one's real feelings to another if they are relatively "uncontrollable."

Related to the question of whether "uncontrollable" feelings may be expressed (even if doing so risks incurring negative interpersonal consequences), is whether children even recognize when a display of feelings has violated a social norm. Johnson, Greenspan, and Brown (1984) studied children's (ages 8–9, 11–12, and 14–15) ability to recognize and improve upon socially inept verbal statements. They found that vignettes involving inept or socially awkward attempts to influence the feelings of another were the most difficult for the children to recognize or to improve upon.

What needs further clarification is why children also believe certain interpersonal relationships and certain settings, which may, in fact, entail controllability or volition, also permit the expression of genuine feelings, as noted in categories (c) and (e) above. It is conceivable that reciprocal interaction is involved here: Both interactants hold expectancies about each other, and each congruently fulfills the other's expectancy (see Ickes et al., 1982). When children did mention specific people to whom they would reveal their real feelings, they always referred to friends, parents, other family members, and, occasionally, their teacher. Paradoxically, the expression of genuine feelings, when interacting reciprocally with *certain* others, may be a highly regulated exchange of ''spontaneous'' emotional-expressive behavior that in fact defines the relationship as a particular kind (intimate, kinship, etc). Settings that were cited as outlets for the expression of genuine feeling were amusement parks or in front of the TV or alone. Again, reciprocity may be operative here: We ''expect'' others to yell and scream on roller coaster rides or during horror movies and the like, just as we may do so ourselves. As for the TV, perhaps it is equivalent to being alone, or at least none of the others is paying attention to one if they are all glued to the set as well. Furthermore, television is often viewed with family members or close friends. Given that one has a close relationship with one's fellow television viewers, it becomes ''OK'' to respond with genuine emotional expression, because this in part defines the relationship as close.

Status differential. The complementary question is also significant: What kinds of interpersonal relationships are viewed by children as being more likely to elicit dissembled or managed emotional-expressive behavior? A recent study (Saarni, in press) indirectly provides a basis for beginning to answer this question. Children (ages 7, 10, and 13) were asked as part of an extensive structured interview whether they thought children like themselves (same age and sex) would be more likely to show their real feelings to other ''kids'' or to adults (parents excluded). The youngest children were more likely to prefer adults as the recipients of genuine displays (61%) rather than show their real feelings to their peers (39%). The two older age groups tended to prefer their peers as recipients of genuine displays (56%), with this pattern being most pronounced among the older girls: 73% of the 10-year-old girls and 62% of the 13-year-old girls preferred peers. When their rationales for their choice of peers or adults were descriptively categorized, children who preferred adults as the audience for genuine emotional displays justified their choice either because they feared peer derision (44%) or because they thought adults were more trustworthy (37%). Children preferring peers thought either that peers were more trustworthy (66%) or that adults were troublesome people who might do something negative to one if they saw one's genuine feelings (34%). Interestingly, it was primarily the 10- and 13-year-old girls who viewed adults as such disagreeable people and therefore preferred to show their real feelings to their peers.

In sum, perception of a difference in status between self (i.e., the child) and target (an adult or peer) seemed to affect management of expressive behavior in two ways: (1) because adults have more age role-related power over a child, there is some inherent risk as to how that power will be expressed if a child reveals genuine feelings to the adult; and (2) to be ridiculed by one's peers over one's expression of genuine emotions constitutes a loss of status within the peer group, although perhaps only temporarily.

Turning briefly to research with adults, Mehrabian is a notable early investigator of adults' nonverbal expressive behavior (reviewed in 1972). He found that differences in status were communicated through variations in patterns of gaze direction, postural tension, and use of space. Thus, when status differs between two individuals, their management of expressive behavior occurs in a somewhat predictable fashion. However, Mehrabian also maintained that interacting with judgments of status were two additional social cognitive categories, namely, judgments of a person as imbued with positive or negative emotional valence and judgment of the person's importance to oneself (e.g., intimate relationship versus a trival transaction with a stranger). These three basic categories of social cognition hypothetically constitute a three-dimensional framework in which adults' interpersonal nonverbal expressive behavior can be described. Mehrabian's work with adults leads us to consider the next feature of social context – degree of affiliation – that may influence preinteraction expectancies and subsequent emotional-expressive behavior management in children. I view degree of affiliation as a combination of Mehrabian's categories of emotional valence and importance or salience of the target to oneself.

Degree of affiliation. In the same descriptive study discussed above (Saarni, in press), how close and/or trustworthy one perceived one's relationship with a communicative target to be was relevant to the kinds of positive rationales offered for whether genuine feelings would be revealed. Thus, degree of affiliation appeared to underlie which audience – adults or peers – was believed to be more trustworthy. For peers the positive expectancy was that they would be understanding and that one could trust one's peers to accept one's expression of real feelings. For adults the positive expectancy included being listened to and taken seriously by adults, and that one could elicit sympathy or help from adults if one showed one's genuine feelings.

Further evidence that supports the dimension of degree of affiliation as underlying emotional-expressive behavior management comes from a study by Yarczower and Daruns (1982) in which first- and sixth-grade children were rated as less expressive while watching affective slides when they were in the company of an adult experimenter versus when they were alone watching the slide. In contrast, when an adult does display warmth and affiliation, children preferred closer proximity toward that adult (Morris & Smith, 1980). In this context, interpersonal distance may also be construed as a form of expressive behavior, subject to regulation, with implications for who becomes a preferred target for genuine emotional displays.

By middle childhood and more thoroughly in early adolescence, children actively take into account the social context in predicting and justifying expressive behavior management. This was demonstrated in Mendelson and Peters' (1983) study on children using relationship knowledge (i.e., parent versus nonparent, friend versus nonfriend) to predict the emotions communicated in a dyadic interaction. They found that by 9–10 years children took into account "relationship information to organize their interpretations of hostile but not affectionate behaviors. . . . Only grade 8 [13–14 years] children were consistently influenced by knowledge of the relationships" (p. 2). Again relevant here is the investigation by Gnepp and Chilamkurti (1987), who documented an age-related increase in grade-school children's use of personality information in predicting and justifying future behaviors and somewhat less consistently (unless they were prompted) in predicting emotional reactions (defined as internal states, not expressive behavior, see also Gnepp & Gould, 1985).

Finally, without regard for developmental issues, social psychologists have also emphasized the significant effect of intimacy or degree of affiliation on adults' nonverbal expressive behavior. Frequency, intensity, and variety of expressive behaviors and immediacy usually increase with affiliation (e.g., Buck, 1984).

Thus, the complexity demonstrated by children in their understanding of social-emotional interaction is guided by their ability to use contextual information that may involve status comparisons, differences in closeness of relationship, and perception of degree of personal control over either or both situational circumstances and internal states.

Conclusion

This chapter has sought to clarify how children come to understand strategic control of emotional expression in social transactions. However, I do not think I have adequately addressed the *strategic* part of this understanding. Strategy has often been linked with the artful or skillful planning and conduct of military combat – which is certainly not what I have in mind as a way of characterizing social interaction! By strategic control I wish to highlight the *shrewd finesse* (i.e., a self-serving subtle or tactful maneuver) that often accompanies deliberate management of emotional-expressive behavior, such as illustrated in the three examples at the beginning of this chapter. In other words, people have motives, based on promoting their presumably healthy self-interest, that are also evident in the management of their emotional-expressive behavior with others. By middle-to-late childhood, children seem well on their way to having a good understanding of what those motives may encompass. They then combine that understanding of motives with their perception of critical features of the interpersonal context and can subsequently articulate rather impressively what our culture would view as art and skill in conducting social transactions. Among the questions I would like to see addressed in future research are (1) sources of individual differences in this multifaceted understanding, and (2) how this understanding is manifested *pragmatically* in actual social transactions as opposed to how it is verbalized in the child's emerging theory of mind and emotion as elicited in experimental interviews.

I would like to conclude with a few comments on conducting empirical research with children about their understanding of emotional experience. First, there is the critical issue of demand characteristics, which obviously affect young subjects. Much of the developmental research on the understanding of emotion uses a structured verbal interview with a forced- choice response format. When we provide standardized and streamlined stimuli to control for situational variability, what we may actually be doing is enlarging the amount of variation contributed by the influence of demand characteristics to the response given by the child. These demand characteristics include the interpersonal transactions that involve control of emotion expression between the experimenter and the child subject. In addition, sparse stimulus questions and response formats press the child still more to figure out what it is that the experimenter wants from her or him.

Second, children also tend to view experimenters as adults who expect compliance. As a result, children often feel they *have* to give an answer, and they will seek to read from the experimenter's expressive behavior what is expected. Whether the answer given is a true indicator of a child's preferred or most sophisticated way of comprehending some facet of emotional experience is quite another matter. Oversimplified stimulus situations that are designed to elicit from children their reasoning about emotional experience may well permit one to analyze one's data more readily, but it is not at all clear that such stimuli actually get at the richness of children's comprehension of emotional experience. Such stimuli may reflect more how the child subjects are coping with the demand characteristics of the particular research study. The experimental interview probably also represents a good example of how children take into account status comparison, degree of affiliation, and controllability as they negotiate their interaction with the experimenter.

Third, relative to research methods for studying children's understanding of emotion, I am obviously biased in the direction of in-depth interviews accompanied by supportive photos or pictures. As part of the interview children may also respond to structured choices but ideally would subsequently have to justify their choices (and that task may well lead to their changing their minds about the original choice). In other words, probes, follow-up questions, counterexamples, comprehension and memory checks, and justifications all provide for greater depth in what sort of responses are given. I am also biased in favor of offering to children a variety of scenarios or situations in which to probe the nuances of their understanding of emotional experience, because different social contexts elicit from children very different viewpoints on what is going on emotionally. Limits on generalizability are particularly important to recognize here, because context has such a pervasive influence on what children give as their interpretations of the social-emotional scenario they are asked to make sense of.

Lastly, we need more observational and ethnographic research (beyond the age of infancy), such as that by Miller and Sperry (1987) and Cummings (1987), both to substantiate our interview and questionnaire methods and to enrich our theoretical positions on the development of understanding of emotion.

At this point I hope a persuasive argument has been presented such that readers of this chapter will be more likely to take into account in their next research project on understanding of emotion what the interpersonal situation is that faces their young subjects. That interpersonal situation includes both the experimental situation, which itself is a social transaction, and the kinds of theoretical issues about emotion that the experimenter is preoccupied with and that the young subject is trying to figure out in order to strategically control the outcome.

References

Barden, R., Zelko, F., Duncan, S., & Masters, J. (1980). Children's consensual knowledge about the experiential determinants of emotion. *Journal of Personality and Social Psychology, 39,* 968–976.

Baumeister, R. F. (1982). A self-presentational view of social phenomena. *Psychological Bulletin, 91,* 3–26.

Bradbury, T. N., & Fincham, F. D. (1987). Affect and cognition in close relationships: towards an integrative model. *Cognition and Emotion, 1,* 59–87.

Breger, L. (1974). *From instinct to identity.* Englewood Cliffs, NJ: Prentice-Hall.

Buck, R. (1984). *The communication of emotion.* New York: The Guilford Press.

Burgess, R., & Conger, R. (1978). Family interaction in abusive, neglectful, and normal families. *Child Development, 49,* 1163–1173.

Camras, L., Grow, G., & Ribordy, S. (1983). Recognition of emotional expressions by abused children. *Journal of Clinical and Child Psychology, 12,* 325–328.

Carlson, C. R., Felleman, E., & Masters, J. C. (1983). Influence of children's emotional states on the recognition of emotions in peers and social motives to change another's emotional state. *Motivation and Emotion, 7,* 61–79.

Cummings, E. M. (1987). Coping with background anger in early childhood. *Child Development,* *58,* 976–984.

Darley, J., & Fazio, R. (1980). Expectancy confirmation processes arising in the social interaction process. *American Psychologist, 35,* 867–881.

Dunn, J., & Munn, P. (1985). Becoming a family member: family conflict and the development of social understanding in the second year. *Child Development, 56,* 480–492.

Ekman, P. (1984). Expression and the nature of emotion. In K. Scherer & P. Ekman (Eds.), *Approaches to emotion* (pp. 319–343). Hillsdale, NJ: Erlbaum.

Emde, R. (1980). Levels of meaning for infant emotions: a biosocial view. In W. A. Collins (Ed.), *Development of cognition, affect, and social relations, Vol. 13, Minnesota Symposia on Child Psychology* (pp. 1–37). Hillsdale, NJ: Erlbaum.

Feinman, S., & Lewis M. (1983). Social referencing and second order effects in ten-month-old infants. *Child Development, 54,* 878–887.

Flavell, J. H. (1986). The development of children's knowledge about the appearance–reality distinction. *American Psychologist, 41,* 418–425.

Gardner, D., Harris, P. L., Ohmoto, M., & Hamazaki, T. (1988). Understanding of the distinction between real and apparent emotion by Japanese children. *International Journal of Behavioral Development, 11,* 203–218.

Gnepp, J., & Hess, D. (1986). Children's understanding of verbal and facial display rules. *Developmental Psychology, 22,* 103–108.

Gnepp, J., & Chilamkurti, C. (1987). *Children's use of personality attributions to predict behavior and emotions.* Paper presented at the meeting of the Society for Research in Child Development, Baltimore, MD, April.

Gnepp, J., & Gould, M. (1985). The development of personalized inferences: understanding other people's emotional reactions in light of their prior experiences. *Child Development, 56,* 1455–1464.

Gordon, S. (1981). The sociology of sentiments and emotions. In M. Rosenberg & R. Turner (Eds.), *Social psychology: sociological perspectives* (pp. 562–592). New York: Basic Books.

Gross, D., & Harris, P. L. (in press). False beliefs about emotion: children's understanding of misleading emotional displays. *International Journal of Behavioral Development.*

Haley, J. (1963). *Strategies of psychotherapy.* New York: Grune and Stratton.

Harkness, S., & Super, C. M. (1985) Child-environment interactions in the socialization of affect. In M. Lewis & C. Saarni (Eds.), *The socialization of emotions* (pp. 21–36). New York: Plenum.

Harris, P. L. (1985). What children know about situations that provoke emotion. In M. Lewis & C. Saarni (Eds.), *The socialization of emotions* (pp. 161–185). New York: Plenum.

Harris, P. L., Donnelly, K., Guz, G., & Pitt-Watson, R. (1986). Children's understanding of the distinction between real and apparent emotion. *Child Development, 57,* 895–909.

Harter, S. (1982). Children's understanding of multiple emotions: a cognitive-developmental approach. In W. Overton (Ed.), *The relationship between social and cognitive development* (pp. 147–194). Hillsdale, NJ: Erlbaum.

Heider, K. (1984). *Emotion: inner state versus interaction.* Paper presented at the meeting of the American Anthropological Association, Denver, November.

Hinde, R. (1985). Expression and negotiation. In G. Zivin (Ed.), *The development of expressive behavior: biology–environment interactions* (pp. 103–116). New York: Academic Press.

Hochschild, A. (1983). *The managed heart.* Berkeley: University of California Press.

Ickes, W., Patterson, M. L., Rajecki, D., & Tanford, S. (1982). Behavioral and cognitive consequences of reciprocal versus compensatory responses to preinteraction expectancies. *Social Cognition, 1,* 160–190.

Izard, C. E. (1977). *Human emotions.* New York: Plenum.

Johnson, R. R., Greenspan, S., & Brown, G. (1984). Children's ability to recognize and improve upon socially inept communications. *The Journal of Genetic Psychology, 144,* 255–264.

Jurkovic, G., & Selman, R. (1980). A developmental analysis of intrapsychic understanding: treating emotional disturbances in children. *New Directions for Child Development, 7,* 91–112.

Kempe, R. S., & Kempe, C. H. (1978). *Child abuse.* Cambridge, MA: Harvard University Press.

Kemper, T. (1978). *A social interactional theory of emotion.* New York: Wiley.

Lazarus, R. S. (1984). On the primacy of cognition. *American Psychologist, 39,* 124–129.

Lewis, M., & Michalson, L. (1983). *Children's emotions and moods.* New York: Plenum.

Linehan, M., Paul, E., & Egan, K. (1983). The Parent Affect Test: development, validity, and reliability. *Journal of Clinical Child Psychology, 12,* 161–166.

Lutz, C. (1985). Cultural patterns and individual differences in the child's emotional meaning system. In M. Lewis & C. Saarni (Eds.), *The socialization of emotion* (pp. 37–53). New York: Plenum.

Malatesta, C. (1985). Developmental course of emotion expression in the human infant. In G. Zivin (Ed.), *The development of expressive behavior: biology–environment interactions* (pp. 183–219). New York: Academic Press.

Malatesta, C., & Haviland, J. (1982). Learning display rules: the socialization of emotion expression in infancy. *Child Development, 53,* 991–1003.

McCoy, C., & Masters, J. (1985). The development of children's strategies for the social control of emotion. *Child Development, 56,* 1214–1222.

Mendelson, R., & Peters, R. D. (1983). *The influence of relationship knowledge on children's interpretations of social behaviour.* Paper presented at the meeting of the Society for Research in Child Development, Detroit, MI, April.

Mehrabian, A. (1972). *Nonverbal communication.* New York: Aldeno Atherton.

Miller, P., & Sperry, L. (1987). The socialization of anger and aggression. *Merrill-Palmer Quarterly, 33,* 1–31.

Morris, E. K., & Smith, G. L. (1980). A functional analysis of adult affection and children's interpersonal distance. *The Psychological Record, 30,* 155–163.

Noble, G. (1983). Social learning from everyday television. In M. Howe (Ed.), *Learning from television: psychological and educational research* (pp. 101–124). New York: Academic Press, 1983.

Patterson, M. L. (Ed.) (1984). *Nonverbal intimacy and exchange.* Special issue of *Journal of Nonverbal Behavior.* New York: Human Sciences Press.

Perry, M., Doran, L., & Wells, E. (1983). Parent characteristics in abusing and nonabusing families. *Journal of Clinical and Child Psychology, 12,* 329–336.

Rosaldo, M. Z. (1984). Toward an anthropology of self and feeling. In R. A. Schweder & S. R. LeVine (Eds.), *Culture theory: essays on mind, self, and emotion* (pp. 137–157). Cambridge: Cambridge University Press.

Saarni, C. (1978). Cognitive and communicative features of emotional experience, or do you show what you think you feel? In M. Lewis & L. Rosenblum (Eds.), *The development of affect* (pp. 361–375). New York: Plenum.

Saarni, C. (1979a). Children's understanding of display rules for expressive behavior. *Developmental Psychology, 15,* 424–429.

Saarni, C. (1979b). *When not to show what you think you feel: children's understanding of relations between emotional experience and expressive behavior.* Paper presented at the meeting of the Society for Research in Child Development, San Francisco, March.

Saarni, C. (1982). Social and affective functions of nonverbal behavior: developmental concerns. In R. Feldman (Ed.), *Development of nonverbal behavior in children* (pp. 123–147). New York: Springer–Verlag.

Saarni, C. (1984). An observational study of children's attempts to monitor their expressive behavior. *Child Development, 55,* 1504–1513.

Saarni, C. (1985). Indirect processes in affect socialization. In M. Lewis & C. Saarni (Eds.), *The socialization of emotions* (pp. 187–209). New York: Plenum.

Saarni, C. (1987). *Children's beliefs about parental expectations for emotional-expressive behavior management.* Paper presented at the meeting of the Society for Research in Child Development. Baltimore, MD, April.

Saarni, C. (1988). *Children's beliefs about emotion.* Paper presented at the meeting of the International Congress of Psychology, Sydney, Australia, September.

Saarni, C. (1988). Children's understanding of the interpersonal consequences of dissemblance on nonverbal emotional-expressive behavior. In B. DePaulo (Ed.), *Deception.* Special issue of *Journal of Nonverbal Behavior, Vol. 12* (Nos. 3–4). New York: Plenum.

Satir, V. (1967). *Conjoint family therapy.* Palo Alto, CA: Science and Behavior Books.

Selman, R., & Demorest, A. (1984). Observing troubled children's interpersonal negotiation strategies: implications for a developmental model. *Child Development, 55,* 288–304.

Shennum, W., & Bugental, D. (1982). The development of control over affective expression in nonverbal behavior. In R. Feldman (Ed.), *Development of nonverbal behavior in children* (pp. 102–121). New York: Springer-Verlag.

Shott, S. (1979). Emotion and social life: a symbolic interactionist analysis. *American Journal of Sociology, 84,* 1317–1334.

Sorce, J., Emde, R., Campos, J., & Klinnert, M. (1985). Maternal emotional signalling: its effect on the visual cliff behavior of one-year-olds. *Developmental Psychology, 21,* 195–200.

Sroufe, A., Schork, E., Motti, E., Lawroski, N., & LaFreniere, P. (1984). The role of affect in social competence. In C. Izard, J. Kagan, & R. Zajonc (Eds.), *Emotions, cognition, and behavior* (pp. 289–319). New York: Cambridge University Press.

Strayer, J. (1985). *Children's knowledge of the situational determinants of emotion.* Paper presented at the meeting of the Canadian Psychological Association, Halifax, Canada, June.

Stern, D. (1974). The goal and structure of mother–infant play. *Journal of the American Academy of Child Psychiatry, 13,* 402–421.

Swann, W., & Snyder, M. (1980). On translating beliefs into action: theories of ability and their application in an instructional setting. *Journal of Personality and Social Psychology, 38,* 879–888.

Watzlawick, P., Beavin, J., & Jackson, D. (1967). *Pragmatics of human communication: A study of interactional patterns, pathologies, and paradoxes.* New York: Norton.

Weiner, B., & Graham, S. (1984). An attributional approach to emotional development. In C. Izard, J. Kagan, & R. Zajonc (Eds.), *Emotion, cognition, and behavior* (pp. 167–191). New York: Cambridge University Press.

Weiner, B., & Handel, S. (1985). A cognition–emotion–action sequence: anticipated emotional consequences of causal attributions and reported communication strategy. *Developmental Psychology, 21,* 102–107.

Yarczower, M., & Daruns, L. (1982). Social inhibition of spontaneous facial expressions in children. *Journal of Personality and Social Psychology, 43,* 831–837.

8 Awareness and self-regulation of emotion in young children

Mark Meerum Terwogt and Tjeert Olthof

After a long period of relative silence, dominated by classical and neobehaviorism, renewed interest in the area of affect was instigated in the sixties by Magda Arnold's phenomenological approach to emotions (Arnold, 1960). She reasserted the idea that emotion is first and foremost a subjective experience and that it is through the subject's immediate experience that it can best be understood. Such a phenomenological approach relies heavily on concious experience in the investigation of affect.

Following in these footsteps, developmental psychologists have recently carried out a rapidly accumulating number of studies on children's insight into their own emotional functioning as well as that of others. Reviews make it clear that, in the course of development, children are increasingly able to talk about many aspects of emotion (Bretherton, Fritz, Zahn-Waxler, & Ridgeway, 1986; Harris & Olthof, 1982). They show an increased understanding of emotion terms (e.g., Barden, Zelko, Duncan, & Masters, 1980; Gilbert, 1969), of the situations that are likely to induce emotions in themselves and in others (e.g., Harris, Olthof, Meerum Terwogt, & Hardman, 1987), of the situational, physiological, and mental cues that enable someone to identify an emotion (e.g., Carroll & Steward, 1984; Harris, Olthof, & Meerum Terwogt, 1981; Shields & Stern, 1979), of the possible effects that emotions have on attitudes and behavior (e.g., Glasberg & Aboud, 1982; Masters & Carlson, 1984; Meerum Terwogt, 1986) and of the integration of successive or simultaneous emotions (e.g., Harter, 1977, 1979, 1983; Meerum Terwogt, 1987; Meerum Terwogt, Koops, Oosterhoff, & Olthof, 1986; Olthof, Meerum Terwogt, van Panthaleon van Eck, & Koops, 1987), of the display rules for emotional expression (e.g., Saarni, 1979, 1984; Taylor & Harris, 1984; Harris, Donnelly, Guz, & Pitt-Watson, 1986), of strategies for simulating or hiding emotion (e.g., Harris et al., 1981; Saarni, 1984), of strategies that change the consequences of emotions (e.g., Masters, Ford, & Arend, 1983; Mischel & Mischel, 1983; Meerum Terwogt, 1986) or change the character of emotion (e.g., Masters & Santrock, 1976; Meerum Terwogt, Schene, & Harris, 1986), and so forth.

209

In much of this research, the reasons for studying children's knowledge of emotion remain implicit. Of course, the child's developing ideas about emotion constitute an interesting and important topic in their own right. Nevertheless, most research in this area seems to imply that studying children's knowledge of emotion is in some way important for our understanding of emotional development and emotional behavior. The precise nature of the relation between knowledge and behavior, however, is left unclear. In the present chapter, therefore, we not only want to consider the development of children's conception of emotion, but also how that conception might influence their actual behavior.

Knowledge about emotion

Before embarking on a discussion about knowledge and behavior, we should specify what we mean by the phrase "knowledge about emotion." We use it to refer to a person's cognitive *representations* concerning emotion and emotional behavior. These representations may contain information about emotion that is relatively explicit and easy to verbalize as well as information that is implicit and difficult to verbalize. The important point is, however, that when using the term "knowledge" we refer to the representational level and not to the level of actual emotional behavior.

An example might clarify the distinction further. Assume that an investigation of the development of anger consists of three parts. First, children's actual anger in real life situations is observed. One might observe, for example, that children get angry in certain types of situations and not in others. Second, children are presented with stories that depict hypothetical anger-arousing situations and are asked how angry they would get in each situation. And third, children simply answer the question: "In what situations do you get angry?" In our view only the data obtained in the second and third part of the procedure reflect children's *knowledge* of anger.

Simply observing that the child gets angry in one situation and not in another does *not* necessarily imply that the child has any knowledge concerning the different anger-arousing potential of both situations. Just as one cannot infer that a car has any knowledge about the distinction between brakes and throttle from the fact that it "behaves" differently depending on which system has been activated by the driver, or that anyone who can preserve an upright position in walking knows the workings of the balance system, one cannot infer children's knowledge about their own emotional functioning just from observing their behavior.

Parallelism

How could the development of children's knowledge about emotion, as defined above, be related to the development of emotional behavior? In our view, several types of relationship are possible.

First, there could be a complete isomorphism between the development of knowledge and of behavior, that is, age-related changes in children's knowledge of emotion could be paralleled by corresponding changes in their emotional behavior. In the above discussion of the definition of the term "knowledge," it was implied that a correspondence between knowledge and behavior is not a *logical* necessity. Behavior is not necessarily mediated by knowledge as defined here. Nevertheless, a correspondence between knowledge and behavior could still be an *empirical* reality. It might, for example, turn out that age-related changes in children's reports about when they get angry are in full agreement with observed changes in the determinants of their actual anger. If found, such an isomorphism would suggest that children have full access to the cognitive processes that underlie their emotional behavior. Asking children about their knowledge would be equivalent to investigating the cognitive determinants of emotional behavior.

A correspondence between knowledge and behavior is often implicitly assumed in much social cognitive research on emotion. For example, attribution theorists (e.g., Graham & Weiner, 1986; Thompson, this volume; Weiner & Graham, 1984) imply that the attributional processes that children bring to bear on hypothetical situations also guide their actual emotional behavior. Despite this widespread acceptance of a correspondence between knowledge and behavior, it is doubtful that such a correspondence applies to all aspects of emotion. Several arguments can be raised against it.

First, emotional behavior occurs even in subjects who are most unlikely to have any explicit knowledge concerning their behavior. For example, Campos and Stenberg (1981) report that 4-month-old infants display an angry expression when their actions are restrained.

Second, it is doubtful whether even adults can report the cognitive determinants of their affect-related behavior (Nisbett & Wilson, 1977; Zajonc, 1980). For instance, the well-known "unresponsive bystanders," described by Latané and Darley (1970), offer all kinds of reasons to justify the fact that they did not help others in distress. However, they all miss the empirical fact that people are increasingly less likely to help as the number of witnesses or bystanders increases. Even when asked directly, they persistently deny that their behavior is influenced by such a factor.

And third, observational studies of children's emotional behavior show that, at the behavioral level, young children have capacities that are reported only at a much later age in studies assessing children's knowledge. For example, attachment theorists describe how some 1-year-old infants display an ambivalent emotional reaction upon reunion with their caretaker after a short separation (Ainsworth, Blehar, Waters, & Wall, 1978; Bretherton, 1985). Yet it is not until several years later that children acknowledge the existence of such ambivalent emotional reactions (Harris, 1983a; Harter, 1983).

The developmental time-lag

Obviously, to validate the argument presented above, studies are needed in which both behavioral and knowledge-based measures are taken. One such study was carried out in the laboratory of one of the present authors (Meerum Terwogt et al. 1986).

The experiment was designed to investigate children's ability to manipulate their emotions on request. In this experiment, 6-year-old children were asked to listen very carefully to a sad story, so that they "could retell it afterward." In addition, some of the children were instructed to listen so that "you make yourself feel sad." Other children were asked to listen so that "you won't become sad yourself." No further instructions were given about the strategies that might be used to reach these objectives. Afterward, the children were interviewed about what happened. That is, questions were asked such as: "Did you find the story sad?", "Were you sad yourself?"; and "What did you do in order to make/stop yourself from being sad?"

Whether or not children reported themselves to be sad is, as argued before, a question of knowledge and not an adequate measure for the effects of the instructions at the behavioral level. Moreover, not only are we dealing with introspective material, but, given the explicit instructions, it was also quite easy for the children to infer what answer the experimenter might want to hear from them. Thus, their answers might have been influenced by variables such as the presence and intensity of the emotion induced, the awareness of these feelings and the wish to live up to the expectations of the experimenter or other socially desirable tendencies.

So, in order to obtain more direct insight into the children's ability to control their sadness we used two emotion-related behavioral measures from which it was not so easy for the children to infer or conform to the behavior as expected by the experimenter. The first measure was based on the conception that a negative emotion generally has deleterious effects on cognitive performance (Easterbrook, 1959). Immediately after listening to the story, children's performance on an unrelated cognitive task was measured. The second measure was based on the assumption that mood provides a helpful retrieval cue for material that reflects that same mood (Blaney, 1986; Bower, 1981). To examine whether such a mood congruity effect occurred, children's recall of the stimulus story was examined for the presence of sadness-related statements.

The behavioral measures showed that children were able to manipulate their sadness on request. Thus, depending on the experimental instructions, children showed more or less deterioration in their performance on the unrelated cognitive task, and a mood-congruent bias in their recall. At the same time, their answers to the question pertaining to the strategy they had used indicated that few children could actually report what they had done. Evidently, most remained un-aware of the strategies that they had used in order to fulfill the request. Thus, knowledge about behavior cannot be used as a reliable predictor of the actual behavior repertoire.

A parallel example has recently been reported by Cole (1986). She found that even 4-year-olds can attenuate the overt display of disappointment when it is socially expected of them (e.g., in the presence of someone who has offered an unexpectedly disappointing gift). The same 4-year-olds were quite incapable of reporting on the display rule that they had adopted. Only one child mentioned that the experimenter might be able to tell how she felt by looking at her facial expression. In addition, there is evidence that 4-year-olds are poor at describing the adoption of display rules in hypothetical situations (Harris, 1988).

If assessing knowledge about behavior is not equivalent to the assessment of the underlying cognitive basis for behavior, how should the relation between knowledge and behavior be conceptualized?

One view is expressed by Piaget in his work on the moral judgment of the child (Piaget, 1977, pp. 106–115). Here Piaget suggests that the development that can be seen at the level of theoretical thought on moral issues is essentially the same development as can be seen at the level of moral behavior itself, except that the first type of development lags somewhat behind the latter. Thus, accord-ing to Piaget, studying the development of knowledge concerning morality is directly relevant to our understanding of the development of moral behavior it-self, provided one takes the developmental time-lag into account. Piaget de-scribes several observations that support this notion of a time-lag between moral development at the level of knowledge and at the level of behavior.

The examples presented above suggest that the same may be true for emotional development. This conclusion is important, because it immediately gives rise to a number of new questions. For example, once knowledge about emotion is conceptually and empirically separated from emotional behavior itself, one may ask about the *origins* of this knowledge. Harris and Olthof (1982) suggest that there are essentially three possible models: a solipsistic, a behavioristic, and a sociocentric model. The first model focuses on the possibility that children ac-quire their knowledge through self-observation. In this conceptualization, they gradually become aware of certain correlations between emotional situations on the one hand and their behavioral and psychological reactions to those situations on the other hand. In the second model, the child is also actively engaged in explaining behavior. Here, however, they use other people's behavior rather than their own experience as a primary source of information. Finally, the sociocen-tric model assumes that many of the relationships that the child has to learn are, more or less explicitly, provided for by the community; in particular the verbal community. At present, we have no means by which to judge which model is true, so we will set this question aside for the time being. Probably, all three models play a role, although the importance of each may differ depending on the child's age.

More important for our purpose is a second question, concerning the *function* of knowledge about emotion. Stated more precisely: What difference does it make for an individual's behavior (emotional or otherwise), if he or she has knowledge about the emotional process? One possible answer to this question is "none." It might be that knowledge about emotion does not affect behavior at all. With Skinner (1958), one might argue that consciousness, and by implication consciously available knowledge, are only epiphenomena of the human capacity for using language with no consequences for behavior. Alternatively, one might reason along the lines of Zajonc (1980) and argue that emotions are too deeply rooted in our evolutionary history and too basic to be really affected by a purely cognitive factor such as knowledge about the emotional process itself.

Accessibility and flexibility

In our view, these positions are unnecessarily restrictive with regard to the concept of emotion and consequently too restrictive with regard to the possible effects of knowledge on emotional behavior. They ignore the constant effort that we make to use our everyday theories of emotion to "reason with our emotional impulses." It seems hard to accept that the availability of conscious knowledge, which is a central characteristic of our species, is only an epiphenomenon without any impact on emotional behavior.

Harris (1985) lists three ways in which children's knowledge about emotion might influence their behavior. First, the acquisition of insight into strategies for self-control is likely to help children when they try to put such strategies into practice. Second, children's knowledge about which situations evoke emotions will enhance their ability to react empathically to other people's distress. And third, important decisions about the future course of one's life are often based on an estimate of how future situations will affect one's feelings. The more accurate one's knowledge is about situation–emotion relationships, the better such choices can be made. In the present chapter we will elaborate on one of these functions of knowledge about emotion, i.e., its effect on the child's ability to exercise self-control.

How can knowledge about emotion enhance children's ability for self-control? One way to approach this question is suggested by Rozin's analysis of the evolution of intelligence (Rozin, 1975). According to Rozin, both the phylogenetic and ontogenetic development of intelligence essentially consist of an increase in the conscious accessibility of preexisting complex information-processing skills. For example, the studies by Von Frisch on honey bees revealed that bees use very complicated systems for orientation and communication. However, in bees these highly organized and precisely calibrated skills are tightly wired into specific types of behavior. That is, they are applicable only in a narrow range of situations. In Rozin's view, the crucial difference between the bee's "intelligent" behavior and human intelligence is not the complexity of the skills that are involved, but the fact that in humans the skills are often consciously accessible, which allows us to make use of them in a flexible and nonspecific way.

Human beings develop a foundational knowledge that is no longer fully embedded in behavior, but that is freely available to be used at will and for different purposes. In short, our knowledge enables us to adapt our skills to a wide range of different situations. Indeed, we could say that this is the general objective of all education. Therefore, Rozin claims that what is taught in the process of education may be described as not only revealing relationships in the outside world (i.e., understanding the Copernican system), but also as "gaining access to knowledge already in the head" (Rozin, 1975, pg. 274).

By analogy, it could be argued that when children, in the course of their development, acquire knowledge about emotion, this acquisition enables them to act in a more flexible and less stereotypical way in emotion-eliciting situations than would have been possible without access to this knowledge. There is, however, no formal education in this area that provides them with such important knowledge in a systematic way.

What does it mean to behave in a flexible way in emotional situations, and how could the acquisition of knowledge about emotion enhance such flexibility? More precisely, in what respect is flexible and presumably knowledge-based emotional behavior different from emotional behavior that is inflexible and not based on knowledge?

As was the case with the honey bees' orientation and communication systems, human emotions can be seen as behavioral programs that are executed in response to specific situations. The relation between the type of situation and the particular emotion elicited by that situation is basically innate (cf. Plutchik, 1980). We run away from frightening situations, we attack when something or someone arouses our anger and we react with approach behavior to joyful events. These bonds between situations and emotional reactions are essentially fixed. Although such fixed bonds may have been useful at some point in our evolutionary history, they are often inadequate in contemporary social life. For example, it is not always a very adaptive reaction to hit one's boss after being angered by his or her behavior. Alternatively, for tactical reasons, it may be useful to express anger in situations that have not actually provoked anger.

Thus, in present day human society there is a need to modify the fixed relation between situations and emotional reactions to these situations, so that emotions can be simulated and emotional reactions can be withheld or acted out more or less deliberately. Withholding emotional reactions requires in its turn the ability to control one's emotional state or at least the expression of that state. The evaluation of an emotional situation goes beyond the immediate emotion-eliciting aspect of the situation (e.g., a nasty remark). One also has to be able to consider numerous other aspects that are relevant to one's "choice" of response (e.g., the fact that this remark was made by the boss). Without this ability we would surely have to face new, maybe even more severe, emotional problems. Phrased in this way, another function of knowledge about emotion comes into sight: It helps us to detect elements in the situation that, although perhaps not emotional in themselves, are made relevant by virtue of anticipation. What is called for in emotion-eliciting situations is the ability to place them in a wider perspective and respond to them in an adaptive way. As is obvious from the examples chosen, this flexibility requires the ability to control emotional states and/or their behavioral expression.

According to our hypothesis, behavioral flexibility in emotion-eliciting situations, and consequently the ability to control emotional states and emotional behavior, is enhanced by acquiring knowledge about emotion. How could this be the case, however, if, as we have already shown above, the control of emotion does *not* depend on conscious awareness of such control strategies?

There is no reason to assume that the control of emotion cannot, like many other behaviors, be learned simply by means of trial-and-error. For example, a child who sees that her immediate emotional reaction to a situation (e.g., getting angry after being hurt by another person) meets with strong disapproval from adults (e.g., because her injury was brought about accidentally), might learn to suppress anger, or at least the expression of anger, if the same event happens again. Nevertheless, we claim that at least two types of knowledge about emotion do influence the control of emotion and thereby enhance flexibility in emotional situations.

The first type of knowledge specifies *when* to control: which emotional reactions are socially acceptable in which type of situation. For example, imagine that the adult in the example mentioned above not only expressed disapproval about the child's anger but also provided the child with a new piece of knowledge by saying: "You should not get angry at Johnny, since he hurt you accidentally. He could not help it." In this way, the child would have acquired the knowledge that getting angry, or at least expressing anger, in response to "accidentally caused harm" (whatever that may mean to the child at that age) is socially unacceptable. This newly acquired piece of knowledge would help the child *generalize* the newly learned response of not getting angry in this particular situation to other cases of accidental injury.

The second type of knowledge that we claim affects control of emotion is knowledge about *how* to control. As pointed out above, this type of knowledge is not a necessary condition for exerting control, because the use of a particular strategy can probably be learned by trial and error. Nevertheless, having knowledge about how to control enables the subject to do something more than just exert control in the situations where he or she has learned to do so by trial and error. It enables the subject to apply other (related) strategies more or less at will in the same situation. Thus, knowing how one exerts control enables the subject to generalize the use of one particular strategy to the use of other strategies. It will be obvious that, with an increasing number of response options available to the subject, the possibility of a truly adaptive reaction is enhanced.

Emotion and cognition

In the preceding section it was argued that children's developing knowledge about emotion might permit more flexible reactions in emotion-eliciting situations. The question to be answered next is how such a view can be integrated with current theories of emotion.

Based upon the foregoing ideas and on Saarni's (1978) more elaborate account of the differentiation of emotional experience, the following picture of emotional development can now be sketched: Initially, the young child's emotional behavior is determined by relatively rigid, wired-in emotional programs. The child has no conscious access to these programs and no knowledge of them. Emotional behavior is entirely determined by environmental input. After this initial "biological" stage, the child reaches a second stage in which affect and expression are coordinated and a third stage in which cognitive representations of events can serve as elicitors of affect (Saarni, 1978). Finally, the child gains insight into the determinants of emotional behavior. These cognitions about affect cause the child's emotional behavior to be no longer entirely "data driven"; it becomes increasingly "knowledge driven."

It is interesting to note that both the beginning and the end of this hypothesized developmental sequence have their counterparts in current theories of emotion. Our characterization of the young child's emotions is strongly reminiscent of Zajonc's view of emotion (Zajonc, 1980), according to which there is a relatively independent emotional system that is unaffected by higher order cognitive processes. The endpoint of our hypothesized developmental sequence, in contrast, can be understood in terms of cognitive theories like those of Arnold (1960), Lazarus (1975, 1982), Lazarus, Coyne, and Folkman (1982), and Frijda (1980, 1987). According to these theories, a person's body of acquired knowledge that is available in long term memory influences emotion via the process of "secondary appraisal" (Lazarus) or "context evaluation" (Frijda). This appraisal process takes place after a more primitive appraisal of the emotion-eliciting situation and often results in a modification of the original emotional impulse that was based on primary appraisal. Thus, according to such cognitive theorists, the acquisition of knowledge about emotion makes the secondary appraisal process more powerful because it provides information that can be used to reevaluate the initial immediate appraisal of the situation. This allows subjects to be less and less bound by their immediate emotional impulses.

In sum, the flexibility in dealing with emotion-eliciting situations that we expect to result from gaining knowledge about emotion can be understood as resulting from the development of the process of secondary appraisal. In the following sections, we will discuss the nature of the knowledge base that children must develop to enlarge the scope of their secondary appraisal. As indicated, we will distinguish between knowledge dealing with the question ''when to control'' and knowledge dealing with the question ''how to control.''

When to control?

Imagine a boy who is wondering how to ask his parents for a new bicycle. He knows enough – maybe he has asked before – to anticipate that his parents will respond to the question with something like ''Why do you always waste your pocket money? If you didn't, you would be able to buy one yourself.'' He warns himself not to start shouting, because he knows that his parents will then refuse to talk about the subject any further. He rehearses all of the arguments about why it is not reasonable to expect him to save enough of his pocket money for this purpose and tries to figure out the best moment to approach his parents. When he brings up the subject they nonetheless immediately start reproaching his supposed habit of ''wasting'' money. He feels his anger rising, and internally starts slowly counting to ten.''

We will not venture to predict the outcome of the boy's attempts, but we might say that his precautions at least enhance his chance of success. What exactly was the nature of the information that made him try to control his emotional response? In the first place, he anticipated a situation that would provoke an emotion. Second, he knew what he would be inclined to do under these circumstances. Third, he anticipated the negative effects that such an action would have on his parents at that particular moment. And finally, he was able to detect the emotional impulse in himself, which allowed him to stop himself from immediately acting out that impulse.

Described in this fashion, the boy used three kinds of knowledge: knowledge about the antecedents of emotion, knowledge about the cues for identifying emotion (which includes the nature of the initial impulse) and knowledge about the consequences of an uncontrolled response. We will discuss these three types of knowledge in the next sections.

Knowledge about the antecedents of emotion

Even 4-year-olds can evisage situations in which familiar emotions, like happiness, sadness, anger, and fear, will occur (Barden et al., 1980; Borke, 1971; Trabasso, Stein, & Johnson, 1981). In our own research (Harris et al. 1987), we tested the development of children's knowledge of situations that provoke emotion across 4 age groups (i.e., 5-, 7-, 10-, and 14-year-olds) in relation to a much wider set of emotions (i.e., 20 emotion terms, including more complicated emotions such as jealousy, guilt, shame, embarrassment, and relief). The emotion terms included were selected to be clear-cut examples of an emotion as judged by adults. All children were asked to describe, for each term, a situation that would be likely to elicit the emotion in question.

Not surprisingly, a considerable number of children in the youngest groups failed to provide an answer for some of the less familiar emotion terms. The quality of the answers that were given was established by a double blind judgment procedure. For each answer, two adult judges were asked to choose, from the complete set of emotion terms used, that emotion term that was most likely to have been the stimulus item for that particular answer.

As might be expected, situations for determinants of happiness, sadness, anger, and fear were given with such explicitness by all age groups that it proved to be quite easy for the adult judges to recognize the situations as such. This might suggest that the link between situation and emotion is most easily made for the set of "basic emotions" that can be associated with discrete facial expressions (Ekman, 1973). Contrary to this interpretation, the determinants of disgust, an emotion that is also widely acknowledged as having a discrete facial expression, are not known to 5-year-olds. On the other hand, children's replies with regard to shyness, an emotion that is not considered to be a "basic emotion" but that is probably often experienced by – as well as explained to – 5-year-olds were just as readily decoded by the adult judges as the replies given by this age group for sadness.

Whatever the explanation, the results show that children's understanding rapidly moves beyond those emotions for which a universal facial expression has been established. For instance, 7-year-olds provided distinctive situations for emotion terms such as guilty, proud, jealous, and worried. Older children extended this list of terms still further.

Analyses of the pattern of mistakes that children made suggested an all-or-none development. That is, there was little support for a model in which more complex terms, such as disappointment, are initially considered as being synonymous with an easier term like sadness, and acquire their status as separate emotions only later on.

These results may have led to an underestimate of children's understanding. Especially within the younger groups, some answers could easily have been misunderstood by the judges because of their idiosyncratic character. In such cases the children may well have understood the situations that provoke the emotion in question. They failed, however, to produce a prototypical situation that was understood by the judges or to express the determinants of that emotion at a sufficiently abstract level. These children possess local introspective knowledge but do not yet acknowledge the general principles that give the situation its emotional impact (Flavell, 1977), or at least fail to describe them in such a way that they may be understood by the adult judges.

Experiments in which children are asked to produce the examples themselves may give a good impression of the knowledge that is available in a more or less generalized form, but they fail to uncover the less well established type of knowledge. Problems of production-deficiency and perspective-taking will prevent this latter knowledge from surfacing. These problems are avoided in experiments in which the children are asked, directly or indirectly, if the presence of certain determinants would influence their affective judgment. This approach was taken in a recent study by one of the authors (Olthof, Ferguson, & Luiten, in preparation). Children's anger was investigated by having them judge how angry they would become in several hypothetical situations in which harm was done to them.

The key idea in this research was that getting angry about someone's behavior is closely related to giving a negative moral judgment on that person's behavior (Averill, 1982; Ferguson & Rule, 1983; Ferguson & Olthof, 1986; Rule & Ferguson, 1984). Therefore, the stimulus situations were varied in terms of three dimensions that each represent one aspect of the assignment of responsibility. These dimensions might be expected to affect children's moral judgments. The dimensions were (a) whether the perpetrator of harm could have avoided causing the harm; (b) whether the perpetrator intended to cause the harm, and (c) whether the perpetrator had good or bad motives in the context of causing the harm. The three dimensions were varied orthogonally and children judged the resulting 8 harmful events on a 7-point rating scale in terms of (a) how naughty they thought the perpetrator of harm to be and (b) how angry they would feel toward the perpetrator if they themselves had been the victim. The subjects ranged from 5 to 15 years of age.

The manipulated dimensions affected judgments of both naughtiness and anger. When the harm was caused unavoidably, unintentionally, or in the context of good motives, children's naughtiness and anger judgments were lower than when the harm was caused avoidably, intentionally, or with bad motives. There were, however, individual differences in the use of these dimensions that were to some extent also related to the child's age. The 5-year-old's judgments were only affected by the acceptability of the perpetrator's motives, although older children also took the avoidability and intentionality dimensions into account. In general, however, the age-related differences were not strong.

More important for our present discussion was an additional analysis in which the relation was examined between, on the one hand, the extent to which children took the responsibility information into account when judging anger, and, on the other hand, the overall value of their anger judgments across all situations. The analysis revealed that, the more that children used the available responsibility information, the lower their overall anger judgments were. Apparently, the judgments of children who made relatively little use of the available responsibility information were not just randomly distributed across the response scale. On the contrary, their ratings were primarily located at the high end of the scale. Thus, these children reported that they would get angry at the perpetrator regardless of the way in which he inflicted the harm. This finding is consistent with the notion that younger children tend not to take the relevant causal analysis into account and concentrate instead on outcomes only (cf. Thomson, this volume). In our study, however, individual differences in the use of responsibility information were only partially related to age.

Obviously these data reflect children's knowledge about when they get angry, and not their actual anger responses. Nevertheless, to the extent that we can assume their knowledge to be veridical, this pattern of findings suggests that children's acquisition of the principles of responsibility and blame assignment enables them to avoid becoming angry in situations where they would have done so before. The effect of acquiring the principles of responsibility and blame assignment seems to be a moderating one, leading toward more differentiated and, in many situations, less extreme anger responses.

A similar conclusion may be drawn from the results of a second experiment (Olthof, Ferguson, Hoeben, & Luiten, in preparation) in which children first received only information about the fact that harm was caused and about who caused the harm. No information was given about the way in which the perpetrator was responsible for causing the harm. At this point in the experiment children judged how naughty the perpetrator was and how angry the victim would be. Virtually all children judged the perpetrator to be extremely naughty and they judged the victim to be extremely angry. Subsequently, children received information about *how* the harm had been caused.

As in the first experiment, whether the harm done was avoidable or unavoidable, intentional or unintentional, and in the context of good or bad motives, was systematically varied. After receiving this information, children judged the perpetrator's naughtiness and the victim's anger. As in the first experiment, these judgments were differentiated depending on the perpetrator's responsibility for causing the harm. Again the responsibility information appeared to have a moderating effect on children's judgments of naughtiness and anger. Thus, providing the children with extra information about the situation induced, even in 5-year-olds, a reappraisal of the situation, which affected the intensity of the emotional impulse.

Obviously, these results are limited in the sense that it remains to be investigated to what extent children's real life anger is actually based on an assessment of a perpetrator's responsibility for causing harm. Similarly, it is an open question whether we can expect these young children to produce this kind of information spontaneously. However, the data do show that, at least at some level of explicitness of knowledge, children have ideas about when to get angry and when not. It remains for future research to show whether and how these ideas are related to behavior.

Knowledge about the cues for identifying emotion

In an interview study (Harris et al., 1981) we asked children, not only about the regulation of emotion, but also about the identification of emotion in the self and in others and about the effects of emotion on behavior.

A marked shift between 6 and 10 years of age was found with respect to the cues mentioned. Younger children tended to focus on the publicly observable components of emotion, that is, the eliciting situation and overt behavioral reactions. Ten-year-olds were more likely to acknowledge the hidden mental aspect of emotion in their replies.

The fact that the internal experience of emotion is considered to play a central role in identification is probably explained by the fact that people come to realize that the other aspects of the emotional process vary from person to person. It is sometimes completely incomprehensible to somebody else, and sometimes even to ourselves, why a certain situation has an emotional impact on us. Also, it is not possible to infer with certainty a person's emotional state on the basis of the presence or absence of any particular emotional expression.

Although it may be highly questionable and hardly possible to prove (see, e.g., Lewis & Michalson, 1983, pg. 111), there is a common conception that we essentially all share the same kind of internal feeling states. Consequently, we think of the eliciting situation and the subsequent expression as less decisive than the internal experience of emotion when we want to identify an emotion, especially in communication with others (Bretherton et al., 1986).

A more important question, in the present context, is why the 6-year-olds present themselves as junior "behaviorists," as we have called them (Harris et al., 1981)? In line with the reasoning given above, one could argue that they do not yet fully realize the eliciting situations are not the same for every person and that an emotional expression is often controlled. This would explain the importance they ascribe to those two aspects.

At this point a cautionary remark should be made. In the Harris et al. (1981) study the children had to answer open-ended questions. Consequently, the findings reflect children's knowledge only to the extent that their knowledge was explicit and could be verbalized. However, a different picture emerges if one does not require the knowledge to be explicit to the extent that it can be verbalized spontaneously. When using responses to structured probing and judgments of hypothetical situations as indices of children's knowledge, Harris (1985, 1988) was able to show that even 6-year-old children can be said to have a mentalistic conception of emotion.

Of course, such findings could be interpreted as an indication that the methods of structured probing and judging hypothetical situations are simply more sensitive than asking open-ended questions. However, this interpretation implies a somewhat arbitrary selection of one particular set of methods and consequently of one particular level of explicitness of knowledge as the "best" indicators of "real" knowledge.

In our opinion, the method-related differences in children's apparent knowledge can also be interpreted as an indication that the concept "knowledge about emotion" is not a unitary construct. It seems that the nature of a child's knowledge differs depending on the level of explicitness and extent of verbalization that is required in its assessment.

Anticipation of the consequences of an emotional impulse

In order to know whether self-regulation of emotion is called for, one also has to anticipate what the consequences of acting out this impulse will be. These consequences are twofold. First, the emotion influences one's own behavior and, second, it elicits a response from the environment.

For the moment, we will concentrate on the question of whether children acknowledge the consequences of an emotional impulse on their own functioning. Our interview study (Harris et al., 1981) included questions concerning the influence of emotions on attitudes (i.e., the perception of others) and behavior (i.e., the production of a drawing). As it happened, even young children acknowledged that a negative emotion would color their attitudes to others negatively ("I wouldn't think they were so nice") and impair their drawing performance ("I wouldn't like to do it then"), whereas a positive emotion would make them more inclined to give positive judgments about others and would improve performance on the drawing task.

We all know from experience that this kind of knowledge can serve as a warning. For instance, when we are driving a car, the realization that we are angry or upset can urge us to slow down and take extra care, because we know that an angry driver is more likely to cause a traffic accident.

In a recent experiment (Meerum Terwogt, 1986), we asked whether young children spontaneously use this kind of knowledge, knowledge that they clearly articulate if asked. We induced an emotion in 5-year-old children by asking them to concentrate for 30 seconds on a happy or sad event in their lives. This mental imagery procedure was developed by Singer and Singer (1976), and it has often proved its effectiveness with children (e.g., Carlson, Swartz, Felleman, & Masters, 1983; Masters, Barden, & Ford, 1979; Meerum Terwogt, 1984; Underwood, Moore, & Rosenhan, 1973).

Immediately after induction, the children were tested on an unrelated memory task. The performance of the "happy" children on the memory task was better, whereas the performance of the "sad" children tended to be worse, as compared to a control group.

Thus far, this experiment can be regarded as a replication of an experiment by Masters, Barden, and Ford (1979), who reported the same phenomena in somewhat younger children. However, in a group of 10-year-old children, we found no influence of the induction procedure on memory performance. We had no reason to assume that the mental imagery procedure should be less effective among older children. If they resisted being influenced by it, or controlled their emotions afterward, the only plausible explanation is that they anticipated the effects of emotion on performance. On the basis of their firmly established knowledge on this point, they might have spontaneously counteracted all negative effects.

To check this idea, we carried out the exact same study again but with one variation. This time we asked the children in advance how they thought that a happy or sad mood would influence their achievements in general and their performance in the forthcoming task in particular. As expected on the basis of the interview study of Harris et al. (1981), even the 5-year-olds were relatively knowledgeable about the general relationship between mood and performance. The present task being no exception to this rule, they predicted exactly what had happened the first time that we ran the experiment.

The striking result was that they nonetheless proved to be wrong this time. The mere activation of their latent knowledge about the possible effects of emotion on performance resulted, even for the 5-year-olds, in an optimal performance, irrespective of the kind of emotion induced in the child. We may infer that, just as the 10-year-olds had already done spontaneously, the 5-year-olds countered the negative effects of emotion.

Thus, immediately accessible knowledge warns the child that self-control is called for. Evidently, however, our 5-year-olds were not yet aware that they were able to counter the interference of emotion in this particular task. By contrast, a considerable number of 10-year-olds, although subscribing to the same general rule, correctly claimed that emotion would have little effect on their performance in this particular task.

An interview among adults (Meerum Terwogt & Kramer, 1981) revealed, not surprisingly, an even more elaborate insight into control strategies: One could speak of a complete incorporation of the extended Yerkes-Dodson Law (Broadhurst, 1957), in which task-difficulty as well as motivational factors are taken into account. Consequently, one could expect adults to spontaneously counteract the consequences of emotion in a wider set of situations.

How is control exerted?

Once an emotion is elicited, how is the automatic emotion program prevented from operating? How do the secondary appraisal activities break into this program in order to exert control?

A possible answer is that the emotion is brought into consciousness: Thinking about an automatism interrupts the program. Thus, most of us are able to keep our balance on a gymnastic bar, but if someone asks us during this process how we do so, we are likely to fall off. Similarly, an experienced driver can change gears quite adequately without thinking, but if he or she tries to explain the movements to someone else, mistakes can intrude.

In both examples, we can easily avoid such disturbances: The automatisms serve only in a specialized set of situations, but in those circumstances they are quite effective. There is no need for further flexibility.

This is not the case for emotion programs. In a limited set of situations we still need a fast, automatic program (for instance, to retreat to the pavement when faced with the immediate threat of an approaching car), but mostly we can take some time to think. The fact that we grant ourselves that time does not mean of course that our consequent behavior will always be sensible or even rational. The original emotional program that is waiting to be executed can easily affect our judgment: We are dealing with so called "hot cognitions" (Abelson, 1963).

Once the execution of the "primitive" program is blocked, there are two possibilities for tackling the situation. We can exercise self-control over the inner mental component of emotion, the feeling itself, in an attempt to get rid of, or at least diminish, the impact of the impulse that troubles us. Alternatively, we can limit our efforts to the modification of the outward expression.

In the Harris et al. (1981) interview these two possibilities were covered by separate questions. For instance, after having sketched a fearful situation, children were asked "Could you pretend not to be afraid?" followed by a request to explain the answer given ("How?" or "How come you can't pretend?"). Subsequently, the following question was posed: "Of course, it would be better if you were really not afraid. Could you do anything to make sure that you are really not afraid?' Again, the subjects were asked to elaborate on the answer.

In their answers to the question of pretense, children of all ages proposed an act, facial expression, or verbal statement appropriate to pretense. Only the older children, however, made the discrepancy between state and expression clear by referring to the inner state that had to be masked. (The conclusion that 6-year-old children do not appreciate the inner-outer discrepancy at all would be premature. Although this conclusion probably still holds for 4-year-old children, as was suggested by a recent study by the same author [Harris, 1988], that same study clearly showed that 6-year-olds, when prompted sufficiently, do acknowledge the difference between what someone really feels and the facial expression that is characteristic but not defining of that emotion.)

With respect to the second question, children of all ages offered strategies that involved an actual change of the emotion-eliciting situation. Once again, only the older children claimed that feelings could also be changed by means of purely mental strategies.

These findings raise several issues that will be elaborated upon in the following two sections.

Control over emotional display

The first issue raised by the Harris et al. (1981) findings is that, even though young children seem to be not fully aware of the inward-outward discrepancy that is consequent upon pretense, they do seem to know *how* to pretend. This suggests that, at the behavioral level, pretense might occur in younger as well as in older children.

This possibility was explored in a study by Cole (1986). Children of 4 to 10 years of age received a disappointing reward (e.g., a broken toy) after having participated in an experiment. It was shown that preschool children made as many attempts to hide their disappointment as did first and third graders. At the knowledge level, however, the age effect became apparent once again. The likelihood of spontaneous references to the discrepancy between actual feelings and outward expressions increased with age.

These results show unambiguously that 4-year-old children possess sufficient skills to control their behavior within this situation. The question is why they do so. Cole suggests that social rules are already effective here and she points out that the preschool years have been noted for the development of socially governed behavior (e.g., Kopp, 1982). Effectiveness, however, does not necessarily imply a complete understanding of the situation. The age differences at the knowledge level indicate that 4-year-olds do not yet have a firm grasp on the problem at a more abstract level. This could be due to a lack of cognitive skills (necessary to combine the several perspectives that are relevant to this problem), to a lack of social skills (they do not fully appreciate the reasons why control is asked for), or both. Whatever the answer, the possibility should be acknowledged that, although expressive control behavior occurred in the fairly prototypical situation that was presented by Cole, young children do not generalize that control behavior to a much wider set of situations.

Cole's study and an earlier study by Saarni (1984) are interesting for another reason as well. In both studies, it was found that girls were more likely to hide their disappointment than boys. Saarni explained these differences in behavior in terms of motivational factors influenced by sex-role pressures. That is to say, in Western society it is considered important for girls to appear to be nice, friendly, and agreeable, despite their real feelings. This conclusion is underlined by Cole's finding that even 4-year-old girls are influenced to a large extent by the pressure of social contexts, i.e., they showed much more expressive control when they received the gift in the presence of the experimenter than when they opened up the gift alone. We cannot ascribe this effect to differential knowledge of when control is asked for, because, in an earlier study (Saarni, 1979), no sex differences in children's *understanding* of display rule usage were found. So males know, to the same extent as females, when control is appropriate, but simply do not feel the same urge to comply with this pressure.

This phenomenon can also be found beyond the behavioral level. In a recent study (Meerum Terwogt, Bannenberg, & Claessen, in preparation) we presented a number of short stories to 6- and 10-year-old children. These stories depicted emotional situations in which the children were asked to imagine themselves to be the protagonist. The theme of the situations was systematically varied in two ways. First, the emotional impact of the stories was varied. They were supposed to induce anger, sadness, or fear in the protagonist. Second, the protagonist experienced these emotions alone or in the presence of acquaintances (i.e., their parents or peers). After each story, the children were interviewed in order to establish how they judged the situation, and how they thought they would handle it.

The first question of the interview was how they would feel if they encountered the situation. The nature of their answers obviously depended on the emotional impact of the story. With respect to the three other predictors that were used to explain the answers, that is, age and sex of the subject and the social context of the situation, mainly gender differences proved to be influential. Although younger and older children alike judged the situations in the same manner (mostly in accordance with the experimenters' intentions, or, alternatively, with a general negative phrase: "I would feel bad"), girls, in their spontaneous answers, ascribed a higher intensity to these emotions than did boys. This effect could, at least partially, be traced to sex differences in the sad and frightening situations. In both cases, a substantial number of boys denied that these situations would have the kind of emotional impact intended by the experimenters. The difference between the two emotions was that, once the boys came to acknowledge their sadness, they were also likely to display this emotion in their anticipated behavioral reactions. In the case of fear, however, they often spontaneously added ''but I wouldn't let it show, otherwise they'll think I'm a coward.''

The next question put to the children was what they themselves would do in such a situation. The answers to this question appeared to be affected by all the independent variables. First, we found a general age effect: Older children described a larger variety of options, predominantly due to the appearance of mental strategies for handling the situations (cf. Harris et al., 1981). Second, among younger children acting out the emotion was mentioned with almost the same frequency in both private and social situations. Among older children, however, the social context was a significant factor in shaping the behavior. Third, it turned out that girls, in particular, made allowances for the presence of others. For instance, in reaction to a situation that involved unjustified withdrawal of pocket money, a 10-year-old girl answered, ''I wouldn't let my anger show, because my father doesn't like that and would yell at me. That would only make things worse.'' Finally, there proved to be an emotion-specific effect in the sense that girls were more likely to suppress overt signs of anger, whereas, as mentioned before, boys were more likely to suppress overt signs of fear.

As is illustrated by the pocket money example, children sometimes spontaneously included the effects their actions might have on others in their answers. If they did not mention these effects spontaneously, we specifically asked for them. Answers to this question varied with age only: Older children were more aware of the effects of their actions on others. That does not mean that they always adapt their behavior accordingly (''OK, then they will think I'm an idiot if they want to''). As noted before, girls are more likely to adapt their strategies than boys, but we must also note that boys are just as capable of acknowledging the consequences of their behavior.

In sum, we can draw three conclusions. First, older children seem to evaluate their emotions and consequent emotional actions in a wider perspective than younger children. Second, in agreement with Saarni (1984), girls seem to be more likely to comply with social pressures but, third, the display rules may be different for the sexes, depending on the nature of the emotion involved.

Control over internal emotional state

As we saw in the Harris et al. (1981) interview, the majority of children – young and old alike – claimed that it is possible to alter one's mood. Older children proposed leaving or changing the eliciting situation, either in reality or just mentally. Younger children almost exclusively answered in terms of an actual change in the situation.

In everyday life, however, we are often simply expected to endure a certain situation. On the basis of their answers, we may expect young children to have difficulties in handling their emotions in such situations. The fact that escaping from a situation is often regarded in our society as "childish" may indicate that young children are not always capable – nor indeed is it expected of them – of enduring certain situations.

Nonetheless, in the experiment carried out by Meerum Terwogt et al. (1986), discussed earlier in relation to "the developmental time lag," we showed that young children are capable of influencing their mood state in situations where an actual change is virtually impossible. Children could not avoid listening to the sad story, because they had to retell it afterward as accurately as possible. The fact that they were able to end up in the mood state requested of them showed that they must have executed some mental strategy in order to "listen in an appropriate fashion."

As mentioned above, over 40 percent of the 5-year-olds could not tell us anything about what they had done in order to follow the instruction "to become/not to become sad." So we concluded that knowledge lags behind behavior.

We shall now take a further look at the reactions of the children who did come up with some kind of answer. First, it was just as difficult for the children to describe strategies for involvement as it was for detachment. However, among the children who were asked about involvement, 25 percent (especially girls) claimed that you do not have to do anything special in order to achieve that state: Involvement for them seems to be a natural attitude. Only a few children (exclusively boys) claimed that the same holds true for detachment.

The remaining children specified very familiar and clearly recognizable involvement or detachment strategies, such as "expanding the story" in a negative manner (to intensify the sadness) or in a positive manner (to reduce the sadness) or "linkage to similar experiences" in their own lives which had turned out to be even worse (intensifying) or better (reducing) than the ones conveyed in the stories. The most frequently mentioned strategies, however, were identification with the protagonist of the story in order to achieve involvement and reminding oneself that it is "just a story" in order to achieve detachment. These results bear a striking resemblance to those reported by Koriat, Melkman, Averill, and Lazarus (1972) with regard to self-control of emotional reactions to a stressful film among (male) adults. Here, too, the most frequently mentioned strategies were identification and emphasis on the fictional nature of the stimulus material respectively. It is interesting to see that Koriat et al. (1972) identified these two strategies not only as the ones most frequently used by their subjects, but also as the ones that proved the most effective.

Thus our results suggest, albeit tentatively, that young children, when dealing with fictional or filmed material, are quite similar to adults with regard to the strategies they use. Development may consist of a more conscious deployment of these strategies, rather than the acquisition of qualitatively new strategies.

This example illustrates that young children's failure to exercise control in certain situations cannot always be attributed to the absence of adequate strategies. An alternative explanation is that such strategies are less accessible to young children. In many situations, young children probably still have too little knowledge about which strategy suits which situation to be able to use the adequate strategy spontaneously. To select the optimal strategy, the child has to have access to information about the constraints in the situation and the effects of different strategies.

In the previous section, we discussed the results of a recent interview study (Meerum Terwogt, et al., in preparation), but without elaborating on the nature and effectiveness of the strategies suggested by the children. The children were not only questioned about what they would do in the situations that were presented, but two additional questions were asked. First, we asked how they thought these actions would affect others, and second, how these actions would affect their own emotional state.

The strategies mentioned by the children could be divided into the following categories: "acting out the emotion," "masking the emotion," "changing the actual situation," "leaving the situation," "mentally changing or leaving the situation," "passivity," and a residual category. Six-year-olds more often chose to act out their emotion. They may have had no other option or, alternatively, they may not have anticipated the effect of this acting out on other people. This last possibility does not mean that children are not aware of such consequences when explicitly asked about them. In fact, we shall see later that they do know these consequences quite well. As in the Harris et al. (1981) study, it was found that the 10-year-olds used more mental strategies than the 6-year-olds. They could also more often anticipate the impact of their strategies on their own feelings and on other people.

Young children found the question concerning the impact of their actions on their own feelings especially difficult to answer. About 70 percent reacted with a "don't know." The question about the possible effects on others proved to be easier to answer, although approximately 40 percent still could not imagine what would happen. However, when the young children did provide an answer, their answers were not much different from those given by the older group.

Acting out and actually or mentally changing or leaving the situation were considered to be effective strategies for reducing one's own emotion, whereas masking and passivity were not. The last two strategies, however, were judged as likely to avoid disapproval from the environment. Acting out, on the other hand, was acknowledged as risking disapproval.

Do certain strategies meet both objectives? Are they both effective and likely not to elicit disapproval? The data suggest that actually changing the situation is sometimes likely to receive an explicit positive reaction from other people but, in other situations, a negative reaction is likely. The same goes for the effectiveness of these strategies: Sometimes they will be very powerful and sometimes little effect is expected.

In terms of both objectives, the most favorable outcome is probably attained by means of mental strategies. They can be applied in almost every situation, without necessarily being noticed by other people. In the set of situations we used, they were, indeed, judged as reducing one's own negative feelings, and at the same time regarded as effective in avoiding negative responses from others.

So, in practice we find that there is often a tension between the inherent tendency toward the execution of an emotional program once it is activated, and the wish to conform to the rules of society. The answers concerning these two objectives show that even young children are aware of each separate objective. However, it is questionable whether they always deploy this kind of knowledge in advance. Is their actual choice of strategy based on these notions or are we dealing with passive knowledge, which is not yet activated at the proper time? And even if this knowledge is active, a further question is: How will children use it in their evaluations? Will one perspective – which is more likely than not to be the "egocentric" one – completely dominate the other, or are they able to weigh both perspectives in a given situation?

The study indicates that this last kind of integration may be incomplete. Older children quite often spontaneously referred, at some point during the interview, to the conflict between these two goals and to their attempts to reach an optimal balance between them. Statements of this nature were completely absent among the 6-year-olds. It should be clear by now, however, that it is hazardous to regard the information that we have acquired at the knowledge level as a direct indicator for actual behavior.

Knowledge and control: a preliminary conclusion

If we now try to reach some preliminary conclusions about the way in which children's knowledge about emotion functions when they control emotional behavior, we need to be very cautious. Most of the studies we referred to were not explicitly designed in order to examine the relationship between knowledge and behavior. Consequently, they have to be regarded as illustrations that fit in with the kind of argument that we are presenting rather than as a direct test of it. Nevertheless, we will try to summarize the picture that emerges and, casting reservations aside, even add more speculations to our theory.

Our account was guided by a functionalist approach (e.g., Arnold, 1960; Plutchik, 1980) in which emotions are considered to be regulatory processes that are

involved in a person's interpretation of the environment and that motivate appropriate actions. Within the constraints and complexity of contemporary society
the expression "appropriate" calls for considerable flexibility in these processes.

Whenever the urge to give way to our most primitive responses can be blocked,
this adaptation is provided for by a secondary appraisal of the situation. In this
way, coping with the emotion eliciting situation involves no direct action and
can be described (cf. Lazarus et al., 1982) as a constant interplay between cognitive appraisal, emotion, subsequent information processing, reappraisal, and
so on.

It is clear that the effectiveness of this mechanism will grow with the development of cognitive abilities, which enable children to switch their attention
smoothly between the inner and outer environment, to integrate several sources
of information, and to take different perspectives with respect to one and the
same situation. Not only is information rearranged in order to deal with the
situation, but new aspects of the situation can also be taken into account.

Another crucial factor, when it comes to the power of this mechanism, is the
amount of knowledge available to the child. In order to go beyond a trial-and-
error approach to the control of emotion, the child has to know where to look for
relevant information in the environment and how to use that information. Such
knowledge is unlimited in scope, but the most direct influence can be expected
from the areas we discussed at length in this chapter: knowledge about when
control is required and knowledge about how it can be done.

If we look at the relationship between knowledge and overt behavior, it is
possible to observe two opposite phenomena. On the one hand, as we argued,
knowledge lags behind competence. That is, on the one hand, the child is able
to use control strategies that it is not yet aware of (e.g., Meerum Terwogt et al.,
1986) and to respond behaviorally to nuances in social context without being
aware of the rules underlying that behavior (Cole, 1986). On the other hand, we
have seen that the child may already possess knowledge that does not show itself
in behavior (e.g., Meerum Terwogt, 1986). This concerns not only information
that could strengthen control strategies, but sometimes even complete strategies.
An example of the last possibility can be found in an experiment of Patterson &
Mischel (1976). These authors observed that young children have great difficulties in resisting temptation. Therefore, they provided their youngest subjects with
a temptation-inhibiting strategy. The children then proved capable of understanding this strategy and used it, immediately after being instructed to do so, effectively. Nonetheless, they were not likely to use this newly provided strategic
knowledge in similar situations later on.

The phenomenon that knowledge lags behind behavior seems to have a certain
logic: One has to be able to do something before one can know that one can do
it. Put in this way, we have assumed that knowledge only arises from observing

one's own behavior. Earlier on, however, we mentioned three possible sources of knowledge (Harris & Olthof, 1982). Not only is this kind of "solipsistic" information available to the child, but "behavioristic" and "sociocentric" sources of information are available as well. The latter source in particular is quite different from the others in at least one respect: The initiative does not always lie with the child.

Whereas in both the other models children act as active "psychologists" who try to construct a theory that fits their observations (Harris, 1983b), they are often passive recipients when it come to (verbal) information provided by their social environment. The social environment undoubtedly can make children sensitive to variations in social context, for example, by communicating how the child is expected to behave in different situations. The problem is, however, that children may not always be ready to digest this information. That is, the knowledge passed to them remains relatively isolated and does not become embedded in a mental structure in which it becomes linked to other information.

Of course, children may also encounter this kind of information when observing themselves or others. Normally it will be ignored or, at least, quickly forgotten. However, when, as in formal schooling, society stresses the importance of the knowledge provided, children are likely, even when they do not acknowledge its importance themselves, to retain the information in order to avoid disapproval.

Such relatively isolated information will be difficult to retrieve. Maybe it will be there when explicitly asked for – like the rule about the general effects of emotions on performance (Meerum Terwogt, 1986) – but, given its loose incorporation, few situations are likely to activate this knowledge spontaneously.

So, here we have the beginning of an explanation for the phenomenon that knowledge sometimes also seems to precede behavior. Normally, however, we can expect little effect from this kind of knowledge on behavior. The child first has to establish through experience a firm bond between this generalized rule and the set of circumstances in which it is applicable.

Here, in fact, we come upon an old educational problem. How do we learn best? We either expect children to discover the general rule from a set of experiences by means of induction – as in the solipsistic and behavioristic models – or we immediately present children with the abstract rule – as can only be done by the social environment – and expect them to discover its relevance to concrete instances by means of deduction.

In addition to the correspondence between learning to manage emotion and other learning situations, we also wish to underline one difference mentioned earlier: The control of emotion essentially means an intervention in deeply rooted programs that link emotional situations, emotional states, and emotional expressions together. Earlier experiences of successful control may weaken these bonds (some situations may lose their emotional value; other ways of expression are added to the repertoire), but in a lot of situations, we are still inclined to give way to these programs. The stronger the impulse, the more quickly secondary appraisal must come up with a behavioral or mental alternative. This time-factor makes it important that control strategies be available.

Initially these strategies will probably concern the expression of emotion, because most social rules are limited to this part of the program: You are allowed to be frightened, as long as you don't show it. Whether or not a different expression will solve the problem depends on the extent to which it serves to reduce the emotion itself. The more remote the strategy is from the original response, the less effective in this it will probably be. Our only hope, then, is to find new information in the situation or new perspectives on the information we already have that alleviate the emotional intensity of that situation. Otherwise, we simply have to endure the impulse – if such a thing is possible – or deal with the dangers of an inadequate response (Meerum Terwogt, Schene, & Koops, 1988).

Thus, emotional control has to be exercised under difficult conditions and is at the same time enormously complicated. No wonder that, even in adult life, it often exceeds our capabilities. For this reason society obviously has to be quite tolerant of the expression of emotion by young children. Quite a lot of learning has to be done.

References

Abelson, R. P. (1963). Computer simulation of "hot cognitions." In S. Tomkins & S. Messick (Eds.), *Computer simulation of personality*. New York: Wiley.

Ainsworth, M. D. S., Blehar, M. C., Waters, E., & Wall, S. (1978). *Patterns of attachment: a psychological study of the strange situation*. Hillsdale, NJ: Erlbaum.

Arnold, M. B. (1960). *Emotion and personality: Vol. 1*. New York: Columbia University Press.

Averill, J. R. (1982). *Anger and aggression: an essay on emotion* New York: Springer.

Barden, R. C., Zelko, F. A., Duncan, S. W., & Masters, J. C. (1980). Children's consensual knowledge about the experimental determinants of emotion. *Journal of Personality and Social Psychology, 39*, 368–376.

Blaney, P. H. (1986). Affect and memory: a review. *Psychological Bulletin, 99*, 229–249.

Borke, H. (1971). Interpersonal perception of young children: egocentrism or empathy. *Developmental Psychology, 5*, 263–269.

Bower, G. H. (1981). Mood and memory. *American Psychologist, 36*, 129–148.

Bretherton, I. (1985). Attachment theory: retrospect and prospect. In I. Bretherton & E. Waters (Eds.), Growing points of attachment theory and research. *Monographs of the Society for Research in Child Development, 50*, Serial No 209.

Bretherton, I, Fritz, J., Zahn-Waxler, C., & Ridgeway, D. (1986). Learning to talk about emotions: a functional perspective. *Child Development, 57*, 529–548.

Broadhurst, P. L. (1957). Emotionality and the Yerkes-Dodson Law. *Journal of Experimental Psychology, 54*, 345–352.

Campos, J. J., & Stenberg, C. R. (1981). Perception, appraisal and emotion: the onset of social referencing. In M. E. Lamb & L. R. Sherrod (Eds.), *Infant social cognition: empirical and theoretical considerations*. Hillsdale, NJ: Erlbaum.

Carlson, C. R., Swartz Felleman, E., & Masters, J. C. (1983). Influence of children's emotional states on the recognition of emotion in peers and social motives to change another's emotional state. *Motivation and Emotion, 7,* 61–79.

Carroll, J. J., & Steward, M. S. (1984). The role of cognitive development in children's understanding of their own feelings. *Child Development, 55,* 1486–1492.

Cole, P. M. (1986). Children's spontaneous control of facial expression. *Child Development, 57,* 1309–1321.

Easterbrook, J. A. (1959). The effect of emotion on cue utilization and the organization of behavior. *Psychological Review, 66,* 183–201.

Ekman, P. (1973). *Darwin and facial expression: a century of research in review.* New York: Academic Press.

Ferguson, T. J., & Olthof, T. (1986). *Children's anger.* Paper presented at the North American ISRA meeting, Chicago, September.

Ferguson, T. J., & Rule, B. G. (1983). An attributional perspective on anger and aggression. In R. G. Green & E. I. Donnerstein (Eds.), *Agression: theoretical and empirical reviews, Vol. I.* New York: Academic Press.

Flavell, H. M. (1977). *Cognitive development.* Englewood Cliffs, NJ: Prentice Hall.

Frijda, N. H. (1980). *Towards a model of emotion.* Paper presented at the N.I.A.S.-Conference on Stress and Anxiety. Wassenaar, The Netherlands, February.

Frijda, N. H. (1987). *The emotions.* Cambridge: Cambridge University Press.

Gilbert, D. C. (1969). The young child's awareness of affect. *Child Development, 40,* 629–639.

Glasberg, R., & Aboud, F. (1982). Keeping one's distance from sadness: children's self-reports of emotional experience. *Developmental Psychology, 18,* 287–293.

Graham, S., & Weiner, B. (1986). From an attributional theory of emotion to developmental psychology: a round-trip ticket? *Social Cognition, 4,* 153–179.

Harris, P. L. (1983a). Children's understanding of the link between situation and emotion. *Journal of Experimental Child Psychology, 33,* 1–20.

Harris, P. L. (1983b). The child as a psychologist. In M. Donaldson, R. Grieve, & C. Pratt (Eds.), *Early childhood development and education.* Oxford: Blackwell.

Harris, P. L. (1985). What children know about the situations that provoke emotion. In M. Lewis & C. Saarni (Eds.), *The socialization of emotion.* New York, Plenum.

Harris, P. L. (1988). Children's understanding of real and apparent emotion. In J. W. Astington, P. L. Harris, & D. R. Olson (Eds.), *Developing theories of mind.* Cambridge: Cambridge University Press.

Harris, P. L., Donnelly, K., Guz, G. R., & Pitt-Watson, R. (1986). Children's understanding of the distinction between real and apparent emotion. *Child Development, 57,* 895–909.

Harris, P. L., & Olthof, T. (1982). The child's conception of emotion. In G. Butterworth & P. Light (Eds.), *Social cognition: the individual and the social in cognitive development.* Sussex: Harvester Press.

Harris, P. L., Olfhof, T., & Meerum Terwogt, M. (1981). Children's knowledge of emotion. *Journal of Child Psychology and Psychiatry, 22,* 247–261.

Harris, P. L., Olthof, T., Meerum Terwogt, M., & Hardman, C. E. (1987). Children's knowledge of the situations that provoke emotion. *International Journal of Behavioral Development, 10,* 319–343.

Harter, S. (1977). A cognitive-developmental approach to children's expression of conflicting feelings and a technique to facilitate such expression in play therapy. *Journal of Consulting and Clinical Psychology, 45,* 417–432.

Harter, S. (1979). *Children's understanding of multiple emotions: a cognitive developmental approach.* Address to the Ninth Annual Symposium of the Jean Piaget Society, Philadelphia, June.

Harter, S. (1983). A cognitive-developmental approach to children's understanding of affect and trait labels. In F. C. Serafica (Ed.), *Social-cognitive development in context.* New York: Guilford Press.

Kopp, C. (1982). Antecedents of self-regulation: a developmental perspective. *Developmental Psychology, 18,* 199–214.

Koriat, A., Melkman, R., Averill, J. R., & Lazarus, R. S. (1972). The self-control of emotional reactions to a stressful film. *Journal of Personality, 40,* 601–619.

Latané, B., & Darley, J. M. (1970). *The unresponsive bystander: why doesn't he help?* New York: Appleton-Century-Crofts.

Lazarus, R. S. (1975). The self-regulation of emotion. In Levi, L. (Ed.), *Emotions – their parameters and measurement.* New York: Raven Press.

Lazarus, R. S. (1982). Thoughts on the relations between emotion and cognition. *American Psychologist, 37,* 1019–1024.

Lazarus, R. S., Coyne, J. C., & Folkman, S. (1982). Cognition, emotion, and motivation: the doctoring of Humpty-Dumpty. In R. W. Neufeld (Ed.), *Psychological stress and psychopathology.* New York: McGraw-Hill.

Lewis, M., & Michalson, L. (1983). *Children's emotions and moods.* New York: Plenum.

Masters, J. C., Barden, R. C., & Ford, M. E. (1979). Affective states, expressive behavior and learning in children. *Journal of Personality and Social Psychology, 33,* 380–390.

Masters, J. C., & Carlson, C. R. (1984). Children's and adults' understanding of the causes and consequences of emotional states. In C. Izard, J. Kagan, & R. Zajonc (Eds.), *Emotions, cognition and behavior.* New York, Cambridge University Press.

Masters, J. C., Ford, M. E., & Arend, R. A. (1983). Children's strategies for controlling affective responses to aversive social experience. *Motivation and Emotion, 7,* 103–116.

Maters, J. C., & Santrock, J. W. (1976). Studies in self-regulation of behavior: effects of contingent cognitive and affective events. *Developmental Psychology, 12,* 334–348.

Meerum Terwogt, M. (1984). *Emotional development in middle childhood: a cognitive view.* Ph.D. dissertation, Vrije Universiteit, Amsterdam.

Meerum Terwogt, M. (1986). Affective states and task performance in naive and prompted children. *European Journal of Psychology of Education, 1,* 31–40.

Meerum Terwogt, M. (1987). Children's behavioral reactions in situations with a dual emotional impact. *Psychological Reports, 61,* 1002.

Meerum Terwogt, M., Bannenberg, A., & Claessen, A. (in preparation). Children's anticipations of the effects of emotional situations on themselves and others.

Meerum Terwogt, M., Koops, W., Oosterhoff, T., & Olthof, T. (1986). Development in processing of multiple emotional situations. *Journal of General Psychology, 113,* 109–119.

Meerum Terwogt, M., & Kramer, L. (1981). Onderkenning van de invloed van stemmingen op taakuitvoering onder volvassenen (Acknowledgment in adults of the influence of mood on task-performance). Internal report, Vrije Universiteit, Amsterdam.

Meerum Terwogt, M., Schene, J., & Harris, P. L. (1986). Self-control of emotional reactions by young children. *Journal of Child Psychology and Psychiatry, 27,* 357–366.

Meerum Terwogt, M., Schene, J., & Koops, W. (1988). Opvattingen over emoties bij uithuis geplaatste en thuis opgevoede kinderen (Children's conceptions of emotion: normal versus institutionalized children). *Nederlands Tijdschrift voor de Psychologie, 43,* 363–375.

Mischel, H. N., & Mischel, W. (1983). The development of children's knowledge of self-control strategies. *Child Development, 54,* 603–619.

Nisbett, R. E., & Wilson, T. D. (1977). Telling more than we can know: verbal reports on mental processes. *Psychological Review, 84,* 231–259.

Olthof, T., Ferguson, T. J., Hoeben, S., & Luiten, A. (in preparation). Account source and person-based expectations as determinants of children's attributions of blame and anger.

Olthof, T., Ferguson, T. J., & Luiten, A. (in preparation). Cognitive determinants of children's attributions of blame and anger.

Olthof, T., Meerum Terwogt, M., van Panthaleon van Eck, O., & Koops, W. (1987). Children's knowledge of the integration of successive emotions. *Perceptual and Motor Skills, 65,* 407–414.

Patterson, C. J., & Mischel, W. (1976). Effects of temptation-inhibiting and task-facilitating plans on self-control. *Journal of Personality and Social Psychology, 33,* 209–217.

Piaget, J. (1977). *The moral judgement of the child.* London: Penguin (originally published by Routledge & Kegan Paul, 1932).

Plutchik, R. (1980). *Emotion, a psychoevolutionary synthesis.* New York: Harper & Row.

Rozin, P. (1975). The evolution of intelligence and access to the cognitive unconscious. In J. Sprague & A. N. Epstein (Eds.), *Progress in psychobiology and physiological psychology, Vol. 6.* New York: Academic Press.

Rule, B. G., & Ferguson, T. J. (1984). The relations among attribution, moral evaluation, anger, and aggression in children adults. In A. Mummendey (Ed.), *Social psychology of aggression. From individual behavior to social interaction.* New York: Springer.

Saarni, C. (1978). Cognitive and communicative features of emotional experience, or do you show what you think you feel? In M. Lewis & L. A. Rosenblum (Eds.), *The development of affect.* New York: Plenum.

Saarni, C. (1979). Children's understanding of display rules for expressive behavior. *Developmental Psychology, 15,* 424–429.

Saarni, C. (1984). An observational study of children's attempts to monitor their expressive behavior. *Child Development, 55,* 1504–1513.

Shields, S. A., & Stern, R. M. (1979). Emotion: the perception of bodily change. In P. Pliner, K. R. Blankstein & J. M. Spigel (Eds.), *Perception of emotion in self and others. Advances in the study of communication and affect, Vol. 5.* New York: Plenum.

Singer, J. L., & Singer, D. G. (1976). Imaginative play and pretending in early childhood: some experimental approaches. In A. Davids (Ed.), *Child personality and psychopathology: Current topics.* New York: Wiley.

Skinner, B. F. (1958). *Verbal behavior.* New York: Appleton-Century-Crofts.

Taylor, D. A., & Harris, P. L. (1984). Knowledge of strategies for the expression of emotion among normal and maladjusted boys: a research note. *Journal of Child Psychology and Psychiatry, 24,* 141–145.

Trabasso, T., Stein, N. L., & Johnson, L. R. (1981). Children's knowledge of events: a causal analysis of story structure. In G. Bower (Ed.), *Advances in learning and motivation, Vol. 15.* New York: Academic Press.

Underwood, B., Moore, B. S., & Rosenhan, D. L. (1973). Affect and self-gratification. *Developmental Psychology, 8,* 209–214.

von Frisch, K. (1968). Honeybees: do they use direction and distance information provided by their dancers? *Science, 158,* 1072–1076.

Weiner, B., & Graham, S. (1984). An attributional approach to emotional development. In C. Izard, J. Kagan, & R. Zajonc (Eds.), *Emotions, cognition and behavior.* New York: Cambridge University Press.

Zajonc, R. B. (1980). Feeling and thinking: preferences need no inferences. *American Psychologist, 35,* 151–173.

Part V

Emotion, empathy, and experience

9 Understanding emotion and experiencing emotion

Paul L. Harris and Mark S. Lipian

Consider a child who is currently facing an emotionally charged situation, such as a separation from parents and friends or entry into a novel or frightening environment. If we conduct an interview to discover how frightened or upset the child is, it will be important to take into account the implicit theory that the child adopts in formulating her or his answers. Does the child realize that it is possible to feel negative as well as positive feelings in response to the same situation? Does the child grasp the distinction between the outer display of emotion and the private experience of emotion? Does the child understand the causal antecedents that elicit guilt as distinct from those that elicit sadness? The way that age changes in the understanding of emotion might influence answers to these questions has been discussed in several chapters of this volume.

There is, however, another important consideration that has not been discussed. The child who is facing an emotionally charged situation is presumably experiencing one or more emotions. Does that current experience of emotion have any influence on the child's understanding? As adults, we often assume that intense affect can produce a temporary change in our judgment. We may postpone important decisions or encounters, knowing the influence that strong emotion can have. It would not be surprising, therefore, if the current experience of emotion had an influence on the child's judgment, particularly about emotion itself. Thus, when we interview a child who is upset or distressed, we may need to interpret the child's replies not just in terms of the way in which the child's conceptualization changes during development; we may also need to consider whether the child's conceptualization exhibits temporary fluctuations when strong emotion is being experienced.

In this chapter, we begin to analyze this issue. We cannot yet do so in an exhaustive fashion, but our initial findings are provocative enough to warrant further investigation. We describe two different studies in which we interviewed children about emotion. In each study, a comparison was made between children facing an emotionally charged situation and children who had faced that situation, or some components of it, earlier but were no longer likely to be experienc-

241

ing the relevant emotions to the same degree. Our question was whether the two groups of children would differ in their conceptualization of emotion. Three outcomes seemed possible: an enhancement of understanding, a reduction of understanding, and no change. We will consider each of these in turn.

An enhancement of understanding appears, at least prima facie, to be a plausible outcome because a child who is currently experiencing emotion may well be confronted by an extended sequence of events: the situation that has provoked the emotion, the physiological and subjective reactions that ensue, and the possibility of attempting to conceal or change those reactions. Confronted by this sequence of events, children might show more insight than when they think about that same sequence hypothetically.

A reduction or contraction of understanding is also conceivable. The experience of emotion may temporarily make the possibility of feeling differently seem utterly remote. For example, the child might mistakenly regard the situation that caused the emotion as a permanent state of affairs, or underestimate the extent to which an initially intense emotion might wane over time. In addition, the intense thoughts and feelings immediately surrounding an emotion-inducing event might distract the child from a carefully reasoned analysis. Thus, current emotion might temporarily constrain or narrow the way that emotional reactions are conceived, impelling the child to consider her or his current emotion as an inevitable and unchangeable reaction to the current situation.

Finally, the current experience of emotion might not bring about any change in the child's understanding of emotion because that understanding is a stable function of her or his current level of cognitive development. Any emotion, whether it is being experienced at the moment, whether it is an emotion that might be felt but not currently, or whether it is an emotion observed in another person, will be understood through the same cognitive lens. Immediate experiential factors will be irrelevant.

In order to assess the impact of current emotion, we selected two naturally occurring situations likely to elicit quite strong emotion in children. In one study, some of the children were in the hospital; in the other study, the children were entering a new boarding school. In certain respects, the children in both studies were facing a similar situation: They were away from home; they were in an unfamiliar environment; and they were separated from their parents. As we shall show, however, there were also important dissimilarities between the two studies and in the pattern of their results.

Children in the hospital

In the first study (Harris & Lipian, 1985; Lipian, 1985), one hundred children were interviewed about their emotional reactions to illness. The children were 6 and 10 years of age. Half the children in each age group were sick. Their illness was sufficiently serious that they were in the hospital at the time of the interview. They were suffering from a variety of acute or suspected medical or surgical conditions, but none of them were life-threatening (abdominal pain; infection following an insect bite; hepatitis; observation for suspected tuberculosis; a broken wrist, and so forth). The remaining children were healthy. They were interviewed at school and asked to think back to the last time that they were sick and to describe their emotional reactions. Thus, both groups were interviewed about the same emotionally charged topic (being sick), but whereas the hospitalized children were currently facing the experience of illness and its sequelae, the healthy children were only asked to consider an illness that they had once had, whose sequelae were long since gone. Finally, it should be emphasized that in other respects the sick and healthy children were comparable. Their teachers rated their educational attainments as similar; they came from the same distribution of social backgrounds, ranging from lower working class to upper middle class; both groups were almost equally divided between males and females.

The interview included a variety of questions about emotion. It was built around a set of structured questions, but the interviewer attempted to put those questions in a conversational style and asked additional, unscheduled questions if the child's answer to the standard formulation was unclear or hesitant. We focus on certain core questions that were included not only in this study but also in the study of children entering a boarding school (described below). These questions concerned the possibility of experiencing mixed or ambivalent feelings; the concealment or masking of emotion; and strategies for making oneself feel more cheerful.

Mixed emotions about illness

At the beginning of the interview the children were asked to say how they felt about being sick. Not surprisingly, the majority claimed to feel one or more negative emotions: sad, bored, fed up, unhappy, angry, and so forth. The interviewer followed up this initial question by asking whether mixed feelings were possible as a reaction to illness. Specifically, children were asked whether being sick could ever make one feel an emotion opposite in valence to the emotion that they had mentioned initially. For example, a child who claimed to feel sad at being sick was asked if being sick could ever make you feel happy.

The replies to this question differed quite sharply for the hospitalized as opposed to the healthy children. The healthy children showed the kind of age change that has been established in other work on children's understanding of mixed feelings (Harris, 1983a; Harter, 1983; Harter & Whitesell, this volume) Thus, only a minority of the 6-year-olds (24%) agreed without further prompting that they could feel such mixed feelings, whereas a large majority (84%) of the 10-year-olds agreed. The picture was quite different for the hospitalized children in that the age change was much reduced. Thus, only a minority of 6-year-olds (20%) but also only a minority of 10-year-olds (40%) agreed without further prompting that illness could provoke mixed feelings.

One plausible interpretation of this result is that it simply reflects the kind of illness that the two groups had in mind: Whereas the healthy children were thinking about a sore throat or chicken pox that might not preclude the elicitation of various positive feelings (for example, those associated with not having to go to school), the hospitalized children were thinking about a more serious illness with few if any mitigating features. A follow-up question is pertinent to this interpretation. The children were asked to envisage that they had gone on an outing to their favorite fun-fair despite being sick. This hypothetical scenario was deliberately concocted to confront the child with a situation where mixed or ambivalent feelings would be more feasible. Children who still insisted that they would feel only negative feelings on such an outing were prompted as follows: "Well, say it was just a little illness – a cold or a little sore throat. What feelings would you have at the fair then?" The customary age change emerged among the healthy children. Thus a minority of 6-year-olds (33%) but a majority of 10-year-olds (72%) agreed that you could feel both positive and negative feelings. The results were quite different for the hospitalized children. This acknowledgment was made by only a tiny fraction of the 6-year-olds (4%) and by very few 10-year-olds (16%). Thus, whether the hospitalized children were asked about their current illness or about a hypothetical but related situation involving a minor illness, they were much less willing than their healthy peers to acknowledge that mixed feelings were possible.

The pattern of results obtaine⁻ with respect to mixed feelings was repeated many times throughout the interview. Thus, whereas the 6- and 10-year-old healthy children showed the usual and expected pattern of developmental change, the hospitalized children gave fewer "mature" replies, particularly in the 10-year-old group.

Hiding negative feelings about illness

A further illustration of this pattern is provided by children's replies to questions about hiding one's feelings. The initial question about hiding feelings was open-ended: "Say you were with your mother or father and you were sick. Could it ever happen that your mother or father didn't know you felt *sad* (or whatever emotion the child had claimed to feel at the beginning of the interview)?" A clear age change emerged among the healthy children. Thus, just under half of the 6-year-olds (40%) but an overwhelming majority of 10-

year-olds (90%) pointed out that it would be possible to hide one's feelings by behaving in a way that was inconsistent with one's actual feelings. This acknowledgement was made by far fewer hospitalized children – a minority of both the 6-year-olds (16%) and the 10-year-olds (33%).

Again, one could interpret this pattern of replies in terms of the particular illness that the two groups were contemplating. The hospitalized children were presumably thinking of a more severe complaint so that the possibility or even the desirability of hiding one's feelings was less obvious to them than it was to the healthy children, who were probably recalling a minor ailment. This interpretation leads to the prediction that hospitalized children would be willing to admit that other people, particularly their parents, might seek to remain outwardly cheerful or unconcerned, however worried they might be, in order not to worry the child. Thus, children facing severe or life-threatening illnesses are often confronted by parents who are reluctant to explicitly acknowledge the gravity of the situation for fear of disturbing the child, even though the child often sees through the parents' supposedly reassuring exterior. To probe their understanding of such efforts at parental concealment, the children were told about another child who allegedly told the interviewer that "sometimes when he was sick, his parents acted cheerful, even when they were very worried about him because he was sick." The children were then asked whether he was right or wrong in what he had claimed about his parents. Among the healthy children, the majority of 6-year-olds (60%) acknowledged that parents could indeed act one way and feel another, and among the healthy 10-year-olds this acknowledgment was universal. Among the hospitalized children, by contrast, there were many children who rejected the possibility of parental concealment. Thus, only a minority of the 6-year-olds (20%) and less than three quarters of the 10-year-olds (72%) agreed that parents might hide their feelings. In summary, the pattern that emerged for the understanding of mixed or ambivalent feelings was repeated for the understanding of whether or not feelings can be hidden. The hospitalized children were less likely to give the more advanced sort of replies that were given by approximately half of the healthy 6-year-olds and by all of the healthy 10-year-olds.

Changing negative feelings about illness

Children were asked not just about changing the overt expression of emotion, but also about devices to change the experience of emotion. The following question was posed: "Say you were sick and you felt sad [or whatever emotion the child had mentioned to describe his or her feelings at the beginning of the interview]. Is there anything you could do to change the way you felt, to change the feeling of being sad?" Among the healthy children, there was a clear age change toward increased optimism about the possibility of strategic intervention. Thus, less than half of the 6-year-olds (44%) but all the 10-year-olds thought that there was something one could do. By contrast, the majority of the hospitalized children were pessimistic, irrespective of age. Less than half of the 6-year-olds (40%) and about the same proportion of the 10-year-olds (36%) thought that there was something that one could do to alter the feelings being experienced in association with her or his illness.

What sort of strategies did children propose when they did accept that strategic intervention was possible? The most popular strategy among the 6-year-olds – whether they were healthy or hospitalized – was engagement in some sort of enjoyable activity such as playing with toys or friends. Young children could not elaborate these proposals very much. The following exchange between the interviewer and a 6-year-old hospitalized girl is typical:

Interviewer: Say you were sick and you felt sad. Is there anything you could do to *change* the way you felt?
Child: I could get someone to play with me.
Interviewer: What would that do?
Child: Make me more cheerful.
Interviewer: How?
Child: Because I could play with them – a game.
Interviewer: What could you do if you were all by yourself?
Child: I could play with my spinning top.
Interviewer: What does that do?
Child: I'm happier.
Interviewer: How come?
Child: 'Cos it's good fun, my spinning-top.
Interviewer: Anything else you could try?
Child: No.

Among the 10-year-olds – again whether they were healthy or hospitalized – mentalistic replies were as common as activity-oriented replies. Instead of merely proposing an enjoyable activity, children were able to explain the psychological mechanism in more detail. Consider, for example, the following exchange between the interviewer and a 10-year-old healthy boy:

Interviewer: Say you were sick and you felt depressed. Is there anything you could do to change the way you felt?
Child: Well, if you read quite a lot.
Interviewer: What would that do?
Child: Well, it'd probably boost my morale a little – reading something; it'd get me away from feeling very sad and get me into the book.
Interviewer: Anything else?
Child: Well, anything to get me away, really – watch the telly or cards with my dad.
Interviewer: "Get you away" . . . ?
Child: Yeah, you know, distract me so I don't think about it all the time.

Pulling together the various results obtained in this interview study, a stable picture emerges. Among the hospitalized children, there is a consistent slippage

Table 9.1. *Mean maturity score as a function of age and status*

	Status	
Age	Hospitalized	Healthy
6-year-olds	0.05	0.15
10-year-olds	0.17	0.49

Note: A two-way ANOVA confirmed the main effects of Age and Status and the interaction between those variables (all $p < .001$). Further analysis of the interaction confirmed the significance of each of the four possible pair-wise comparisons (all $p < .01$).

or regression. The more sophisticated replies that are found in a minority of healthy 6-year-olds and a majority of healthy 10-year-olds are found much less often in the hospitalized children. The sick 10-year-olds give replies that are more characteristic of healthy 6-year-olds, and there are even fewer indications of such advanced thinking among the hospitalized 6-year-olds. This difference between the groups emerged for the three domains discussed above – mixed feelings, the concealment of emotion, and deliberate efforts to change one's emotion – as well as for other domains addressed during the interview.[1] Although some of these differences between the healthy and ill children might be due to a difference in the severity of the illness being considered, the same pattern persists even in response to questions pertaining to a less severe illness or centering on supposedly healthy people, such as the subjects' parents.

In order to obtain an overview of the results, responses to each question were allocated to one of three levels. Level 1 responses were those characteristic of 6-year-olds; level 2 responses were those characteristic of 10-year-olds; and level 3 responses were those characteristic of 15-year-olds (the full study carried out by Lipian, 1985, included a group of healthy 15-year-olds). Each child could be given an overall score that reflected the extent to which he or she had responded in a more or less mature fashion to the 28 questions of the interview. Scores could range from zero (consistent responding at the 6-year-old level) to one (consistent responding at the 15-year-old level).[2] The mean ''maturity'' scores are given in Table 9.1 as a function of age and status. Table 9.1 indicates, as might be expected, that in general 10-year-olds give more mature responses than 6-year-olds. In addition, healthy children give more mature responses than hospitalized children, the effect of status being especially marked among the 10-year-olds.

Entering a new boarding school

How should the slippage phenomenon among the hospitalized children be explained? They differ from the healthy children in a variety of ways: They are sick, probably in some distress, separated from their parents and in a strange environment. None of these factors apply to the healthy children. In order to narrow down the set of possiblities, we carried out a study of boys entering an English boarding school (Harris & Guz, 1987). Such schools are of two types: preparatory schools, which typically admit boys at 8 years of age, and public schools, which admit boys at 13 years of age. We interviewed 8-year-olds who were just starting at a preparatory school and 13-year-olds who were just starting at a public school. Most public school boys have been at a preparatory school before entering their public school; this was true of the majority of the 13-year-olds that we talked to. Accordingly, although they were entering a new school, many of the 13-year-olds had already had a good deal of experience with life at a boarding school. For the 8-year-olds, on the other hand, this was the first experience of being away from home and living at a boarding school. In preliminary discussion with teachers at boarding schools, we learned that the first two to three weeks at the school were regarded as a settling-in period. By the end of this period, the boys had typically become more adjusted to the routine of the school; they had usually made some friends and seemed less obviously homesick. Accordingly, we interviewed half the boys in each age group at some point during their first two weeks at the school; the remaining boys were interviewed after five or six weeks. Irrespective of the time of the interview, the boys were asked about their feelings during the first few days following their arrival at the school. Thus, the boys interviewed in the first couple of weeks were effectively asked about their current feelings and we shall refer to them as the current group. The boys interviewed later in the term were asked to look back retrospectively to feelings that had presumably subsided in intensity and they will be referred to as the retrospective group.

As in the earlier study, the interview consisted of a structured series of questions, but the interviewer again made every effort to keep the atmosphere of the interview relaxed. Additional questions were posed if a reply was not initially clear. Many of the questions ranged over the same issues as before: the possibility of feeling mixed or conflicting emotions, the possibility of hiding one's feelings from other people, and potential strategies for altering one's feelings.

Mixed feelings about boarding

We anticipated that the boys would be quite likely to feel ambivalent about entering the new school. Arrival signaled the start of a lengthy period away from home (about 13 weeks for most boys); on the other hand, most of the boys regarded themselves as fortunate or privileged in being able to go to a boarding school that offered ample educational and recreational opportunities. We did not know, however, if the boys would be more or less willing to acknowledge their mixed feelings depending on the time when we interviewed them. The results were unequivocal. Irrespective of the time when they were interviewed, the majority of the boys readily acknowledged that mixed feelings were possible. They either spontaneously admitted such feelings themselves in reply to an initial, open-ended question about their reaction to starting at the new school, or they did so in response to the following prompt: "Some of the other boys said that they felt happy or sad or afraid or excited. Do/Did you feel any of those feelings as well?" Thus, following either the first open-ended question or the second more explicit question, approximately three-quarters of the boys acknowledged their own mixed feelings, irrespective of the time of the interview. Moreover, in response to a third question ("Do you think that someone could feel/could have felt excited but also worried at the same time about starting at this new school?"), there was almost universal assent.

The most notable age change was in the way the boys justified their belief in mixed feelings. The boys sometimes cited a single situation with two conflicting aspects ("You could be excited about the new class but worried about whether you'd do well in it"), and sometimes two distinct albeit concurrent situations ("You're excited about what's going to happen but worried 'cos you miss your mum)". Among the older boys, the citation of a single situation with two conflicting aspects was more common. Such a shift with age toward the citation of a single situation has also been reported by Harter and Buddin (1987).

This initial series of questions suggested that the experience of having just started at a new boarding school did not have the same impact as hospitalization. The relatively mature response of acknowledging ambivalence was spontaneously given by many of the boys and elicited from the majority with minimal probing. This pattern was repeated throughout the rest of the interview.

Hiding negative feelings about boarding

Boys who are settling into a boarding school may well feel anxious or homesick, but there is also some pressure on them not to express those feelings too openly for fear of being teased or ridiculed. Accordingly, the boys were posed a series of questions in which the interviewer hinted more and more explicitly at the possibility of such feelings of distress or anxiety being concealed from the other boys. Throughout this series of questions, there were very few boys who claimed that it was impossible to hide or at least try to hide their feelings. One of the questions in the series illustrates this general pattern. In this question, the possibility of hiding one's feelings was put to the boys quite explicitly: "Some of the other boys have said that they're sad at this school because they miss their friends at home, but they hide it by smiling and acting cheerful. Is that possible, do you think, to hide the fact that you feel sad about starting school by acting cheerfully at the same time?" Among the current group, only a few 8-year-olds (18%) or 13-year-olds (15%) claimed that it was impossible to hide one's feelings or that those feelings would show through in any case, or gave uninformative replies. The majority in each age group agreed that feelings could be hidden by deliberately adjusting one's social behavior, facial expression, or conversation – or by trying to change the sad mood itself. A similar pattern emerged among the boys tested retrospectively. There were few 8-year-olds (27%) and few 13-year-olds (8%) who were unable to suggest a strategy for concealing emotion or thought that it could not be done; the majority suggested strategies similar to those proposed by boys in the current group.

Changing negative feelings about boarding

Another series of questions was directed at the boys' strategies for cheering themselves up. Within this series, the boys were asked to comment on the effectiveness of two potential strategies – a strategy directed at the outward display of emotion rather than its mental component ("Does it help to smile or do you still feel sad?") and a strategy directed at the mental component rather than the outward display ("Does it help to think about certain things or do you still feel worried?"). In response to the first question, only a minority – just over a quarter of the boys – agreed that smiling per se might help to alleviate negative affect. Moreover, this proportion was similar for both age groups and for boys tested both currently and retrospectively. In response to the second question about the use of a mental or cognitive strategy, a much larger proportion of the subjects agreed that such an approach would help. Among boys in the current group, a clear majority of the 8-year-olds (77%) and of the 13-year-olds (92%) agreed that deliberately attempting to change the direction of one's thought processes could be helpful. A similar picture emerged for the boys in the retrospective group. Again, a clear majority of the 8-year-olds (73%) and of the 13-year-olds (77%) agreed that a cognitive strategy could be helpful. Taken together, the replies to these two questions show that even 8-year-olds can make a distinction between two possible strategies for changing one's mood. They are more willing to agree that efforts to control or redirect one's thought processes will be beneficial than they are to accept that a change in one's overt facial expression will alter one's actual feelings.

Summarizing over the various questions that were put to the boarding schoolboys, there was no indication of any slippage or regression when their replies were compared to those obtained from similarly aged subjects in other studies. Moreover, when the boys from the current group were compared to those from the retrospective group, a very similar pattern of responding was obtained: a willingness to admit to mixed or ambivalent feelings, a willingness to acknowledge the possible concealment from others of certain emotions such as worry or homesickness when a more positive front was socially acceptable, and a widespread endorsement of cognitive strategies as opposed to overt expressive changes as an efficacious technique for actually altering one's mood. Even though boys in the current group had been at the school for about a month less than had boys in the retrospective group, and hence were presumably less used to being away from home, had made fewer friends, and were less familiar with the routine and environment of the school, there was no systematic indication that their replies were any less subtle or advanced than those proposed by the more seasoned "veterans" populating the retrospective group.

Why does slippage occur?

If we combine the results of the two studies described above – the study of children newly admitted to a hospital and the study of children newly arrived at a boarding school – it is clear that the regression or slippage that was found among the hospitalized children is not an inevitable reaction to parental separation nor to immersion in a strange environment. No obvious signs of slippage were observed among the boys who had recently started at a new boarding school. The negative results obtained in the second study help us in trying to pin down the variable or variables that are responsible for slippage. Because neither parental separation nor entry into a strange environment seem responsible, what likely factors remain? There are at least three plausible candidates. First, the hospitalized children were sick. Second, they saw their hospital stay as a short-term event. Third, the majority were unhappy about being in the hospital. In our judgment, it is the third of these candidates – the children's emotional status at the time of the interview – that accounts for the pattern of results. Let us now examine each of the three candidates in turn to see why negative emotional status would seem to offer the most plausible explanation.

By definition, the hospitalized children were sick, whereas the children with whom they were compared (i.e., the children asked about their most recent illness) and also the boys interviewed in the boarding school study were in good health. Observation of very young children suggests that illness often provokes regressive behavior in the form of increasing clinging and dependency (Bowlby, 1971, pp. 258–259). Conceivably, we were observing a more cognitive version, in older children, of the type of overt regressive behavior that has been docu-

mented in toddlers. In future studies, this possibility could be tested by comparing sick and healthy children who are otherwise enjoying the same environment.
Thus, it would be feasible to interview children suffering from one of the common childhood illnesses, such as measles or chicken pox, at home and to compare their reports with those obtained from children who had had such an illness
in the preceding weeks but who had fully recovered.

Such an empirical investigation is the final arbiter. In the meantime, there are
various considerations that make it unlikely that illness, per se, provokes slippage. Consider first the wide variety of conditions that led to admission for the
hospitalized children: multiple fractures following a bicycle accident, abdominal
pain and suspected appendicitis, circumcision, multiple tooth extractions, infection following an insect bite. It is unlikely that these disparate complaints have
a common physiological impact. Yet the results of the interview suggested that
the hospitalized children were exhibiting a fairly uniform pattern of slippage.
Even if a common physiological impact could be identified – for example, a
high temperature – it is not obvious how such a physiological state could in itself
alter the child's cognitive processing in such a way as to produce a regression or
slippage effect.

There is, however, one possible physiological change that should be seriously
considered. Although the children had entered the hospital for a variety of conditions, a sizable proportion had undergone surgery before the interview. Of the
6-year-olds, just over a quarter (28%) had undergone surgery. Of the 10-year-
olds, just under half (48%) had undergone surgery. These children had been
given a general anesthetic during surgery and were interviewed on the day there-
after. Accordingly, even though they had undergone a diversity of surgical procedures, there was one common factor: They were all recovering from the effects
of a general anesthetic. Physiologically, the effects of general anesthesia may
persist for 12 hours or more (Gilman, Goodman, Rall, & Murad, 1985). If we
assume that children recovering from anesthesia exhibit an impairment in their
cognitive functioning, we would expect the score of the hospitalized group as a
whole to be lower than that of the healthy children, and, given the larger proportion of postoperative children among the 10-year-olds, we would expect this
slippage to be greater among the older hospitalized children. This is, of course,
exactly the pattern of findings that was obtained (cf. Table 9.1).

To check this interpretation, the hospitalized children who had undergone surgery were compared to those who had not by means of the maturity index described earlier. Mean maturity scores are given in Table 9.2 as a function of age
and surgical status. Table 9.2 shows clearly that surgery had little effect on the
hospitalized children. Within each group, the children exhibit comparably low
scores, irrespective of whether they had undergone surgery. Given these negative
findings, we doubt that illness, or some physiological concomitant of illness,
explains the slippage phenomenon.

Table 9.2. *Mean maturity score as a function
of age and surgical status*

	Status	
Age	No surgery	Postsurgery
6-year-olds	0.05	0.06
10-year-olds	0.20	0.15

Note: Two separate *t*-tests indicated that there was no effect of surgical status for either age group (t [23] <1.0, p n.s.).

A second possible explanation for the difference between the hospitalized children and the boarding schoolboys concerns the expectations the two groups bring with them. Hospitalization is viewed by children as a highly abnormal interlude in their lives during which a variety of strange procedures are enlisted so as to allow the child to leave as quickly as possible to return to the normal world outside. By contrast, the boarding-school pupil is frequently convinced well ahead of entry that the opportunity to go to a boarding school is a privilege. The child may have taken tests or examinations and passed them at a certain level to gain entry. This inevitably leads the child to view attendance at a boarding school as a positive achievement rather than as an unfortunate and distressing accident, even if the process of settling into the school turns out to be more stressful than anticipated. Once the boarder is at the school, he or she must acknowledge that the routine of the school will govern daily life for the foreseeable future. Admittedly, there are the vacations to look forward to, but those appear quite remote at the beginning of term. These various considerations mean that the hospitalized child is likely to think of hospitalization as an unexpected but temporary departure from normal life, whereas the boarder is likely to view entry into the school as the start of a challenging but desirable new adventure in life. Given these differences in outlook it is possible that the hospitalized children regard their situation as one that inevitably provokes entirely negative emotion, which there is no reason to hide and will only be relieved when their situation is altered – i.e., by their leaving the hospital. Boarders, on the other hand, knowing that they will be living in the school for the next few years, may make a deliberate effort to conceal their negative emotion from the other boys, to enjoy the school that they already hold in high regard. Moreover, they may accept the need to look to their own mental resources for relieving distress because the status quo is unlikely to change. This interpretation has some plausibility and makes some interesting predictions. Consider the child who is suffering, not an acute illness, as was the case for the hospitalized children, but rather a chronic illness such as diabetes or asthma. Such a child will presumably come to see his or her illness as a relatively permanent state of affairs to which an internal, mental adjustment must be made. An interpretation like that outlined above would predict that children suffering from a chronic illness, or more precisely children who have accepted that their illness is likely to remain chronic, may well describe and interpret their emotional reactions differently from children who have not reached such a state of acceptance. This analysis also raises the possibility that slippage will be found among children facing any kind of setback or distress that they view as temporary or undesirable. Consider, for example, children who have not yet accepted that their parents have permanently separated. They may well see their distress as unavoidable so long as the loss is not restored, and therefore view their emotional reactions in quite a different way from those children who have become convinced that a reconciliation is impossible.

Plausible though the above interpretation may be, it does not readily explain certain results. Recall that when the hospitalized children were asked to think about going to the fair with a mild cold, they typically anticipated predominantly negative rather than mixed feelings. Similarly, when they were invited to consider whether their parents might seek to conceal their anxieties, they denied that their parents would – or could – do that. Neither of these findings can be explained by assuming that the hospitalized children think of their distress as an inevitable reaction to an unusual and temporary situation. In the question about the fun-fair, they were explicitly invited to imagine a situation quite different from that surrounding hospitalization. In the question about their parents, they were explicitly invited to consider the emotional reactions of other people rather than their own. In short, the slippage effect appears to be too pervasive to be easily explained simply in terms of the child's judgment about the cause and duration of her or his current distress.

A third possible interpretation concerns the emotional status of the hospitalized children. Although there was considerable heterogeneity in the complaints that brought them to the hospital, there was a good deal of uniformity in their emotional reactions once they were there. Most children described themselves as sad, unhappy, bored, fed up, and so forth. The healthy children, interviewed at school about a past illness, were presumably in a normal emotional state. What about the boarding-school pupils? As noted earlier, the reactions of the boys entering boarding school were not uniformly negative. The majority readily acknowledged that they felt a mixture of positive and negative feelings. Only two or three showed overt signs of distress when they were interviewed, and then in connection with questions about missing their parents and feeling homesick.

Thus, it is possible that the slippage observed in the hospitalized children is a consequence of their predominantly negative feelings. How would such feelings change children's conceptualization of emotion? The following model appears to make sense of the results. We may suppose that strong emotion and the thoughts that accompany it (concerning either the event that precipitated the emotion or its likely consequences) exert a pervasive filtering effect on consciousness. Other more positive concerns are either subverted to fit this one central preoccupation or are ignored. Subjectively, this effect would seem to vary with the intensity of the emotion being experienced; the more intense the distress the more complete the flooding of consciousness. Work with adults confirms that once a depressed or negative mood has been induced, a variety of cognitive biases are likely to come into play. First, there is a bias toward the retrieval of negative events, particularly those involving failure (Blaney, 1986). Second, there is an association between sad or depressed mood and the tendency to see the self as a likely cause of bad but not good events both in adults (Brewin, 1985) and children (Seligman & Peterson, 1986). Third, the induction of a negative mood increases the expectation of negative events even when the events are naturally occurring disasters quite unrelated to the event that elicited the negative mood (Johnson & Tversky, 1983). In sum, a negative mood appears to lead subjects to recall negative events from the past, to expect negative events in the future, and to blame them upon the self irrespective of whether they might in fact be attributable to the self or to some quite unconnected, natural accident or calamity.

If the hospitalized children in our sample were distressed or sad, they would presumably be prone to all these negative biases. Such biases might be especially pertinent to expectations about emotion itself, be it the experience or the display of emotion. If this line of argument is valid, then children in distress might temporarily underestimate the possibility of feeling a positive emotion not just currently but also in relation to some hypothetical future event. Hence, they would effectively deny the possibility of mixed feelings. Similarly, they might underestimate the efficacy of any strategy whereby a negative emotional reaction might be hidden and a more positive expression displayed instead. Thus, both in their own cases and in those of their parents they would tend to assume the inevitability of a negative emotional expression. Finally, they may find it hard to recall positive thoughts or activities. Thus, they would find it more difficult to conceive of strategies that would alleviate their current sadness or distress and bring about a more positive mood.

This hypothesis predicts that slippage will occur in a variety of circumstances, not just when children are sick or hospitalized. Whenever children are sad, be it in reaction to loss, failure, or conflict, they should show some sign of slippage or ''negative bias'' in their understanding of emotion. Indeed, if the hypothesis of emotion-induced bias is correct, it might be fruitful to explore the impact of other emotional states. To the extent that other negative emotions such as anger, or indeed positive emotions such as joy or pride, flood consciousness, a different set of biases may come into play. Introspection lends some credence to this notion. Overwhelmed with relief or with love, it is often difficult to acknowledge that our positive emotional state may not be permanent, and must gradually yield to the more prosaic and cautious expectations that govern our day-to-day lives.

So far we have discussed the origins of the slippage effect. We also need to consider the nature of the effect itself. Two distinct issues will be considered: the pervasiveness of the effect and its duration. So far as its pervasiveness is concerned, we may envisage the slippage effect as having an impact on events and emotions that are closely associated with the event and emotion that is currently active or we may envisage a more widespread impact. If the slippage phenomenon were extremely local, it might influence the child's conceptualization of only the events and emotions associated wtih his or her current illness. A wider impact can be envisaged, however. The effect might spread to any event associated with sadness, or to any event associated with negative emotion. At its most pervasive, the effect might obtain for events in general, whether affectively charged or neutral. Thus, hospitalized children might show signs of regression or slippage in their understanding of conservation or visual perspective-taking. Further research will be needed to resolve this issue. In the meantime, we may note several pointers from the results that we have already obtained. First, as we noted in describing the results for the hospitalized children, the slippage effect not only manifests itself when the children are questioned about what they feel here and now in relation to their current illness; it is also apparent when they are questioned about hypothetical situations such as a day at the fair while suffering from some other illness, or parents' concealing anxiety about their child's illness. At the very least, therefore, the effect extends to the child's thoughts about illness in general. We would speculate that the effect might be still more pervasive, extending to thoughts about any sad or distressing event. Certainly, the research on mood-induced cognitive bias in adults shows that a sad mood alters the subject's judgment about the likelihood of negative events quite unrelated to the one that initially provoked the negative mood (Johnson & Tversky, 1983).

Finally, we may consider whether and for how long slippage is likely to persist. The answer to this question depends on our diagnosis of the underlying cause of the phenomenon. For example, if illness is assumed to be the underlying mechanism, then one might expect any observed slippage effect to recede following recovery from illness. If, on the other hand, it is the tendency to think of illness as a temporary, undesirable state that leads to slippage, then it would be possible for the slippage effect to recede provided the child accepted that the illness might be permanent rather than temporary. Finally, if, as our preferred interpretation suggests, the slippage is a result of the state of sadness or distress, then the phenomenon should recede as soon as the negative emotion that maintains it begins to wane. In future research, a longitudinal study in which children were interviewed at various points after the onset of either an acute or a chronic illness could help to assess the relative validity of these three interpretations.

Conclusions

At the beginning of this chapter, we asked whether children's understandng of emotion is influenced by the current experience of emotion. The results of the hospital study suggest that such an influence does exist. Hospitalized children exhibit a slippage or negative bias in their conceptualization of the way in which emotional reactions may be combined, concealed, or altered. Such an influence was not observed among children starting at a new boarding school. Apparently, entry into a new environment and separation from parents do not inevitably influence children's understanding of emotion. Although we have by no means firmly established the exact circumstances under which the slippage effect will be observed, nor have we ascertained its breadth and persistence, it is clear that the child's understanding of emotion is not of the classical type familiar from work in cognitive development. The classical picture of cognitive development is that of a progressive and more or less irreversible sequence. Such, at least, is the picture that emerges from the study of object permanence (Harris, 1983b), pretend play (Watson & Fischer, 1977) and moral judgment (Colby, Kohlberg, Gibbs, & Lieberman, 1983). Compared with the ratchetlike progress that children seem to make in those domains, the development of an understanding of emotion would appear to be strikingly volatile.

Notes

1. Children were also questioned about psychosomatic causality – whether or not one's emotional state might help or hinder recovery from illness. Healthy children, particularly in the older group, were more likely than their hospitalized peers to claim that emotion might influence the rate of recovery and to offer a mentalistic interpretation of that influence.
2. Children were given zero points for a level 1 response, one point for a level 2 response, and two points for a level 3 response across each of the 28 questions of the interview. Each child could then be given a single maturity index where the number of points obtained was expressed as a proportion of the maximum number of points obtainable (i.e., $2 \times 28 = 56$).

References

Blaney, P. H. (1986). Affect and memory: a review. *Psychological Bulletin, 99,* 229–246.

Bowlby, J. (1971). *Attachment and loss: Vol. 1, Attachment.* London: Pelican.

Brewin, C. R. (1985). Depression and causal attributions: What is their relation? *Psychological Bulletin, 98,* 297–309.

Colby, A., Kohlberg, L., Gibbs, J., & Lieberman, M. (1983). A longitudinal study of moral judgment. *Monographs of the Society for Research in Child Development,* Serial No. 200.

Gilman, A. G., Goodman, L. S., Rall, T. W., & Murad, F. (1985). *Goodman and Gilman's: the pharmacological basis of therapeutics* (7th ed.). New York: Macmillan.

Harris, P. L. (1983a). Children's understanding of the link between situation and emotion. *Journal of Experimental Child Psychology, 36,* 490–509.

Harris, P. L. (1983b). Infant cognition. In P. Mussen (Ed.), *Handbook of child psychology: Vol II Infancy and developmental psychobiology.* (M. M. Haith and J. J. Campos, Vol. Eds.) (pp. 689–782). New York: Wiley.

Harris, P. L., & Guz, G. E. (1987). *How boys report their emotional reactions upon entering an English boarding school*. Unpublished manuscript, Department of Experimental Psychology, University of Oxford.

Harris, P. L., & Lipian, M. S. (1985). *Distress and the loss of insight into emotion*. Paper presented at the Society for Research in Child Development, Toronto.

Harter, S. (1983). Children's understanding of multiple emotions: a cognitive–developmental approach. In W. Overton (Ed.), *The relationship between social and cognitive development* (pp. 147–194). Hillsdale, NJ: Erlbaum.

Harter, S., & Buddin, B. (1987). Children's understanding of the simultaneity of two emotions: a five-stage developmental acquisition sequence. *Developmental Psychology, 23,* 388–399.

Johnson, E. J., & Tversky, A. (1983). Affect, generalization, and the perception of risk. *Journal of Personality and Social Psychology, 45,* 20–31.

Lipian, M. S. (1985). *Ill-conceived feelings: developing concepts of the emotions associated with illness in healthy and acutely ill children*. Unpublished doctoral dissertation, Yale University.

Seligman, M. E. P., & Peterson, C. (1986). A learned helplessness perspective on childhood depression: theory and research. In M. Rutter, C. E. Izard, & P. B. Read (Eds.), *Depression in young people* (pp. 223–249). New York: Guilford.

Watson, M. W., & Fischer, K. W. (1977). A developmental sequence of agent use in late infancy. *Child Development, 48,* 828–836.

10 What children know and feel in response to witnessing affective events

Janet Strayer

Witnessing affective events involving others, like seeing a delighted youngster at a circus or a disabled person struggling to walk, typically elicit in us different thoughts and, often, feelings. On occasion, such events may also elicit our empathy or feelings that are triggered by and are more appropriate to the other person's experience and situation than to our own external context. These topics are central to this chapter, in which we examine children's experience of emotion in response to witnessing affective events and how this experience changes as a function of children's age, gender, and the kind of emotion witnessed.

The vantage gained from this examination is basic to understanding both *whether* the witnessing of such events elicits empathy and *how* empathy is experienced by children of different ages. The experiential component of emotions conjoins what we feel and what we know about feelings (Lewis & Michalson, 1983). Empathy, as a bridging of one's own and the other person's experience, is an interpersonal transaction that further conjoins, between ourself and other persons, what we feel and what we know about feelings. Typically, and particularly in empirical investigations, the experiential component of emotions and of empathy necessarily entails what a person can and chooses to say about this subjective experience. Our aim is to integrate the affective and cognitive responses entailed in this verbal material in terms of a new research tool: the Empathy Continuum. Our position is that what children feel and know about their own and others' emotions changes as a function of both cognitive and social development.

In order to set the context for this chapter, we will begin by presenting the conceptual and methodological features of the Empathy Continuum. Because empathy is discussed in terms of children's emotional responses and their rec-

Funding from the Social Sciences and Humanities Research Council of Canada (Grant 498830027) for research on which this chapter is based is gratefully acknowledged, as is the assistance of the National Film Board of Canada. My special thanks to graduate students working with me and to colleagues who read and offered helpful comments on this chapter.

259

ognition of emotions in others, and because points made concerning the empirical data relevant to the Empathy Continuum build upon data relevant to both children's recognition of others' emotions and their emotional self-attributions, the second section of this chapter will focus upon these data. In this section we will also consider our findings in light of previous measures of children's empathy, in which affective matching between self and the other person is the criterion. Empirical findings specific to the Empathy Continuum will then be presented in the last section of this chapter.

Our focus is on one aspect of children's emotional experience – their responsiveness to witnessing emotional events in which other persons are the main participants. This responsiveness, of course, is only a part of the child's emotional experience, which often centers more directly on the self. Nevertheless, I believe it is an important part, in the sense that emotions are not only "private" events, but that they develop with reference to a social context that explicitly and incidentally informs us about what we do feel or should feel. In this way, our own emotional experience is linked to what we may know and experience of the emotions of others. In particular, empathy permits us to "live through" many emotional events as if we were a participant.

A cognitive-affective continuum for empathy

In past research with children, empathy has been operationalized either as a match between a child's own and her or his reported emotion for a stimulus character's identified emotion (e.g., Feshbach & Roe, 1968) or as a general disposition, reported via questionnaire responses, to be emotionally responsive to affective events (Bryant, 1982). The present focus is, in part, similar to the first approach. That is, empathy is assessed as an affective response to emotionally evocative events. It differs from previous emotional match procedures in that empathy is operationalized as *both* an affective response concordant with someone else's emotions and/or situation, *and* one that entails different cognitive mediators that necessarily affect the empathic experience. My interest is to examine empathy from the subjective viewpoint of the child experiencing it and to present an empirical model for organizing the cognitive-affective experience of empathy along a developmental continuum. I shall first present the proposed framework for organizing affective and cognitive data relevant to children's experience of empathy, and then examine the relation between that framework and more traditional emotional matching procedures.

Empathy is primarily an affective reaction; but, like other affective processes, it is likely to be mediated by different kinds of cognitive appraisals, which may be ordered in terms of increasing complexity (Hoffman, 1975, 1982). For example, shared affect may occur at all ages with little or no deliberate cognitive mediation. Certainly, examples of "emotion contagion" via involuntary motor mimicry and the absence of self–other differentiation – such as newborns crying upon hearing another newborn cry (Sagi & Hoffman, 1976) are of this sort. These examples may be precursors to, but are not necessarily evidence of empathy as it is currently construed (Strayer, 1987c). Once cognitions become involved, there is likely an affective-cognitive feedback loop (Feshbach, 1982; Hoffman, 1975), in which affective arousal primes attention and cognition, and cognition influences what is understood about these feelings, as well as what further affect-related information is sought and processed.

On one level, shared affect with another person may be experienced as a direct response to the contextual cues impinging upon both oneself and the other person. The focus is not so much upon the other person as upon the stimulus events themselves. However, given that these events are experienced vicariously (e.g., the observer is not being hit, but is reacting to the hit observed), these responses are within the domain of empathy, defined by Hoffman (1982) as responses more appropriate to someone else's context than to one's own. At this point, I think an important distinction for discerning different kinds of empathic experience becomes whether the observer's reaction stems mostly from the event (e.g., cringing at witnessing a blow being delivered), the person-by-event interaction (e.g., cringing along with a frail person seen being hit by a strong person), or even more personalized cues regarding the target person (e.g., having previously observed the target act courageously and nonviolently in the face of provocation).

I would propose that less complex levels of empathy are characterized by an event-focus, with little person-based inference operating to mediate the feelings provoked. At more complex levels, the experience of another person involved in events, rather than the events themselves, is paramount. Thus, at a somewhat more complex level, the fact that another person actually is involved in the events witnessed would explicitly be noted in children's responses. Empathy may then be experienced as a *parallel* response mediated by personal experiences elicited by and associated with those witnessed for the stimulus person. And, at the most complex level proposed, empathy is experienced as a *participatory* response (Staub, 1979) focused upon the other person's internal experience. This would entail a particular focus upon the reactions, general characteristics, and point of view of the other person, more than upon either the objective events themselves or a simple person-in-event recognition.

Taking these considerations into account, the Empathy Continuum (EC) has been designed (Strayer, 1987a,b,c) as a multidimensional measure. The EC considers a subject's reports of affective arousal concordant with another person's emotion together with the reported cognitive mediation for that arousal. The basic structure of the EC is shown in Table 10.1. The ordering of the seven EC levels, together comprising 20 categories, is based upon theories asserting a pro-

Table 10.1. *The Empathy Continuum (EC) scoring system*

EC score	EC level (cognitive mediation)	Affect-match	Description	Attribution
0	I	0	No emotion reported for character	*No report of matched emotion; no empathy*
1		0	Accurate emotion reported for character, but no (or discordant) emotion for self	
2	II	1	Similar emotion for self and character	*No attribution or irrelevant reasons are provided for matched emotion: e.g., "I just didn't like it."*
3		2	Same emotion, different intensity	
4		3	Same emotion, same intensity	
5,6,7	III	1,2,3	Similar emotion for self and character Same emotion, different intensity Same emotion, same intensity	*Attribution based on story events only, not characters: e.g., "I felt scared of that creepy, old house."*
8,9,10	IV	1,2,3	Similar emotion for self and character Same emotion, different intensity Same emotion, same intensity	*Attribution refers to a specific character's situation: e.g., "I felt scared when he went up to that old house."*
11,12,13	V	1,2,3	Similar emotion for self and character Same emotion, different intensity Same emotion, same intensity	*Attribution indicates transposition of self into situation and/or association to one's own experiences: e.g., "Well, I'm scared but curious, like him, about stuff like that."*
14,15,16	VI	1,2,3	Similar emotion for self and character Same emotion, different intensity Same emotion, same intensity	*Attribution indicates responsiveness to character's internal state: e.g., "I felt sad because she felt so put down."*
17,18,19	VII	1,2,3	Similar emotion for self and character Same emotion, different intensity Same emotion, same intensity	*Attribution indicates semantically explicit role taking: e.g., "If I were in her place, I'd be angry at him for treating me like that."*

gression along the following lines: (a) from no evident awareness of another's affect, to affective awareness but no emotional responsiveness, to awareness and concordant responsiveness; (b) from direct personal reaction to stimulus events to increasingly greater focus upon the other person; (c) from centering on external events, to acknowledging the other person as object, to considering the other person a subject (i.e., focusing upon what they may be experiencing); (d) from parallel responses along with the other person to participatory empathy, with role taking proposed as the highest cognitive mediator of participatory empathy (Hughes, Tingle, & Sawin, 1981; Feshbach, 1975, 1982; Hoffman, 1975, 1982; Staub, 1979).

It is assumed that both recognition of a character's affect and an emotional response concordant with her or his situation are necessary for empathy (Feshbach, 1978; Hoffman, 1978). The first level of the Empathy Continuum is composed of two initial categories that make necessary distinctions between a person being either unaware or aware of the character's affective experience. The lowest EC category, EC 0, indicates that a character's affect has not been recognized (e.g., responses such as "I don't know" or such clearly erroneous identifications as reporting a sad person as "happy"). The second category, EC 1, indicates that a character's affect has been recognized, but there is no similar affect reported in oneself (responses such as "She feels sad"; "I feel OK"). EC 1 represents a cognitive advance over EC 0, given the recognition of affect evidenced, but neither EC 0 nor EC 1 indicates empathy because the critical criterion of similar affect between self and character is not met. Scores of EC 2 – EC 19 all reflect empathy, given that similar affect has occurred. These scores occur in groupings of three degrees of affective match between self and character at each of six subsequent levels of cognitive mediation. The numerical values for the three degrees of affective match change as a function of their cognitive mediation. Thus, each value in the EC represents an interaction of affective and cognitive factors, such that the experience of similar affect at EC Level II, for example, is considered to be different from the experience of similar affect at EC Level III.

The Empathy Continuum attempts to delineate affective responses that are mediated at progressively more complex levels of cognitive involvement, as based upon models of empathy development (Hoffman, 1975) and age-related findings for children's interpersonal reasoning (Hughes et al, 1981; Shantz, 1983). The last six EC levels progress from no attributions or irrelevant reasons provided by the person for her or his experienced emotion (EC Level II), to attributions based upon direct responses, to story events that do not implicate any specific character in the story (e.g., "I felt scared because the house was creepy" – EC Level III); to EC Level IV attributions made with reference to a specific character's external situation (e.g.,"I felt scared watching *him* go up to the house"); to EC Level V attributions indicating transposition of oneself into the situation and/or association to one's own experience (e.g., "I'd sure feel scared in old haunted houses"; "Being in places like that scares me."); to EC Level VI attributions indicating a response to the character's internal experience, motivations or general lot in life (e.g., "I felt scared for that little kid trying to take on that spook"; "I felt sad for her having to face so much with her handicap"); and EC Level VII attributions indicating semantically explicit role-taking to the character (e.g., "If I were she . . ."; "If I were in her place, I'd feel mad at him treating me like that"; "I'd try my best, too, but I'd feel sad if I were handicapped like her").

Three progressively ordered categories of concordant affect in self and character are nested within each of the six empathy-mediation levels: (a) general match reporting similar, generally positive or negative emotions for self and character; (b) specific match reporting the same emotion but different intensities for self and character; (c) the same emotion and intensity for self and character. For example, at EC Level II, which indicates no evident cognitive mediation, the three scores of EC 2, EC 3, and EC 4 each represent increasing degrees of matched affect with a character. EC 2 denotes similar, but not the same, emotion as the character, in terms of general positive or negative valence, for example, "afraid" and "sad." EC3 denotes the same emotion but at different intensities; and EC 4 denotes the same emotion with same intensity. At EC Level III, the scores of EC 5, EC 6, and EC 7 respectively again represent these three degrees of affective responses but occur at a mediational level explained as in direct response to the stimulus events. Similar groupings of these three affective distinctions occur at the remaining EC levels, and reflect different kinds of cognitive-affective mediation, as shown in Table 10.1.

The levels of the Empathy Continuum exhaust all the responses given by children of different ages we studied, as well as those of a pilot sample of adults. Reliabilities for the Empathy Continuum scores (EC 0 to 20) were good for three different sets of raters scoring 25% of randomly selected children's responses across the three age ranges. Agreement ranged from 87% to 96%.

Developmental models of empathy agree that the six mediational levels included in the Empathy Continuum are not mutually exclusive, and that all may occur in the mature empathizer. However, there has been no systematic information in the extant research literature to determine their relative prevalence among children of different ages. Given a common set of stimuli, it has been suggested that quantitative differences exist in *how much* empathy is experienced by children of different ages and genders (Feshbach & Roe, 1968; Feshbach & Feshbach, 1969; Feshbach, 1982; Iannotti, 1978). In addition, we are concerned with the qualitative differences in *how* empathy is mediated and experienced. Finally, it is proposed that differences in empathy mediation, as reflected by EC levels, will relate to the amount of empathy experienced. Entailed in the generally progressive ordering of the EC levels is the expectation that attainment of

Table 10.2. *Description of televised stimuli*

Title	Description
Old House	Three children sneak into a fenced-in yard at night. A boy climbs up creaking stairs to peer through a window into the house. A looming shadow of a man appears above him, and the children run away.
Spilled Milk	A husband and a wife have an angry exchange while their daughter is watching TV in the background. The man slams the door as he leaves; the woman shouts at the girl to come to dinner; the girl accidentally knocks over a glass of milk and the mother slaps her.
Jeannie	A young woman is shown talking directly to the viewer about the difficult life she and her children had on an isolated farm with her abusive husband.
Skates	A girl and boy argue over taking turns on her new skates. The boy calls her names and threatens to tattle. She pushes him down and he runs crying to the girl's mother. The father is called in to pursue the issue. The boy lies, and the father believes his story. The girl defiantly maintains her story, is punished, and her skates are given away to the boy. The girl is shown crying.
Canes	A girl introduces herself to viewers and talks pleasantly about her life and fun, despite her physical disability. She is then shown practicing walking up and down stairs with canes while joking with the adult physiotherapist.
Circus	A father and daughter go to see the circus train on stopover one night. The elephant is let out to perform some tricks. The girl jumps and laughs excitedly, and is even lifted up on the elephant's trunk.

higher EC levels presumes access to lower levels of mediation as well. Thus, it is expected that children with higher mean EC levels will report both a greater amount of total empathy, measured traditionally as a general or specific concordance of emotion between self and character and access to a greater range of empathic experience at different levels of cognitive mediation.

Method for administering the Empathy Continuum

Granting that our interest in a person's subjective experience of empathy is necessarily constrained by what they can tell us about this experience, the following discussion is based upon the verbal reports of 74 children in response to the stimulus vignettes presented in Table 10.2. These vignettes display children and adults in dramatic interactions consensually agreed by a panel of adults (and also by the children's data) as portraying primary emotions such as happiness, anger, sadness, fear, and surprise.

Children in three age groups from preschool to early adolescence participated.

Group 1 comprised 34 5-year-olds (16 boys; 18 girls; mean age = 5 years, 2 months); Group 2 comprised 20 8- to 9-year-olds (11 boys; 11 girls; mean age = 8 years, 10 months); and Group 3 comprised 20 12- to 13-year-olds (10 boys; 10 girls; mean age = 13 years, 1 month). All were from middle-class families who were recruited by means of local media announcements for a study of emotional development. Parents were invited to preview the films, but did not discuss films with their children.

After children and parents had been familiarized with the setting and interviewer, children were escorted to a comfortably furnished room at the university equipped with a TV. The introductory preamble was as follows:

We're interested in children's and young people's reactions to people and events. What you're going to see on the TV in front of you are different brief scenes. There will be a blank screen for a few seconds [10 sec.] between each scene and then a beep will remind you to pay attention to the next one. I won't be watching, and will be busy finishing some work I have to do over there (behind and facing back to the child), but I'm here just in case you need anything. So, just sit back, relax, and watch the TV.

Two main lines of inquiry were pursued to assess children's attention to and understanding of others' emotional experience. First, children's attention to and inferences about emotional events were provided by their free descriptions of the videotapes, from which their use of affective labels, inferences regarding motivations, and explanations for others' affect was coded. In addition, the children's own emotional experience in response to these stimuli was of particular interest.

After viewing the videotapes, the interviewer asked the child to relate in his or her own words what had happened in each of the six vignettes described in Table 10.2. Children were then asked to identify whether the character felt neutral ("Ok"; "nothing much") or whether a character felt happy, sad, surprised, angry, afraid and/or disgusted. They also indicated the intensity of this emotion as either "a little" (1) or "a lot" (2). Children who attributed more than one emotion to a character were asked to identify which was primary (i.e., most prevalent and intense). Line drawings of facial expressions with labels of the main emotions mentioned above, as well as small and large dots to represent intensities, were available for the younger children. Children also were asked, "Did you feel anything watching that, or just neutral ('OK'; 'nothing much')? What made you feel that way in what you just saw on TV?" Children's answers were tape recorded and then transcribed.

The EC permits scoring of empathy according to the traditional criterion of affective matching between self and character and also according to the level of cognitive mediation involved. Although the EC was designed as an integrative measure of both affect and cognition working together, these two components can be considered separately for investigative purposes. Let us first examine how children distinguish between their own emotions and the emotions of others they witness in emotionally evocative events. Then we can proceed to the affective matching scores from the EC in order to examine similarities in emotions re-ported for oneself and for the character in the emotional events witnessed. Such affective matches, regardless of their cognitive mediation, both accord with how children's empathy has been operationalized in the past and provide the neces-sary affective component of the Empathy Continuum. In addition, they provide evidence of how the affective component of empathy is influenced by different emotional contexts as a function of children's age and gender. Subsequently, findings pertaining specifically to EC scores are considered.

The specific questions to be examined include:

1. How well do different aged children recognize the emotions of others presented in this context?
2. Are they emotionally affected and, if so, are their emotions similar to or different from the emotions attributed to the characters observed?
3. Do different emotions differently affect their emotional responsiveness and affective empathy?
4. How empathically responsive are different aged children to different emotions – that is, to what extent do they exhibit affective matching?
5. What differences are there in how empathy is mediated and experienced at different ages?

We shall begin by considering topics concerning the first two items jointly, and then proceed to each of the remaining items.

How well are others' emotions recognized and do they evoke similar or different emotions in children of different ages?

The first conclusions to be drawn from children's emotional attributions to the video characters and to themselves is that most children, even the young-est: (1) recognized the characters' emotions; (2) reported feeling an emotion in response to the stimulus vignettes (at least 75% of all responses per group); and (3) clearly differentiated between emotions attributed to characters and to the self. For instance, even though only a minority of children's responses reported that they felt "nothing much" or neutral across the stimulus vignettes, this per-centage was much higher for self-attributions than the 3% neutral attributions reported for characters. It appears, then, that children of all ages sampled both appropriately recognized that emotions were being experienced by others in these vignettes and could distinguish the emotional context as pertaining to the char-acter rather than to themselves. Furthermore, for each age group there were significant differences in attributions to self versus character across the seven emotions investigated: happy, sad, angry, afraid, surprised, disgusted, or neu-tral.

Although there were differences in the relative frequency with which particu-

Table 10.3. *Percentages for different emotions attributed to self and characters by children of different ages*

	Emotions						
	Happy	Sad	Angry	Afraid	Surprised	Disgusted	Neutral
Group 1							
Character responses (306)	22	28	33	13	1	1	4
Self responses (204)	52	10	7	11	4	2	13
Group 2							
Character responses (180)	25	29	23	21	1	0	1
Self responses (120)	21	18	8	17	5	7	25
Group 3							
Character responses (180)	25	29	18	23	2	0	3
Self responses (120)	21	26	13	10	7	2	21

Note: Percentages are calculated as cell frequency divided by total row responses. Children were asked to identify emotions for 9 characters across a total of 6 vignettes and to identify their own most prevalent emotion for each vignette.

lar emotions were attributed to characters, it was rare for characters' emotions to be inappropriately identified by children when appropriateness was defined either in terms of the prevalent emotions identified by older children or the similar consensus of a panel of adults on the emotions possible within each vignette. For example, both sadness and anger were appropriate to describe a girl's emotions in a vignette showing her father wrongly punishing her by giving away her prized skates. Only 2% of responses across vignettes were considered to be misattributions, and, interestingly, all were made by 5-year-olds and occurred in response to the only vignette (i.e., "Jeannie") in which there was only a character's personal narration of events and no contextual enactment was presented. This finding adds some support to the suggestion that young children may need to witness the context of an emotion-provoking event rather than just to be exposed to a character, particularly if the character is unfamiliar (Wilson & Cantor, 1985).

What did differ as a function of age were the particular emotional attributions identified for characters and for oneself in response to the same vignettes. In addition, not only did the extent of concordance of emotional responses for self and characters increase with children's age, as a number of researchers have found (Feshbach & Roe, 1968; Iannotti, 1978; Knudson & Kagan, 1982), but this was also found to vary as a function of the specific emotion attributed.

First, let us consider the emotions attributed to the self and to the nine characters across the vignettes. Table 10.3 shows the percent attribution of different emotional responses for each age group. Differences within each age group were examined using response contingency tables, and age differences in percentage attributions for each emotion were assessed. Examination of the frequencies across the six vignettes for seven emotional categories attributed to oneself and to characters yielded significant findings. There were no gender-related differences, pooled across age, in proportional attributions of different emotions to characters. Thus, boys and girls perceived characters' emotions similarly. Interestingly, however, gender-related differences occurred for emotions attributed to the self. These age- and gender-related differences will be discussed in light of more specific investigation of the four most prevalent emotion categories: happy, sad, angry, afraid.

Emotions attributed to the self

Starting with emotional attributions to the self, there were notable differences in emotions reported for oneself as a function of age, as shown in Table 10.3. For example, significant age differences, pooled across gender, occurred in reports of oneself as feeling happy. Proportions for happiness in response to stimulus vignettes were significantly higher for 5-year-olds than for either 8- or 13-year olds. In contrast, reports of sadness were significantly higher for both 8- and 13-year-olds than for 5-year-olds. These findings accord with reports in the literature that happy attributions are particularly prevalent as a general response tendency of young children (Carlson, Felleman, & Masters, 1983; Mood, Johnson, & Shantz, 1978). Furthermore, given the prevalent dysphoric content across these vignettes, the greater frequency with which older children reported themselves to feel dysphoric emotions is consistent with their greater responsiveness to the material presented.

That 5-year-olds were more likely to report being happy and less likely to report being dysphoric is not due to their inability to attribute dysphoric emotions. They were able to do so appropriately for the characters, as shown in Table 10.3. Thus, it appears that 5-year-olds recognized dysphoric emotions in others, but were less personally affected by this, particularly in terms of feeling sad, than were older children. This interpretation is confirmed by comparisons of emotions attributed to the self versus to characters.

As for the other emotions, the age-related differences noted for proportions of self-reported anger are not significant. Summing responses across all children, anger was the least likely emotion of the four main emotions listed in Table 10.3 to be either evoked or reported by children. Perhaps this reflects the greater personal risk associated with both the report of anger (which is unlikely to elicit nurturant responses from others) and the experience of anger, particularly in response to this vicarious rather than direct involvement with events. The goals and consequent ''fight-or-flight'' adaptive responses that are typical for anger in response to actual events would seem less appropriate, and likely to be frustrated, when there is no direct route for action (Campos, Barrett, Lamb, Goldsmith, & Stenberg, 1983).

Gender differences in emotional self-attributions were also found, and may be explained in terms of sex-role socialization. Pooled across age and focusing upon the three main negative emotions of anger, sadness, and fear, boys reported more anger than did girls: 66% of all self-reported anger occurred for boys, in contrast to 44% for girls. Differences between boys' and girls' percentages of anger given their total responses were marginally significant (27% versus 14%). Such findings are consistent with the generally greater tolerance for the expression of anger in boys than girls (Maccoby & Jacklin, 1974). Likewise, socialization differences in maintaining a "stiff upper lip" might lead boys to report significantly less sadness and fear than did girls.

Both expectations were confirmed. Girls reported both more sadness and more fear than boys: 69% of all self-reported sadness occurred for girls, in contrast to 31% for boys, with the same percentages noted for fear. Relative sadness as a percentage of each group's total self-reported emotions also indicated that girls reported significantly more sadness than did boys (22% versus 10%), and results for fear were marginally significant (16% versus 8%). No differences were expected, or occurred, for happiness. In general, girls reported more emotions than did boys, who reported significantly more "neutral" responses: 70% of all neutral responses were made by boys, and the percentage neutral responses of total emotional responses was significantly higher for boys (27%) than girls (11%). These findings accord with socialization expectations and differences in gender-related "feeling rules" and "display rules," which in our culture generally may permit or encourage more emotional awareness and/or demonstrativeness in females than in males (Saarni, 1985).

Emotions attributed to characters contrasted with self-attributions

The emotions attributed to characters were similar across the different age groups. Thus, across these ages, similar emotional meanings are drawn from the characters and events depicted. This conclusion is supported by recent evidence of a general consensus in simple emotional attributions across adults and children of different ages (Barden, Zelco, Duncan, & Masters, 1980; Strayer, 1986). However, each age group attributed different emotions to the characters as opposed to the self. That is, even young children recognize that affective situations can evoke different emotions for different persons (Gnepp, Klayman, & Trabasso, 1982) – in this case, for the person (character) experiencing the affect versus the person (child) witnessing their situation.

Our particular interest is in differences in each of the four main emotions (happiness, sadness, anger, fear) relative to the target of attribution: self or other person. Even when they similarly perceive others' emotions, are children of different ages affected differently by, and do they report differences in, the emotions they experience in response to those perceived in others?

As shown in Table 10.3, children differentiated and were not necessarily drawn into, or similarly affected by, the characters' emotions, even though the children recognized these emotions. This finding confirms a basic theoretical distinction between emotional recognition and empathy (Feshbach, 1975). Knowing how other persons feel does not ensure affective empathy with them. I maintain (Strayer, 1987c) that both knowing (cognitively inferred or occurring at a more basic, noninferential level) how others feel and sharing their emotional experience are necessary for empathy (a translation of the original German term, *Einfühlung*), defined as "feeling into" the emotion of another.

As might be expected from the data reported above for self-attributions, only 5-year-olds attributed happiness to themselves more often than to the characters. Thus, they recognized that a character was not happy, but nevertheless maintained that they were. This disparity between self and other is also reflected in their overall frequency of attributions across the dysphoric emotions. Five-year-olds made attributions of sadness and anger less often to themselves than to the characters. However, similar frequencies occurred for fear attributed to self and to the characters, suggesting either that the same stimulus events leading to the characters' fear were fearful to 5-year-olds as well, or that empathy, in which the characters' fear is shared to some extent, was involved. In contrast to this youngest group, both 8- and 13-year-olds attributed sadness to self and to characters nearly equally often. Only 13-year-olds attributed anger to self and the characters nearly equally often, whereas both 5- and 8-year-olds reported the self as less angry than characters.

Speculatively, it can be suggested that the youngest children, whose self–other differentiation and emotional coping experiences may be less well developed and less flexible than those of older children, must guard or distance themselves from the distress of contagion by others' dysphoric emotions. In contrast, older children, with greater emotional experience and cognitive control, may participate in others' emotions with less risk. Furthermore, in the face of likely socialization pressures against children reporting angry feelings to their elders, by age 13 these children may feel more assured regarding when and how it is appropriate to express anger, particularly "righteous" anger on behalf of others (e.g., a girl who was unfairly punished). In fact, it seems precisely this type of anger that Hoffman (1987) discusses as one affective motivator for moral judgment and action.

Fear, which was attributed with similar frequency to self and characters by both 5- and 8-year-olds, was the only main emotion that 13-year-olds reported themselves to experience significantly less frequently than characters reportedly did. Various interpretations for this finding can be given. First, the oldest children, although recognizing others' fear, may have recognized clearly that there was nothing for them, personally, to fear – that is, they clearly identified themselves as observers rather than participants. Such differentiation of self and other is neither necessary for rudimentary forms of empathy to occur (e.g., emotional contagion, Hoffman, 1975), nor, I would argue, for initiating the empathic process (Strayer, 1987c). However, I believe that self–other differentiation is necessary at some phase in the empathic process in order for *the other person's* feelings and attendant motivations, limitations, and perspective to be more specifically identified and addressed.

This shift from overidentification with or "engulfment"[1] by others' emotion to engagement in and sharing of others' emotion, while self–other awareness is maintained, strikes me as one of the major ways in which empathy may change with age. Thus, young children may be more likely to experience the televised fear stimuli *directly,* rather than *vicariously* (Wilson & Cantor, 1985), as may have occurred in response to our vignette showing a large shadow looming over a frightened child. At this point, empathy measured by affective matching alone could not distinguish between fear that both the child and the character are reported to feel in response to the shadow versus fear that the child feels for, or along with, the character who is the shadow's target. Examining children's cognitive mediation of their fear response enables us to distinguish these alternatives, as we shall see in a later section.

A second possibility is that older children have acquired the "feeling rule" (Saarni, 1985) that it is important and adaptive to master fear in our society; therefore, as noted in their empathic reports, they responded to characters' fear with other emotions. A third and final possibility is that although older children experience fear they encounter more socialization pressure to deny or conceal it from others. The first two alternatives are more plausible, given that older children did report themselves as feeling angry, despite likely socialization pressures against this. Moreover, when they did report fear it was usually fear in terms of the other person, rather than personal fear in direct response to the situational events witnessed. Having discussed the distinctions evident in children's reports of their own and others' emotions, in the remainder of this chapter our focus turns to the concordance of one's own and others' emotions, discussed in terms of empathy.

Empathy and emotional responses to others' emotions

How likely are children of different ages and genders to feel in consort with another person whom they witness and identify as experiencing happiness, anger, fear, or sadness? This has often been regarded in the developmental literature as a question of empathy. It has generally been assumed that the greater the degree of emotional match reported for self and the character, the greater the empathy with the character. The necessity for such an emotion-based measure of empathy became apparent to developmental researchers (Feshbach, 1975; Hoffman, 1975) who recognized that the empathy construct had become inappropriately merged with and undifferentiated from cognitive constructs, such as role taking. The essential component of affective participation had been forgotten or neglected.

Does empathy develop with age?

There is not yet a definitive answer, in part due to ambiguity surrounding what we mean and measure by "empathy." For example, we know from some, but not all, studies that reported empathy to characters, measured as degree of match between the child's and the character's emotion, seems to increase during the preschool to early elementary school ages appropriate for such measures (Feshbach, 1982; Feshbach & Roe, 1968; Feshbach & Feshbach, 1969; Iannotti, 1978). With the present procedures, we can expand the age span investigated to older children as well. In contrast, studies employing a different conceptualization of empathy as a dispositional trait, and a methodology based upon a global, empathy questionnaire score (Bryant, 1982), have not found significant differences between first grade and fourth grade children. Only by seventh grade were children found to score higher than both younger groups. Given that the items in this questionnaire assess self-reports of general emotionality, expressivity, and caring about others, as well as empathy, differences in results using these two methods and conceptualizations of empathy might be expected.

Some issues concerning the generalizability and meaning of such age differences in trait measures are important to consider. For example, why should empathy, defined as a dispositional trait, increase with age? Perhaps because dispositions, like personality traits, are considered to become first integrated only at adolescence, with the emergent construction of self-concepts into an identity formation (Erikson, 1950). If so, however, the construct validity of a dispositional measure applied at preadolescent ages seems tenuous. In any case, dispositional measures would seem more appropriate for examining individual differences within, rather than between, age groups.

Additional issues pertain to the responsive empathy measures, as assessed by tasks such as those of Feshbach and Iannotti. For example, are the reported increases in children's scores on these tasks due mostly to the cognitive skill in identifying the specific emotion determined for a character? Or is it the increasing affective responsiveness to others' emotions that is most responsible for the noted age changes? The latter, which is closest to what we generally mean by empathy, could equitably be assessed only among those children of different ages who accurately identified the character's emotion, discarding the scores of those children who did not.

A related issue in designing measures using this paradigm is that an identification of a character's emotion may be plausible, even if it is not consensually the one most often judged to be the "correct" identification. This range of plausible options has not been used in scoring specific affect matches in previous studies, but is recognized and permissible in the present one. More importantly, because there are few measures assessing interpersonal affective responsiveness that are applicable across a wide enough age and stimulus range, we cannot be confident in concluding at present whether or not empathy increases with age.

Lastly, it seems important to consider whether empathy as a capacity increases with age and/or whether empathy as a process is experienced differently with age. This issue pertains to considerations of empathy both in terms of quantitative response frequencies and of qualitative terms described by particular cognitive-affective developments. There are not sufficient developmental data on the empathy construct to answer this question. Present data will provide a start in this direction. My viewpoint is that, whereas there may indeed be biological "givens" (e.g., affective responsivity thresholds, aspects of intelligence) that influence one's empathic "capacity" and disposition, more weight should be given to the life experiences that enlarge one's cognitive-affective perspective and contribute to the qualitative, experiential factors involved in empathy.

First, let us examine the affective matching criterion of empathy, given that this is the traditional criterion of empathy in most developmental research. It is also the condition that must be met for empathy to be scored and for different degrees of empathy to be differentiated at the same mediational level using the Empathy Continuum. Our first expectation is that matching of a child's and character's emotion will vary as a function of the emotion attributed to characters. It should be easiest to share emotion with someone who is happy, thus empathically experiencing happiness ourselves. However, empathy most often is considered in terms of sharing negative or dysphoric emotions, with the resulting negative emotion experienced hypothesized to act as a prosocial motivator on behalf of the other person (Feshbach, 1975; Hoffman, 1975; Staub, 1979).

In the discussion to follow, the results of our study will be presented. It is important to recall that our procedures are different from past methods in both the nature of the stimuli and the response interview used. Our results will be discussed both in light of measures that have been used in the past (i.e., affect matching), and in light of the new Empathy Continuum scores, which are based upon affective-matching and cognitive mediation. First, empathy as affective matching was scored as follows. A score of 0 indicates that an emotion was attributed to a character, but no concordant emotion was reported for oneself. Similar to earlier affective operationalizations of empathy, a score of 1 indicates a general concordance in either positive (e.g., character was happy; child was pleasantly surprised) or negative tone (e.g., character was afraid; child was sad). A score of 2 indicates a specific match in emotion, but differences in its intensity for self and character (e.g., character was very sad; child was a little sad). A score of 3 indicates a specific match in both emotion and intensity.

Preliminary findings are described for differences in empathy as a function of the emotion attributed to characters, children's age, and gender. Separate examination was made of scores indicating general concordance or better (scores equal to or greater than 1), and scores indicating specific matches (scores equal to or greater than 2). Unless noted, our findings for empathy assessed in these ways are similar. As we shall see, empathy is different for different emotions, and varies as a function of children's age and gender.

Is affective empathy different for different emotions?

How empathic are children in the contexts assessed across the four main emotions reported? Our preliminary findings[2] that 40% of total responses across these emotions were empathic suggest selective rather than ubiquitous empathic feeling. This finding accords with previous research (Feshbach & Roe, 1968; Feshbach, 1982), and contributes to our confidence that children could identify characters' emotions without responding to social desirability or other demands to report feeling similarly themselves when they felt neutral. Additional evidence comes from a related study, using similar procedures and stimuli, which found that children's responses on this task were not significantly related to their scores on a social desirability questionnaire (Chovil, 1985).

The first major finding is that empathy differs as a function of the four main emotions examined. Of the total empathic responses given across age groups, and taking into account the different base rates for report of each emotion, empathy was most prevalent for happiness (55%), fear (50%), and sadness (44%), and least prevalent for anger (17%). This pattern holds for both general concordance and specific matching procedures. The relative distribution of responses shows some accord with naturalistic studies of preschoolers' behaviors in response to others' emotions in a natural context (Denham, 1986; Strayer, 1980). As such studies suggest, it may be more immediately rewarding to share in others' happy experiences, so that empathy to this emotion may be expected at higher levels than to dysphoric emotions. This was especially so for the youngest age group. Of the four main emotions, by far the largest percentage of empathic responses was with others' happiness: 60% in contrast to 12%–39% for the dysphoric emotions (based on different base rates of report for each emotion).

Nevertheless, "feeling into" others' sadness and dysphoria is what is most commonly referenced in ordinary usage of the term empathy. This was attested to informally by parents and adult students who were asked what emotion they typically felt when they were feeling empathy: "Sad" was a model answer. Our findings for children's empathy with others' dysphoria accord increasingly with this view as children get older. With age, children were increasingly responsive to others' sadness. In fact, 8- and 13-year-olds reported equal or more empathy with sadness than happiness. Of the remaining two dysphoric emotions, fear was empathized with much more than was anger.

Shared feelings of anger, especially, appear to be problematic. It may seem paradoxical and counterproductive to feel empathic anger. Yet we do experience empathic anger, for example, in responding to a friend who is being unjustly treated. Such vicarious experience of others' emotions, particularly anger, may even impel us to moral or prosocial action on their behalf. We can, motivated by the shared anger or frustration felt, and guided by the recognition that we are not under the same conditions as they, do something on their behalf. Similarly, sharing another's fear while recognizing that we are, at most, participators in their experience but not ourselves at risk, may prompt us to ameliorate their fear, and at the same time reduce our own negative feelings. Martin Hoffman (1982, 1987) has discussed this process in describing how these empathically experienced emotions may motivate prosocial and moral acts.

All emotions, theoretically, can be empathized with. Nevertheless, anger seems a particularly difficult emotion to harbor empathically. From a philosophical perspective, anger has been considered a particularly hazardous emotion, even if empathically engendered, given the challenge it poses for self-control (Smith, 1789/1887). Anger in others is often a threatening intrusion, and children, especially, may avoid rather than empathize with anger. Managing our anger is an early maturity demand placed upon us. In order to empathize in a constructive fashion with another person's anger it is necessary to focus upon the needs of that person rather than of the self. The relatively lower empathic responsiveness to anger than to other emotions may reflect the difficulty of making this shift of focus, given the higher arousal or activation levels posited for anger, in contrast to other dysphroric emotions such as sadness, in circumplex models of emotion (Russell, 1980). Once anger is instigated, it may be harder for us, and particularly for children, to maintain the self–other distinction necessary for empathy, and it may put us at greater risk for self-overinvolvement.

Affective empathy as a function of both age and emotion

Empathic responses as a percentage of the frequency of attributions to characters of each of the four main emotions are shown in Table 10.4 for each

Table 10.4. *Percentage empathy to four emotions attributed to characters*

	Emotions			
	Happy	Sad	Angry	Afraid
Group 1				
Frequency of emotion	68	85	99	36
% No empathy	39	75	90	61
% General empathy	61	25	10	39
% Specific empathy	57	14	8	31
Group 2				
Frequency of emotion	45	53	33	41
% No empathy	60	40	81	41
% General empathy	40	60	19	59
% Specific empathy	30	33	10	41
Group 3				
Frequency of emotion	44	53	33	41
% No empathy	43	43	70	49
% General empathy	57	57	30	51
% Specific empathy	52	43	27	29

Note: Frequencies of general empathy (scores = 1, 2, and 3) and specific empathy (scores = 2 and 3) are divided by the frequency listed for each emotion to obtain percentages.

age group. There were significant increases in total empathy (summed across emotions) with age. Age differences in empathic versus nonempathic responses to the different emotions suggest that these changes are due mainly to increasing responsivity to dysphoric emotions rather than to happiness. Comparing findings shown in Table 10.4, age-related changes in empathy with characters' happiness decreased from 60% of responses for 5-year-olds to 40% and 57% for 8- and 13-year-olds. In contrast, empathy with others' sadness increased from 25% for 5-year-olds to 60% and 57% for 8- and 13-year-olds, respectively. Similarly, empathy with others' fear increased from 39% to 59% and 51% for these age groups.

As we have noted, children across age groups tended to respond with high frequencies of empathy to characters' happiness, with younger children responding most often. It is unlikely that our capacity to share in others' happiness diminishes with age. Rather, older children seem to have perceived the same stimulus events in more complex ways than did the younger children, thus making their appraisals of certain "happy" events more equivocal. For example, although there were no age differences in happy appraisals of a girl at a circus (a fairly common happy "social script" in our culture), with whom the majority of all children shared happiness, there were meaningful age-related differences in appraisals of a cheerful, physically disabled girl who joked around while working out with an adult. Whereas 65% to 73% of children in the three groups identified this girl as happy, only a minority of the two older groups (25%–45%), in contrast to 79% of the 5-year-olds, responded with concordant happy affect themselves.

Thus, it appears that, whereas 5-year-olds were responding to the girl's smiles and playful demeanor, the older children, who also saw the girl as happy, were responsive to the less immediate context of the girl's "lot in life." Hoffman (1987) discusses this reaction in terms of an appraisal of and sympathetic responsiveness to the other person's general life conditions (e.g., disability, poverty, oppression), an appraisal that goes beyond the current context and feelings shown by the character. This vignette was included for precisely these reasons; and our results here suggest some contrast between empathy (concordant emotions *with* a character) and sympathy (sad affect *for* a character). All age ranges empathize, but the older children seem to go beyond the girl's immediate display of cheerfulness to sympathize with her disability and difficulties. For example, only 3% of the youngest group reported themselves as sad in response to this vignette, in contrast to 15%–20% of older children who sympathized with the girl. Vignettes such as this one demonstrate that the stimulus context responded to by children of different ages may be different, even when the same objective information is displayed.

As we have seen, the relative frequency of empathic versus nonempathic responses to characters' dysphoria generally increased with age. What might contribute to this development? Several plausible directions for answers are suggested by theories concerning social–emotional development and empathy. First, children unavoidably experience an increasing range of emotions in their own lives with increasing age and social experience. Cognitively, they become better able to differentiate emotional cues and to understand emotions. Pertinent to both individual differences and increasing empathy with age is greater exposure to, rather than protection from, a variety of different emotional situations. Such increasing familiarity with a range of different emotions should lower the threshold for both recognition and responsiveness to those emotions in others. Responsiveness, in particular, would be reinforced by having witnessed and experienced a range of emotions that have been successfully managed. Thus, vicariously experiencing others' distress may be more likely for children once they have learned that such experiences can be alleviated. Such learning across a range of different emotions is likely to increase as a function of both cognitive development and social experience.

Similarly relevant to both individual differences and age increases, empathy may be enhanced if children's attention to events involving emotional cues and interpretations, and their autonomous efforts to participate in such events, has been supported and guided by parents, and with increasing age by an expanded realm of significant others including peers and educators. With age children's interpersonal understanding is increasingly focused upon the psychology of individuals and social–emotional events occuring within and between people. This represents a major development, evident in Piaget's views (1932; 1981), regarding the "socialization of intelligence" and the construction with age of multiple possibilities and perspectives concerning both internal and external events. It also reflects views regarding the importance to personal and social growth of the mirroring of one's own and others' experiences, attributions, and processes such as empathy (e.g., Cooley, 1902; Harter, 1986; Mead, 1934; Selman, 1980).

With age, a child's sense of self typically becomes better defined (Erikson, 1950; Loevinger & Wessler, 1970), thus functioning to permit, without self-confusion, the internalization of emotions perceived in others. It would also enable the necessary self–other differentiation posited for empathy as more appropriate to the other's situation than to one's own. Thus, with age, an increasing frequency and wider range of such experiences should also increase both the child's tolerance for empathic engagement with others and the extent of its occurrence.

Additional explanations for increasing empathy with age are based on the proposal that empathy is marked by a shift from involuntary to increasingly voluntary mediators. Thus, with age the individual has more control over and can to a greater extent modulate her or his experience of empathy. For example, motor mimicry and rudimentary associations based upon classical conditioning are under no, or only minimal, voluntary control. These are the only mediators of empathy theoretically proposed for the very young child (Hoffman, 1975, 1987). Even the next mediator developmentally available to somewhat older children – direct associations based upon immediate and concrete events – offers only slightly greater voluntary control. I would argue that this concept of voluntary control incorporates the idea of cognitive "distancing" (cf. Sigel, 1984), which permits an event to be apprehended at several levels at once (e.g., real and symbolic; actual and vicarious). Using Hoffman's model of empathy development, associations drawn from symbolic material (e.g., books), for instance, should involve greater distancing than the previous modes. With the availability of voluntary mediators, such as symbolic association and role taking, the child "acts" (is an agent) in the empathic process. This increasing capacity for voluntary mediation of the empathic experience with age may make it more likely for the empathizer to attend to and become engaged in the other person's experience and less likely for him or her to feel "overwhelmed" (personal distress) by the feelings engendered by the other person's experience.

In sum, factors in age-related increases in empathy are likely to include developments in recognition of different emotions, detection of different cues to

emotion, familiarity with an increasing range of interpersonal emotional interactions and provisions of emotional comfort or redress to self and others, development of perspectival and "psychological" thinking directed at the other person's experience, increasing self-development, autonomy, and use of voluntary
empathic mediators. Although there are consistent theoretical grounds for proposing each of these as developmental factors, research on their contribution to
empathy is still nascent and fairly unintegrated (see Barnett, 1987; Feshbach,
1978, 1987; Hoffman, 1978; Staub, 1979; Zahn-Waxler, Radke-Yarrow, & King,
1979).

Sex differences in empathy with different emotions

Consideration of socialization factors relevant to emotional responsiveness and empathy calls for a consideration of sex-role differences. Previous studies (Eisenberg & Lennon, 1983; Feshbach & Roe, 1968; Feshbach, 1982), have
indicated that girls generally report more empathy than boys. This difference has
been interpreted in terms of socialization practices that tend to encourage or
permit more self-reported emotions in girls than in boys (Eisenberg & Lennon,
1983). The same sex difference also emerged in our own findings. The explanation seems to rest more upon gender-related differences in emotional self-
attributions than upon differences in attention to others' emotions. For example,
although there were no sex differences in the report of some emotion versus
"neutral" emotion attributed to vignette characters, there were sex differences
in self-reported emotions. Boys reported significantly more neutral self-attributions
than did girls.

Sex-role socialization differences seem appropriate to explain girls' greater
overall self-attributions of emotions than boys'. Socialization differences would
also lead us to posit differences in experienced empathy with particular negative
emotions, given the expectations that we are more likely to empathize with emotions we find familiar and are encouraged to express. Expected socialized sex
differences were that boys would report more empathy with anger than girls,
whereas girls would report more empathy with sadness and fear. Our descriptive
data indicate support for these expectations. Empathic responses to characters'
anger was considerably higher for boys than girls (20% for boys versus 12% for
girls, out of each group's total attributions of anger to characters). In contrast,
girls' empathic responses to characters' fear were higher than boys' (61% versus
38%); this occurred similarly but less so for sadness (51% versus 35%).

How much emotional matching is required for empathy?

Empathy thus far has been examined in terms of affective matching.
This is consistent with most earlier developmental research, and is also important

for examining emotional response differences as a function of different emotional stimuli, as we have seen. But how much of a match is required for us truly to empathize with others' emotions and does this differ in degrees for different emotions? Although the degree of match required for a response to be truly empathic has been debated, most researchers agree on the appropriateness of at least a generally concordant response (Feshbach, 1975; Hoffman, 1975; Stotland, 1969). This seems appropriate because allowance must be made for differences between one's own "feeling into" and the character's direct experience of the affective material, and also because there may be more than one emotion experienced by the character in a given context.

In the present study, a comparison of the percentage of general versus specific matches may also inform us of the differential effect that our four main emotions have upon the observer. For example, from naturalistic studies it seems that happiness is the emotion most likely to receive a specific rather than a general match from children (Denham, 1986; Strayer, 1980). This is also apparent in present findings, as was shown in Table 10.4. Pooling responses across age groups, there were more specific matching than general concordant responses for happiness (95%) than for sadness, anger, or fear (63%–70%). These findings seem plausible in light of emotions considered in terms of the previously discussed goal- and action-oriented perspective (Campos et al., 1983). It has been argued that empathic arousal of dysphoric rather than euphoric emotions is more likely to direct our attention away from the other person and toward overcoming these negative emotions in ourselves. However, given that sadness, in particular, often elicits nurturant responses (Campos et al., 1983), when others' sadness arouses empathy, we should be more likely to keep the other person in mind, even if we do not report sharing the same specific emotion with her or him.

Interpretations consistent with these ideas are provided when we examine the kinds of cognitive mediation for empathic responses, based upon the Empathy Continuum. The rare occurrence among 5-year-olds of empathic responses expressly mediated by a focus upon the other person's internal feelings (see EC Level VI, Table 10.1) was in response to sadness, in contrast to the other emotions. Although such mediation was more prevalent among the two older groups, especially among 13-year-olds, the greatest proportion of all children's responses focusing "inside" the other person similarly was for sadness. When empathy with anger occurred, its modal cognitive mediation reflected a somewhat more distant position referring to the character's situation (see EC Level IV). Only among the oldest children was the modal response to anger based upon a focus upon the character's internal feelings. And for fear, as well, the modal responses (see EC Level III) of most children were more removed from a particular person and were based upon story events (without mention of a character), except for the oldest group, who referenced the character's situation as the reason for their own feelings. From these initial findings it seems that *how* empathy is experienced depends both upon the children's age and the particular emotion elicited.

Thus far, we have seen that empathy may be more or less forthcoming as a function of the particular emotion perceived in the other person and as a function of age- and gender-related variables. In the next section we continue to examine empathy from the subjective viewpoint of the child experiencing it. These data are assessed in terms of the Empathy Continuum.

How empathy is mediated and experienced at different ages: empirical findings using the Empathy Continuum

The aim of this section is to integrate the preceding with additional information concerning children's reasoning about their empathic experiences within the framework of the Empathy Continuum (EC). First, our results indicate that empathy increases with age using both traditional affect-matching and the EC scoring methods. Empathy scored as an affective match between self and character increased significantly for the three age groups, and was significantly greater for girls than for boys pooled across age. Using the EC scoring continuum, empathy was also found to increase significantly with age. However, although girls report more empathic responses than do boys, as reported above, when only empathic responses are considered (i.e., EC 2 and above) there are no sex differences for the Empathy Continuum responses. Thus, the EC results permit us to conclude that sex differences obtained using affective matching procedures alone – in this and previous studies – are likely due to girls' versus boys' greater reporting of emotions in the self (Eisenberg & Lennon, 1983). Once emotions have been reported for oneself, EC findings indicate that boys' and girls' experience of empathy is similar.

A summary of the predominant empathic responses (modal response out of total responses for each subject) is shown in Figure 10.1. Most 5-year-olds' (G1-56%) predominant responses were at EC I, at which the character's affect is recognized but no concordant affect is experienced oneself. In contrast, only 35% of 8-year-olds' (G2) and 20% of 13-year-olds' (G3) predominant responses were at this level. Examination of the predominant responses of the two older groups indicates further progression along the Empathy Continuum. The greatest number of 8-year-olds' (45%) predominant responses were at EC Level IV, in which the child's own emotions are attributed to the character's external events. The greatest number of 13-year-olds' predominant responses were divided between EC Level IV (40%) and EC Level VI (40%), in which responses are based more upon the character's internal state (e.g., feelings or attributed internal reactions) than upon external events.

These findings indicate that with age there is a move toward empathic expe-

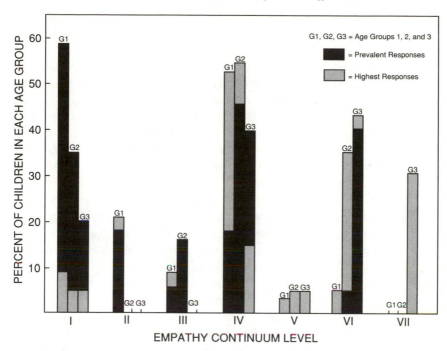

Figure 10.1. Prevalent and highest level Empathy Continuum response for three age groups.

rience becoming more focused upon characters than upon events, and more focused upon internal psychological perspectives relative to other persons than upon external events involving them. This direction of movement supports the expected increase with age to a quality of empathy that participates in the character's experience, rather than remaining a reaction parallel to it because of attention to events external to the character, as was the case for 5-year-olds. Nevertheless, even when 5-year-olds offer attributions for their emotions, these are more often based upon an explicitly stated focus on the other person's situation rather than on just the situation itself: The predominant responses of only 6% of 5-year-olds were attributed to story events without mention of characters (EC Level III), whereas three times as many children (18%) mentioned characters (EC Level IV). Thus, there is reason to conclude that these young children's responses reveal the self–other differentiation necessary to distinguish empathy from direct, personally centered emotional reactions. Contrary to suggestions that young children respond directly to the events themselves (as Wilson & Cantor, 1985, concluded for young children's fear responses to video stimuli), the present findings indicate that empathy, as a response more appropriate to another's situation than to one's own is found in some youngsters most of the time (i.e., predominant responses) or in most youngsters some of the time (i.e., highest responses).[3]

In contrast to predominant responses, which indicate the modal response across different stimuli, the highest response level attained by each child (the gray areas in Figure 10.1) was also examined in order to determine the "ceiling" for empathic experience as assessed by the Empathy Continuum. The highest level attained by most (53%) 5-year-olds was EC Level IV, indicating that a focus upon "characters-in-situations" is possible, although not predominant, in the responses of many young children. However, for only 9% of these young children did their highest responses occur at levels above EC IV. In contrast, 95% of both older groups' highest responses were at EC Level IV or higher. The differences between these two groups again helps to confirm the increase with age for empathy focused upon internal attributes rather than upon the external context of characters. Whereas most of 8-year-olds' (55%) highest responses were at EC Level IV, the greatest number of 13-year-olds' (45%) highest responses were at EC Level VI, with a notable 30% of their responses at the highest EC Level VII, indicating explicit role taking. These findings suggest that empathy is experienced in a qualitatively different fashion with age, and they accord with developmental views that children's social-cognitive understanding becomes increasingly focused with age upon internal dimensions of the person (Harris & Olthof, 1982; Selman, 1980).

Given age-related increases in empathy using the simpler affect-matching system and the Empathy Continuum, are there any advantages to the EC system? There appear to be at least five advantages that can be summarized as follows. First, the issue of whether or not empathy is experienced, particularly how it is experienced by children of different ages and in response to different stimuli, requires a verbal report measure. Despite the shortcomings of such procedures (Strayer, 1987d), they nevertheless permit access to "subjective" or personal experience. The EC is a more comprehensive system than verbal report measures in current use, and is designed to examine *how*, as well as how much, empathy is experienced. Thus, qualitative, as well as quantitative, aspects of empathic experience are addressed. This may permit us, for example, to distinguish direct emotional arousal to stimulus events (that perhaps only coincidentally matches the character's emotion) from an emotional reaction that acknowledges the character to differing degrees. The cognitive mediation accompanying affective matching (e.g., "I share the girl's anger at her father") versus complementary affective arousal (e.g., "I feel sad for the girl with the mean father") may also help to distinguish empathy from sympathy for a person.

Second, use of the EC provides insight into both the cognitive mediational and affective arousal components of empathy. These components can be examined separately, although they are integrated into one system. The interaction among affective and cognitive factors is crucial to empathy and to considerations regarding the development of emotional understanding. Third, there is support for the expectation that higher mean scores on the EC will relate to higher frequencies of empathic responsiveness. That is, higher EC scores, reflecting greater affective concordance (the affective component of EC) together with increasing cognitive involvement (the cognitive component of EC) indicate a higher total frequency of empathy. Fourth, the EC is applicable to a range of dramatically or naturalistically presented affective stimuli. By learning what children of different ages are responsive to in affective events witnessed by them, we may be better able to assess the relationships among their emotional understanding, affective responsivity, and both the extent and qualitative features of their empathy. Extending the EC interview procedure to a range of different affective events, the meanings of which are derived from the children's own reports, seems most likely to relate to their behavior in real life situations. Fifth, the EC permits a fine-grained developmental analysis applicable across a wide range of stimuli and ages. The most prevalent EC categories can be assessed for each age group in order to answer questions regarding *what* it is that may change in empathy with age: affective and/or cognitive involvement in others' affective experience. The EC may similarly be helpful in assessing changes in empathy as a function of different stimulus content and modes of presentation: for example, seeing fearful versus sad events or seeing only a distressed person narrating the critical events versus seeing these events taking place. These, and hopefully other, questions may encourage future applications of the Empathy Continuum across a wider sample of both stimuli and children, as well as adults.

Concluding comments

In conclusion, I would answer the five questions we started out with in the following way:

1. Children as young as 5 years of age generally recognize very well the characters' emotions in dramatic vignettes. What happens with age seems more a refinement of emotional complexity and subtlety rather than an increase in basic accuracy (for example, multiple emotions and affective role taking are reported more by older than younger children).

2. For all children, emotional attributions to oneself and to characters are different. Thus, even though they do empathize with characters' feelings, children also differentiate between themselves and characters, rather than egocentrically or overinclusively assuming similar reactions.

3. Children are more responsive to some kinds of emotions than others

(e.g., positive more than negative) and show different kinds of emotional responses and degrees of emotional matches to different kinds of
emotions, depending upon their age and sex.

4. There are quantitiative increases in empathy with age, based upon affective matches.

5. There are also qualitative differences in how empathy is experienced
with age, as assessed using the Empathy Continuum, reflecting a progression from empathic mediation focused more upon external events
to mediation based more upon events internal to a specific character.

I end this chapter with confidence that there is much we can learn about developments in responsiveness to others' emotions by letting children tell us this
and by organizing in theoretically relevant ways what they tell us in reaction to,
and in empathy with, others' emotions. The Empathy Continuum is an initial
attempt to operationalize theoretical views concerning how empathy is developmentally organized and how its experience may change with age. It has offered
a new and more comprehensive means of investigating empathic responses across
a wider age and stimulus range than has previously been the case. This has been
made evident in terms of both the continuity of issues in past and present work,
such as the extent of emotional matching, and the new issues addressed, such as
how to assess the experience of empathy at different ages.

Present findings, resulting from applying the Empathy Continuum to richer
stimuli than have been used in most past research, have increased our understanding of children's emotional recognition, their attributions of affect in others
and in themselves in response to different emotional evocations, and the cognitive-affective mediators of empathy at different ages. These are the present
achievements. In addition to extending these data across ages and stimuli, there
are promissory notes to be expected from new measures. One particular such
note is that, because different mediators may have different effects on prosocial
motivation, the Empathy Continuum may prove expecially useful in future investigations of the links between empathy and prosocial behavior, and, in general, in investigating relations among feelings, cognition, and action.

Notes

1. Perceptual development researchers have noted that very young children are often best described
   as "captured by" rather than as in more active control of the stimulus (Gibson, 1969).
2. All findings presented are based on an initial review of the data in an ongoing project.
3. Simple mention of a character is sufficient to score a response at EC Level IV. Neither identification with, nor adoption of, characters' viewpoints is necessarily implied at this level, in contrast
   to successive EC levels. It is included as a basic differentiation from EC III, in which events are
   referenced *without* mention of a character. That young children do and do not make this basic
   differentiation is noted in Figure 10.1, showing that reference to events only, without mention of

characters, is the predominant or highest level response for some 5- and 8-year-olds, but for no 13-year-olds.

References

Barden R. C., Zelco, F. A., Duncan, S. W., & Masters, J. C. (1980). Children's consensual knowledge about the experiential determinants of emotion. *Journal of Personality and Social Psychology, 39,* 968–976.

Barnett, M. A. (1987). Empathy and related responses in children. In N. Eisenberg & J. Strayer (Eds.), *Empathy and its development.* New York: Cambridge University Press.

Bryant, B. K. (1982). An index of empathy for children and adolescents. *Child Development, 53,* 413–425.

Campos, J., Barrett, K. C., Lamb, M. E., Goldsmith, H. H., & Stenberg, C. (1983). Socioemotional development. In P. H. Mussen (Ed.), *Handbook of child development* (Vol.2, pp. 783–915). New York: Wiley.

Carlson, C. R., Felleman, E. S., & Masters, J. C. (1983). Influence of children's emotional states on the recognition of emotion in peers and social motives to change another's emotional state. *Motivation and Emotion, 7,* 61–79.

Chovil, N. (1985). *An investigation of sex differences in empathy and imaginal involvement.* M.A. thesis, Simon Fraser University, Burnaby, B.C., Canada.

Cooley, C. H. (1902). *Human nature and social order.* New York: Scribners.

Denham, S. (1986). Social cognition, social behavior, and emotion in very young preschoolers: contextual validation. *Child Development, 57,* 197–201.

Eisenberg, N., & Lennon, R. (1983). Sex differences in empathy and related capacities. *Psychological Bulletin, 94,* 100–131.

Eisenberg, N., & Strayer, J. (Eds.) (1987). *Empathy and its development.* New York: Cambridge University Press.

Erikson, E. H. (1950). *Childhood and society.* New York: Norton.

Feshbach, N. D. (1975). Empathy in children: some theoretical and empirical considerations. *Counseling Psychologist, 5,* 25–30.

Feshbach, N. D. (1978). Studies on empathic behavior in children. In B. A. Maher (Ed.), *Progress in experimental personality research* (Vol. 8). New York: Academic Press.

Feshbach, N. D. (1982). Sex differences in empathy and social behavior in children. In N. Eisenberg (Ed.), *The development of prosocial behavior* (pp. 315–338). New York: Academic Press.

Feshbach, N. D. (1987). Parental empathy and child adjustment/maladjustment. In N. Eisenberg & J. Strayer (Eds.), *Empathy and its development.* New York: Cambridge University Press.

Feshbach, N. D., & Feshbach, S. (1969). The relationship between empathy and aggression in two age groups. *Developmental Psychology, 1,* 102–107.

Feshbach, N. D., & Roe, K. (1968). Empathy in six- and seven-year-olds. *Child Development, 39,* 133–145.

Flapan, D. (1968). *Children's understanding of social interactions.* New York: Teachers College Press.

Gibson, E. J. (1969). *Principles of perceptual learning and development.* New York: Appleton-Century-Crofts.

Gnepp, J., Klayman, J., & Trabasso, T. (1982). A hierarchy of information sources for inferring emotional reactions. *Journal of Experimental Child Psychology, 33,* 111–123.

Harris, P. L., & Olthof, T. (1982). The child's conception of emotion. In G. Butterworth & P. Light (Eds.), *The individual and the social in cognitive development.* Sussex: Harvester.

Harter, S. (1986). Cognitive-developmental processes in the integration of concepts about emotions and the self. *Social Cognition, 4,* 119–151.

Hoffman, M. L. (1975). Developmental synthesis of affect and cognition and its implications for altruistic motivation. *Developmental Psychology, 11,* 607–622.

Hoffman, M. L. (1978). Toward a theory of empathic arousal and development. In M. Lewis & L. A. Rosenblum (Eds.), *The development of affect.* New York: Plenum.

Hoffman, M. L. (1982). The measurement of empathy. In C. E. Izard (Ed.), *Measuring emotions in infants and children.* New York: Cambridge University Press.

Hoffman, M. L. (1987). The contribution of empathy to justice and moral judgment. In N. Eisenberg & J. Strayer (Eds.), *Empathy and its development.* New York: Cambridge University Press.

Hughes, R., Tingle, B. A., & Sawin, D. B. (1981). Development of empathic understanding in children. *Child Development, 52,* 122–128.

Iannotti, R. J. (1978). Effect of role-taking experiences on role-taking, empathy, altruism, and aggression. *Developmental Psychology, 14,* 119–124.

Izard, C. E. (1977). *Human emotions.* New York: Plenum.

Knudson, K. H. M., & Kagan, S. (1982). Differential development of empathy and prosocial behavior. *Journal of Genetic Psychology, 140,* 249–251.

Loevinger, J., & Wessler, R. (1970). *Measuring ego development* (Vol. 1). San Francisco: Jossey-Bass.

Lewis, M., & Michalson, L. (1983). *Children's emotions and moods: developmental theory and measurement.* New York: Plenum.

Maccoby, E. E., & Jacklin, C. N. (1974). *The psychology of sex differences.* Stanford, CA: Stanford University Press.

Mead, G. H. (1934). *Mind, self and society.* Chicago: University of Chicago Press.

Mood, D. W., Johnson, J. E., & Shantz, C. U. (1978). Social comprehension and affect matching in young children. *Merrill-Palmer Quarterly, 8,* 99–104.

Piaget, J. (1932). *The moral judgment of the child* (M. Gabain, Trans.). London: Kegan Paul.

Piaget, J. (1981). *Intelligence and affectivity: their relationship during child development.* (T. A. Brown & C. E. Kaegi, Trans.). Palo Alto, CA: Annual Reviews.

Russell, J. A. (1980). A circumplex model of affect. *Journal of Personality and Social Psychology, 34,* 1161–1178.

Saarni, C. (1985). Indirect processes in affect socialization. In M. Lewis & C. Saarni (Eds.), *The socialization of emotions* (pp. 187–209). New York: Plenum.

Sagi, A., & Hoffman, M. L. (1976). Empathic distress in newborns. *Developmental Psychology, 12,* 175–176.

Selman, R. L. (1975). Level of social perspective taking and the development of empathy in children: speculations from a social-cognitive viewpoint. *Journal of Moral Education, 5,* 35–43.

Selman, R. (1980). *The growth of interpersonal understanding: developmental and clinical analyses.* New York: Academic Press.

Shantz, C. U. (1983). Social cognition. In P. H. Mussen (Ed.), *Handbook of child psychology* (Vol. 3, pp. 495–555). New York: Wiley.

Sigel, I. E. (1984). Reflections on action theory and distancing theory. *Human Development, 27,* 188–193.

Smith, A. (1759/1887). *The theory of moral sentiments.* London: George Bell & Sons.

Staub, E. (1979). *Positive social behavior and morality* (Vol. 2). New York: Academic Press.

Stotland, E. (1969). Exploratory investigations of empathy. In L. Berkowitz (Ed.), *Advances in experimental social psychology* (Vol. 4, pp. 271–314). New York: Academic Press.

Strayer, J. (1980). A naturalistic study of empathic behaviors and their relation to affective states and perspective-taking skills in preschool children. *Child Development, 51,* 815–822.

Strayer, J. (1986). Children's attributions regarding the situational determinants of emotion in self and others. *Developmental Psychology, 17,* 649–654.

Strayer, J. (1987a). *Children's responses to others' emotions and situations considered in terms of an empathy continuum.* Unpublished manuscript. Simon Fraser University, Burnaby, B.C. Canada.

Strayer, J. (1987b). *Empathy and sympathy in a social context*. Paper presented at meetings of the Society for Research in Child Development, Baltimore, April.

Strayer, J. (1987c). Affective and cognitive perspectives on empathy. In N. Eisenberg & J. Strayer (Eds.), *Empathy and its development*. New York: Cambridge University Press.

Strayer, J. (1987d). Picture-story indices of empathy. In N. Eisenberg and J. Strayer (Eds.), *Empathy and its development*. New York: Cambridge University Press.

Wilson, B. J., & Cantor, J. (1985). Developmental differences in empathy with a television protagonist's fear. *Journal of Experimental Child Psychology, 39,* 284–299.

Zahn-Waxler, C., Radke-Yarrow, M., & King, R. (1979). Child rearing and children's prosocial initiations toward victims of distress. *Child Development, 50,* 319–330.

Part VI

The role of culture and socialization practices

11   Culture, scripts, and children's understanding of emotion

James A. Russell

Jean Briggs (1970) spent 17 months in the Canadian north studying the emotional lives of a non-English-speaking Inuit band, the Utku. One of her observations was that the "Utku do not classify emotions exactly as English speakers do: their words for various feelings cannot in every case be tidily subsumed under our words" (p. 311). The Utku sometimes distinguish kinds of emotion not distinguished in English, and some of their emotion terms have no precise equivalent in English. Rather than one word, *fear,* the Utku distinguish fear of physical calamity, *iqhi,* from fear of being treated unkindly, *ilira.* Their word *qiquq* labels a feeling that cannot be described in English with a single word: *qiquq* is the feeling of being on the verge of tears because of bottled-up hostility (perhaps a common feeling in a culture that condemns all expression of hostility).

If Briggs's simple observations are correct, they have fundamental implications concerning the nature of emotion categories and the development of children's understanding of emotion. If Briggs is correct, emotion categories must be the sorts of things that allow cultural variation. Utku-speaking children must have to learn to categorize and label emotions in the Utku way. And English-speaking children must have to learn to do so in the English-speaking way. Yet, by and large, the psychological literature on this topic ignores the role of culture in the acquisition of emotion categories and ignores the possibility that how emotions are categorized and labeled varies with culture.

The psychological literature tends to presuppose what I shall call the *standard view.* I don't know if any psychologist accepts all of the assumptions of the standard view, especially in the extreme form in which I shall state them, but it may be useful to make explicit what may be often implicit. I take the standard view to include these assumptions:

1.   Emotions divide naturally into a small number of discrete kinds.
2.   English words like *fear* and *anger* are names given to these natural kinds. Other languages may use other words, but they denote the same natural kinds. Emotion words thus can be translated one-to-one between languages.

293

3. Human beings easily recognize the natural kinds of emotion both in themselves and in others. Although younger children seem to make errors when trying to recognize emotions, these errors are gradually eliminated, leaving accurate recognition.

Because the standard view is so widely shared, it is rarely stated. But, it can be seen in the kinds of words that most psychologists use when writing about children's understanding of emotion – words like *recognition, accuracy, correctness*. We read of children's *recognition* of a facial expression of anger or fear, and of the *accuracy* of their emotion labels. Some labels are considered *correct*, the rest *errors*. Such words have their place, but used as they are they tend to imply an absolute truth rather than a culturally relative one. They imply that the understanding of emotion is a straightforward registration of that truth. And they imply that *anger, fear* and other English language categories of emotion are universal, indeed the only conceivable means of classifying emotions. The ambiguity of the word *category* – both a set of real events or objects and a mental representation of that set – reinforces this view.

In this chapter, I discuss children's understanding of emotion from an alternate point of view. I take the standard view to be part of our Western heritage, rather than a universal truth. Because we psychologists share this cultural background, and presuppose its truth, the child's acquisition of these ideas tends to appear to us as the child's growing recognition of the nature of things, the growth of accuracy. To step back from the standard view, my first task is to distinguish the concepts we have about emotion from the emotions themselves. I take no position on the first premise of the standard view. Whatever the reality of emotion events may be, the child must still interpret that reality. Whether or not emotion reality consists of discrete units does not tell us how children (or adults) conceptualize emotion. If emotion reality is discrete, children may or may not know this. If reality is not necessarily discrete, children might still impose discrete categories. Too often writers have assumed without argument that human emotion and human conceptualization of emotion must coincide and therefore that one can be inferred from the other.

I believe that emotions are difficult to understand – sufficiently so that scientists have yet to have an adequate grasp of them. Like a scientist, a child is developing a theory – I use the word loosely – about emotions rather than recognizing some obvious truth about them. By a theory, I mean that children are developing a set of interrelated concepts and propositions that constitutes their basis of understanding. These theories of emotion, whether "accurate" or not, guide children's interpretation of their own experience and of the conduct of those around them. Words such as *anger, fear,* and *happiness* are labels for conceptual categories that are part of the child's theory – that is, for English-speaking children. Rather than labels for inevitable and obvious categories, *anger, fear,* and other words of the English language are a means of classifying emotions that is part of our Western cultural heritage, just as the Utku children rely on their cultural heritage for *iqhi, ilira,* and *qiquq.* More generally, children's theories of emotion rely on and are part of their culture's indigenous psychology (Heelas & Lock, 1981), their culture's folk theory of mind.

In contrast to the standard view, I shall assume:

1. Emotions may or may not divide into natural kinds. In either case, neither children nor adults have direct knowledge on this topic.
2. Emotion words express culturally influenced concepts that are embedded in a culturally influenced theory of mind.
3. Human beings must, in part, learn their emotion concepts and theory from their culture.

I shall begin by looking at additional cross-cultural evidence, with which I hope to convince the reader that Briggs's observations are plausible; that is, that there are differences as well as similarities in the way in which emotions are categorized in different cultures. I then hope to use these similarities and differences as a source of hypotheses on the nature of human conceptualization of emotion. Goethe said that people who know no foreign tongue do not know their own. From the vantage point provided by cross-language evidence, we can get a fresh view of *anger, fear, happiness,* and other English language categories for emotion. I shall then discuss how emotion categories, so viewed, might change in the course of development. If emotion concepts vary with culture, then culture must play a role in their acquisition, and I shall suggest what sort of role this might be. At several points, I focus on human understanding of facial expressions because evidence on this topic is widely regarded as favoring the standard view I am questioning.

Cross-cultural research

The ethnographic record

Jean Briggs's (1970) observations on the Utku are not atypical of the observations made by ethnographers whose reports I was able to obtain. Each language studied provides a means of referring to types of emotion, but not necessarily the same types found in English. Let us consider some examples of the kinds of differences reported.

One difference among languages is that some do not distinguish between emotions labeled separately in English. Some African languages use the same word for *anger* and *sorrow* (Leff, 1973; Orley, 1970). Samoans do not distinguish *hate* from *disgust,* and they use one word, *alofa,* for *love, sympathy,* and *liking* (Gerber, 1975). Neither the Tahitians nor the Newars of Nepal distinguish *shame* from *embarrassment* (Levy, 1973). The Javanese do not distinguish *shame* from *guilt* (Geertz, 1959).

Conversely, some languages provide distinctions unavailable in English. I've already mentioned the Utku distinction between *iqhi* and *ilira.* The Tahitians distinguish fear caused by a ghost from fear of natural objects (Levy, 1973).

Not all differences among languages can be described simply as divisions within or combinations of English concepts. There is no precise equivalent for *guilt* among the Tahitians (Levy, 1973), nor among the Pintupi, an aboriginal Australian people (Morice, 1978). Marsella (1981) reviewed various studies and concluded that there is no precisely equivalent term for *depression* among many non-Western cultural groups. Cheng (1977) found no term in Chinese precisely translatable as *anxiety,* although some words (translated as *tension* and *worry)* come close. There are apparently no words precisely equivalent to *anxiety* or *depression* among the Eskimos and Yorubas, either (Leff, 1973; Murphy, 1973).

Conversely, some languages include emotion concepts that have no exact equivalent in English. Doi (1973) concentrated years of study on a single Japanese concept, *amae,* for which no word exists in English. *Amae* is a pleasant feeling of dependence on someone: The feeling Catholics have toward Mary, the mother of Jesus, or an infant has sucking the sweet milk of its mother. Doi (p. 20–21) remarked that the closest he has come to hearing this idea expressed in Western thought was the psychoanalytic notion of passive object love, with the emphasis on passive. In her study of the Javanese, H. Geertz (1959) wrote: *"Wedi* and *isin,* although complex, are close enough to American ideas to be translated as 'fear' and 'shame' or 'guilt,' but *sungkan,* a feeling state associated with respect, is something peculiarly Javanese" (p. 233). In her study of the Ifalukians, a people of Micronesia, Lutz (1985) studied the word *nguch,* which captures what in English must be said metaphorically as "sick and tired" or "fed up." *Nguch* also includes feelings of boredom and lethargy due, for example, to extreme heat, weariness, or illness.[1]

The most thorough analysis of a single term may be Rosaldo's (1980) study of the Ilongot concept of *liget,* which is translated *anger.* Rosaldo wrote:

I began to see in a term that I had understood initially to mean no more than "anger" a set of principles and connections with elaborate ramifications for Ilongot social life. (p. 45)

Like anger, *liget* can be caused by insult or injury, and can be manifested in irritability or violence. But *liget* can also be aroused by a communal, all-night song fest, pride of accomplishment, or the loss of a loved one, and *liget* can be manifested in the sweat of hard work. *Liget* is shown when a man hunts with courage and concentration or when a woman prepares a good meal. *Liget* is a highly valued force, vital to social and personal life.

Bilingual friends have told me that their native language contains emotion terms for which there is no exact English translation. Two examples given to me from Japanese were the words *itoshi*, which refers to longing for an absent loved one, and *ijirashi*, which refers to the feeling associated with seeing someone praiseworthy overcoming an obstacle. An example from German was *Schadenfreude*, which refers to pleasure derived from another's discomfort. These examples would suggest that emotions named in other languages can be translated into English, although not with a single word. Lutz (1980) provides a possible counterexample, however, in her analysis of the Ifalukian word, *fago*, which seems to defy translation.

Lutz's (1980) observations on how *fago* is used in daily life, interviews about experiences of *fago*, and requests for explicit definitions of *fago* leave little doubt that it is a concept difficult to translate into English. *Fago* is felt when someone dies, is needy, is ill, or goes on a voyage, and thus resembles the English word *sad*. But *fago* is also felt when in the presence of someone admirable or when given a gift. *Fago* is used in some situations in which English speakers would use *love, empathy, pity, sadness,* and *compassion* – but not in all such situations.

Discussion

Without more rigorous testing and confirmation of these various observations, it is difficult to say how much credence they deserve. To begin with, it is difficult to know which terms in another language should be thought of as referring to emotions. Neither the Tahitians (Levy, 1973), the Ifalukians (Lutz, 1980), nor the Samoans (Gerber, 1975) have a word precisely equivalent to *emotion:* The word *emotion* itself appears to be culture-bound.

Ethnographers may also tend to report differences more than similarities. Similarities may be less noticeable. Or because of the doctrine of the psychic unity of mankind, especially when emotion is the topic, ethnographers may sometimes take similarities for granted and not report them. Thus, similarities tended to be mentioned in passing, often to contrast with the differences. Before describing in great detail differences in certain emotion concepts, Lutz (1985) mentioned that "relatively adequate American English glosses can be found for many Ifalukian emotion words" (p. 43).

There has also been very little work testing the actual equivalence or nonequivalence of emotion categories across languages, and perhaps there are equivalences that have escaped notice. The trend of accumulating evidence appears to go in the opposite direction, however. Closer examination of non-English emotion terms has suggested that where translation equivalents initially appear to exist, they may not really be equivalent. Tanaka-Matsumi and Marsella (1976) compared *depression* with its commonly given Japanese translation *yuutsu*. The free associations given by English speakers to *depression* were quite different from the free associations given by Japanese speakers to *yuutsu*, raising the possibility that the psychological meaning of the two terms may not be quite the same. They also asked subjects to rate *depression* and *yuutsu* on semantic differential scales. Separate analyses for the terms yielded different factor structures – a more damning piece of evidence if, as Osgood (1969) argues, the semantic differential measures affective meaning. Marsella, Murray, and Golden (1974) obtained similar evidence for differences in meaning between other English emotion words and what had been thought to be their equivalents in Japanese.

What about facial expressions?

The idea of differences in how cultures conceptualize emotions may also be viewed with skepticism by psychologists who have read that "recognition" of facial expressions of emotion is pancultural. Smiles, frowns, and certain other facial expressions are similarly labeled (assuming translation equivalents) in widely different cultures (Ekman, 1972; Izard, 1971). And, indeed, I take the cross-cultural evidence on perception of emotion in facial expressions as among the best evidence we have that there are similarities across cultures in the way in which emotions are categorized. Similarities, not identities.

First, labeling a facial expression is of course not the same as conceptualizing emotion. Second, some studies on this topic found clear cultural differences. When Paul Ekman (1980), who emphasizes cross-cultural universals in his writing, reviewed five of the early studies (Triandis & Lambert, 1958; Cúceloglu, 1970; Dickey & Knower, 1941; Winkelmayer, Exline, Gottheil & Paredes, 1971; Vinacke, 1949), he concluded that although all five of these studies found evidence of universals, "four of them also found evidence of cultural differences in judgment of facial expression" (pp. 122–123).

Third, even the research cited as evidence that "recognition" of emotion is pancultural (Ekman, 1972; Ekman & Friesen, 1986; Izard, 1971) found less than perfect agreement between cultures, especially where the languages were not of Indo-European origin. In Izard's (1971) studies, for example, African and Japanese subjects showed a substantially lower proportion of agreement with English-speakers than did speakers of Indo-European languages. (Ekman, 1980, points to methodological differences that may account for this finding.)

Fourth, the method used in these studies, even if they had yielded 100 percent agreement, cannot be taken to show precise equivalence of the concepts in the different cultures. To illustrate, imagine you are a subject in one of the studies.

You are shown a photograph of a young woman with a bright smile. You are asked to describe how she feels by selecting one word from the following list: *sad, angry, disgusted, afraid, surprised, happy*. Most likely, you'd select *happy*. But now suppose that *happy* was replaced on the list with *overjoyed*. Given the alternatives, you'd have little choice but to select *overjoyed*. Suppose *happy* were successively replaced with *satisfied, excited, grateful*, and *triumphant*. Given the alternatives, you'd again probably select each of these words in turn. Indeed, substitute for *happy* any clearly positive word (or perhaps any subcategory of *happy*) from *contented* to *ecstatic* and the conclusion remains the same. If so, the judgment task used in these studies is insensitive to the precise meaning of the terms involved. Cross-cultural evidence gathered with this judgment method therefore shows at best that people from different cultures give *similar* interpretations to facial expressions.[2]

Conclusion

Anthropologists and psychologists have investigated emotion across cultures for different purposes, with different methods, and from different perspectives. Rarely have the studies focused on emotion *concepts*. Still, enough cross-cultural evidence has accumulated to warrant a tentative conclusion: Much about emotion concepts is similar, but something is often different. I turn next to examine the nature of these concepts, asking how it is possible for them to be both similar and different from one language to the next.

The nature of emotion concepts

Cultural-specific features

What might be culture-specific about emotion concepts? One possibility seems to concern the cause of the emotion. Recall the examples from German and Japanese of terms for which there is no monolexemic equivalent in English. The German *Schadenfreude* specifies that the cause of the pleasure is another's displeasure. The Japanese *ijirashi* specifies that the cause of this feeling is seeing someone praiseworthy overcoming an obstacle. The Utku word *iqhi* specifies that the cause threatens physical harm, whereas *ilira* specifies that the cause threatens social or psychological harm. Anthropologists have described how people of other cultures attribute emotions to such things as the soul leaving the body, a curse from an enemy, bewitchment, demonic possession, disfavor of the gods, and visitations of ghosts. For example, the Tahitian word *mehameha* refers to an uncanny fear caused by a ghost (Levy, 1973).

Causal antecedents also appear to be involved in emotion terms in English:

Fear implies that a danger has appeared, whereas *anxiety* implies that the cause is vague or unknown. *Guilt* implies that you yourself are the causal agent of an outcome, whereas *anger* implies that another has caused some harm. Weiner (1982) has provided evidence and a conceptual analysis of the role of causal thinking in English language emotion concepts. (Thompson, this volume, discusses causal attributions and children's understanding of emotion.)

People react emotionally to different things in different cultures: what is disgusting to one culture may be enjoyable to another (Averill, Opton, & Lazarus, 1969; Lazarus, Tomita, Opton, & Kodama, 1966; Lazarus, 1967; Mead & Bateson, 1942) – although there may also be pancultural elements in the causes of emotion (Boucher & Brandt, 1981). Presumably, then, what people *believe* to be the causes of their emotion can vary with culture, and this believed cause can be incorporated into the meaning of an emotion-descriptive term. In short, I propose that causal antecedent can be an aspect of the meaning of an emotion term, and that this aspect of meaning can be part of what varies with culture.

Another sort of culture-specific aspect seems to concern the behavioral consequences of emotion, such as emotionally expressive gestures. For example, we find that there are different terms in Tahitian for when an expression is inhibited and when it is displayed (Levy, 1973). Similarly, the Samoan word *'o'ona* refers to anger that is not expressed (Gerber, 1975). According to Ekman (1972, 1980), different cultures establish different norms about the control of emotional expressions. These "display rules" might dictate that at a funeral, for example, grief should be inhibited, displayed, or exaggerated. (Saarni, 1982, has discussed children's understanding of display rules.) Peoples of different cultures thus expect different behavioral consequences of specific emotions. Again, I propose that these expectations are incorporated into the meaning of terms, and that this aspect of meaning can vary with culture.

In general, we might suppose that any culture-specific folk belief or practice about emotion could be incorporated into that culture's emotion vocabulary. One topic, for example, that I have not discussed here but that shows large cross-cultural variation concerns ideas about the physiology of emotion.

Pancultural features

What about emotion concepts might be pancultural? The most comprehensive, although least direct, evidence on this question stems from the semantic differential technique. In the over twenty languages studied, the dimensions of evaluation, activity, and potency appeared as primary features of meaning (Osgood, May, & Miron, 1975) – dimensions Osgood (1969) has interpreted as affective in nature. Evaluation and potency have appeared as pancultural dimensions in the conceptualization of interpersonal behavior, a domain closely linked to emotion (White, 1980). Evaluation and activity have appeared as pancultural dimensions of aesthetic judgments, another related domain (Berlyne, 1975; Berlyne, Robbins, & Thompson, 1974).

When the semantic differential technique is applied directly to English-language emotion terms, the same three dimensions emerge (Averill, 1975; Block, 1957; Russell & Mehrabian, 1975), although sometimes renamed pleasure or positivity, arousal or activation, and control or dominance. Block's semantic differential (1957) study of 15 English emotion words, for example, revealed underlying dimensions of pleasure and arousal. More important, when Block's study was repeated in Norwegian, the same two dimensions were found. A multidimensional scaling study of emotion-related words in English (Russell, 1980), which yielded two dimensions – degree of pleasure and degree of arousal – was replicated in Chinese, Japanese, Croatian, and Gujarati. Quantitative assessment showed that both dimensions were available in all five languages (Russell, 1983). (Because the words scaled were not a representative sample of emotion-related words in each language, the *salience* of these two dimensions remains to be established. Nevertheless, we know at least that these two dimensions exist and are dominant within some set of emotion-related words in each language studied.)

Other multidimensional scaling studies have corroborated the first dimension. G. Ekman (1955) used multidimensional scaling with 23 Swedish emotion-denoting words. These data have been analyzed in various ways, often with slightly different results (Ekman, 1955; Fillenbaum & Rapoport, 1971; Lundberg & Devine, 1975; Micko, 1970; Shepard, 1962; Stone, 1971; Stone & Coles, 1970). Nevertheless, one bipolar dimension closely related to pleasure–displeasure emerged in most of the analyses and a clear arousal dimension emerged in at least one (Micko, 1970). Fillenbaum and Rapoport (1971) multidimensionally scaled 15 Hebrew words denoting emotions, but only a single dimension was interpretable: pleasure–displeasure. A multidimensional scaling of 35 Japanese words yielded pleasantness–unpleasantness as a first dimension, but no further dimension analogous to dimensions found in studies of English (Yoshida, Kinase, Kurokawa, & Yashiro, 1970). Lutz (1982) used multidimensional scaling in her study of the emotion words spoken by the Ifaluk. Her analysis of the 31 words most commonly used to describe emotions yielded two dimensions: pleasure–displeasure and strength–weakness. Lutz specifically noted the absence of anything like the dimension of arousal seen in studies of English emotion words.

Cheng (1977) interviewed Chinese residents of Hong Kong, one group in English and another in Chinese. Subjects were asked to describe various emotional experiences, to label the emotion, and to rate it on various verbal scales. These verbal scales were specifically aimed at dimensions such as pleasantness–unpleasantness, level of activation, and five others derived from studies of the English lexicon. The result:

The pleasant–unpleasant dimension . . . was the only dimension of the entire seven dimensions that the author believed as definitely present in the subjects' construction of emotion. None of the subjects of the entire sample had difficulty in understanding it and in indicating that their emotions were pleasant or unpleasant. (p. 192)

In short, studies on what is similar in emotion concepts across cultures seem to point to dimensions of feeling: pleasure–displeasure surely, arousal–sleepiness probably. Most psychologists are familiar with the extensive work done with English language emotion concepts in which just such dimensions of feeling have been argued to be the principal features of their meaning. Some English words for emotion can be defined principally as combinations of pleasure and arousal. Thus, *excitement* is the combination of pleasure with high arousal, *calm* the combination of pleasure with low arousal, *nervousness* the combination of displeasure with high arousal, *depression* the combination of displeasure with low arousal (Russell & Mehrabian, 1977). I am suggesting that this same conclusion will be reached in other languages.

Interim summary

Let me pause to summarize where I have been and to hint where I am going. Concepts that people use to taxonomize the domain of emotion do not appear to be universal, although there is good reason to believe they are often similar. If we are to account for cultural differences in emotion concepts, we cannot think of them as unanalyzable elemental units – as mental atoms. Rather, we must analyze each concept into its constituents. We can refer to these constituents as *features,* provided we make no assumptions that features must be panhuman or discrete or whatever. Causes and consequences are among culture-specific features of emotion words, but they may not be the only ones, because there is no reason to suppose that there is some small number of features. Emotion terms also incorporate features specifying degree of pleasure and degree of arousal, and these features may be part of the reason for the similarity across cultures.

Of course, the available evidence is sparse and what there is does not force us to a single conclusion. Any number of hypotheses could be proposed to account for this evidence, but I will focus my attention here on one such possibility. The key idea is that of a *script* (Abelson, 1981). I shall elaborate on this idea in the next section, but let me first state it briefly.

Concepts of types of emotion consist of features. The features describe the subevents that make up the emotion: causes, feelings, physiological changes, overt actions, and vocal and facial expressions. These subevents, or features, are ordered in a causal sequence – in much the same way that actions are ordered in a playwright's script. To know the meaning of a term like *happiness, fear,* or *jealousy* is to know a script for that emotion. In other words, the present hypothesis is that the meaning of each such word, the concept it expresses, *is* a script.

Scripts

A script is a knowledge structure for an event in which the event is thought of as a sequence of subevents. Although we often speak of an emotion as a thing, a more apt description is a sequence of subevents. For example, consider the prototypical case of anger:

> You are working hard to get something you want. Someone intervenes to prevent you from having it. You stop and stare. You feel your heart pounding, your muscles tightening. You race forward, knocking the person to the ground.

The sequence just narrated might never have actually occurred in just that way, but for each emotion concept, we know some such sequence. Fear, we know, is typically caused by a danger and typically leads to some sort of running away. For some concepts, the story is simple. In happiness, one desires something, gets it, feels pleasure, smiles, and, perhaps, feels kind toward others. For other concepts, the story is more complicated. Consider jealousy:

> A teenage boy is in love with a girl. One day, he sees her flirting with another male. The boy stops and stares at them. He feels his muscles tighten, his heart beat. Unkind thoughts race through his head. He runs toward them and demands that she come with him.

In this story, the boy's central feeling is extreme unhappiness and arousal. But *jealousy* implies a surrounding situation, a social relationship between two people, motives, behaviors, and consequences. These implications must be understood to know what the word *jealousy* means.

As a knowledge schema, a script is brought to bear on the interpretation of emotional events. An actual event is examined as a possible instantiation of the script. The actual event may resemble the script to varying degrees and in various ways. The features of the script are neither necessary nor sufficient; rather, the more features present, the closer the resemblance and the more appropriate the script label. Moreover, each feature of the script has a prototypical value. Features/subevents of events in the world can resemble the feature prototype in the script again to varying degrees and in various ways. For example, Tomkins and McCarter (1964), Izard (1971), and Ekman and Friesen (1976) have isolated a prototypical fear face, and yet a range of different facial expressions count, to varying degrees, as fear (Russell & Bullock, 1986a).

Unfortunately, the word *script* means different things to different writers. (For example, I am using the term in a different sense than does Lewis, this volume.) I am also treating emotion scripts somewhat differently than did Abelson (1981) when he first proposed them. Abelson (1981) thought of emotion scripts as involved both in understanding (a knowledge schema) and in behavior (a response program); I am restricting my treatment to the former. I am also leaving my treatment somewhat vague. It remains an empirical question just how abstract or concrete are the features that constitute the script. Moreover, it is possible that different people within the same culture possess slightly different scripts for the same emotion word. There may be more agreement for *fear* and *anger* than for less common concepts, like *ennui* and *envy*.

On the other hand, other writers have expressed a similar idea but used a different word. Stein and Trabasso (this volume) describe each emotion word as a *narrative structure:* anger – you wanted something, but some agent intentionally prevented you from having it; now you want revenge; fear – you anticipate something unwanted happening. They told 6-year-olds brief stories and questioned them about the emotional responses of the story characters. The children's answers seemed to reveal tacit knowledge describable as these narrative structures.

The present script hypothesis is also closely tied to Rosch's (e.g., 1973, 1975, 1977) prototype theory of natural language categories of objects. A script is to an event what a prototype is to an object. Elsewhere my colleagues and I have pointed to aspects of the emotion domain clarified by Rosch's theory (Bullock & Russell, 1984, 1986; Fehr & Russell, 1984; Fehr, Russell, & Ward, 1982; Russell & Bullock, 1986a). Rather than properly defined, *happiness, sadness, fear, anger,* and other natural language categories of emotion are fuzzy. By this, I mean that: (a) Borders between categories are vague, rather than clear-cut. Although some actual events are clear cases of, for example, anger, and other actual events are clearly not anger, some events straddle the fence and are difficult to decide one way or the other. (b) Membership within a category is a matter of degree rather than all or none. Actual events that are cases of anger vary in how well they exemplify the concept. Some are prototypical, some are good, and some are mediocre cases. (c) Different categories tend to overlap one another rather than to be mutually exclusive. Actual events tend to be categorizable into more than one category; the same case can be anger, fear, disgust, and sadness. There can exist any degree of overlap between categories. Some categories overlap each other almost completely, others to a high degree, others to a minimal degree, and some not at all. If concepts of emotion are scripts, then it would not be surprising for them to be fuzzy in the sense just described. The script could represent an idealized case of the emotion, which actual events may resemble to varying degrees. Membership in a category like *fear* or *anger* would therefore be a matter of degree. Different scripts could share certain features in common and therefore overlap. Actual events could resemble more than one script and therefore be categorizable as more than one emotion.

The development of children's concepts of emotion

Different positions could be taken on how the child develops a set of concepts for emotions. At one extreme would be the position that there are something like innate emotion categories. Biological theories of emotion emphasize the evolutionary advantages of the communication of emotion (Andrew, 1963; Darwin, 1872/1965). Perception and interpretation of facial expressions has been said to have evolved as part of this function (e.g., Oster, 1978). If a facial expression is thought of as a releasing mechanism, again something like an emotion detector is implied. At the opposite extreme would be the position that the child must construct from experience every aspect of her or his conceptual scheme for emotions. Perhaps the culture or language community must teach this scheme. Perhaps the child constructs it via general cognitive mechanisms. The cross-cultural similarities we have seen favor a position more toward the first extreme; the cross-cultural differences favor one more toward the other. If there are both similarities and differences, then we might favor a position somewhere in the middle.

Merry Bullock and I (1986) have suggested such a possibility. We suspect that children do not possess innate emotion categories, but they do not begin as blank slates either. The child begins with a number of general constraints on how to interpret the emotion world. The particular constraint we have emphasized is that matters of emotion are initially perceived in terms of those dimensions that are pancultural: pleasure–displeasure and arousal–sleepiness. A subjective experience might be felt as pleasant and aroused; the word *fear* might be interpreted as meaning unpleasant and aroused; the caregiver's sad demeanor appears unpleasant and unaroused. This hypothesis does not deny that very young children discriminate and categorize different emotions. What it does is specify the initial basis of discrimination and categorization as pleasure and arousal dimensions, rather than the adultlike categories implied by such labels as *anger, fear,* and the like. As an analogy, consider the words *big* and *little*. When we discriminate and categorize objects as *big* or *little,* we are relying on a single quantitative dimension of size rather than on two separate and discrete categories.

If our assumption is correct, every child the world round initially interprets an emotional event in a way that can be described as global and relatively "undifferentiated." The child's developmental task, then, is to differentiate within this global interpretation to reach the culture's taxonomy for emotional states. Recall the case we English-speaking adults would classify as jealousy: the teenager who glares when his girlfriend flirts with another boy. Our hypothesis implies that the teenager's infant brother would not interpret this scene in terms of *jealousy,* but would perceive his brother as in a state of displeasure and high arousal. How in the course of development does the younger brother move from this global interpretation to the particular one? This question, if our reasoning is sound, is central to the development of emotional understanding. Our answer, of course, is that the child learns a script about jealousy. And so we must ask how the child acquires scripts.

There are two general, complementary, answers to this question. The first answer focuses on the structure of emotion events: The features that make up each emotion script are likely to be at least somewhat correlated in emotion reality. When children face a danger, they may see a fear expression on their caregiver's face. When they soil a diaper, they may see a disgust expression; When they disobey a command, they may see an anger expressio: Thus, reality is not random but structured, and the child will encounter these associations. Episodes initially experienced as unpleasant and aroused can come to be differentiated into fear, disgust, and anger. (I am not here taking a position on what accounts for this structuring of emotion reality. Some psychologists emphasize a biological basis for the links, others emphasize culture's role. However emotion reality comes to be structured, the structure provides one means for the child to differentiate and conceptualize emotions.)

The second answer focuses on the child's surrounding culture. The associations that the child encounters are often labeled and interpreted by caregivers. The caregiver labels some episodes as *fear*, some as *anger*, some as *disgust*. Parents and others interpret the young child's own emotional states as well as those of others the child may observe (Miller & Sperry, 1987). English-speaking children are told stories about *romantic love* and *jealousy*, *fear*, and *courage*. Japanese children are told stories of *itoshi* and *ijirashi*. Utku children of *iqhi*, *ilira*, and *qiquq*.

Levels of understanding

Based on these general considerations as well as on prior conceptual and empirical investigations by Bullock and Russell (1986) and Nelson (1987), the following possible sequence of steps is proposed.

Level 1: Infants discriminate particular gestures and changes in others' face and voice. Infants as young as 2 months, possibly including newborns, can respond differentially to such events (Field, Woodson, Greenberg, & Cohen, 1982; Nelson & Horowitz, 1983; LaBarbera, Izard, Vietze, & Parisi, 1976).

Some writers have used this evidence to argue that very young infants can "recognize," "discriminate," and "imitate" happy, sad, and perhaps other facial expressions of emotion. However, the ability to perceive different physical features is not the same as the ability to perceive a class of expressions as a class.

Nor is it the same as giving special status to those features we as adults consider communicative of emotion. Nor is it the same as finding meaning in these features. Consideration of separate evidence on infants' lack of visual perceptual sensitivity, their limited ability to scan human faces, and their lack of a schema for faces, all led Nelson (1987) to a similar conclusion. He suggests that before 4 months, infants may not distinguish expressions as such, but only distinguish such features as open versus closed mouth.

Level 2: Infants show the ability to discriminate classes of expressions (e.g., smiles or frowns), responding differently to exemplars of different classes and responding similarly to exemplars of the same class despite variations in such extraneous features as the sex of the person posing the expression. Nelson and his associates (Nelson, Morse, & Leavitt, 1979; Nelson & Dolgin, 1985; Nelson & Ludeman, 1986) suggest that infants between 4 and 8 months have formed such expression classes. Nevertheless, at this level, infants may still not find any meaning in the patterns they detect.

Level 3: Infants begin to attribute meaning to the classes of expressions of emotion. By an adult standard, the meanings that infants give to facial or vocal expressions are relatively undifferentiated. The meaning is quantitative, distinguishing emotions only in terms of degree of pleasure and (either simultaneously or slightly later) degree of arousal. Still, this meaning serves to facilitate social interactions and to guide infants' reactions to ambiguous events.

For example, infants as young as 10 months use their mother's facial expression as a guide for their own behavior, in what is termed "social referencing." Infants approach or withdraw from a novel toy, a visual cliff, or a stranger, depending on their mother's facial expression (e.g., Boccia & Campos, 1986; Klinnert, 1984; Klinnert, Campos, Sorce, Emde, & Svejda, 1983; Sorce, Emde, Campos, & Klinnert, 1985; Zarbatany & Lamb, 1985). Not all infants in these studies show social referencing, and not all infants who do reference alter their behavior accordingly. Still, some infants do reference and do alter their behavior accordingly.

Investigators who have carried out these studies tend to interpret their findings in terms of the standard view. Mothers are asked to appear afraid, sad, angry, or happy, and the infants are assumed to interpret their mother's facial expressions in the same terms. But some of the results are puzzling from this point of view. Consider, for example, the Sorce et al. (1985) study, in which infants faced a visual cliff. As expected, mother's fear expression resulted in avoidance of the visual cliff in all 17 infants tested. But an anger expression produced a similar result in 16 of 18 infants, and a sad expression did so in 12 of 18 infants. Nelson (1987) comments: "As is the case with anger, it is baffling why sad would deter crossing. It thus may be the case that infants group fear, anger, and sad into a broader category of 'negative' expressions, and interpret all such expressions as a warning'' (p. 900). Nelson's categorical interpretation fails to account for why fear was more powerful than anger, and why anger was more powerful than sad. The explanation I would offer is that the infant interprets the mother's facial expression in terms of dimensions of pleasure and arousal. Deterrence is greatest at displeasure-and-high-arousal, falling off the farther the expression is from this point – hence the order: fear, anger, sad, and, last, happy.

Level 4: The child now associates pairs of meaningful elements. Children might first begin to associate a type of facial expression with a particular type of vocal cue, or with the immediate context in which it occurs. For example, the child notices that smiles come with gifts or with a certain tone of voice. Although at this point differentiation is primitive and the child's concepts may not be organized into temporal or causal sequences, these two-element combinations are probably the precursor for more differentiated meaning attached to emotional events. Two different expressions, although similar in pleasure and arousal, may now be associated with different contexts, different vocal expressions, or different outcomes. For example, the child finds that the caregiver's unpleasant and aroused expression in the context of spilled milk is different from the caregiver's equally unpleasant and aroused expression in the context of soiled diapers. The child can also now pair an expression or tone of voice with a particular word, such as *angry* or *happy*. Because, to the child, the meaning of the facial or vocal expression is in terms of pleasure and arousal, the meaning of the emotion word will be understood in the same way. Put another way, children at this level are constrained to pleasure and arousal dimensions in their initial hypotheses on the meanings of the emotion words provided by their language community.

Level 5: The child now comes to string together emotion sequences, consisting of behaviors, expressions, situations, and words. This involves two related processes. One is that the child associates multiple elements together. The second is that the child begins to combine the elements according to temporal order and causal links. These sequences are the basis for emotion scripts, but at this point they may not be highly abstract. Rather, they are a collection of specific sequences observed. The culture's language of emotion may be important at this level, as the child now has a good basis for distinguishing different emotion words according to the different sequences associated with them. That parents use different words may stimulate the child to look for differences in events. Also, to the extent that parents use the same word in seemingly different situations, they may stimulate the child to look for similarities and form more abstract concepts.

Level 6: From the collection of remembered sequences, the child forms more generalized scripts. In the emerging script for fear, for instance, the collection of frightening situations is summarized by the concept of danger, the collection of ensuing behaviors by the concept of avoidance. At the same time, the child's growing sophistication in social and moral matters is incorporated into the scripts. In the emerging script for anger, for instance, the collection of frustrating situations focuses on those involving deliberate and illegitimate frustration. The child also learns which emotions and which displays of emotion are socially permissible or obligatory (Hochschild, 1983; Saarni, 1982) under what circumstances. When emotion scripts are formed is unknown. We do know that 3-year-olds have established reasonably accurate scripts for at least a half dozen basic emotion terms (Trabasso, Stein, & Johnson, 1981). This finding is consistent with the fact that 3-year-olds are establishing accurate scripts about other important event sequences in their lives as well, such as the daily routines of the daycare (Nelson & Gruendel, 1981).

The end product. The developmental sequence just outlined is, of course, over-simplified and overly general. Within each level, skills improve and develop. These levels thus overlap and may be out of order. Some emotion concepts never develop to the end. Some concepts, even in adults, may be understood solely through several exemplars (Level 5). Some concepts may develop beyond the generalized folk scripts of Level 6, as when experts propose ever finer distinctions. The differentiation of emotions according to their scripts does not, in my view, lead to a fixed set of emotion types. Thus, there is no end point in the developing taxonomy of emotion concepts. Nor is it helpful to dichotomize taxonomies as correct or incorrect. Rather, taxonomies of different ages and different cultures – like scientific theories – are useful for different purposes.

The 2-year-old's understanding of facial expressions

At this point, it may be helpful to examine a bit of evidence. Let me therefore return to the interpretation of facial expressions, with a focus on 2-year-olds. Although interpreting a facial expression is but one context in which the developing child categorizes the emotion of another, it is a context that has been extensively studied and is a cornerstone of the standard view. I will focus on the primary meaning of emotional facial expressions. By primary meaning I refer to the meaning of the expression alone – even when we believe a smile is hiding grief or is insincere we understand the meaning of the smile by itself.

According to the standard view, to interpret a facial expression is to understand it in terms of *discrete categories.* Seeing the three facial expressions shown in Figure 11.1, for example, the child would have to interpret their meaning

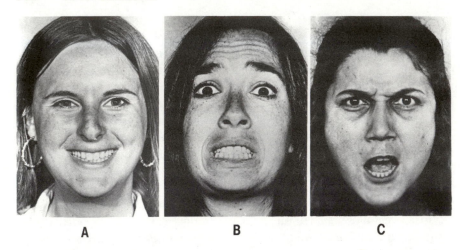

Figure 11.1. Three facial expressions of emotion (reproduced with permission from Ekman & Friesen, 1976).

according to qualitatively different categories, appropriately labeled *happiness, fear,* and *anger,* respectively. Beginning with a study published in 1923 by Gates, children have been asked to label facial expressions (Izard, 1977). Almost all these studies presupposed the standard view by adopting adult norms on category choices against which to assess children's "accuracy." From this perspective, 2-year-olds and indeed all preschoolers look bad. The general conclusion has been that adult "accuracy" is not achieved until the early *teens.* Up until then, slow steady improvement is seen. Preschoolers do poorly and young pre-schoolers score at chance levels. From this evidence, it appears that either 2-year-olds do not understand facial expressions, or, if they do, their performance is obscured by random errors. Put another way, children were like sloppy adults: Their basic way of understanding facial expressions is in principle like that of adults. Yet, they were prone to confusion, poor memory, mistakes of vocabulary, lapses of attention, and lack of motivation – hence their frequent errors.

According to the account I have been describing in this chapter, when children begin understanding facial expressions, they do so in terms of pleasure and arousal. When they begin acquiring vocabulary items, the meaning they give to emotion words (e.g., *happy, mad, sad)* is in terms of pleasure and arousal. In neither case is the meaning equivalent to the meaning adults give. If so, the criterion for accuracy in these studies has been inappropriate.

To interpret facial expressions according to bipolar dimensions, the child would think in terms of quantitative distinctions. Seeing the three facial expressions shown in Figure 11.1, for example, the child might see face *A* as expressing pleasure and moderate arousal, face *B* as expressing displeasure and high arousal, and face *C* as similarly expressing displeasure and high arousal. That *B* and *C* receive similar interpretations by my account is a key to differentiating it empirically from the standard account. The standard account treats these as separate and distinct, *fear* for *B*, *anger* for *C*. Indeed, by the standard account, *B* is as distinct in meaning from *C* as it is from *A*.

We should therefore be able to find that, given the opportunity to use dimensions, 2-year-olds have established a way of understanding facial expressions overlooked by studies based on the standard view. Just such a result occurred in a study in which we got 2-year-olds to judge the similarity between facial expressions (Russell & Bullock, 1986b). The children worked with ten photographs, each a prototypical expression of ten separate categories of feeling: sadness, disgust, anger, fear, surprise, excitement, happiness, calm, and sleepiness. Through a slow step-by-step process, 38 2-year-olds placed together the expressions that they thought were alike. This method allowed us to explore children's understanding with a method that has nothing to do with emotion labels. The children were asked to group together people who felt alike. Their groupings allowed us to estimate the similarity they perceived between different expressions. And the estimates of similarity allowed us to use multidimensional scaling to produce a portrait – a geometric metaphor – of the children's perceived similarity structure of emotion. The result was a two-dimensional structure, the axes of which were interpretable as pleasure and arousal. We have obtained similar results for 3-, 4-, and 5-year-olds (Russell & Bullock, 1985, 1986b).

We have also asked 2-year-olds to associate faces with words like *happy* or *angry*. In an unpublished study, each child was trained to place objects in a special box, leaving aside any inappropriate objects. In the first session, green cards go in the box, other colors do not. In the second session, happy people go in the box, others do not. (At this task, our 20 2-year-olds showed remarkable skill. Happy expressions were put in the box 100% of the time. Angry, afraid, sad, and disgusted expressions were put in the box an average of only 10% of the time. If we define a *hit rate* as correct positives minus false negatives, this session revealed a 90% hit rate, i.e., 100% − 10%.) In the third session, angry people go in the box, others do not. (Anger was defined for the child by both a word, *angry*, and a picture of an angry facial expression.) The children put angry faces in the box 63% of the time. They put happy faces in the box only 8% of the time. (So, once again, the children were clearly differentiating angry from happy expressions; there was a 55% hit rate, i.e., 63% − 8%.) The important trials were negative but nonangry emotions: expressions of sadness, fear, and disgust. The children put these expressions in the box 63% of the time: a 0% hit rate (i.e., 63% − 63%). In short, the 2-year-olds distinguished positive from negative facial expressions, but did not distinguish among the negative expressions.

Studies of this sort – and we found similar results for older preschoolers –

suggest a deeper reason for preschoolers' errors observed by Gates (1923) and others. The standard interpretation was wrong in one fundamental way: Their "errors" were *not* random. "Errors" (i.e., responses that did not agree with the adult-defined criterion) were not due to the extraneous factors as previously thought – they were part and parcel of children's interpretation of facial expressions. Sad, disgusted, and afraid expressions are put in the angry box because the 2-year-old interprets those expressions and the word *angry* as similar in meaning: unpleasant.

In describing these findings, I do not mean to imply that 2-year-olds cannot differentiate different emotions. In another study of 2-year-olds using a forced-choice method (Bullock & Russell, 1985, Study 1), we found very slight differentiation among negative expressions, which we could interpret in terms of degree of arousal. Given richer stimulus input, such as vocal cues, situation, and behavioral consequences, 2-year-olds would almost certainly differentiate more than they did in our study when given only facial expressions. At least this is the prediction we make from the idea that a concept such as anger is understood in terms of a script – for it is just the information about causes, concomitants, and consequences specified by the script that is lacking when the child is given only a facial expression.

Conclusion

Understanding how children develop the ability to interpret emotion requires a thorough understanding of the ability itself. In other words, we must know where adults end up if we are to get a handle on how children get there. At the same time, we must not assume that children are doing just what adults do, but with more errors.

In this chapter, I have argued that all adults do not end up in the same place. Anthropologists and psychologists have found what appear to be telling examples of different languages and cultures categorizing the emotion world somewhat differently. At the same time, there are obvious similarities across cultures in emotion concepts. I do not want to resurrect an outdated Whorfian claim that language coerces thought; not do I claim here that different cultural conceptions of emotion necessarily produce different emotional experiences; not do I claim that culture is the sole determinant of emotion concepts. Differences across language and culture in the way in which emotions are categorized do, however, mean that culture plays a role in children's acquisition of those categories.

Psychologists have come to think about the human understanding of emotions largely through some simple metaphors, drawn, I believe, from our cultural heritage. In the *discrete category* metaphor, people sort emotions into mental pigeon holes, which are called categories and which are labeled such things as *anger, fear, happiness,* and the like. In the *dimension* metaphor, people place emotions on internal scales, which are called dimensions and which are thought to represent such attributes as amount of pleasure, power, or physiological arousal felt during the emotion. In the *mechanistic* metaphor, people perceive that one event causes the emotion and that the emotion causes subsequent actions: A bear appears before you, the bear elicits fear, and that fear causes the person to shoot it – in much the same mechanistic way that pulling the trigger causes the action of the bullet.

Each metaphor has provided a means of approaching a difficult subject. Each metaphor has been heuristic, guiding research and unearthing new information about emotional understanding. Thus, we know that children can categorize the emotions of others, can specify how pleasant another's emotion state is, and can specify the causes and consequences of emotions. Still, we must not become overly attached to one or the other metaphor. We must remember that metaphors are ladders to be thrown away once we've climbed to the top. With this attitude, we can better benefit from new metaphors as they come along.

I believe the most promising new metaphor is that of a *script.* That is, when we say that someone is, for example, afraid, we combine in one word a series of consecutive events dependent on one another. To know the meaning of the word *fear,* to have the concept expressed by that word, is to know that sequence. The metaphor of a script subsumes the discrete category, dimension, and mechanistic metaphors: Categories such as *anger* and *fear* are mentally represented as scripts. Dimensions like pleasure–displeasure are among the features of the scripts. And the features are related to one another in a causal sequence. Emotions are panculturally represented as scripts, the dimensions of pleasure and arousal may be the panhuman features in those scripts, but other features in the script are culture-specific. The pancultural dimensions of pleasure and arousal are among the earliest devices available to children for interpreting emotional experiences. *Anger, fear,* and other emotion concepts develop out of this less differentiated means of interpretation with the help of the surrounding culture.

Notes

1. There are also numerous descriptions of pathological states, labeled by the culture, for which there is no equivalent English term (Gobeil, 1973; Johnson & Johnson, 1965; Langness, 1965; Kiev, 1968; Rubel, 1964; Westermeyer, 1972). For example, *amok* is a term found mainly in the Malay archipelago. It refers to an intense state characterized by delusions and violent assaults directed against friend and foe alike, followed by amnesia and deep sleep (Carr & Tan, 1976). We are not inclined to include such states as *amok* among the emotions, but perhaps this is simply because *amok* is not an emotion term in English.
2. The most celebrated studies on this topic were of nonliterate, relatively isolated groups in Borneo and New Guinea. The first such study reported (Ekman, Sorenson, & Friesen, 1969) used the forced-choice method just described and found modest correspondence across culture. Two fur-

ther studies (Ekman, 1972; Ekman & Friesen, 1971) used a brief story with or in place of the emotion term. Rather than to select a picture of "disgust," for example, the subject would be asked to select the picture of the person who smelled something bad. This method, although providing interesting information, cannot tell us much about how the people of these cultures conceptualize emotions.

References

Abelson, R. P. (1981). Psychological status of the script concept. *American Psychologist, 36,* 715–729.

Andrew, R. I. (1963). Evolution of facial expression. *Science, 142,* 1034–1041.

Averill, J. R. (1975). A semantic atlas of emotional concepts. *JSAS Catalog of Selected Documents in Psychology, 5,* 330 (Ms. No. 421).

Averill, J. R., Opton, E., & Lazarus, R. (1969). Cross-cultural studies of psychophysiological responses during stress and emotion. *International Journal of Psychology, 4,* 83–102.

Berlyne, D. E. (1975). Extension to Indian subjects of a study of exploratory and verbal responses to visual patterns. *Journal of Cross-Cultural Psychology, 6,* 316–330.

Berlyne, D. E., Robbins, M. C., & Thompson, R. (1974). A cross-cultural study of exploratory and verbal responses to visual patterns varying in complexity. In D. E. Berlyne (Ed.), *Studies in the new experimental aesthetics: steps toward an objective psychology of aesthetic appreciation.* Washington, DC: Hemisphere.

Block, J. (1957). Studies in the phenomenology of emotions. *Journal of Abnormal and Social Psychology, 54,* 358–363.

Boccia, M. L., & Campos, J. J. (1986). *Maternal emotional signals, social referencing, and infants' reactions to stranger.* Manuscript submitted for publication. (Cited by Nelson, 1987.)

Boucher, J. D., & Brandt, M. E. (1981). Judgment of emotion: American and Malay antecedents. *Journal of Cross-Cultural Psychology, 12,* 272–283.

Briggs, J. L. (1970). *Never in anger: portrait of an Eskimo family.* Cambridge, MA: Harvard University Press.

Bullock, M., & Russell, J. A. (1984). Preschool children's interpretation of facial expressions of emotion. *International Journal of Behavioral Development, 7,* 193–214.

Bullock, M., & Russell, J. A. (1985). Further evidence on preschoolers' interpretation of facial expressions of emotion. *International Journal of Behavioral Development, 8,* 15–38.

Bullock, M., & Russell, J. A. (1986). Concepts of emotion in developmental psychology. In C. E. Izard & P. Read (Eds.), *Measuring emotions in infants and children, Vol. 2.* New York: Cambridge University Press.

Carr, J. E., & Tan, E. K. (1976). In search of true amok: amok as viewed within the Malay. *American Journal of Psychiatry, 133,* 1295–1299.

Cheng, T. (1977). *A phenomenological study of emotional experience: a search for cultural differences and similarities in the construction of emotion by a Hong Kong Chinese sample.* Unpublished master's thesis, University of Hong Kong.

Cüceloglu, D. M. (1970). Perception of facial expressions in three cultures. *Ergonomics, 13*(1), 93–100.

Darwin, C. (1872/1965). *The expression of the emotions in man and animals.* London: John Murray, (Reprinted by University of Chicago Press).

Dickey, E. C., & Knower, F. H. (1941). A note on some ethnological differences in recognition of simulated expressions of emotions. *American Journal of Sociology, 47,* 190–193.

Doi, T. (1973). *The anatomy of dependence.* Tokyo: Kodansha International.

Ekman, G. (1955). Dimensions of emotion. *Acta Psychologica, 11,* 279–288.

Ekman, P. (1972). Universal and cultural differences in facial expressions of emotions. In J. K. Cole (Ed.), *Nebraska Symposium on Motivation, 1971.* Lincoln: University of Nebraska Press.

Ekman, P. (1980). *The face of man: expressions of universal emotions in a New Guinea village.* New York: Garland STPM Press.

Ekman, P., & Friesen, W. V. (1971). Constants across cultures in the face and emotion. *Journal of Personality and Social Psychology, 17,* 124–129.

Ekman, P., & Friesen, W. V. (1976). *Pictures of facial affect.* Palo Alto, CA: Consulting Psychologists Press.

Ekman, P., & Friesen, W. V. (1986). A new pan-cultural facial expression of emotion. *Motivation and Emotion, 10,* 159–168.

Ekman, P., Sorenson, E. R., & Friesen, W. V. (1969). Pan-cultural elements in the facial displays of emotions. *Science, 164(3875),* 86–88.

Fehr, B., & Russell, J. A. (1984). Concept of emotion viewed from a prototype perspective. *Journal of Experimental Psychology: General, 113,* 464–486.

Fehr, B., Russell, J. A., & Ward, L. M. (1982). Prototypicality of emotions: a reaction time study. *Bulletin of the Psychonomic Society, 20,* 253–254.

Field, T. M., Woodson, R., Greenberg, R., & Cohen, D. (1982). Discrimination and imitation of facial expressions by neonates. *Science, 218,* 179–181.

Field, T. M., Woodson, R. W., Cohen, D., Greenberg, R., Garcia, R., & Collins, K. (1983). Discrimination and imitation of facial expressions by term and preterm neonates. *Infant Behavior and Development, 6,* 485–489.

Fillenbaum, S., & Rapoport, A. (1971). *Structures in the subjective lexicon.* New York: Academic Press.

Gates, G. S. (1923). An experimental study of the growth of social perception. *Journal of Educational Psychology, 14,* 449–461.

Geertz, H. (1959). The vocabulary of emotion: a study of Javanese socialization processes. *Psychiatry, 22,* 225–237.

Gerber, E. (1975). *The cultural patterning of emotions in Samoa.* Unpublished Ph.D. dissertation, University of California, San Diego.

Gobeil, O. (1973). El susto: A descriptive analysis. *International Journal of Social Psychiatry, 19,* 38–44.

Heelas, P., & Lock, A. (Eds.) (1981) *Indigenous psychologies: the anthropology of the self.* Toronto: Academic Press.

Hochschild, A. R. (1983). *The managed heart.* Berkeley: University of California Press.

Izard, C. E. (1971). *The face of emotion.* New York: Appleton-Century-Crofts.

Izard, C. E. (1977). *Human emotions.* New York: Plenum.

Johnson, D., & Johnson, C. A. (1965). Totally discouraged: a depressive syndrome of the Dakota Sioux. *Transcultural Psychiatric Research Review, 2,* 141–143.

Kiev, A. (1968). *Curanderismo: Mexican-American folk psychiatry.* New York: Free Press.

Klinnert, M. D. (1984). The regulation of infant behavior by maternal facial expression. *Infant Behavior and Development, 7,* 447–465.

Klinnert, M. D., Campos, J. J., Sorce, J. F., Emde, R. N., & Svejda, M. (1983). Emotions as behavior regulators: social referencing in infancy. In R. Plutchik & H. Kellerman (Eds.), *Emotion: theory, research, and experience,* Vol. 2. New York: Academic Press.

LaBarbera, J. D., Izard, C. E., Vietze, P., & Parisi, S. A. (1976). Four- and six-month-old infants' visual responses to joy, anger, and neutral expressions. *Child Development, 47,* 535–538.

Langness, L. L. (1965). Hysterical psychosis in the New Guinea highlands: a Bena Bena example. *Psychiatry, 28,* 258–277.

Lazarus, R., Tomita, M., Opton, E., & Kodama, M. (1966). A cross-cultural study of stress-reaction patterns in Japan. *Journal of Personality and Social Psychology, 4,* 622–633.

Lazarus, R. (1967). Cognitive and personality factors underlying threat and coping. In M. Appley (Ed.), *Psychological stress*. New York: Appleton-Century-Crofts.

Leff, J. (1973). Culture and the differentiation of emotional states. *British Journal of Psychiatry, 123*, 299–306.

Levy, R. I. (1973). *Tahitians*. Chicago: University of Chicago Press.

Lundberg, U., & Devine, B. (1975). Negative similarities. *Education and Psychological Measurement, 35*, 797–807.

Lutz, C. (1980). *Emotion words and emotional development on Ifaluk Atoll*. Unpublished Ph.D. dissertation, Harvard University.

Lutz, C. (1982). The domain of emotion words in Ifaluk. *American Ethnologist, 9*, 113–128.

Lutz, C. (1985). Cultural patterns and individual differences in the child's emotional meaning system. In M. Lewis & C. Saarni (Eds.), *The socialization of emotions* (pp. 37–53). New York: Plenum.

Marsella, A. J. (1981). Depressive experience and disorder across cultures. In H. Triandis & J. Draguns (Eds.), *Handbook of cross-cultural psychology*. Boston: Allyn & Bacon.

Marsella, A. J., Murray, M. D., & Golden, C. (1974). Ethnic variations in the phenomenology of emotions. I. Shame. *Journal of Cross-Cultural Psychology, 5*(3), 312–328.

Mead, M., & Bateson, G. (1942). *Balinese character*. New York: Academy of Sciences Press.

Micko, H. C. (1970). A "halo"-model for multidimensional ratio scaling. *Psychometrika, 35*, 199–227.

Miller, P., & Sperry, L. L. (1987). The socialization of anger and aggression. *Merrill-Palmer Quarterly, 33*, 1–33.

Morice, R. (1978). Psychiatric diagnosis in a transcultural setting: the importance of lexical categories. *British Journal of Psychiatry, 132*, 87–95.

Murphy, H. B. M. (1973). History and the evolution of syndromes: the striking case of Latah and Amok. *Psychopathology: contributions from the social, behavioral and biological sciences*. New York: Wiley.

Nelson, C. A. (1987). The recognition of facial expressions in the first two years of life: mechanisms of development. *Child Development, 58*, 889–909.

Nelson, C. A., & Dolgin, K. (1985). The generalized discrimination of facial expressions by 7-month-old infants. *Child Development, 56*, 58–61.

Nelson, C. A., & Horowitz, F. D. (1983). The perception of facial expressions and stimulus motion by 2- and 5-month-old infants using holographic stimuli. *Child Development, 54*, 868–877.

Nelson, C. A., & Ludemann, P. (1986). *The categorical representation of facial expressions by 4- and 7-month-old infants*. Manuscript submitted for publication (Cited by Nelson, 1987).

Nelson, C. A., Morse, P. A., & Leavitt, L. A. (1979). Recognition of facial expressions by seven-month-old infants. *Child Development, 50*, 1239–1242.

Nelson, K., & Gruendel, J. (1981). Generalized event representation: basic building blocks of cognitive development. In M. E. Lamb & A. L. Brown (Eds.), *Advances in developmental psychology* (Vol. 1). Hillsdale, NJ: Erlbaum.

Orley, J. H. (1970). *Culture and mental illness*. Nairobi, Kenya: East Africa Publishing House.

Osgood, C. E. (1969). On the whys and wherefores of E, P, and A. *Journal of Personality and Social Psychology, 12*, 194–199.

Osgood, C. E., May, W. H., & Miron, M. S. (1975). *Cross-cultural universals of affective meaning*. Urbana: University of Illinois Press.

Oster, H. (1978). Facial expression and affect development. In M. Lewis & L. A. Rosenblum (Eds.), *The development of affect* (pp. 43–75). New York: Plenum.

Rosaldo, M. Z. (1980). *Knowledge and passion: Ilongot notions of self and social life*. Cambridge: Cambridge University Press.

Rosch, E. (1973). On the internal structure of perceptual and semantic categories. In T. E. Moore (Ed.), *Cognitive development and acquisition of language*. New York: Academic Press.

Rosch, E. (1975). Cognitive representations of semantic categories. *Journal of Experimental Psychology: General, 104*, 192–233.

Rosch, E. (1977). Human categorization. In N. Warren (Ed.), *Studies in cross-cultural psychology* (Vol. 1, pp. 1–49). London: Academic Press.

Rubel, A. (1964). The epidemiology of a folk illness: *susto* in Hispanic America. *Ethnology, 3*, 268–283.

Russell, J. A. (1980). A circumplex model of affect. *Journal of Personality and Social Psychology, 39*, 1161–1178.

Russell, J. A. (1983). Pancultural aspects of human conceptual organization of emotions. *Journal of Personality and Social Psychology, 45*, 1281–1288.

Russell, J. A., & Bullock, M. (1985). Multidimensional scaling of emotional facial expressions: similarities from preschoolers to adults. *Journal of Personality and Social Psychology, 48*, 1290–1298.

Russell, J. A., & Bullock, M. (1986a). Fuzzy concepts and the perception of emotion in facial expressions. *Social Cognition, 4*, 309–341.

Russell, J. A., & Bullock, M. (1986b). On the meaning preschoolers attribute to facial expressions of emotion. *Developmental Psychology, 22*, 97–102.

Russell, J. A., & Mehrabian, A. (1975). The mediating role of emotions in alcohol use. *Journal of Studies on Alcohol, 36*, 1508–1536.

Russell, J. A., & Mehrabian, A. (1977). Evidence for a three-factor theory of emotions. *Journal of Research in Personality, 11*, 273–294.

Saarni, C. (1982). Social and affective functions of nonverbal behavior: developmental concerns. In R. Feldman (Ed.), *Development of nonverbal behavior in children*. New York: Springer-Verlag.

Shepard, R. N. (1962). The analysis of proximities: multidimensional scaling with an unknown distance function. *Psychometrika, 27*, 125–139, 219–246.

Sorce, J. F., Emde, R. N., Campos, J. J., & Klinnert, M. D. (1985). Maternal emotional signaling: its effects on the visual cliff behavior of 1-year-olds. *Developmental Psychology, 21*, 195–200.

Stone, L. A. (1971). Congruent multidimensional scaling results obtained using the Halo-model and the Stone-Coles Method model. *Perceptual and Motor Skills, 33*, 524–526.

Stone, L. A., & Coles, G. J. (1970). Correlational similarity: the basis for a new revised method of similarity analysis. *Studia Psychologica (Bratislava), 12*, 258–265.

Tanaka-Matsumi, J., & Marsella, A. J. (1976). Cross-cultural variations in the phenomenological experience of depression: I. Word association studies. *Journal of Cross-Cultural Psychology, 7*(4), 379–396.

Tomkins, S. S., & McCarter, R. (1964). What and where are the primary affects? Some evidence for a theory. *Perceptual and Motor Skills, 18*, 119–158.

Trabasso, T., Stein, N. L., & Johnson, L. R. (1981). Children's knowledge of events: a causal analysis of story structure. In G. H. Bower (Ed.), *The psychology of learning and motivation* (Vol 15). New York: Academic Press.

Triandis, H. C., & Lambert, W. W. (1958). A restatement and test of Schlosberg's Theory of Emotion with two kinds of subjects from Greece. *Journal of Abnormal and Social Psychology, 56*, 321–328.

Vinacke, W. E. (1949). The judgment of facial expressions by three national-racial groups in Hawaii: I. Caucasian faces. *Journal of Personality, 17*(4), 407–429.

Weiner, B. (1982). The emotional consequences of causal attributions. In M. S. Clark & S. T. Fiske (Eds.), *Affect and cognition*. Hillsdale, NJ: Erlbaum.

Westermeyer, J. (1972). A comparison of amok and other homicides in Laos. *American Journal of Psychiatry, 6*, 703–709.

White, G. M. (1980). Conceptual universals in interpersonal language. *American Anthropologist, 82*, 759–781.

Winkelmayer, R., Exline, R. V., Gottheil, E., & Paredes, A. (1978). The relative accuracy of U.S., British, and Mexican raters in judging the emotional displays of schizophrenic and normal U.S. women. *Journal of Clinical Psychology, 34,* 600–608.

Yoshida, M., Kinase, R., Kurokawa, J., & Yashiro, S. (1970). Multidimensional scaling of emotion. *Japanese Psychological Research, 12,* 45–61.

Zarbatany, L., & Lamb, M. E. (1985). Social referencing as a function of information source: mothers vs. strangers. *Infant Behavior and Development, 8,* 25–33.

12   The socialization of children's emotions: emotional culture, competence, and exposure

Steven L. Gordon

In societies and times other than our own, children cringed in terror over damnation, boasted proudly about social status, enjoyed lewd and cruel humor, languished in profound grief, and generally displayed what we may regard now as an unchildlike repertoire of emotions. The vast range of emotions that children can potentially experience, express, and recognize has been documented in historical narratives and diaries (e.g., Ariès, 1962; deMause, 1974; Greven, 1977; Kett, 1977; Pollock, 1983; Schorch, 1979; Stearns & Stearns, 1986) and in anthropological ethnographies (e.g., Levy, 1984; Lutz, 1983; Rosaldo, 1984). The emotional life of children seems so diverse as to raise a question whether any universal developmental principles can possibly account for this variety. Although little direct evidence is available about how these children understood emotions, substantial information has been recorded about their social position. For example, we have cross-cultural and historical data on the circumstances under which children were accepted by adults as emotional equals and about children's exposure to events that would evoke various emotions.

This chapter will examine social structural variables that influence what children learn about emotions and how they learn it. Society determines children's understanding of emotions by inducting them into an emotional culture, defining the criteria of emotional competence, and regulating their exposure to emotional episodes. Although my effort is necessarily speculative, I will use the available evidence to argue that children's understanding of emotions reproduces the interactional adaptations required by their social environment. As the economy shifted from farming to entrepreneurial work, for example, American parents increasingly socialized children to inhibit angry displays to prepare them to compete later for business customers (Stearns & Stearns, 1986). I will identify crosscultural dimensions of social structure that determine socialization practices that, in turn, shape children's conceptualization of emotions. Research from *cognitive* constructionism, focusing on the development of reasoning about emotions, will

For their helpful comments on earlier drafts of this chapter, I thank Francesca Cancian, Arlie Hochschild, Dave Kemper, Anne Peplau, and Peggy Thoits.

319

be connected with *social* constructionism, which holds that interpretations of emotions emerge from the dynamics of social interaction.

Social and cognitive construction of emotions

It is remarkable that the study of children's cognitive construction of emotions has developed rather independently of social constructionist theories of emotions. Both theories argue that individuals "construct" or interpret the meanings of emotions, and that in turn these meanings shape emotional experience and expression. Social constructionists have studied variations in emotional experience and expression linked to social structure and child-rearing practices, but their findings have not been linked to the development of children's understanding of emotion.

To argue that emotions are socially constructed is to say that emotional experience and expression depend primarily upon the meanings assigned to emotions through social interpretation (Armon-Jones, 1985; Averill, 1982; Denzin, 1984; Gordon, 1981, 1985; Harré, 1986; Hochschild, 1979, 1983; Levy, 1984; Rosaldo, 1984; Shott, 1979; Thoits, 1985). From this view, emotions are responses to social definitions, particularly about the personal implications of a situation or relationship. Society pervades this process of constructing meaning. The facial expressions and bodily gestures that communicate emotions are largely, although not entirely, the product of social learning. When people discuss emotions, they necessarily employ the cultural vocabulary of emotion concepts. Emotions are regulated by social norms that prescribe the conventionally appropriate quality, intensity, duration, and target for emotions in particular situations and relationships.

In contrast to social constructionism's broad perspective, cognitive constructionism aims at the microanalytic level, where psychologists have focused on two basic connections between cognition and emotion in children. First, as cognitive functions mature, new emotions emerge and become available to the child as *experiences* (e.g., Kagan, 1984). A toddler may feel shame, for example, only after having developed a rudimentary self-concept, together with some understanding of others' reactions to one's deeds, of causal responsibility for behavior, and other mental prerequisites for shame. In a second line of research, psychologists have identified cognitive developmental transitions as preconditions for a child to be able to *think about* an emotion – for example, to distinguish between inner feeling and outer expression (e.g., Harris, 1985; Harris & Olthof, 1982; Harter, 1982; Michalson & Lewis, 1985; Saarni, 1979) or to know that an emotion will wane over time (Harris, Guz, Lipian, & Man-Shu, 1985). Although a few developmental studies have examined gender differences in emotional understanding, comparisons are rare across social classes, ethnic subcultures, or historical eras.

The social and cognitive versions of constructionism differ in research methods and theoretical assumptions, but these incompatibilities should not be exaggerated. The perspectives have been speaking past one another more than they have argued. Cognitive constructionism emphasizes *processes* of conceptualization and reasoning about emotions, as related to cognitive development. Social constructionism focuses on the *content* of emotional socialization, particularly as it reflects the requirements of social interaction. Whereas cognitive studies have focused on children and their immediate environment, social constructionists have usually analyzed adult emotions in the larger community, such as in occupations (Hochschild, 1983).

Every social constructionist theory must adopt some model of cognition, at least implicitly, but usually makes only minimal assumptions about any developmental timetable for the unfolding of emotional understanding. It is not surprising, therefore, that social constructionism has had little influence on the mainstream of research on children's construction of emotion. A closer integration of social and cognitive constructionism should be mutually beneficial. As I shall argue below, children's emotional behavior and knowledge change not only because of developmental progress but also in response to their entry into new social groups and roles.

The "social" in social constructionism sets it apart not from cognitive constructionism, but rather from *biological* constructionism. Social constructionism posits that social interaction integrates emotion components that otherwise would be unassociated – for example, a particular facial expression with a certain appraisal in a specific situation. Thus, connections among components are an *open system,* in which social interaction determines which components become associated. Therefore, the number of different emotions is potentially infinite, contingent only upon the possible permutations of social variables and cultural interpretations (see Gordon, 1981, for a discussion).

Research on cognitive construction of emotions has tended toward a *closed* system perspective, in which the social context accelerates or retards the inevitable emergence of universal cognitive abilities. The issue becomes one of when and how children develop abilities to conceal or to label "embarrassment," for example, not how and why such an emotion is socially available for children to conceptualize. That is, the social construction of the emotion, a version of which the individual child constructs, is not regarded as problematic.

This closed-system developmental approach is sometimes joined with a closed-system biological viewpoint, which assumes that connections among components of basic emotions are universal and biologically fixed by evolutionary constants (Izard, 1977; Ekman, 1982, 1984; Plutchik, 1980). For example, developmental research on how children learn to "dissociate" external expressive behavior from inner experience seems to assume that emotional components were naturally linked in the first place (e.g., Saarni, 1979). This assumption may be tenable for primary emotions such as fear and sadness (although not all social constructionists would concede this point). However, the assumption should be reformulated for secondary or complex emotions (e.g., jealousy, guilt, pride), which even closed system theorists admit emerge from socialization and vary across cultures. Although some components of certain emotions may be universal (e.g., a surprised face), components of other emotions are socially constructed (e.g., a jealous face). Similarly, the link between emotion components (the jealous face and a particular situation) is socially constructed, not a closed system. Research on cognitive dissociation of components could explore new possibilities by regarding any prior association of components as socially problematic, not as a fixed biological given.

A closer look at social constructionism may expand the range of emotions for which cognitive processes are being investigated. Focused on infancy and early childhood, developmental psychologists have concentrated on primary emotions, mainly fear, anger, sadness, surprise, disgust, and joy. With notable exceptions (e.g., Harter & Whitesell, this volume; Thompson, this volume), few studies have examined the socialization of emotions emerging in middle or late childhood – shame, guilt, pride, pity, hatred, jealousy, and grief, for example. We know little about how children come to understand these complex emotions, or *social sentiments,* which are the product of both social and cognitive construction (Cooley, 1902/1964; Gordon, 1981; Turner, 1970). The social bases of cognitive construction of emotions can be examined through three concepts I will introduce here: emotional culture, emotional competence, and differential exposure to emotions.

Emotional culture

The concepts that children form about emotion are of course not entirely their own creation, but usually represent widespread cultural ideas. *Emotional culture* is a group's set of beliefs, vocabulary, regulative norms, and other ideational resources pertaining to emotion (Gordon, in press). Children may be exposed to beliefs, vocabulary, and norms about an emotion as often as they are to actual episodes of the emotion.

The vocabulary and norms in emotional culture record a society's history of experiences and interpretations regarding an emotion. Emotion norms specify ranges of permissible expression and feeling for a situation or relationship (Gordon, 1981; Hochschild, 1983). When controls over anger became more stringent in the eighteenth century, for example, the new word "tantrum" came into common usage, referring first to adult loss of temper and later to childish outbursts (Stearns & Stearns, 1986, p. 29). A vocabulary of emotion includes not only terms and meanings, but also symbolic metaphors. English language metaphors for anger include images of heat and internal pressure, for example (Lakoff & Kovecses, 1987). People make inferences on the basis of these metaphors, such as to decide whether someone is angry.

Emotional culture includes *ethnopsychology,* a group's folk beliefs about emotions in human nature and about the development of the child's abilities to feel and behave emotionally like an adult (Lutz, 1983). Ethnopsychology provides the interpretive principles for adults to attribute meaning to children's emotional development and to organize children's emotional socialization (Briggs, 1970; H. Geertz, 1959; Harkness & Super, 1985; Heelas & Lock, 1981; Levy, 1984; Lutz, 1985; Lutz & White, 1986; Rosaldo, 1984).

Emotional culture, I suggest, is learned by children as a cumulation of knowledge, norms, metaphors, and ethnopsychology pertaining to an emotion. These elements become cognitively organized around the vocabulary term for an emotion. Emotions may be culturally encoded and mentally represented as prototypes, emotion categories defined by their typical features: typical antecedents, responses, and self-control procedures (Fehr & Russell, 1984; Schwartz & Shaver, 1987; Shaver, Schwartz, Kirson, & O'Connor, 1987). People use prototypes to distinguish among emotions and to understand emotion events. In sum, what children construct out of social interaction is a molar or complex unit of prototypical components for each emotion identified by the culture.

It must be emphasized that emotional culture does not always describe actual experience and behavior accurately. Parents' behavior toward their children often differs from the advice given in a period's childrearing manuals (Mechling, 1975). English Victorians held a belief in childhood innocence, but nonetheless imposed severe discipline and exploited the labor of many children (Coveney, 1957). For this reason I treat emotional culture as a category distinct from social interaction.

Emotional competence

Acquisition of emotional culture is essential for children to become effective and valued participants in social relationships – to be *emotionally competent*. Children form concepts of emotions not mainly out of theoretical curiosity, but as part of everyday interaction. Their understanding of emotions emerges as they adapt to socially patterned demands placed upon them. Caregivers aim at teaching emotional competence through institutionalized socialization to prepare children to function as members of society (Inkeles, 1966, 1968). Although socialization often involves intentional reinforcement, modeling, and explicit training of emotion, children are more often socialized indirectly by learning emotional behaviors, norms, and symbols as an unintended consequence of interaction (Gordon, 1981; Inkeles, 1968; Lewis & Saarni, 1985a). By learning to understand caregivers' use of verbal and nonverbal symbols of emotion, children become more effective in obtaining rewards, gaining interpersonal advantage, defending self-esteem, and other benefits of emotional competence.

Children infer an emotion's meaning by conceptualizing its place in recurrent social interactions, relying on emotional culture for vocabulary, norms, and other explanatory tools. Having understood the cultural meaning of an emotion, children become able to act *toward* it – magnifying, suppressing, or simulating it in themselves, and evoking or avoiding it in other people. Like social competence (Smith, 1966; Waters & Sroufe, 1983), emotional competence requires abilities, knowledge, and behavioral skills. Emotional competence entails the demonstration of abilities to: (1) express and interpret emotional gestures as nonverbal messages about a social situation or relationship (Saarni, 1982); (2) control overt expression of impulsive but socially disapproved feelings; (3) feel and express socially appropriate emotions spontaneously; (4) recognize the vocabulary of terms linking emotions symbolically to cultural meanings; (5) cope with distressful emotions, for example, by knowing how to distract oneself from feeling sadness over separation from loved ones (Harris & Lipian, this volume). This ability to manage distressful emotions permits the child to maintain social poise and direct attention to the tasks at hand.

The concept of emotional competence is a theoretical bridge between social and cognitive constructionism. As children grow older, they are more likely to view their feelings from the perspectives of others, to understand multiple emotions, and to regard themselves as able to change or hide their emotions (Carroll & Steward, 1984; Harris & Olthof, 1982; Harter, 1982; Saarni, 1979). Attainment of these abilities depends upon both cognitive development and transitions in social experience, as argued below.

Differential exposure to emotions

Being exposed to an emotion – having the opportunity to experience or observe an emotion or to be told about it – seems to be an obvious precondition for conceptualizing the emotion. Exposure to the emotions occurs through the opportunities and demands imposed by the structural patterning of interaction (for a related concept of a "developmental niche," see Harkness & Super, 1983, 1985; Whiting & Whiting, 1978). For example, researchers have traced the effects on children of being exposed to anger and sadness by their parents' divorce (Hetherington, Cox, & Cox, 1982) and parental fighting (Cummings, Zahn-Waxler, & Radke-Yarrow, 1981, 1984). On a larger structural scale, exposure occurs through widespread social trends (an increase in divorce, for example) and historical events (e.g., wars, natural disasters) that affect birth cohorts differently. Depending on their social position (cohort, social class, or gender, for example), children receive *differential* exposure to emotions through caregivers' behavior, environmental events, or the child's autonomous activity. Through differential exposure, a particular set of emotions is selected, elaborated, and interpreted for children from the potential range of human emotional experience (H. Geertz, 1959).

Socialization agents attempt to regulate children's exposure to events and persons – such as danger, death, sexuality, or strangers – because of concern about the emotions that might be elicited. Thus, exposure depends upon a society's or subgroup's emotional culture and its requirements for emotional competence. An intensive ethnography of three mothers' socialization of their daughters in a working-class South Baltimore neighborhood found that teaching self-defensive retaliation and toughening the children were major child-rearing goals (Miller & Sperry, 1987). The mothers told narratives of anger and aggression in their daughters' presence and intentionally teased them to elicit retaliation and to suppress their hurt feelings. Maternal beliefs about emotional competence were realized through the children's exposure to anger and aggression.

Patterns of exposure shift over history. In colonial America, for example, children participated in adult work and frequently moved among households, being "exposed to the emotional concerns of their elders" (J. Demos, 1986, p.100). By the mid-nineteenth century, however, middle-class American caregivers made "systematic attempts to purify the environments of the young, to withdraw them from debasing community temptations, and to immerse them in networks of good influence" (Finkelstein, 1985, p. 117). Children were placed under the protection of full-time mothers and female teachers because women were regarded as inherently gentle, morally superior, and models of self-control. In modern times, controversy arises over children's exposure to sexual desire, violent anger, horror, or grief through television and other media, because these emotions are believed to be "too intense" or otherwise inappropriate for children (Dorr, 1985).

Exposure to an emotion allows a child to experience, observe, or indirectly learn its components (Gordon, 1981; Lewis & Saarni, 1985a). To measure exposure, we may ask: (1) How often does the *stimulus situation* of an emotion occur in the child's presence? Do caregivers direct the child's attention to the situation? (2) Are facial, gestural, and vocal *expressions* of the emotion visible to the child? Are these expressions spontaneous, masked, or exaggerated? From infancy, emotion is guided, for example, by observing others' emotional response in an unfamiliar situation (Klinnert, Campos, Sorce, Emde, & Svejda, 1983). (3) Is the child's attention called to the experience of the emotion's *phys-*

iological state or distracted from it? The interpretation learned for an emotional experience may determine whether it is enjoyable or aversive – anger may be interpreted as feeling either "sweet" or "insufferable," for example (Stearns & Stearns, 1986, p. 42). (4) Which *norms and beliefs* about the emotion are taught to the child, and which are concealed? (5) How elaborate or sparse are the *vocabulary terms* learned for the emotion?

The concept of exposure encompasses more specific socialization processes: reinforcement, modeling, identification, and direct teaching (Lewis & Saarni, 1985a; see also Saarni, this volume). The concept also includes the three main models of how children develop emotional knowledge: observing others' behavior, self-observation, and verbal explanations by others (Harris & Olthof, 1982). This simplifying assumption, for purposes of my argument, shifts our focus away from the details of cognitive and learning processes instead to the social structuring of exposure to emotion. I will describe three structural ways in which emotional exposure can vary, in sequence, constraint, and diversity.

Dimensions of exposure

Historical and cross-cultural accounts by adults reveal a vast spectrum of differences in children's exposure to emotions and in their society's definition of emotional competence. However, except for modern developmental studies, we have few direct reports from children about their understanding of emotion. Many indirect descriptions exist. For example, Puritan diaries and sermons "were filled with references to . . . childhood responses to the terrors of separation, mortality, and damnation" (Stannard, 1977, p. 69). Of all the facets of emotional socialization across cultures and history, we have the most information about children's social relationships and about the cultural content of emotional socialization.

Knowing something about children's social position and about what they were supposed to learn from their emotional culture, we could make inferences about their understanding of emotion. We would have to assume that specific conceptual outcomes result universally from specific dimensions of exposure to emotions. Our next problem is to identify these dimensions of exposure, which must be sufficiently abstract to apply across divergent social contexts and socialization modes.

To identify relevant variables in emotion socialization, we may turn to more established areas of socialization research. Comparative studies suggest that the cultural content to which a child is exposed from multiple socialization agents can vary from strong consistency to confusing contradiction (Benedict, 1938; Inkeles, 1968; Stonequist, 1937). General socialization theory suggests that the degree of consistency in exposure affects the range of beliefs developed by the child and the strength with which those beliefs are held. I will leave to cognitive psychology the question of whether in fact people worldwide respond similarly to discrepant information, and similarly to consistent information. Yet the consistency dimension can be extrapolated to emotion socialization. For example, do children conceptualize anger differently if their parents tolerate angry outbursts but schoolteachers punish anger than if all socialization agents are consistent in responding to anger?

Although early cognitive developmental research was preoccupied with the conceptualization of the physical properties of objects, the development of emotional understanding parallels the development of *moral* judgment more closely. Piaget (1932) set forth a social constructionist model that can be generalized usefully to emotional understanding. Exposure within an authoritarian parental context leads young children to conceive of rules as unalterable, Piaget argued. When later exposed to rules during reciprocal, egalitarian relations with peers, older children realize that many rules are conventional and alterable. Intentions and feelings become more salient, partly because of their significance in negotiation and cooperation in peer relationships.

Contrary to Piaget, children can distinguish between rules about morality and justice and social conventions requiring behavioral uniformity prior to peer interaction as early as age 3 (Turiel, 1983; Smetana, 1984). Piaget's valuable insight, however, was that children's concepts reflect the social context of exposure (authoritarian or egalitarian), and also reflect the concept's function in group life (a way to avoid punishment or to organize a game, for example). Development of thinking about emotions resembles moral development and socialization in other ways as well. Emotions are evoked by rule-bound appraisals or evaluative judgments of social situations (Averill, 1982; Lazarus, Kanner, & Folkman, 1980; Solomon, 1977). Learning a rule may be a prerequisite for feeling an emotion, at least for moral emotions of shame, guilt, or embarrassment, which rest upon norms of responsibility, maintenance of self-esteem and poise, and so forth. Furthermore, rules about socially appropriate emotion represent a morality of self-control, conveyed through socialization into an emotional culture (Gordon, 1981; Hochschild, 1983; Thoits, 1985). Hence moral development seems a promising starting point for identifying dimensions of exposure to emotions.

Moral development and socialization research finds the sequence, constraint, and diversity of exposure to social interaction to be highly significant (e.g., Baumrind, 1971; Hoffman, 1970; Kohlberg, 1969; Piaget, 1932). For example, if a child's moral reasoning is advanced by contact with individuals who are at higher levels of moral reasoning (Kohlberg, 1969; Turiel, 1966), perhaps emotional understanding may be advanced by exposure to older peers' or adults' emotional expression or self-regulation. I propose that variation in the sequence, constraint, and diversity of exposure to an emotion strongly influence children's cognitive construction of the emotion. These dimensions of exposure are inter-related complexly; therefore, I shall define the dimensions briefly before examining each in detail.

Sequence

Children will be exposed to the various emotions, their components, vocabulary, and norms in many different sequences, depending on the organization of their social group. Children in one society may be told about an emotion long before they observe or experience it, although elsewhere the direct experience of the emotion usually precedes the verbal labeling, for example. A group's typical sequence of exposure should cause children to conceptualize different emotions in a particular order (happiness before anger, for example), and to know more about some emotional components than about others (such as expression more than feeling). It may also be hypothesized that early exposures influence children's understanding differently than later exposures, which must be conceptualized in relation to what has already been learned.

Sequence of exposure reflects the adaptations required of a child as he or she moves through a sequence of groups, such as from family to peers, then to school, etc. Each group reveals a different emotional life, inspiring new conceptualizations of emotion by the child. In fact, what may appear to be cognitive developmental timetables in emotional understanding may be children's adaptations to a sequence of group memberships (Maccoby, 1984). The sequence of exposure depends partly on emotional culture, which defines some emotions as more appropriate than others for exposure to children at different ages. When discussed in detail below, some structural determinants of sequence of exposure will be discussed in relation to emotional culture and emotional competence.

Constraint

Children's exposure to emotions may be constrained overtly by discipline or subtly by limiting their emotional interactions. Patterns of emotional constraint result from societal requirements for emotion competence, as translated into socialization beliefs and practices. Japanese mothers, for example, try to avoid expressing anger in their children's presence, in the expectation that this will lead to the inhibition of anger in their children (Lebra, 1983; Miyake, Campos, Kagan, & Bradshaw, 1986). Caregivers' attempted concealment or suppression of an emotion leads children to think of the emotion as something to be stifled or hidden.

Child-rearing practices also can intentionally expose children to a valued emotion, constraining them to become aware of, feel, and adapt to the emotion.

Among the Ifaluk islanders of the Pacific, parents encourage the emergence of *metagu,* roughly translated as "social fear and anxiety" (Lutz, 1983). Parents frequently and approvingly label children's reactions as *metagu* in the presence of strangers, large groups, and other appropriate situations. Through consistent and reinforcing exposure, an emotion becomes an approved and often spontaneous reaction. It also serves as a culturally accepted explanation for a wide range of behaviors congruent with social values and needs.

The origin of exposure constraints can be traced upward to social structural requirements. In industrializing nations, for example, the changing function of the family from a workplace to a refuge from work required stronger standards of anger control as an obligation among family members (Stearns & Stearns, 1986). Children were exposed to anger less frequently than in earlier times, but exposures were now assigned more negative significance by parent and child alike. In sum, socialization agents establish the possibilities for children's understanding of emotions, setting constraints on exposure that may become part of the emotion concept itself.

Diversity

Children's exposure to emotion can vary from consistent to diverse content, as discussed above. The social distribution of caregiving can be a major source of diversity. Children's emotional knowledge is socialized by multiple caregivers: parents, siblings, extended family, peers, nonfamily adults, and others, who provide diverse socialization. Developmental psychology has emphasized only the mother as the socialization agent for emotions (Campos, Barrett, Lamb, Goldsmith, & Stenberg, 1983; Field & Fogel, 1982; Lewis & Michalson, 1983; Lewis & Saarni, 1985b; Plutchik & Kellerman, 1980; Scherer & Ekman, 1984; Zahn-Waxler, Cummings, & Cooperman, 1984). This overemphasis on a single caregiver overlooked specialization and contradiction among socialization agents. We need to ask questions such as whether fathers are especially influential in the socialization of anger, and whether peers are the key agent in knowledge about sexual feelings. From such findings we could then ask how a child's emotional understanding is affected by contradictory behavioral demands or socialization messages from different agents. On a sociocultural scale, diversity of exposure occurs through social class mobility, regional migration, or national immigration, when children move between groups with contrasting emotional cultures and standards of emotional competence.

A comparative analysis of children's exposure to emotions should begin with children's statuses and roles in social institutions, especially in the family, economy, education, and religion. These universal institutions structure children's lives and the distribution of emotions around them, representing a large-scale "ecology of human development" (Bronfenbrenner, 1979). Children's exposure to emotions depends on such measureable factors as composition of the household, the age at which children begin work, the division of society into age grades, and other variables reviewed below. The set of variables considered is suggestive, not exhaustive. My presentation is organized to focus on sequence, constraint, and diversity, in that order, although each structural variable usually has some effect on all three dimensions of exposure.

Age-grading

All societies divide the life cycle into age grades, defining culturally meaningful stages such as infancy, adolescence, and adulthood, each with distinctive rights and obligations (Benedict, 1938; Eisenstadt, 1956; Keniston, 1971). Age-grading is explained and justified in a society's emotional culture, particularly in ethnopsychological ideas about stages of emotional development. Emotional culture specifies which emotions caregivers take for granted as natural to children and which emotions become the focus of socialization at each age (Harkness & Kilbride, 1983).

The organization of society into age grades segregates children's interactions according to age. The less the age-grading, the more that children are exposed to adult emotional culture. Preindustrial societies generally do not recognize age grades other than infancy and general adulthood. Meyer Fortes (1970, p. 18) noted that in traditional African societies, "the social sphere of adult and child is unitary and undivided. . . . Nothing in the universe of adult behavior is hidden from children or barred to them." In medieval Europe, children and adults expressed and observed the same emotional reactions, such as grief, sexual desire, and lewd or cruel jokes (Ariès, 1962; but see Pollock, 1983). A shared emotional culture facilitates interaction between age groups. Early American children and adults alike could indulge their temper freely when playing games together. By Victorian times, adults sought stronger restraints on anger, reporting discomfort over children's angry outbursts during play, and even seeking to avoid sharing games with children (Stearns & Stearns, 1986). It may be hypothesized that lesser age-grading accelerates the sequence of conceptualizing emotions, letting children become aware of the gamut of adult emotions.

Modern societies recognize more age grades, such as preschool, school-age, and adolescent stages. Age-grading restricts the child's opportunities to observe and experience particular emotions. Age-grading schedules the age sequence in which children are exposed to different emotions. Where their interaction opportunities are sharply demarcated by age, children's emotional socialization is usually discontinuous across age periods. As children grow up, new knowledge about emotions often contradicts the knowledge acquired at a younger age. For example, primary-group norms of emotional intimacy, trust, and support during early childhood can be useless or even harmful when the older child enters more formal, impersonal institutions such as school, workplace, or public settings (Dreeben, 1968). Thus, emotional competence cannot be carried over as children grow up, but must be demonstrated anew at each age grade. Modern societies have few rites of passage – ritualized transitions between age grades to clarify new expectations for emotions. Discontinuous and vague socialization intensifies children's uncertainty about how to achieve emotional competence (Harkness & Super, 1985).

Complex structural and economic forces determine age-grading, but a provocative speculation about one factor is illustrative. The invention of the printing press helped distinguish children from adults by defining literacy as a major criterion of adulthood (Postman, 1982). From books, adults were exposed to new, different emotional vocabulary and norms than were children. The highly literate classes gradually defined emotional competence as being quiet, self-controlled, and immobile – qualities necessary for reading. In our century, however, the spread of television reduced the utility of these traits, while exposing children and adults to similar emotional episodes, styles, vocabulary, and other emotional culture.

Age-grading is manifested in socialization during emotional exemptive stages and anticipatory socialization into emotions.

Emotional exemptive stages

Most societies designate emotional exemptive stages – periods during which children are allowed to express emotions more freely than will be permitted later. The moratorium is confined to a specified age period and may not apply in certain situations, such as formal ceremonies involving high-status adults. It may apply only to particular emotions within a certain range of expressive intensity, such as being playful but not "wild." The exemptive stage provides an opportunity for the child to conceptualize emotions by associating spontaneous expression and feeling with a social situation and label.

The exemptive period may be justified by beliefs that children of that age are unable to control their emotions or are not ready to understand social norms. Probably all cultures exempt infants and very young children from certain expectations about emotional control (although research is needed to identify the earliest cultural socialization efforts). Deficient in emotional competence, children may be seen as being "oblivious, unaware, deaf, or unheeding to social circumstances – particularly to what is happening and who is present" (Myers, 1979). Children may even be viewed as not being fully human or civilized during the exemptive period. Young children in Java, for example, were thought of as "not yet Javanese'' – not yet a full member of the society because of incomplete socialization into their culture's complex expressive norms and styles (Geertz, 1959).

Exemptive stages vary across cultures. In the U.S. and Western Europe, exemption from emotional control has been accompanied, paradoxically, by an exemption or protection from certain emotional knowledge. Protection from premature knowledge about devalued emotions was exemplified by nineteenth century child-rearing literature's concern about "precocity" – feeling and knowing too much too soon (Finkelstein, 1985). Children's innocence was protected by isolating them from persons outside the family household. Both freedom and protection derive from the increasingly favored status accorded to children, reflecting stronger parental attachments as children's survival chances improved (Ariès, 1962) and more benign religious beliefs about children's nature (Greven, 1977). An enhanced sentimental value for children has also been attributed to a decline in their purely economic, utilitarian functions in turn-of-the century America (Zelizer, 1985).

Free expression accelerates knowledge of gestural and feeling components of an emotion; such awareness is retarded by concealment of the emotion, although concealment may familiarize children with the normative component. The concealment of emotions is discussed further below under Constraint.

Anticipatory socialization of valued emotions

Children are exposed early and often to emotions that are culturally valued as interactional techniques and as desired personality traits. This *anticipatory socialization* occurs even before children are old enough to enter situations and roles in which the emotion will be normally expected. These emotions may hold greater functional significance to the society or reflect its basic values. Illustrations are the Japanese emotion of *amae* – feeling mutually dependent on another person (Doi, 1973) – and the Eskimo emotion of *naklik* – wanting to care for and protect a person who appears pathetic (Briggs, 1970). Collective pride and shame are promoted for children in Soviet nurseries and schools, who are socialized to work cooperatively and accept collective responsibility (Bronfenbrenner, 1970).

Caregivers may intentionally arouse valued emotions in children by creating realistic situations to elicit the emotions. For example, the Chewong of Malaysia value fear and shyness and try to evoke those emotions in children frequently. Adults call out explicit rules governing appropriate expression, and comment approvingly when fear and shyness are displayed (Howell, 1981). In literate societies, the desired emotions may be elicited by requiring or encouraging children to read juvenile fiction, primers, catechisms, advice books, religious tracts, and other prescriptive literature. This literature also documents shifts in the particular emotions of greatest cultural concern. In early nineteenth-century America, children's fiction shifted away from the Puritan focus on the pain and fear of sin to the pain and fear of earthly dangers caused by disobedience to parents (Francis, 1985).

Children often cooperate eagerly in the anticipatory socialization of emotion. When an emotion has been idealized in fantasy and play, and its display brings pleasure and esteem, children want to understand and experience it. For example, many U.S. children seem to anticipate and feel passionate love as early as kindergarten age (Broderick, 1966; Easton, Hatfield, & Synodinos, 1984). They conceive of it similarly to adults, evaluate it as desirable, and often report having already been in love with specific boyfriends and girlfriends. Of course age-grading may reserve certain valued emotions for adults (e.g., sexual desire and moral indignation, in our society). Through anticipatory socialization, however, children develop an adult understanding of most valued emotions earlier than most other emotions.

Sequence of exposure and emotion concepts

Early and frequent exposure to an emotion should foster an early conceptualization of it. Most U.S. children probably observe and feel positive emotions – happiness, joy, pleasure, and glee – more than negative emotions such as anger or sadness. For example, U.S. children appear to form a concept of "happiness" and recognize it facially and in story characters earlier than sadness, anger, or fear (Borke, 1971, 1973; Demos, 1974; Feshbach & Roe, 1968; Field & Walden, 1982; Izard, 1971). U.S. children pose positive expressions more accurately and intensely than negative expressions (Buck, 1975; Odom & Lemond, 1972). Children aged 18–23 months and 24–29 months knew the meaning of *happy* earlier than *sad, afraid,* or *angry* (Ridgeway, Waters, & Kuczaj, 1985). In conversations of 28-month-olds, the most commonly used emotion words were *love* and *like* (although next most frequent are *mad, scared, happy,* and *sad;* Bretherton & Beeghly, 1982). This primacy in understanding happiness may reflect the relatively pleasant child-raising conditions of most U.S. children. As Charles Cooley (1902/1964, p. 102) noted, "The faces that children see are mostly full of the expression of love and truth. Nothing like it occurs in later life, even to the most fortunate."

Children in less favored settings should conceptualize negative emotions more readily. Children in earlier times may have understood more about anger and fear than happiness because they often were "battered children" by today's standards (Stone, 1979; but see Pollock, 1983). Contemporary middle-class Chinese preschoolers identify fearful and sad situations more accurately than U.S. preschoolers, perhaps reflecting Chinese emphasis on anxious parenting and punishment through shame (Borke, 1973). Abused children are less accurate than nonabused children in identifying facial expressions of happiness, possibly because they engage in fewer happy interactions with their parents (Camras, 1985). We need more information about conceptual sequence among children from a range of contrasting social environments.

Normative constraints on exposure

Socialization agents impose constraints upon children's exposure to emotions. Caregivers restrict exposure to instill expressive control. For emotions that are culturally devalued, socialization agents may even try to prevent the child from acquiring the emotion in his or her expressive repertoire. Limited exposure also may be an incidental result of the child's social position, such as an only child who is not exposed to sibling jealousy. Constraint is manifested in *display norms* governing overt expression in a situation or relationship (Ekman, 1984), and in *feeling norms* defining the appropriate mental and physiological reaction (Hochschild, 1979, 1983). The older the child, the more norms she or he can name (Saarni, 1979). Patterns of constraint often become part of the child's concept of the emotion, as I shall argue below.

Group effects on emotion norms

Emotion norms of varying levels of generality are learned by children in different group contexts. Intimate interaction with family members and close peers exposes the child to *primary-group norms*. The rules often are idiosyncratic to the small group and apply mainly or exclusively to specific individuals (e.g., laugh at Daddy's jokes). As children's social worlds expand beyond the primary group, they become aware of more widely-accepted *societal norms* that apply equally to all, such as to not feel happy over anyone's death. From the broader social context children also acquire *status norms* that govern expression and feeling between persons in particular social positions, such as a rule to display interest and respect for teachers.

Each group exercises a different form of constraint, and these forms occur in varying sequences, depending on the child's social position. Most middle-class U.S. children, for example, may not have to adjust their emotions according to status differences until they enter the more formal, impersonal relations of school. Thus, primary-group norms may retain a primacy or salience because of early learning. Each type of norm potentially contradicts the other types. Nonfamily caregivers and teachers try to revise the expressive norms that children bring from home, for example. Family and peers give their own slant to societal and status norms through selective emphasis; to illustrate, a peer group may discount the importance of family and school norms about controlling excitement. Or a boys' group may emphasize norms prescribing suppression of signs of fear. Socialization agents can exploit the specialized effects of different social environments. The Javanese think of children's residence with an extended family as a technique for teaching obedience and good manners in a household that is less permissive than the nuclear family (Geertz, 1959). Becoming sensitized to status distinctions through the new demands of interaction, children learn to display respectful "shame-shyness," a fundamental value in Javanese emotional culture.

Valued and devalued emotions

Culturally valued emotions are appropriate responses to a broad range of situations and hence are readily available for observation. Socialization agents will aim to ensure that children develop an understanding of moral, religious, patriotic, and other valued emotions that symbolize major social institutions. Caregivers restrict children's exposure to certain other emotions by preventing circumstances that might evoke those feelings, reinterpreting the proscribed emotion with a more acceptable label, and controlling children's access to alternative sources of knowledge about the emotion. Distraction, for example, deflects a child's attention away from inappropriate emotions toward more acceptable emotions. Emotional equanimity is valued in Javanese society where, through distraction of the child's attention, "adults try to structure the child's affairs so as to minimize the emergence of impulses disruptive of social life" (H. Geertz, 1959, p. 259).

Socialization agents may permit exposure to a problematic emotion under circumstances believed to promote control over it. They may denigrate an emotion episode. Victorian parents sought to stimulate anger and then teach children to channel it constructively (Stearns & Stearns, 1986). Beginning in the 1940s, however, parents taught children to avoid or dissipate anger, advising them that anger does not achieve desired outcomes and is an unpleasant, disagreeable feeling. No longer was there any advantage in eliciting children's anger; thus exposure was to be minimized and denigrated.

Constraints on exposure are mediated by the emotional culture. A belief in childhood determination of adult character intensifies concern about permissive and restrictive exposure. Many nineteenth-century U.S. parents believed in a child's *tabula rasa,* leading them to avoid displaying anger so as to avoid "implanting evil" (anger) in the innocent child's character (Stearns & Stearns, 1986, p. 92). Caregivers must weigh long-term socialization priorities for teaching emotional competence against the immediate strains of child-rearing. In order to inculcate religious dread and piety, many American Colonial parents read books to their children contrasting the happy deaths of pious children against the frightful deaths of irreligious children (Newson & Newson, 1976). Children were allowed to witness the deaths of their siblings and peers. Exposure to grief, suffering, terror, and horror was a deliberate means of character-building, even though parents often reported feeling distressed over this harsh duty (Pollock, 1983). Other Colonial children's exposure to emotions was more sheltered and gentle, in families whose religions held less stringent views about children, the body, the will, and the self (Greven, 1977).

Ideas about emotional competence are important considerations for socialization agents. Parents employed in bureaucracies encourage emotional expressiveness and sensitivity and well-controlled temper (Miller & Swanson, 1958; Stearns & Stearns, 1986). They aim to make their children emotionally competent for the kind of social interaction known by the parents in their own work lives (Kohn, 1969). In traditional societies, display and feeling norms are defined by elites, whose ways of expression and feeling filter down the stratification hierarchy (Stearns & Stearns, 1986). Higher status brings a privilege of greater leeway from norms, allowing the development of new emotional patterns and styles that diffuse to less powerful groups. In modern societies, however, television and films also may shape emotional norms by presenting the "lowest common denominator" of emotional expressions and situations that the mass public can comprehend and accept. Partly because of mass media influences, social classes are converging toward shared expressive norms, and in child-rearing beliefs and practices generally (Bronfenbrenner, 1958).

Effects of constraint upon emotion concepts

Constraint on exposure may influence children's emotional understanding through at least three dimensions: (1) the merger of secondary moral emotions with the original emotion, (2) effects of concealment upon integration of emotion components, and (3) generalization of socialization processes or modes to the emotion itself.

The shame, guilt, embarrassment, or fear that often surround socialization to control other emotions may become part of children's concepts for the latter emotions. Self-conscious moral reactions, based upon negative social responses to emotional display, become merged with the initial emotion and are experienced together in the future. For example, expressions used to mask an inappropriate facial display may be learned as a component of the emotion. Devalued emotions may be experienced mainly as "affect blends," combining emotions (Zahn-Waxler, Cummings, & Cooperman, 1984). For socially *approved* emotions, I would expect that feelings of pride or happiness might become part of their meaning and experience when those approved emotions are effectively displayed.

Children will observe culturally valued emotions expressed spontaneously and are more likely to conceive of those emotions as units of correlated elements. But the more concealed an emotion, the less children will associate its components as a unit. Expression, feeling, and situation do not become organized around the emotion label. Furthermore, children find it difficult to even acquire the vocabulary for these culturally invisible emotions. For example, parents rarely discuss their own guilt feelings with their children, who therefore cannot detect consistency among parental expressions, social situation, and reported feelings of guilt (Hoffman, 1979). Emotions may require social support and validation to be experienced as real or legitimate (Thoits, 1985).

If children are openly exposed to an emotion so that they may learn to control it, they must learn to distinguish among its components. Children can follow display rules most effectively if they have learned to dissociate or conceptually isolate expression, feeling, and situation (Saarni, 1979, 1985). This cognitive differentiation may result partly from caregivers' communication of sanctions. For example, a child who is admonished, "Don't laugh at strangers even if they look funny," learns to discriminate among feeling, expression, and situation. Caregivers' communications about an emotion may typically refer to *connections* among its components – for example, "You don't look very happy" – rather than to the whole emotion. In the ethnography, discussed above, of three mothers' socialization of their daughters, the mothers exposed them primarily to the instigating events and the instrumental retaliation in anger and aggression (Miller & Sperry, 1987). Consequently, those were the most salient components in the daughters' concepts of anger and aggression, instead of emotion labels, feelings, or a need to express feelings, because these latter components were rarely exposed to the children.

The more that a child focuses on managing one component, the more salient it becomes in the child's concept of the whole emotion. Colonial American parents sought to control the *expression* of anger, but early nineteenth-century parents aimed their constraint at the child's angry *feelings* (Stearns & Stearns, 1986). A shift in the child's understanding of anger appears in parental reports of socialization and anger episodes during the historical transition. An emphasis on managing feeling more than expressions may account for the modern Western conception of emotions as internal states of individuals, instead of as social relationships and events (Lutz, 1985).

Integrative socialization patterns and emotion concepts

If children are to learn to regulate their emotions according to social norms, they must learn the pattern or association among each emotion's components. If, for example, a child is to mask a particular emotional expression by changing his or her thoughts, the child must understand that specific expressions, thoughts, a situation, and a rule belong together. This linkage of components is promoted, I suggest, through integrative socialization patterns that portray the set of components constituting an emotion, and that become part of the emotion concept itself.

Integrative patterns provide imagery and associations from which children can infer an emotion's constituent elements. Two integrative patterns to which I will call attention here are personal emotional models and emotional social types. *Personal emotional models* are individuals who frequently evoke an emotion from the child or express it for him or her. The younger the child, the more concretely personal are the child's emotional models. Discussing the child in family or friendship group, Charles Cooley (1902/1964, p. 118) suggested, "To think of love, gratitude, pity, grief, honor, courage, justice, and the like, it is necessary to think of people by whom or toward whom these sentiments may be entertained." Young children's emotion concepts are not abstractions, but are defined by their personal source or target. As a child's exposure to an emotion broadens to encompass many different individuals, personal models become merged with more general categories of people and situations. From early life, the personal models for an emotion function to unify feeling, expression, and situation around a concrete example for the child.

Emotional social types such as "scaredy-cat" or "bully" mark the boundaries of appropriate emotion by symbolizing deviant forms of expression or feeling. Social types tend to be negative labels that children seek to avoid. A social type personifies a violation of an emotion norm, naming excesses of intensity ("hothead"), inappropriate situation ("party-pooper"), or gender role ("bitch," "wimp"). These types serve as powerful sanctions to correct children's expression or feeling (for use of "crybaby," see Miller & Sperry, 1987). Social types unify emotional components by indicating which feelings, displays, and situations belong together. Also, it becomes difficult to think about a norm ("boys don't show fear") apart from the image of a type of person who violates the norm (a "scaredy-cat").

Diversity of exposure to emotions

Children's interactions may expose them to diverse vocabulary, norms, and expressive styles for emotions. Some communities and households provide children with more opportunities for interaction with diverse persons and novel ideas than do other child-raising environments. Children's neighborhood and school contacts with ethnic groups, for example, may make them aware of very different emotional subcultures. As hypothesized above, children think about emotions differently if their socialization is contradictory or diverse than if consistent. I shall focus on four structural sources of diverse socialization: social distribution of caregiving, consistency across socialization agents, shifts in group participation, and exposure to strangers and subcultures.

Social distribution of caregiving

Caregivers who are heterogeneous in gender, age, and ethnicity expose children to more varied emotion norms, vocabulary, and expressive styles. A mother and father may reinforce and label emotions differently; for example, fathers may be more tolerant of anger in children, especially in sons (Stearns & Stearns, 1986). Therefore, in situations where such disparity would exist, consistent socialization is enhanced by one parent's absence or noninvolvement in caregiving. In Japan, fathers typically work away from home; mother and child form a coalition to resist the father's authoritarian discipline (Miyake, Campos, Kagan, & Bradshaw, 1986).

The gender of siblings also may be an important exposure variable. Children with cross-sex siblings tend to acquire traits associated with the other sex (Brim, 1958); therefore, children's emotional understanding may incorporate the other gender's emotion norms and vocabulary. Cross-cultural research suggests that having many siblings reduces children's face-to-face contacts with adults, but increases exposure to both nurturant and aggressive emotions from siblings (Whiting & Whiting, 1978). Contemporary trends toward increasing divorce and declining family size call our attention to variation in emotional exposure due to household composition.

Adults can conceal their own emotions if their interaction settings can be segregated by age, but emotional privacy has been rare historically. In medieval Europe, the typical household had perhaps two dozen members, who did not live in the house so much as camp in it (Rybczynski, 1986). The traditional European peasant household exposed children to episodes of affection, anger, and violence, with all indoor activities in one room (Shorter, 1975). Unlike today's smaller, isolated family, early American children were exposed to the gamut of emotions in household interaction (Boocock, 1976; Modell & Hareven, 1973). In a small household, children mingled with lodgers, apprentices, and servants. Their father and adult siblings also usually lived and worked at home. To be interactionally competent, children developed a broad and flexible emotional repertoire. As family life changed, however, middle- and upper-class families excluded nonfamily cohabitants. Children were restricted to home nurseries, limiting their opportunities to observe adult emotions. A "protective isolation" sentimentalized children as innocent and easily impressionable (Ariès, 1962; Zelizer, 1985). Caregiver diversity declined as the concept of "home" emerged, but children were now exposed to emotions related to the privacy, comfort, and coziness signified by the domestic home (Rybczynski, 1986).

Consensus across socialization agents

In traditional societies, the authority of the parent is supported by the kinship group and the community (Davis, 1940). Emotional socialization is consistent because parents face no competing authorities such as peer subcultures, schools, or mass media. Of course other institutions than the family may dominate emotional culture. Institutionalized theological emotions of awe and dread permeated moral instruction for eighteenth-century American children, reflecting the "sovereignty of religion in every phase of a child's life" (Kiefer, 1948).

Consistent socialization can derive from overdetermination or redundant controls when children receive the same socialization from several dependable sources (Levy, 1978). Tahitians, for example, teach children to inhibit anger and aggression by means of child-rearing practices, community attitudes, the vocabulary for emotions, ways of interpreting nature, and providing alternatives to anger and aggression for expressing and labeling feelings (Levy, 1978). In modern societies, consistency is introduced whenever emotion norms are generalized from one life domain to another. Emotion norms, such as the belief that anger should be avoided or dissipated, are extrapolated to child-rearing from the workplace and from marriage (Kohn, 1969; Stearns & Stearns, 1986).

In modern, heterogeneous societies, children are exposed to divergent ideas about emotions. Parents strive to isolate children from alien, unfamiliar notions, but socialization for competence may have to take institutional diversity into account. Families cannot repress anger completely when the emotion may be an effective interpersonal tool in peer group, school, or workplace (Stearns & Stearns, 1986).

Shifting group participation

Modern societies draw a sharp boundary between the culturally homogeneous family household and the heterogeneous world of nonfamily peers and adults. Gradually moving from interaction with parents to the peer group and adults, children are exposed to emotional diversity through this shifting balance in group participation.

Peers. Children's emotion concepts emphasize those components that directly facilitate their effective adaptation to recurrent interaction with others. Peer relations are more egalitarian than interaction with parents, emphasizing negotiation and reciprocity. Children regard peers as more receptive and understanding targets for emotional disclosure than most adults, who appear to lack understanding and may react punitively (Saarni, 1985). Whereas children's first emotion concepts emphasize situations and expressions, a later reconceptualization adds feeling and normative components. For example, younger children frequently attribute their emotions to actions directed by others toward themselves, in answers like, "[I get angry] when my brother wrecks my toys." (Wolman et al., 1972a, 1972b). Older children's answers show self-initiated activity and subjective reactions, as in "I get mad when I fall down and hurt myself." Although this changing conceptualization stems partly from cognitive transformations such as emergence of a self-concept, it also incorporates the younger child's powerlessness with adults, and the older child's sense of agency and reciprocity with peers.

The peer group can be emotionally diverse, and their norms and vocabulary also diverge form those of parents. This heterogeneity requires children to infer peers' emotional reactions instead of simply projecting their own. The child becomes aware that people can have different emotional responses to the same situation or person (Harris & Olthof, 1982). Furthermore, by regarding a situation from the perspectives of different groups (i.e., family and peers), the child becomes aware of feeling mixed emotions. Peer groups allow experimentation with roles such as leader or adviser that cannot be played with adults, increasing the child's awareness of emotional self-presentation.

Generational change. The rapid pace of social change may expose children to new emotion norms and vocabulary, setting them and their peers apart from the parental generation. Some emotional domains – romantic and erotic relations, for example – change more rapidly than others. For these emotions, peer-influenced children will notice discrepancies from the teachings of older generations (Troll & Bengtson, 1979). An *emotional culture lag* may develop, as cultural norms and vocabulary fail to keep pace with new patterns of emotional experience (Keniston, 1971).

Exposure to the public and subcultures

As children grow older, their interactional domain expands into public society at large – to contacts with persons outside the intimate family circle. Intense attachments with early caregivers become supplemented or replaced by relationships with extended family, schoolmates, teachers, childcare professionals, casual acquaintances, and strangers. For example, in eras when U.S. parents sought to conceal their anger from children, schoolteachers displayed anger at students much more freely, contrasting home and school emotion norms in the child's mind (Stearns & Stearns, 1986).

Public interaction expands the child's emotional range. Some encounters elicit intense emotions such as terror, awe, hatred, and infatuation. The child may be able to isolate these emotions conceptually for the first time because they are intense and simple, unlike their complex, ambivalent reactions felt for family and friends. Task-oriented, transient contacts with acquaintances and strangers also expose the child to emotions of a low intensity unknown in family interaction. Entry into public life is a major transition today, but historically many children served in apprecticeships or as housemaids under the discipline of a master, and were exposed to nonfamily emotional life (Beales, 1985; Schulz, 1985).

As a newcomer to public life, the child becomes aware of being a target for the emotions of casual acquaintances and strangers. These emotions may be directed at the child in terms of visible characteristics like attractiveness or height, or as a representative of social categories such as race or gender. The child becomes exposed to racial prejudice, social class contempt or envy, even sexual desire, and other emotions that broaden her or his vocabulary of emotions. For example, wealthy or attractive children are targets of envy and become sensitized to recognize and deflect envy (Foster, 1972; Schoek, 1966). Children may develop a sense of being an object of unpredictable emotions from others, no longer as a unique individual for whom emotions are expressed only by family and friends known intimately.

Children first learn their own group's emotional culture, but gradually their expanding scope of interaction exposes them to emotional subcultures. Modern societies are differentiated by ethnicity, social class, religion, region, and deviant or alternative life styles. Each subculture presents children with a unique variant of the society's emotional culture. Subcultural diversity is especially apparent to children who are socially mobile across national, regional, ethnic, or class boundaries.

Effects of diversity on emotion concepts

Diversity of exposure might be expected to produce at least the following consequences. First, the child's understanding of the emotion becomes more complex and differentiated. For example, the more varied the persons with whom a child comes into contact, the more the child is sensitized to status distinctions and the vocabulary for varieties of respect (Geertz, 1959; Ochs, 1982).

Second, diverse exposure makes the child's understanding more situationally adaptable and potentially competent in different groups. This hypothesis has support from other socialization fields. The Soviet boarding school's monolithic authority contrasts with the pluralistic day school in which socialization agents compete and balance one another, advancing moral judgment (Bronfenbrenner, 1970). Children from isolated farms were poorer at perspective taking than village or town children in Norway and Hungary (Hollos, 1975). The capacity for empathy is spurred by "socialization that permits children to experience many emotions rather than protects them from emotional experience," wrote Martin Hoffman (1982, p. 7). Children may generalize their emotional understanding from one group to another. Children from divorced families overperceive anger and underperceive happiness in judging the emotions of their peers (Reichenbach & Masters, 1983).

Third, diversity of exposure causes strain and self-consciousness in learning and expressing emotional culture. Children learn emotion norms and vocabulary more readily when their socialization is consistent. Children and adolescents often realize the contradictions between early ideals and the pragmatic, even cynical, content of later socialization (Davis, 1940). For example, young children's books on manners portray friendships idealistically as based on politeness and honesty. Manners books for adolescents focus on instrumental strategies for coping with selfish, jealous, or unwanted friends, and pretense as in concealing one's real eagerness for intimacy (Cavan, 1970).

Finally, exposure to diversity alters a child's conception of emotional components. Observing how expression of an emotion differs from one social group to another, the child becomes sensitized to distinctions among expression, feeling, and social context. Seeing an emotion's components arranged in different patterns across groups implies that the emotion's structure is relative or arbitrary, and hence perhaps can be manipulated or managed by the child.

Conclusion

This chapter has presented a theoretical framework for tracing social structural and cultural variables downward in scale to socialization practices and children's resultant understanding of emotions. Scientific analysis requires variation in the central phenomena of interest; to locate substantial variation in emotional socialization, we must look to other societies and other time periods. My objective has been to delineate structural and socialization variables that can be applied in comparative cross-cultural research.

The wealth of cross-cultural and historical information about emotional socialization should be explored to promote a convergence between social constructionism and cognitive constructionism. Yet even more information is required about very basic issues. Although infants and young children have been studied extensively, we know little about the emotional socialization of older children and adolescents. Research has concentrated on a small set of primary

344   S. L. Gordon

emotions, neglecting the complex emotions or sentiments that constitute most of a society's emotional vocabulary. And greater attention should be given to socialization agents besides the mother, especially to the effects of fathers, peers, schools, and mass media. Finally, we need a clearer vision of the important functions of emotion for social interaction – what is it that emotions do for social life? – if we are to understand why societies have constructed such elaborate and demanding interactional systems to socialize children's emotions.

References

Ariès, P. (1962). *Centuries of childhood: a social history of family life.* New York: Vintage Books.
Armon-Jones, C. (1985). Prescription, explication and the social construction of emotion. *Journal for the Theory of Social Behavior, 15,* 1–22.
Averill, J. R. (1982). *Anger and aggression: an essay on emotion.* New York: Springer-Verlag.
Baumrind, D. (1971). Current patterns of parental authority. *Developmental Psychology Monographs, 4* (1, part 2).
Beales, R. C., Jr. (1985). The child in seventeenth-century America. In J. M. Hawes & N. R. Hiner (Eds.), *American childhood: a research guide and historical handbook* (pp. 15–56). Westport, CT: Greenwood.
Benedict, R. (1938). Continuities and discontinuities in cultural conditioning. *Psychiatry, 1,* 161–167.
Boocock, S. S. (1976). Historical and sociological research on the family and the life cycle: methodological alternatives. In J. Demos & S. S. Boocock (Eds.), *Turning points: historical and sociological essays on the family* (pp. 366–394). Chicago: University of Chicago Press.
Borke, H. (1971). Interpersonal perceptions of young children: egocentrism or empathy. *Developmental Psychology, 5,* 263–269.
Borke, H. (1973). The development of empathy in Chinese and American children between three and six years of age: a cross-cultural study. *Developmental Psychology, 9,* 102–108.
Bretherton, I., & Beeghly, M. (1982). Talking about internal states: the acquisition of an explicit theory of mind. *Developmental Psychology, 18,* 906–912.
Briggs, J. L. (1970). *Never in anger: portrait of an Eskimo family.* Cambridge, MA: Harvard University Press.
Brim, O. G., Jr. (1958). Family structure and sex role learning by children: a further analysis of Helen Koch's data. *Sociometry, 21,* 1–16.
Broderick, C. (1966). Sexual behavior among pre-adolescents. *Journal of Social Issues, 22,* 6–21.
Bronfenbrenner, U. (1958). Socialization and social class through time and space. In E. T. Maccoby, T. Newcomb, & E. Hartley (Eds.), *Readings in social psychology* (pp. 400–425). New York: Holt.
Bronfenbrenner, U. (197j0). *Two worlds of childhood.* New York: Russell Sage Foundation.
Bronfenbrenner, U. (1979). *The ecology of human development.* Cambridge, MA: Harvard University Press.
Buck, R. (1975). Nonverbal communication of affect in children. *Journal of Personality and Social Psychology, 31,* 644–653.
Campos, J. J., Barrett K. C., Lamb, M. E., Goldsmith, H. H., & Stenberg, C. (1983). Socioemotional development. In P. H. Mussen (Ed.), *Handbook of child psychology: Vol II, Infant development* (M. M. Haith & J. J. Campos, Vol. Eds.) (4th ed., pp. 783–915). New York: Wiley.
Camras, L. A. (1985). Socialization of affect communication. In M. Lewis & C. Saarni (Eds.), *The socialization of emotions* (pp. 141–160). New York: Plenum.

Carroll, J. J., & Steward, M. S. (1984). The role of cognitive development in children's understandings of their feelings. *Child Development, 55,* 1486–1492.

Cavan, S. (1970). The etiquette of youth. In G. Stone & H. Farberman (Eds.), *Social psychology through symbolic interaction* (pp. 554–565). Waltham, MA: Ginn-Blaisdell.

Cooley, C. H. (1902/1964). *Human nature and the social order.* New York: Scribner.

Coveney, P. (1957). *Poor monkey: the child in literature.* London: Rockliff.

Cummings, E. M., Zahn-Waxler, C., & Radke-Yarrow, M. (1981). Young children's responses to expressions of anger and affection by others in the family. *Child Development, 52,* 1274–1282.

Cummings, E. M., Zahn-Waxler, C., & Radke-Yarrow, M. (1984). Developmental changes in children's reactions to anger in the home. *Journal of Child Psychology and Psychiatry, 25,* 63–75.

Davis, K. (1940). The sociology of parent–youth conflict. *American Sociological Review, 5,* 523–535.

deMause, L. (Ed.). (1974). *The history of childhood.* New York: Psychohistory Press.

Demos, E. V. (1974). *Children's understanding and use of affect terms.* Unpublished Ph.D. dissertation, Harvard University.

Demos, J. (1986). The rise and fall of adolescence. In J. Demos (Ed.), *Past, present, and personal: the family and the life course in American history* (pp. 92–113). New York: Oxford University Press.

Denzin, N. K. (1984). *On understanding emotion.* San Francisco: Jossey-Bass.

Doi, T. (1973). *The anatomy of dependence.* Tokyo/New York: Kodansha Institute.

Dorr, A. (1985). Contexts for experience with emotion, with special attention to television. In M. Lewis & C. Saarni (Eds.), *The socialization of emotions* (pp. 55–85). New York: Plenum.

Dreeben, R. (1968). *On what is learned in school.* Reading, MA: Addison-Wesley.

Easton, M., Hatfield, E., & Synodinos, N. (1984). Development of the juvenile love scale. Manuscript submitted for publication.

Eisenstadt, S. N. (1956). *From generation to generation: age groups and social structure.* Glencoe, IL: Free Press.

Ekman, P. (1982). *Emotion in the human face* (2nd ed.). Cambridge: Cambridge University Press.

Ekman, P. (1984). Expression and the nature of emotion. In K. R. Scherer & P. Ekman (Eds.), *Approaches to emotion* (pp. 319–341). Hillsdale, NJ: Erlbaum.

Fehr, B., & Russell, J. A. (1984). Concept of emotion viewed from a prototype perspective. *Journal of Experimental Psychology-General, 113,* 464–486.

Feshbach, N., & Roe, K. (1968). Empathy in six- and seven-year-olds. *Child Development, 39,* 133–145.

Field, T., & Fogel, A. (Eds.). (1982). *Emotion and early interaction.* Hillsdale, NJ: Erlbaum.

Field, T., & Walden, T. A. (1982). Production and perception of facial expressions in infancy and early childhood. In H. W. Reese (Ed.), *Advances in child development and behavior* (Vol. 16). New York: Academic Press.

Finkelstein, B. (1985). Casting networks of good influence: the reconstruction of childhood in the United States, 1790–1870. In J. M. Hawes & N. R. Hiner (Eds.), *American childhood: a research guide and historical handbook* (pp. 111–52). Westport, CT: Greenwood.

Fortes, M. (1970). Social and psychological aspects of education in Taleland. In J. Middleton (Ed.), *From child to adult* (pp. 14–74). Garden City, NY: Doubleday.

Foster, G. M. (1972). The anatomy of envy. *Current Anthropology, 13,* 165–202.

Francis, E. A. (1985). American children's literature, 1646–1880. In J. M. Hawes & N. R. Hiner (Eds.), *American childhood: a research guide and historical handbook* (pp. 185–233). Westport, CT: Greenwood.

Geertz, H. (1959). The vocabulary of emotion. *Psychiatry, 22,* 225–237.

Gordon, S. L. (1981). The sociology of sentiments and emotion. In M. Rosenberg & R. H. Turner (Eds.), *Social psychology: sociological perspectives* (pp. 562–592). New York: Basic Books.

Gordon, S. L. (1985). Micro-sociological theories of emotion. In H. J. Helle & S. N. Eisenstadt

(Eds.), *Microsciological theory: perspectives on sociological theory* (Vol. 2, pp. 133–147). London: Sage.

Gordon, S. L. (in press). Institutional and impulsive cultural orientations in the selective appropriation of emotions to self. In D. Franks & E. D. McCarthy (Eds.), *The sociology of emotions: original essays and research papers*. Greenwich, CT: JAI Press.

Greven, P., Jr. (1977). *The Protestant temperament: patterns of child-rearing, religious experience, and the self in early America*. New York: Knopf.

Harkness, S., & Kilbride, P. L. (1983). Introduction: the socialization of affect. *Ethos, 11*, 215–220.

Harkness, S., & Super, C. M. (1983). The cultural construction of child development: a framework for the socialization of affect. *Ethos, 11*, 221–231.

Harkness, S., & Super, C. M. (1985). Child-environment interactions in the socialization of affect. In M. Lewis & C. Saarni (Eds.), *The socialization of emotions* (pp. 21–36). New York: Plenum.

Harre, R. (Ed.) (1986). *The social construction of emotions*. Oxford: Basil Blackwell.

Harris, P. L. (1985). What children know about the situations that provoke emotion. In M. Lewis & C. Saarni (Eds.), *The socialization of emotions* (pp. 161–185). New York: Plenum.

Harris, P. L., Guz, G. R., Lipian, M. S., & Man-Shu, Z. (1985). Insight into the time-course of emotion among Western and Chinese children. *Child Development, 56*, 972–988.

Harris, P. L., & Olthof, T. (1982). The child's concept of emotion. In G. Butterworth & P. Light (Eds.), *Social cognition: studies of the development of understanding* (pp. 188–209). Chicago: University of Chicago Press.

Harter, S. (1982). Children's understanding of multiple emotions: a cognitive developmental approach. In W. F. Overton (Ed.), *The relationship between social and cognitive development*. Hillsdale, NJ: Erlbaum.

Heelas, P., & Lock, A. (Eds.) (1981). *Indigenous psychologies: the anthropology of the self*. London: Academic Press.

Hetherington, E. M., Cox, M., & Cox, R. (1982). Effects of divorce on parents and children. In M. Lamb (Ed.), *Nontraditional families*. Hillsdale, NJ: Erlbaum.

Hochschild, A. R. (1979). Emotion work, feeling rules, and social structure. *American Journal of Sociology, 85*, 551–575.

Hochschild, A. R. (1983). *The managed heart: commercialization of human feeling*. Berkeley: University of California Press.

Hoffman, M. (1970). Conscience, personality, and socialization techniques. *Human Development, 13*, 90–126.

Hoffman, M. (1979). Development of moral thought, feeling, and behavior. *American Psychologist, 34*, 958–966.

Hoffman, M. L. (1982). Affect and moral development. In D. Cicchetti & P. Hesse (Eds.), *Emotional development* (pp. 83–103). San Francisco: Jossey-Bass.

Hollos, R. (1975). Logical operations and role-taking abilities in two cultures: Norway and Hungary. *Child Development, 46*, 638–649.

Howell, S. (1981). Rules not words. In P. Heelas & A. Lock (Eds.), *Indigenous psychologies*. London: Academic Press.

Inkeles, A. (1966). Social structure and the socialization of competence. *Harvard Educational Review, 36*, 265–283.

Inkeles, A. (1968). Society, social structure, and child socialization. In J. A. Clausen, O. G. Brim, Jr., A. Inkeles, R. Lippitt, E. E. Maccoby, and M. B. Smith (Eds.), *Socialization and society* (pp. 73–129). Boston: Little, Brown.

Izard, C. E. (1971). *The face of emotion*. New York: Appleton-Century-Crofts.

Izard, C. E. (1977). *Human emotions*. New York: Plenum.

Kagan, J. (1984). *The nature of the child*. New York: Basic Books.

Kemper, T. D. (1987). How many emotions are there? Wedding the social and the autonomic components. *American Journal of Sociology, 93*, 263–289.

Keniston, K. (1971). Youth: a "new" stage of life. *The American Scholar, 39,* 815–820.

Kett, J. (1977). *Rites of passage: adolescence in America, 1790 to the present.* New York: Basic Books.

Kiefer, M. (1948). *American children through their books, 1788–1835.* Philadelphia: University of Pennsylvania Press.

Klinnert, M., Campos, J. J., Sorce, J., Emde, R. N., & Svejda, M. (1983). Emotions as behavior regulators: social referencing in infancy. In R. Plutchik & H. Kellerman (Eds.), *Emotions in early development: Vol. 2, The emotions* (pp. 56–83). New York: Academic Press.

Kohlberg, L. (1969). Stage and sequence: the cognitive development approach to socialization. In D. Goslin (Ed.), *Handbook of theory and research in socialization* (pp. 347–480). Chicago: Rand-McNally.

Kohn, M. (1969). *Class and conformity: a study in values.* Homewood, IL: Dorsey.

Lakoff, G., & Kovecses, Z. (1987). The cognitive model of anger inherent in American English. In D. Holland & N. Quinn (Eds.), *Cultural models in language and thought* (pp. 195–221). Cambridge: Cambridge University Press.

Lazarus, R. S., Kanner, A. D., & Folkman, S. (1980). Emotions: a cognitive-phenomenological analysis. In R. Plutchik & H. Kellerman (Eds.) (1980), *Emotion: theory, research, and experience* (pp. 189–218). New York: Academic Press.

Lebra, T. S. (1983). Shame and guilt: a psychocultural view of the Japanese self. *Ethos 11,* 192–209.

Levy, R. I. (1978). Tahitian gentleness and redundant control. In A. Montague (Ed.), *Learning non-aggression,* (pp. 222–235). New York: Oxford University Press.

Levy, R. I. (1984). Emotion, knowing, and culture. In R. A. Shweder & R. A. LeVine (Eds.), *Culture theory: essays on mind, self, and emotion* (pp. 214–237). Cambridge: Cambridge University Press.

Lewis, M., & Michalson, L. (1983). *Children's emotions and moods: developmental theory and measurement.* New York: Plenum.

Lewis, M., & Saarni, C. (1985a). Culture and emotions. In M. Lewis & C. Saarni (Eds.), *The socialization of emotions* (pp. 1–17). New York: Plenum.

Lewis, M., & Saarni, C. (Eds.). (1985b). *The socialization of emotions.* New York: Plenum.

Lutz, C. (1983). Parental goals, ethnopsychology, and the development of emotional meaning. *Ethos, 11,* 246–262.

Lutz, C. (1985). Cultural patterns and individual differences in the child's emotional meaning system. In M. Lewis & C. Saarni (Eds.), *The socialization of emotions* (pp. 37–53). New York: Plenum.

Lutz, C., & White, G. M. (1986). The anthropology of emotions. *Annual Review of Anthropology, 15,* 405–436.

Maccoby, E. (1984). Socialization and developmental change. *Child Development, 55,* 317–328.

Mechling, J. (1975). Advice to historians on advice to mothers. *Journal of Social History, 9,* 44–63.

Michalson, L., & Lewis, M. (1985). What do children know about emotions and when do they know it? In M. Lewis & C. Saarni (Eds.), *The socialization of emotions* (pp. 117–139). New York: Plenum.

Miller, D. N., & Swanson, G. E. (1958). *The changing American parent.* New York: Wiley.

Miller, P., & Sperry, L. L. (1987). The socialization of anger and aggression. *Merrill-Palmer Quarterly, 33,* 1–31.

Miyake, K., Campos, J. J., Kagan, J., & Bradshaw, D. L. (1986). Issues in socioemotional development. In H. Azuma, K. Hakuta, & H. Stevenson (Eds.), *Kodomo: child development and education in Japan.* San Francisco: Freeman.

Modell, J., & Hareven, T. K. (1973). Urbanization and the malleable household: an examination of boarding and lodging in American families. *Journal of Marriage and the Family, 35,* 467–479.

Myers, F. R. (1979). Emotions and the self: a theory of personhood and political order among Pintupi Aborigines. *Ethos, 7*, 343–370.

Newson, J., & Newson, E. (1976). *Seven years in the home environment*. New York: Wiley.

Ochs, E. (1982). Talking to children in Western Samoa. *Language and Society, 11:* 77–104.

Odom, R. D., & Lemond, C. M. (1972). Developmental differences in the perception and production of facial expressions. *Child Development, 43*, 359–369.

Piaget, J. (1932). *The moral judgment of the child*. New York: Harcourt Brace and World.

Plutchik, R. (1980). *Emotion: a psychoevolutionary synthesis*. New York: Harper and Row.

Plutchik, R., & Kellerman, H. (Eds.) (1980). *Emotion: theory, research and experience*. New York: Academic Press.

Pollock, L. A. (1983). *Forgotten children: parent–child relations from 1500 to 1900*. Cambridge: Cambridge University Press.

Postman, N. (1982). *The disappearance of childhood*. New York: Delacorte.

Reichenbach, L., & Masters, J. C. (1983). Children's use of expressive and contextual cues in judgments of emotion. *Child Development, 54*, 993–1004.

Ridgeway, D., Waters, E., & Kuczaj, S. A., II. (1985). Acquisition of emotion-descriptive language: receptive and productive vocabulary norms for ages 18 months to 6 years. *Developmental Psychology, 21*, 901–908.

Rosaldo, M. Z. (1984). Toward an anthropology of self and feeling. In R. A. Shweder & R. A. LeVine (Eds.), *Culture theory: essays on mind, self, and emotion* (pp. 137–157). Cambridge: Cambridge University Press.

Rybczynski, W. (1986). *Home: a short history of an idea*. New York: Viking.

Saarni, C. (1979). Children's understanding of display rules for expressive behavior. *Developmental Psychology, 15*, 424–429.

Saarni, C. (1982). Social and affective functions of nonverbal behavior: Developmental concerns. In R. Feldman (Ed.), *Development of nonverbal behavior*, (pp. 123–147). New York: Springer-Verlag.

Saarni, C. (1985). Indirect processes in affect socialization. In M. Lewis & C. Saarni (Eds.), *The socialization of emotions* (pp. 187–209). New York: Plenum.

Scherer, K. R., & Ekman, R. (Eds.) (1984). *Approaches to emotion*. Hillsdale, NJ: Erlbaum.

Schoeck, H. (1966). *Envy: a theory of social behavior*. New York: Harcourt Brace and World.

Schorch, A. (1979). *Images of childhood: an illustrated social history*. Pittstown, NJ: Main Street Press.

Schulz, C. B. (1985). Children and childhood in the eighteenth century. In J. M. Hawes & N. R. Hiner (Eds.), *American childhood: a research guide and historical handbook* (pp. 57–109). Westport, CT: Greenwood.

Schwartz, J. C., & Shaver, P. (1987). Emotions and emotion knowledge in interpersonal relations. In W. Jones & D. Perlman (Eds.), *Advances in personal relationships* (Vol. 1, pp. 197–241). Greenwich, CT: JAI Press.

Shaver, P., Schwartz, J., Kirson, D., & O'Conner, C. (1987). Emotion knowledge: further exploration of a prototype approach. *Journal of Personality of Social Psychology, 52*, 1061–1086.

Shorter, E. (1975). *The making of the modern family*. New York: Basic Books.

Shott, S. (1979). Emotion and social life: a symbolic interactionist analysis. *American Journal of Sociology, 84*, 1317–1334.

Smetana, J. G. (1984). Toddlers' social interactions regarding moral and conventional transgressions. *Child Development, 55*, 1767–1776.

Smith, M. B. (1966). Competence and socialization. In J. A. Clausen, O. G. Brim, Jr., A. Inkeles, R. Lippitt, E. E. Maccoby, & M. B. Smith (Eds.), *Socialization and society* (pp. 270–320). Boston: Little, Brown.

Solomon, R. C. (1977). *The passions*. Garden City, NY: Doubleday.

Stannard, D. E. (1977). *The Puritan way of death: a study in religion, culture, and social change*. New York: Oxford University Press.

Stearns, C. Z., & Stearns, P. (1986). *Anger: the struggle for emotional control in America's history.* Chicago: University of Chicago.

Stone, L. (1979). *The family, sex, and marriage in England 1500–1800.* New York: Harper and Row.

Stonequist, E. V. (1937). *The marginal man: a study in personality and cultural conflict.* New York: Russell and Russell.

Thoits, P. A. (1985). Self-labeling processes in mental illness: the role of emotional deviance. *American Journal of Sociology, 91,* 221–249.

Troll, L., & Bengtson, V. (1979). Generations in the family. In W. Burr (Ed.), *Contemporary theories about the family* (Vol. 1). New York: Free Press.

Turiel, E. (1966). An experimental test of the sequentiality of developmental stages in the child's moral development. *Journal of Personality and Social Psychology, 3,* 611–618.

Turiel, E. (1983). *The development of social knowledge: morality and convention.* Cambridge: Cambridge University Press.

Turner, R. H. (1970). *Family interaction.* New York: Wiley.

Waters, E., & Sroufe, L. A. (1983). A developmental perspective on competence. *Developmental Review, 3,* 79–97.

Whiting, J., & Whiting, B. (1978). A strategy for psychocultural research. In G. D. Spindler (Ed.), *The making of psychological anthropology* (pp. 41–61). Berkeley: University of California Press.

Wolman, R. N., Lewis, W. C., & King, M. (1972a). The development of the language of emotions: I. Theoretical and methodological introduction. *Journal of Genetic Psychology, 120,* 167–176.

Wolman, R. N., Lewis, W. C., & King, M. (1972b). The development of the language of emotions: IV. Bodily referents and the experience of affect. *Journal of Genetic Psychology, 121,* 65–81.

Zahn-Waxler, C., Cummings, E. M., & Cooperman, E. M. (1984). Emotional development in childhood. *Annals of Child Development, 1,* 30–72.

Zelizer, V. (1985). *Pricing the priceless child: the changing social value of children.* New York: Basic Books.

13 Cultural differences in children's knowledge of emotional scripts

Michael Lewis

The notion of scripts is a very useful one. Scripts are complex schemata involving knowledge of situations, actions, and motives of others and the self. They allow for action in the world, including emotional responses. Because scripts are complex and integrated systems of knowledge, a minimal amount of information is needed for their activation. With respect to emotional scripts, if I know about a situation I also have knowledge of the appropriate emotions that are likely to be elicited in others and myself; conversely, if I have knowledge about an emotion, I can describe a situation that is likely to have produced that state. This chapter is about such scripts and the ways in which emotional scripts vary as a function of development and culture.

Emotional scripts in childhood have been studied (for example, Borke, 1973; Gnepp & Gould, 1985; Harris, 1983, 1985). However, the origins of these scripts in early childhood – 2 to 6 years – have received little attention. Moreover, cultural differences have been relatively unexplored, in part due to methodological limitations, an issue we shall return to in some detail. The study of cultural differences in script learning serves as a useful reminder of both general script knowledge and the role of socialization in specific scripts.

Let us first consider an example of emotional script knowledge that will be the focus of our comments: A friend's mother has died, and we have been invited to the funeral. There are many pieces of information having to do with emotional behavior known to us. We know, for example, that in the Western world, we are to wear certain types of clothing: a dark suit, or a suit without bright colors. We are to act in a certain way; laughing and smiling are inappropriate, and a serious, somber and even sad face is more in keeping with what is expected. Moreover, we know not only how we should behave but what to expect in the behavior of others, in particular, in our friend's behavior. We would expect that the death of his mother would produce a sad face rather than joy. Moreover, we

This research was supported in part by a grant from W. T. Grant Foundation. Appreciation is given to Despina Laverick for data reduction and analysis and to Sing-Jen Chen for conducting the study in Japan.

350

can anticipate what his internal emotional state might be like although we cannot be sure.

Thus, we know how we are to act and how others will act in this situation. Emotional scripts inform us about emotional behavior and, at times and to some extent, they inform us about the internal state of others. However, as we have repeatedly pointed out, the relationship between the expressed emotional behavior and the internal state may be quite discrepant (Lewis, 1987; Lewis & Michalson, 1983, 1984). Thus, although I assume that my friend is sad, he may not be so. Emotional scripts, then, are very useful in that they inform us about manifest behavior; they do not necessarily inform us about internal state, although of course they well may do so.

Knowing about situations and emotional states

Scripts inform us most about the external features or expressions of emotional behavior more readily than emotional states themselves. However, our knowledge of emotional scripts may itself play a role in our emotional states and experience. For example, if I know I should be sad for my friend since his mother has died, then I may have an experience of sadness because I know that I should feel this emotion. This suggests that the elicitor of an emotional state can be a particular situation, but it can also be my knowledge about what emotion that situation should elicit. In the case of my friend's mother's death, my sadness may be a direct consequence of the elicitor, her death, or my knowledge of what is appropriate given her death. Models that assume a direct relationship between elicitors and emotion in the absence of cognition (cf. Zajonc, 1980; Izard, 1977) need to be evaluated in light of this potential cognitive interface between any elicitor and the emotional expression observed. To the degree that adults as well as children know, independent of an actual elicitor, what responses are appropriate and what responses most people are likely to show, one must also consider the possibility that it is not the elicitor that produces the emotional response but people's knowledge of what is appropriate behavior. These factors play an important role in any theory of the development of emotions, because in the simplest models of emotional development elicitors are considered to produce specific emotional responses in some one-to-one "automatic" fashion whereas in socialization models it is the socialization of behavior that leads to the elicitation of specific emotional behavior (Lewis & Michalson, 1982). Whereas automatic elicitors, such as the loss of a love object, can lead directly to specific emotional behavior, most of our emotional experience is the product of *both* the basic eliciting situations and the socialization experience of the individual. Emotional script learning in young children has been explored through what children know about the situations that produce emotions.

What children know about situations

Most of the work done on children's knowledge about emotions has concerned children 6 years of age and older. In part, this reflects the methodology that has been used to study children's knowledge about situations. The methodology requires that children be asked directly what it is that they know about situations and emotions. Although such procedures enable us to describe children's verbal knowledge about emotion, there are at least two methodological concerns about the procedure that need to be addressed. The first is that such techniques are limited to verbal children. Young children are unlikely to understand the question or to be able to supply a verbal response to indicate their knowledge. This methodology, then, is not appropriate for assessing what young children know.

A second and perhaps more important concern is that children's verbal ability and understanding increases with age. The developmental changes that we observe in the apparent sophistication of children's knowledge about emotions may reflect either a genuine increase in sophistication or an increase in verbal expressive ability. This is a particularly worrisome point and one that needs further investigation with alternative methods. Harter, for example, has been interested in the question of whether or not children can appreciate that two different emotions can occur at the same time (Harter, 1982; Harter & Whitesell, this volume). The type of procedure used to obtain an answer to this question influences the responses obtained. What does the "same time" mean to children of different ages? Without addressing this issue, we cannot be sure that there are changes in the understanding of mixed emotions. There are a variety of procedures that could be used to measure knowledge that do not require a verbal response and it would certainly further our study of development if we used such procedures in addition to those already reported. In much work in children's emotional knowledge the issue of competence versus performance is a very critical one (Wellman, 1985). Thus, although there is ample evidence to show several important developmental trends in children's knowledge about emotions, it is not clear whether this knowledge is due to age changes in performance or competence.

Even with these limitations, we do know something of what children know about situations and emotions. In a series of studies, Harris and his colleagues (Harris, Olthof, & Meerum Terwogt, 1981; Harris & Olthof, 1982; Harris, 1983, 1985) have shown that children's knowledge of emotional situations, at least in the 6- to 15-year range, undergoes several important changes. By 6 years, children know what kinds of situations are linked to particular emotional responses; they know, for example, that angry facial expressions are provoked in quarreling situations. Moreover, Harris et al. (1981) have shown that there is a significant change between 6 and 11 years. Whereas the 6-year-old child sees situations as the primary elicitor for emotional expression, older children are more aware that emotional expressions are produced by inner states and are not necessarily provoked by particular situations. In general, the development of children's knowledge about emotions changes from a belief that external situations and external expression of emotional behavior are likely to have a one-to-one correspondence with the elicitation of emotion and emotional states to a belief that emotional expression and its control is related to internal representations and control of emotions. Moreover, rather than a simple emotion, complex sets of emotion are acknowledged to be a consequence of any specific situation. In addition to the information on the elicitation of emotion, Harris has investigated children's notions of multiple emotions as a consequence of situational constraints, and their understanding of strategies for the control of the emotion itself rather than its display.

The described developmental change is very similar to changes in other aspects of social cognition. For example, children are very likely to describe people in terms of physical characteristics and only later to describe them in terms of inner states using such features as personality variables. This general shift from external feature characteristics to internal motives and processes characterizes much of the child's learning about people, situations, interactions, and emotions from early childhood through adolescence.

Methodological problems and bias

All of the studies of emotional development tend to use verbal instructions and verbal responses. These studies of emotional script knowledge can be divided into two types of methodology. In the first, children are presented specific situations and asked about the emotions that characterize the actors in the situation. In the second, children are presented with specific emotions and asked about the kinds of situations likely to produce these emotions. Both types of methodology share some difficulties. In both types of study, the findings might be different if children were offered nonverbal tasks. Moreover, in most studies children's responses to these types of question are not compared to those of adults. It is assumed that adults' responses would be the same as those of the older children in the study. Although this may be the case, one should be prepared for the possibility that adults' responses do not necessarily match those of older children. Moreover, they may not match those which the supposedly rational experimenter thinks is the "correct" adult response. This is an error likely to lead to incorrect assumptions about the developmental function.

The lack of information about what adults know about emotion may lead to several problems. It is often assumed that a particular situation has a correct emotion or emotions associated with it. Michalson and Lewis (1985) looked at young people's script knowledge and assumed that a particular emotion was likely to go with a particular situation. For example, they presented 2- to 5-year-old children and adults with a story about a child being lost in a store and asked the subjects to select which facial expression was likely to go with the story character. The authors assumed that the correct response would be "fear." An analysis of children's responses to that story indicated that only a few children selected fear. Indeed, only 50 percent of the adults agreed with the experimenters in choosing fear as the correct script. In this example, two issues are visible; experimenter bias and developmental bias. We analyze each of these biases in turn.

The experimenter script bias. This bias occurs because the experimenter assumes what the "correct" emotional response of children should be. For example, Gnepp and Hess (1986) looked at children's script knowledge, namely, which facial expression went with a particular story. Scoring was based on what the authors perceived as the correct response. This experimenter bias is also present in many other studies (for example, Gnepp & Gould, 1985; Harris et al., 1981; Harris & Olthof, 1982; Michalson & Lewis, 1985). In all these cases, the authors assumed that a certain response is more correct vis-à-vis the situation than others or, in the case of the other methodology, the authors assumed that a certain response is more correct vis à vis a particular emotion than another. The trouble with this assumption is that the experimenter's belief may not match that of other adults. Moreover, the experimenter's or adult's belief may not match that of the child. This brings us to the developmental bias.

The developmental script bias. From a developmental perspective, there may be a discrepancy between what children believe and what adults of the culture believe is the correct response to a particular situation. This will be pursued in more detail as we present cultural and age differences in script knowledge.

These problems of bias cannot be solved by treating other children's judgments as correct responses, in part, because it is important from a developmental perspective to know what the correct script is from an adult point of view (Borke, 1973). By observing what other children consider the correct response, one is able to compare an individual child's response to other children, but one is still not able to look at the developmental consequences. Moreover, adult experimenters, although reflecting the knowledge of the culture at large, probably do so to a limited degree because they may be biased by their *own* research experience. In the Michalson and Lewis study, for example, the adults did not respond as the experimenters anticipated. In the "Lost in the store" script, only 50 percent or so of the adults responded with a "fear" response, which is the response the experimenters thought correct. This argues for the need to obtain data on adults as well as children. For example, in a recent study (Lewis, Michaelson & Goetz, unpublished manuscript), we were able to show that by 5 years of age children's knowledge of facial expression matches that of the adults for the same facial stimuli. Even though only 60 percent of the children get the correct solution, our data showed that adults also get the correct solution only 60 percent of the time. Without knowing the adult percentage, we might have assumed that the developmental process is incomplete by 5 years. It is essential that the adult perspective in terms of situational knowledge be obtained. Most of the studies looking at children's knowledge of situations and emotions have suffered from ignoring that perspective or taking it for granted.

Cultural differences in knowledge

Not only are there developmental differences in the learning of emotional scripts; there are cultural differences as well. We would expect to find that these scripts differ across cultures in ways that reflect the specific features of that culture. Returning to our example of the death of a friend's mother, we can see an interesting script difference in terms of dress. In Western culture, the appropriate color for funerals is black, in contrast to Eastern cultures, where the appropriate dress for funerals is white. Red is used to reflect happiness and is used in marriage ceremonies in Chinese and Japanese cultures, whereas white is used in Western weddings. It is obvious that there are important cultural differences in emotional script learning and differences in how cultures organize and express their emotional lives.

Lutz (1982), for example, argues that the meaning of words, especially emotional words, is embedded in their cultural context and therefore the same word has very different meaning depending on the nature of the culture. The work of Harkness and Super (1985) supports this view of cultural differences in emotional words. They looked at children and adults from Kipsigis and from Massachusetts and asked them to associate the term "happy" with two drawings. Although there were few differences between the groups at 3 years of age, there were marked differences by adulthood. All adult Americans labeled a large curved line as happy, whereas only 35 percent of the Kipsigis adults did so. In contrast, the Kipsigis labeled a flat line as happy whereas the American adults did not. By middle childhood, certainly by the age of 6 or 7 years, Kipsigis children had learned to associate a flat line with happy and had learned that the large swooping figure was "trouble." The opposite was true for the American children. This study, looking at cultural differences in association, points out the need to gather data on the adults of a culture in order to fully understand cultural differences in developmental trajectory.

Borke (1973) studied age and cultural differences in children's knowledge of emotions and situations. In general, she found that the stories for happiness resulted in the most "correct" choices and that there were very few age changes. Children by the age of 3 years had a good understanding of what emotional expression is likely to occur with stories pertaining to happiness. The emotion showing the most change across age was fear, with 3-year-old children having only 50% "correct" (as designated by the experimenter) responses and 6-year-olds about 90%. The emotional scripts that children had the most trouble with were those concerning anger. As to cultural differences, it appeared that Chinese children, at least the younger ones, were able to recognize fearful situations more readily than American children, with 70% of the Chinese children identifying frightening situations at 3 years versus only 40% of the American children. The Chinese children also did better than American children in correctly identifying the sad situation; Chinese children were 70% correct whereas American children were 50% correct. Borke reports no sex differences in this ability. Overall, it would appear that the Chinese children agreed with the predetermined criteria of a "correct" script more than the American children, at least at the youngest ages. Exactly why this is so is hard to know, especially because we have no comparable cross-cultural data on adults of these two cultures. However, there are some problems with this study.

Borke (1973) solved one of the problems of choosing "correct" versus incorrect responses by first asking kindergarten children to suggest situations likely to produce the four different emotions. She took those situations, made up stories, and tested facial expression stimuli against those stories with a group of second graders. Thus, what is called "correct" or "incorrect" emotion for a particular story is based upon what the majority of second graders had suggested. However, what other children think is "correct" may not be what adults think is "correct." Moreover, even 10-year-old children might not have chosen the same response. Thus, the technique used suffers from the problem of developmental bias. Considering the fact that Borke was also interested in cross-cultural differences in knowledge between Chinese and American children, this problem is even more acute because no attempt was made to discern how the children of the two cultures differed in what was considered correct or incorrect *within* the two cultures.

In a series of studies, Harris et al. (1981) and Harris, Olthof, Meerum Terwogt, and Hardman (1987) looked at Dutch, English, and Himalayan children in order to determine whether the same developmental processes reported earlier were to be found across different cultures. Summarizing the findings of these studies leads to two conclusions: (1) Developmentally, English and Dutch children at 6 years have a relatively simplistic notion of emotion as related to specific situations and are not mentalistic in their approach, whereas by 15 years, the children are more mentalistic and believe that the cause of emotion is not simply situationally elicited; and (2) young children of all three cultures were able to signify situations that were appropriate to emotional terms not associated with a particular facial expression. Although these data inform us about the general abilities of children across different cultures and the changes over age (surely there was no reason to think otherwise), they do not address the issue of the universality of particular situations to elicit particular emotions. Given the task and methodology, we cannot conclude that there is a lack of cultural specificity for the relationship between specific emotions and the situations likely to elicit them. More research on cross-cultural differences and similar emotional scripts is needed, particularly in light of the limited number of studies exploring this issue and because of the methodological constraints that appear to exist. Data from the few studies that exist on the topic suggest that there are general developmental trends as well as some differences in script learning. However, without methodological changes, we must be cautious in reaching these conclusions.

The nature of script acquisition

We have tended to think of emotional script acquisition across emotions, age, and culture as following a single path. However, it is useful for us to consider the different kinds of scripts that are likely to exist in different kinds of developmental sequence. In order to do so, we will use data gathered on a cross-cultural study of scripts that observed Japanese and American children 2 to 6 years old and their Japanese and American mothers.

Study features

In order to study this problem, we first examined children's knowledge of emotion labels. Ninety-two American children, varying in age from 2 to 6 years, and their mothers were shown pictures of a 10-year-old girl (Felicia), posing the facial expressions of happiness, sadness, anger, fear, surprise, and disgust. These six expressions were chosen because they are believed to represent primary emotions that appear early in life (Izard, Huebbner, Risser, McGinnes, & Dougherty, 1980). The validity of the expressions was established by subjecting them to the MAX facial-coding system (Izard, 1979).

Although the results of this phase of the study are not relevant for our discussion of scripts, we did find that for both children and adults of both cultures, there are few differences in the ability to label or comprehend the different facial expressions. The 5- and 6-year-olds in general did as well as the adults and there were no differences between American and Japanese subjects. Two-year-olds did least well and were generally unable, except for happy and sad faces, to correctly label the faces. Comprehension was significantly better across age with over 50 percent of the 2-year-old children being able to identify at least three of the six expressions. By 3 and 4 years, children's ability across both cultures showed marked improvement.

The results indicated that there were significant age effects for both cultures in the ability to label or comprehend facial expressions of the primary emotions. Moreover, the failure patterns of the two cultures did not differ. When subjects of both cultures are unable to provide the correct response, their errors are either random, as in the case of the 2-year-olds, or show some systematic bias as in choosing disgust for anger or anger for disgust. It is possible to explore situational knowledge keeping in mind that across cultures there is little difference in children's (and adults') knowledge of facial expression.

To explore children's knowledge of facial expressions of emotion as related to situational contexts, an experimenter told the subjects six simple stories in which a little girl (Felicia) was involved in situations likely to elicit an emotional response. The stories were illustrated by line drawings in which the faces of the characters were left blank (see Figures 13.1a,b,c,d,e,f). Each story focused on a simple situation that might occur in the life of a child of both cultures or, as in some cases, more likely to occur in one culture than the other. Although the stories are unique examples of situations likely to elicit particular emotions, they cannot be considered prototypic of all situations likely to elicit that emotion. The methodological procedure of presenting unique and limited sets of stories, although used by others, does not allow for the exploration of all likely situations. Even so, it does present the opportunity to explore script knowledge for a limited range of situations. Table 13.1 presents the stories themselves. After each story, the experimenter asked the child to point to the face that Felicia would have made in that situation. Using this procedure, we can explore the various types of scripts that are possible, both within and across different cultures.

Culturally universal scripts

For universal scripts, all members of the culture recognize the likelihood of a particular relationship between emotional expression and a situation; that is, there is general agreement among the adult members of the culture on this association. Within this first class of script, there are several variants.

Single or multiple responses. For any situation, there may be one single emotion considered prototypic or there may be more than one. For example, either anger or sadness is appropriate when someone violates some personal space and every member of the culture recognizes that both responses are possible. Alternatively, there may be a script in which everyone recognizes a single possibility; for example, one's birthday party where one is happy to receive many gifts. In both cases,

Figure 13.1. The six situations used to elicit various emotional scripts: a) Birthday Party; b) Pink Hair; c) Dog Runs Away; d) Awful Food; e) Blocks; f) Lost in Store.

Table 13.1. *Situation stories*

Blocks	In this picture Felicia has some blocks. She was building a tower with the blocks, but her sister came over and knocked the tower down. How did Felicia look when her sister knocked over her blocks? Can you point to the face that Felicia made?
Pink Hair	Felicia's mommy went to the beauty parlor to have her hair cut. When her mommy came home, Felicia saw that her mommy's hair was all pink. How did Felicia look when she saw her mommy's pink hair? Can you point to the face that Felicia made?
Birthday Party	Felicia had a birthday party and all of her friends were there. At the party, everyone ate ice cream and cake and Felicia got lots of presents. How did Felicia look at her birthday party? Can you point to the face that Felicia made?
Lost in the Store	Felicia went to the store with her mommy to buy some food for dinner. She got lost in the store and couldn't find her mommy anywhere. How did Felicia look when she got lost in the grocery store? Can you point to the face that Felicia made?
Dog Runs Away	Felicia has a pet dog named Bingo. One day Bingo ran away from home and Felicia never saw Bingo again. How did Felicia look when she never saw Bingo again? Can you point to the face that Felicia made?
Spinach	It's dinner time and Felicia's mommy made her eat something awful. It's spinach and Felicia hates spinach. How did Felicia look when she had to eat something awful? Can you point to the face that Felicia made?

there is cultural universality, but it is recognized that some situations may have one or more emotions associated with them.

Developmental trajectory. Within this cultural universality of knowledge, there are two types of developmental sequence. In the simplest, the emotional script is learned early and there is intergenerational agreement about it. Both the children and the adults of the culture share the same emotional script. Thus, the first and only emotional script that the child learns matches that of the adult. There is no transformation, and the development of that script is only accretional, with increased knowledge over age. In the second case, there is an intergenerational difference such that children have a different emotional script than that of the adults of the culture. The children acquire an emotional script that does not match that of the adults, and it is only later in development that there is a transformation of the script; the child switches from a child's to an adult's script. This transformation of an emotional script may take place at any point in the devel-

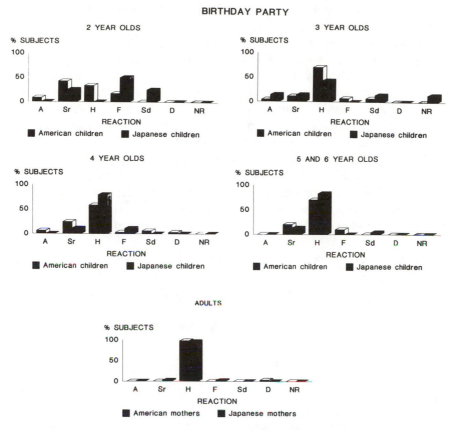

Figure 13.2. Age by culture effects for children's and adults' reactions to the Birthday Party story.

opmental cycle. For some scripts, it is likely to occur when the members of a culture become parents. Here the transformation occurs at a particular experiential point in the life cycle. Emotional script transformation might also occur as a function of cognitive development. Given that Harris and his colleagues have shown a transformation in children's knowledge about emotional situations, it could well be that emotional scripts undergo transformation as a function of cognitive development. One might expect emotional script change to occur some time around the acquisition of the relevant cognitive abilities.

Let us consider examples of these two types of scripts. Figure 13.2 presents by age and culture the responses for the script "Birthday party." This is an example of a universal script, having a single emotional response that is non-transformational in that young children appear to acquire the adult's response as soon as they demonstrate an ability to respond. As found in the Michalson and Lewis study, 2-year-olds do not appear to understand the task, possibly because the verbal instructions are too difficult to follow, they cannot recognize the emotion on the face, or they have not learned the script. Rather than combining them with the 3-year-olds, they are presented separately, because we have reported 2- and 3-year-old age differences in another study (Michalson & Lewis, 1985). Nevertheless, the small number of subjects requires that we treat the data with some caution. The responses of adults of both cultures indicate that this script has only a single primary emotion associated with it. Adults of both cultures believe that children would be happy to receive presents on their birthdays; 97% of American and 95% of the Japanese mothers thought their children would be happy. By 3 years of age, children of both cultures have script knowledge pertaining to children's response to their birthday celebration. Moreover, the single emotion believed to be elicited by the situation is consistent for all subjects of both cultures.

The loss of a pet in the "Dog runs away" story also appears to be a universal script. In this story, the overwhelming choice of adults in both cultures is the emotion of sadness as a consequence of the loss of a loved pet. Ninety-seven percent of American mothers and 93% of Japanese mothers select the sad face. This is a well scripted response and the developmental pattern should be relatively clear.

By 3 years, children of both cultures show high levels of sadness as their choice although the percent showing this response is still less than that for adults of both cultures (average children, 60%; average adult, 92%). The alternative responses distribute themselves evenly across all other facial stimuli except happiness, which is not selected. Losing one's pet evokes a consistent response that shows agreement both between children and adults of a culture as well as across the two cultures.

A third example of a universal script is the "Pink hair" story. This script differs from the first two in several respects. First, although adults of both cultures have a single emotional response (79% of American, 85% of Japanese mothers respond with surprise), American children (and to some extent the Japanese children) appear to have multiple responses, including surprise and happiness. Second, whereas the 5- and 6-year-olds respond like the adults of their cultures, younger children appear either not to have learned a specific script or are likely to have a more varied response repertoire. This age difference might be an indication of a transformation in script learning, but is more likely to be either a lack of a clear-cut script until 5 or 6 years or an example of multiple emotional response in younger children.

A final example of a universal-type script is found in the "Spinach" story. Like the "pink hair" story, adults of both cultures believe that their children will show disgust when presented with an unpleasant food. Whereas both Japanese and American adults select the disgust face for this script (there are no differences between them), there are differences between Japanese and American children. Beyond 3 years of age, American children increasingly choose the disgust face (3 years = 48%; 4 years = 55%; 5–6 years = 60%). Japanese children also show an increase in their "disgust" choice by age (3 years = 0%; 4 years = 26%; 5–6 years = 30%); however, even by 5–6 years they appear to have multiple emotional responses.

It is apparent that adults of both cultures have a similar script; they believe that children presented with a food which they do not like will express disgust. The children of both cultures also appear to be learning this script, and in this sense the script can be assumed to be of a culturally universal type. That Japanese learn this script less quickly than American children may be due to many factors. These differences may be due to the differential ability to discriminate the disgust face, in which case it does not represent differences in script learning. The verbal production data gathered on the children indicate that this is not the case. Differences in this particular disgust script learning may be culturally based because Japanese parents do not try to force their young children to eat the foods they do not like, whereas American mothers may be more insistent. Such cultural differences around eating behavior and food preferences may be of importance because the prototypic situation for eliciting disgust is in the spitting out of unpleasant food. Cultural differences in script learning about disgust would be interesting to explore further.

In general, these four scripts, at least for the adults, show little effect of cultural difference. The universal quality of specific scripts within a culture appear to operate across cultures as well. To some extent, then, there is support for the belief that some situations elicit similar emotional responses across cultures; that is, there are situations that are not culturally specific.

Nonuniversal idiosyncratic emotional scripts

Although the discussion of emotional scripts is usually thought of in terms of uniformity, that is, the acquisition of a single script, it is clear that some scripts are idiosyncratic, specific to individuals, families, or cultures. Within culture for some scripts there is less interest, success, or need to convey a uniform emotion for particular situations. That is, there is either no social pressure or insufficient pressure for every adult member of the culture to have the same script. Such scripts seem as likely and as probable as the culturally universal ones. These idiosyncratic scripts may have similar features to those described for universal ones. In terms of single or multiple emotions associated with particular situations, we can conceive of such idiosyncratic scripts as being of both kinds. In terms of intergenerational difference, idiosyncratic scripts might also be of both kinds. For example, it may be that for adults the script is idiosyncratic, whereas for children the script is universal, or vice versa. These scripts differ from the former set in the amount of cultural demand that is placed on the members of the culture to learn one script over another.

Across cultures, differences in scripts and script learning exist so that there may be uniformity (or universality) within a culture, but not across cultures. In addition to the examples presented earlier, particular differences between Japanese and American culture have been noted in two areas – child care and the control of aggressive behavior – and these may be related to different script behavior.

Until recently and still to a large extent, Japanese children are cared for by their mothers (or grandmothers) and are cared for at home. Separation from parents occurs, but more slowly and in fewer situations. For example, infant day care is rare in Japan and more common in the United States. Moreover, in Japan, children are likely to sleep in the same room (and even in the same bed) with their parents whereas the American child, from birth, most often has its own bed and frequently its own room as well (or a room different from the parents' bedroom). Babysitters are quite common in the United States but rare in Japan. These differences in separation practices of the two cultures are manifested in laboratory research, where mothers are instructed to leave their children alone in a strange room (Takahashi, 1986).

The use of aggressive behavior is another example of culture difference between Japan and America. Although the expression of anger is acceptable in the United States, it is unacceptable in Japan. This difference is reflected, in part, in everyday interpersonal interactions and, at the cultural level, in terms of the differences in violent crimes, including murder, rape, and aggravated assault. Given these differences, both in separation and aggression, we would expect to find script differences between the two cultures, although there might be uniformity within the cultures.

Within culture, from where might the demand for particular but nonuniversal emotional scripts derive? If we ignore random variations, there are two possibilities for the origins of such scripts. First, they could derive from particular familial scripts that are not consistent across the culture. An emotional script that is not universal is likely to be influenced by the child's unique experience. This might be observed by looking at children's scripts that are not universal and looking at the response of the parents of particular children, and seeing whether or not the parents' scripts are similar to those of their children. For example, although some children believe that a beautiful event such as a sunset is likely to elicit joy and sadness (including crying), others do not. One could observe whether mothers (or fathers) of these children share the same script.

Second, personality characteristics may call forth a particular script in an individual. Personality variables may produce nonuniversal scripts in the absence of cultural pressure. In this case, a depressed child is likely to believe that an angry event such as someone grabbing a desired object from another is likely to elicit sadness, whereas an angry or nondepressed child is likely to believe that this event is likely to elicit anger. In this regard, there is some evidence that personality characteristics influence how individuals perceive the emotional behavior of others, although the relationship between script knowledge and personality has not been explored.

Psychopathology and emotional scripts. One other type of idiosyncratic script is possible. This may have to do with psychopathology (Lewis & Michalson, 1984). It is possible that parents attribute an incorrect emotion in a particular situation. Thus, the child may learn that *A* emotion is elicited by *Y* situation, whereas most other children learn that *B* emotion is elicited by that situation. In this case, children who learn *A* acquire a unique script and are likely to produce, themselves, responses that are idiosyncratic vis à vis others of the same culture. This idiosyncratic script and behavior pattern may be viewed as psychopathic by other members of the society. Since it is in disagreement with the normative values of the society it puts children "at risk" with respect to their behavior toward others. Moreover, such script learning may teach children inappropriate knowledge about their own internal states. Examples of such deviation occur within clinic settings where, for example, delusional patients may consider that laughter (an emotional expression) that occurs in a situation of happiness (as defined by others) does not mean joy but terror. Here the patient has a script that is discrepant from the norm, both in terms of its misinterpretation of the emotional state marked by the expression and in terms of the situation-behavior script.

The last two stories, "Lost in store" and "Knocking down the blocks," provide examples of nonuniversal scripts. The "Lost in the store" story is an example of between-culture differences, whereas the "blocks" story is an example of within-culture differences.

The story of a child becoming separated from its mother in a strange place is an example of the complexity of script learning (see Figure 13.3). From a cross-cultural perspective, the adults have a different script. American mothers believe that their children would be fearful if separated from them in the store (70%), whereas Japanese mothers believe that their children would be sad (76%). Thus, the adults of the two cultures differ on the emotional responses likely to be elicited by this situation. The cause of these cultural differences cannot be determined without further study using more examples of situations involving separation. This is an example of the disadvantage of using a single story. However, as an exploratory device it does allow for the targeting of specific script areas

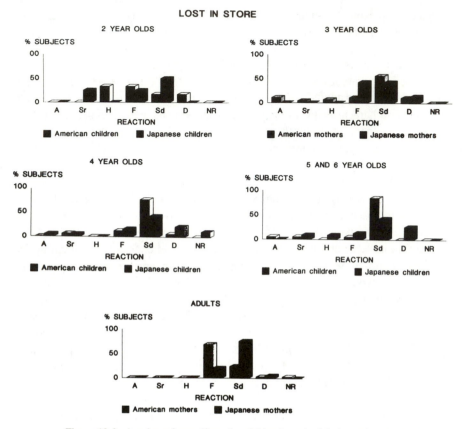

Figure 13.3. Age by culture effects for children's and adults' reactions to the Lost in Store story.

which may reflect cultural differences. We consider this story to be a probe for determining whether cultural differences in scripts relating to separation exist. Given the cultural differences in child-care practices and the differences reported in the separation literature (Takahashi, 1986), we are not surprised by the cultural differences.

The adult data further indicate that two major emotional responses are likely to be elicited by this situation. Although American mothers choose fear as their primary response, sadness is the next highest (and for the most part, the only other response). For the Japanese mothers, the reverse is the case. Thus, the responses of fear and sadness are both likely to be elicited by this situation. There appears to be a cross-cultural agreement that fear and sadness are the two likely emotions elicited by this situation; the difference in their mixture appears to be culturally specific.

This story also presents an example of a transformation across age in script learning, especially for the American sample, but to some extent for the Japanese as well. Whereas American mothers overwhelmingly choose fearfulness, their children choose sadness and do so increasingly with age (3 years = 56%; 4 years = 76%; 5–6 years = 85%). Thus, at no age do American children's scripts match that of the adults'. We can only assume that the transformation from the child to the adult script takes place after 6 years. It would be interesting to explore exactly when this transformation occurs. Such a transformation is unlikely to be related to cognitive ability but may be more related to role change. American parents often leave their children for work, vacation, and recreation, and it may be the case that the separation requirements of American parents lead them to adopt a script about their children that makes the adults more comfortable about leaving. It would seem that thinking one's child fearful would be less painful than thinking them sad because the parents know that their children are safe. Again, this particular story cannot address the causes of the difference but does provide a probe for the study of intergenerational differences within the culture.

The intergenerational difference for the Japanese is also evident but does not appear to be transformational. Japanese children show sadness as a modal response. Although it does not increase with age (3 years = 43%; 4 years = 42%; 5–6 years = 43%) the sadness response never reaches the adult level, at least not by 5–6 years. Whether this level increases between childhood and adulthood cannot be determined, but the Japanese appear to have a more culturally universal response across age than do the Americans for this script.

The story about one child knocking down the tower of blocks of another child produces the most deviant responses both within and across cultures and age. We consider this to be an example of an idiosyncratic script. Although some American and Japanese mothers select anger as the child's most likely response to the situation, the percentage who do so is rather low; 59% of Japanese mothers chose this emotion, and 38% of American. Whereas Japanese mothers select anger significantly more than the other emotions, there is no dominant choice among American mothers. Besides anger, American mothers choose surprise (24%), sadness (21%), and disgust (14%).

In general then, adults show a complex pattern, with four emotions all showing some degree of likelihood as a consequence of a physical transgression of one child toward another. The lack of a clear script for the response to aggression in the American culture is surprising in that one thinks of American culture as apt to be aggressive, especially to an aggressor (Izard, 1977). The findings for Japanese mothers are also surprising given the lack of overt aggression found in Japanese society and the cultural rules against the expression of anger, even when the victim of aggression. These findings suggest that, although angry

Table 13.2. *The relationship between mother and her child's choice of emotional expression*

		Mother						
		Anger	Surprise	Happy	Fear	Sad	Disgust	No response
Child	Anger	7 (3)	2 (2)	—	— (1)	2 (1)	2 (—)	(1)
	Surprise	2 (—)	1 (1)	—	—	1 (1)	2 (1)	
	Happy	— (1)	— (1)	—	—	— (—)	— (1)	
	Fear	3 (—)	— —	—	—	1 (4)	1 (2)	
	Sad	10 (4)	1 (2)	—	—	1 (—)	— (—)	
	Disgust	1 (3)	— (—)	1	—	— (—)	— (—)	

Japanese 9/41 22%
( ) American 8/30 27%

expressions may be prohibited, anger per se is still acknowledged as an emotional state. This is supported by our finding no difference in the adults' (and children's) ability to label the anger faces. These findings taken together suggest that even though the Japanese are being trained not to express the emotion itself they can recognize the expression and have some script knowledge as to the situations likely to elicit anger.

It is clear that neither culture insists that only one or two emotions be chosen for this situation. The emotion thought most likely to occur by a given individual has to be accounted for by other factors. Two factors suggest themselves. First, individual mothers may influence how the child behaves. Thus, if a mother is likely to respond to such a situation with anger, then her child will be taught to express anger. Alternatively, if the mother responds with sadness or surprise, the child will be taught sadness or surprise. The script would be learned not as a function of a cultural rule but as a function of a particular familial rule.

The second possibility has to do with the particular personality type of the child or adult. Some adults or children might be inclined to respond to such a situation with aggression or with self-blame.

Table 13.2 presents the matrix of mothers' choices as compared to their children's choices for this situation. The data for the American sample is in parentheses. Notice that there is no lawful relationship between what a mother chooses and what a child chooses for this situation; they agree on only 24 percent of the responses. For example, eight American children chose anger as the likely emotion, whereas 11 of the mothers chose anger. The overlap between child and parent is only three. The situation does not improve as one looks over age; that is, the agreement does not change as a function of the child's age. Familial socialization rules of script learning cannot be excluded, but the data lend little support to the belief that maternal–child patterns are similar. The data indicate that this script is not determined by the culture at large nor by the maternal pattern. Other possibilities of individual characteristics as determinants of idiosyncratic responses need to be further explored.

There are intergenerational differences to this story. Whereas the adults are more likely to choose anger, both American and Japanese children choose sadness, although this pattern is less clear for the Japanese children, who fluctuate between sadness and anger. This type of script is unique in this study because there does not appear to be a universal script within or across cultures, and therefore there is no clear adult standard to be compared. In contrast, the children appear to have a stronger script that will become less fixed with age.

Why is there a discrepancy between the children and adults in the expression of anger and sadness? The adults of both cultures assume that children would express more anger than the children themselves state they would express. That children appear to exhibit more sadness than anger at a transgression may have to do with many factors. First, they may be reluctant to indicate anger in front of an adult examiner because adults usually punish anger expression in children. The level of anger that the children select may not represent what they would choose if the adult was not present. Second, the story includes a sibling knocking over the tower, and it may be inappropriate to express anger toward a sibling, especially in front of an adult. Third, young children may be more likely to consider what they themselves might have done to elicit the attack or they may withhold anger because they are unsure if the sibling deliberately knocked over the blocks. The attack may appear more warranted from the adult's point of view than from the child's point of view. Finally, adults of both cultures may have more aggressive feelings than do children, as expressed in their choices. Whatever the reasons, the story indicates the lack of both a within-cultural and cross-cultural universal script and, perhaps even more interesting, it exemplifies the possibility that children may have a universal script when adults do not.

The development of script knowledge

The data on children's and adults' choices allow us to find examples of the development of various types of scripts. Some scripts are learned early. In general, using this technique, it is not until 3 years of age that children show they have knowledge of emotional scripts. This finding is in agreement with other studies, which suggest that 3-year-olds have already formed complex schemata about the relationship between emotional responses and situations. There are few data to support the belief that younger children have these scripts. However, because this technique requires that children be able to follow a story and to point to a picture of a face it may be that they have scripts but not the abilities they need to indicate this. There is evidence that children younger than 2 years use emotional expression instrumentally, suggesting that they already know what responses are appropriate for what situations and what emotional responses are likely to bring about the action they wish to produce. Thus, the 15-month-old who cries in order to get a parent to come into his or her room may have emotional script knowledge. Unless we can tap this knowledge without using verbal ability, we will be hard put to answer the question of whether children younger than 3 years have emotional knowledge about situations.

It is clear that by 5–6 years, children understand some scripts as well as do adults of their culture. That is not to say that all script learning is completed by this age. Considering that scripts depend upon a general knowledge base, children's scripts will be different from those of adults because they do not know as much as adults do. This general knowledge pertains to simple information as well as to role understanding. Children's script knowledge will also differ from that of adults as a function of general intellectual level and reasoning ability. The work of Harris and colleagues supports the transformation of this ability in respect to situations and emotion and is similar to the transformation that occurs in other aspects of social cognition.

It is possible that scripts marking different emotions emerge at different rates as a function of the type of emotion. From the data that exist on usage of emotion concepts, language knowledge, facial recognition, and the like, it is clear that happiness, for example, should be better understood so far as the situations likely to produce it are concerned than disgust. Likewise scripts involving secondary emotions, such as shame, guilt, and pride are likely to emerge after scripts about the primary emotions. In order to explore this difference in scripts by emotion, a much larger set of situations is needed. Another method to explore this would be to determine whether some emotions are associated more readily and consistently with situations than are others. The use of this methodology would be particularly relevant for this question.

The belief that some emotional scripts undergo little developmental change once they emerge whereas others undergo significant transition received support from the data. This suggests that classes of scripts can be studied around the issue of transformational change. The pressure for change obviously comes from two sources: first, the increased cognitive capacities of children as they become older; and second, the change in roles and status (and therefore perspective) as children develop. Both factors play a part, and script differences as a function of role (e.g., gender or parental status) would be of interest to explore.

Idiosyncratic scripts are particularly interesting to study because the lack of universality of response allows us to explore how scripts are formed. Some idiosyncratic scripts may be related to familial factors rather than to general cultural ones. This possibility suggests that script knowledge may be a function of smaller units than the culture at large. Thus, there should exist scripts by socioeconomic group, by region of the country, by occupation of the parents, by religion, and so forth. Across these groups, one would observe this diversity and conclude that there were only idiosyncratic responses. However, consistency might be observed when group membership is considered. Some scripts that appear idiosyncratic may turn out not to be if an appropriate unit of comparison is used. However, some scripts clearly remain at the family level.

In our analysis of an idiosyncratic script we were not able to find any consistency within the family. Although we have data on mothers and children, fathers may play an important role in this regard and we need more information before being able to rule out familial impact. Even so, the few data we have on fathers is not encouraging. Nevertheless, it is obvious that families socialize unique scripts and that children acquire some knowledge in this manner. However, if the familial script is too deviant from the culture at large, it is possible that the child may appear not only deviant but pathological. As we have suggested, the creation of such pathology may be best treated by redefinition of these scripts (Lewis & Michalson, 1984). If a child believes that someone will be angry if x occurs and in fact people will not be angry given x, then the child's response to x may be deviant. This deviance may itself be pathological or it may lead to pathology through disrupted social interactions. If we could teach the child the emotion most people have to x, then we might alter the pathological condition.

Cultural differences in scripts, both as an outcome and in terms of the developmental course, are an obvious fact. A particular meaning and the system of the network of meanings is not the same across cultures, nor are the associations between situations and emotions. The relationships between situations and emotions are cultural artifacts. Certainly some few basic situations have a one-to-one association with emotions; for example, loud, sudden noises with startle and fear. Other situations may not have such an association – being lost in a store, for example. Part of our difficulty in understanding the association between situations and emotions is the weakness in our definition of situation: As we already have discussed, definitions of "correct" situations lead to developmental and experimenter bias. There is another problem with situation that has to do with the size of the unit. If we define situation very specifically, more cultural deviation appears than if we use a broader definition. For example, the appearance of a loved one may be associated with happiness in all cultures, but the definition of who is a loved one (mother, grandmother, sister, other, etc.) is culturally determined. Situations are best associated with particular emotions at the level of the broadest definition of situations. Culture operates to define the exact nature of the situations, as well as the nature of the emotional response, including expression and experience.

The technique used here to explore specific cultural differences allows us to find universal situations as well as situations that produce different emotions for the different cultures. Two of the scripts presented allow for this comparison of cultural specificity and four for cultural universality. This technique is useful in this regard. The specifics of these differences need to be studied further using sets of situations thought to represent the general script. Even so, these specific cases are useful as probes, and the results suggest that different scripts around parenting practices and aggressive behavior may characterize, in part, important aspects of the differences in Japanese and American culture. The specific results of this study have only limited generalization to all scripts. What these findings do underline are methodological considerations regarding children's growing knowledge of emotional scripts, the need to further develop our understanding of the types of scripts that are possible, and the various possible growth patterns in script development. Individual differences and cultural patterns of socialization as well as characteristics of individuals impact on the relationship between situations and emotions and provide the meaning system for the development of complex schemas of emotional knowledge. Script acquisition studies allow for the generation of information about emotional knowledge, developmental and individual, as well as cultural differences. Given the importance of emotional knowledge in the creation and maintaining of emotional behavior, its study provides an important interface between cognition and affect.

References

Borke, H. (1973). The development of empathy in Chinese and American children between three and six years of age: a cross-cultural study. *Developmental Psychology, 9*, 102–108.

Bridges, K. M. B. (1932). Emotional development in early infancy. *Child Development, 3*, 324–334.

Gnepp, J., & Gould, M. E. (1985). The development of personalized inferences: understanding other people's emotional reactions in light of their prior experiences. *Child Development, 56*, 1455–1464.

Gnepp, J., & Hess, D. L. R. (1986). Children's understanding of verbal and facial display rules. *Developmental Psychology, 22*, 103–108.

Harkness, S., & Super, C. M. (1985). Child development interactions in the socialization of affect. In M. Lewis & C. Saarni (Eds.), *The socialization of emotion*. New York: Plenum.

Harris, P. L. (1983). Children's understanding of the link between situation and emotion. *Journal of Experimental Child Psychology, 36*, 490–509.

Harris, P. L., Olthof, T., & Meerum Terwogt, M. (1981). Children's knowledge of emotion. *Journal of Child Psychology and Psychiatry, 22*, 247–261.

Harris, P. L. (1985). What children know about the situations that provoke emotion. In M. Lewis & C. Saarni (Eds.), *The socialization of emotion*. New York: Plenum.

Harris, P. L., & Olthof, T. (1982). The child's concept of emotion. In G. Butterworth & P. Light (Eds.), *Social cognition: studies of the development of understanding*. Chicago, IL: University of Chicago Press.

Harris, P. L., Olthof, T., Meerum Terwogt, M., & Hardman, C. E. (1987). Children's knowledge of the situations that provoke emotion. *International Journal of Behavioral Development, 10*, 319–343.

Harter, S. (1982). Children's understanding of multiple emotions: a cognitive developmental approach. In A. Collins (Ed.), *Proceedings of the Piaget Society, June 1979*. Hillsdale, NJ: Erlbaum.

Izard, C. (1977). *Human emotions*. New York: Plenum.

Izard, C. E. (1979). *The Maximally Discriminative Facial Movement Coding System (MAX)*. Newark, DE: Instructional Resources Center, University of Delaware.

Izard, C. E., Huebner, R. R., Risser, D., McGinnes, G. C., & Dougherty, L. M. (1980). The young infant's ability to produce discrete emotion expressions. *Developmental Psychology, 16*, 132–140.

Lewis, M. (1987). Thinking and feeling: the elephant's tail. In C. A. Maher, M. Schwebel, & N. S. Fagley (Eds.), *Thinking and problem solving in the developmental process: international perspectives*. New Brunswick, NJ: Rutgers University Press.

Lewis, M., & Michalson, L. (1982). Socialization of emotions. In T. Field & A. Fogel (Eds.), *Emotion and early interaction: normal and high risk infants*. Hillsdale, NJ: Erlbaum.

Lewis, M., & Michalson, L. (1983). *Children's emotions and moods: developmental theory and measurement*. New York: Plenum.

Lewis, M., & Michalson, L. (1984). The socialization of emotional pathology in infancy. *Infant Mental Health Journal, 5*, 121–134.

Lewis, M., & Michalson, L. (1985). Faces as signs and symbols. In G. Zivin (Ed.), *Development of expressive behavior: biology environmental interaction*. New York: Academic Press.

Lewis, M., Michalson, L., & Goetz, N. *Children's ability to label emotions*. Unpublished manuscript.

Lutz, C. (1982). The domain of emotion words on Ifaluk Atoll. *American Ethologist, 9*, 113–128.

Michalson, L., & Lewis, M. (1985). What do children know about emotions and when do they know it? In M. Lewis & C. Saarni (Eds.), *The socialization of emotions*. New York: Plenum.

Miyake, K., Chen, S. J., & Campos, J. (1985). Infant temperament, mother's mode of interaction, and attachment in Japan: An interim report. *Monograph of the Society for Research in Child Development, 50 (1–2)* 276–297.

Takahashi, K. (1986). Examining the strange-situation procedure with Japanese mothers and 12-month-old infants. *Developmental Psychology, 22*, 265–270.

Weinraub, M., & Lewis, M. (1977). The determinants of children's responses to separation. *Monographs of the Society for Research in Child Development, 42*.

Wellman, H. M. (1985). The child's theory of mind: the development of conceptions of cognition. In S. R. Yussen (Ed.), *The growth of reflection*. San Diego, CA: Academic Press.

Zajonc, R. B. (1980). Feeling and thinking: preferences need no inferences. *American Psychologist, 35*, 151–175.

Author index

375

Subject index